PEARSON EDEXCEL INTERNATIONAL AS/A LEVEL
BUSINESS
Student Book 1

Rob Jones

Published by Pearson Education Limited, 80 Strand, London, WC2R 0RL.

www.pearsonglobalschools.com

Copies of official specifications for all Edexcel qualifications may be found on the website:
https://qualifications.pearson.com

Text © Pearson Education Limited 2018

Designed by Pearson Education Limited 2018

Typeset by Pearson CSC

Edited by Jeremy Toynbee and Sarah Wright

Original illustrations © Pearson Education Limited 2018

Cover design by Pearson Education Limited 2018

Picture research by Aptara Inc.

Cover photo/illustration © Getty Images/David McLain

Inside front cover photo: Shutterstock, Dmitry Lobanov

The rights of Rob Jones to be identified as author of this work have been asserted by him in
accordance with the Copyright, Designs and Patents Act 1988.

First published 2018

25 24

10

British Library Cataloguing in Publication Data
A catalogue record for this book is available from the British Library
ISBN 978 1 292239 17 0

Endorsement statement

In order to ensure that this resource offers high-quality support for the associated Pearson
qualification, it has been through a review process by the awarding body. This process confirms
that this resource fully covers the teaching and learning content of the specification or part of a
specification at which it is aimed. It also confirms that it demonstrates an appropriate balance
between the development of subject skills, knowledge and understanding, in addition to
preparation for assessment.

Endorsement does not cover any guidance on assessment activities or processes (e.g. practice
questions or advice on how to answer assessment questions), included in the resource nor does
it prescribe any particular approach to the teaching or delivery of a related course.

While the publishers have made every attempt to ensure that advice on the qualification and its
assessment is accurate, the official specification and associated assessment guidance materials
are the only authoritative source of information and should always be referred to for definitive
guidance.

Pearson examiners have not contributed to any sections in this resource relevant to examination
papers for which they have responsibility.

Examiners will not use endorsed resources as a source of material for any assessment set by
Pearson.

Endorsement of a resource does not mean that the resource is required to achieve this Pearson
qualification, nor does it mean that it is the only suitable material available to support the
qualification, and any resource lists produced by the awarding body shall include this and other
appropriate resources.

Acknowledgements

The authors and publisher would like to thank the following individuals and organisations for their
kind permission to reproduce copyright material.

Photographs

(Key: b-bottom; c-centre; l-left; r-right; t-top)

123RF.com: Fiphoto 137, 123RF 148, Yoanna Boyadzhieva 174, Jens Brüggemann 200,
odessa4 239; **Alamy Stock Photo:** Philip Game vii, 6, Matthew Richardson 20b, Clive Horton
29, Travelib pakistan 46, Kathy deWitt 52t, Xinhua 55, Richard Cummins/Destinations/Design
Pics Inc 57, Simon Turner 73b, Radharc Images 73c, Ashley Cooper 75, Alberto Grosescu 80,
Danita Delimont 89, BJ Warnick/Newscom 110, Aurora Photos 160, Jorge Pérez 166, Best View
Stock 177, Rafael Ben-Ari 183, Oxana Oleynichenko 198, Rob Crandall 203, HD SIGNATURE
CO., LTD 220, Christopher Kimmel/Aurora Photos 222, JG Photography 252, Cynthia Farmer
258, Richard Milnes 262, Ka Wing Yu 295, Monty Rakusen 308, Katharine Rose 311, Markus
Mainka 319, Germany 322, Taina Sohlman 327; **AP Images:** DANTE PIAGGIO 226; **Corbis:**
Reuters 271; **Fotolia:** yolfran 52b, Michael Jung 115, xy 126, Darren Baker 139, Picture-Factory
157, doble.d 264b; **Getty Images:** Nihat Sinan Erul vi, 2, Bloomberg vii, 4, 19, 22, iStock/360

31, AtomicSparkle/Vetta 91, Westend61 112, DarioEgidi 131, AFP Contributor/Contributor
195, Jose A. Bernat Bacete 199, Sjo 215, Amir Mukhtar/Moment Unreleased 228, Jasper
Juinen 249, Peeterv/iStock 283, iStock/360 288, Xavierarnau/E+ 30, @by Feldman_1/
Moment 56, Sarah Franklin/Moment 97, Suranto Riadi/EyeEm 140, Lars Ruecker/Moment
165, Malorny/Moment 205, Alexander Spatari/Moment 240, aaaaimages/Moment 263,
Howard Kingsnorth/Stone 294; **PhotoDisc:** Brofsky Studio Inc 277; **Rex Features:** Nicholas
Bailey 161; **Shutterstock:** LightField Studios 18, Sorbis 27, Beros919 38, Iurii 40, Yuliya
Yesina 42, Lenakov 47, Bea Rue 50, WithGod 51, CandyBox Images 66, Bogdanhoda 67,
ImagineStock 71, Tom Burlison 76, REDPIXEL.PL 79, nd3000 82, Abir Abdullah 84, Tumarkin
Igor – ITPS 85, Dmitry Kalinovsky 103, tsyhun 108, ProStockStudio 117, Shutterstock
120, Monkey Business Images 122, Matt Trommer 128, Dragon Images 144, Stock-Asso
145, wavebreakmedia 150, g-stockstudio 153, Marina Shanti 154, Ayman alakhras 162, Mila
Supinskaya Glashchenko 168, xiao yu 170, Monkey Business Images 172, Eviled 176, Jaroslav
Pachy sr 180, Mavo 182, Yulia Grigoryeva 187, Fascinadora 188, Stuart Jenner 192, Sergey
kolesnikov 193, Iakov Filimonov 207, Coronado 212, Adrin Shamsudin 213, Wkst 218, Africa
Studio 232, Syda Productions 241, Maridav 245, science photo 247, Ricantimages 248, ESB
Professional 255, Daxiao Productions 256, RedTC 264t, wzlv 266, Paul Vinten 275, James Steidl
278, SasinT 279, Xieyuliang 285, Mr Max 286, Jens Buettner/Epa/REX 287, Aun Photographer
300, Pingphuket 313, ArtStudioHouse 318, Maria Savenko 323; **Specialized:** Specialized.com
68; **Thomson Reuters:** Thomas Mukoya 45; **Volkswagen UK:** Volkswagen UK 20t.

All other images © Pearson Education

The Publisher would like to thank the following individuals and organizations for their
approval and permission to reproduce their materials:

p. 35 Graph from ABS data used with permission from the Australian Bureau of Statistics,
www.abs.gov.au; National Commission of Audit, Australian Government; **p. 35** From Why
Australia needs to get real on population growth, http://www.afr.com/news/politics/
national/why-australia-needs-to-get-real-on-population-growth-20131129-ij9ym; **p. 296**
Bank of England; **p. 134** Extract from Berkshirehathaway.com. This material s copyrighted
and used with permission of the author; **p. 134** From Berkshire Hathaway Inc; **p. 80** The
CPO, purvey - Highlights and Insights Report, Figure 5.1, February 2015; **p. 306** From
Budget 2017-2018, The Commonwealth of Australia; **p. 23** Adapted from Corporate Eye;
p. 10 Graphs from EV Volumes.com. Used with permission; **p. 164** Extract from a report
by the European Environment kency (E-EA); **p. 10** From ElectricCarsReport.com; **p. 21**
Adapted from Failuremag and Sun Pharma, Research and Development, Evolving Better
Being Stronger Moving Faster, Sun Pharmaceutical Industries Ltd; **p. 27** Adapted from Fly10
Emirates; **Pages 162, 203, 270** Extract from adapted from the Financial Times, all rights
reserved; **p. 5** Egham, Gartner Says Worldwide Smartphone Sales Grew 3.9 Percent in First
Quarter of 2016. Gartner Inc., 2016; **p. 32** Graph from Gulf News Community and Global
Plug-in Sales for 2017-Q4 and the Full Year. Used with permission; **p. 32** From Adapted from
Gulf News Community and Global Plug-in Sales for 2017-Q4 and the Full Year;
p. 145 From Adapted from Why did Google abandon 20% time for innovation? and Google's
Intrapreneurship Program; **p. 17** From Adapted from Wearable Tech Market To Be Worth
$34 Billion By 2020, Forbes, Virtual Reality Headset Market - Global Industry Analysis,
Size, Share, Growth, Trends and Forecast 2016 – 2023; **p. 29** Adapted from Rebranding
Strategy: Gems of Wisdom from 5 Successful Brand Revitalizations and Marketing Strategy
of Harley Davidson – Harley Davidson Strategy; **p. 3** International Civil Aviation Organization,
Civil Aviation Statistics of the World and ICAO staff estimates. CC BY-4.0; **p.192** www.
khanacademy.org; **p. 19** Adapted from Mintel; **p. 20** Extract from M&M'S®, is a registered
trademarks of Mars, Incorporated and its affiliates. The M&M'S® trademark and associated
slogan is used with permission. Mars, Incorporated is not associated with Edexcel; **p. 298**
From Adapted from What is MUJI?, 2016 Annual report March 1, 2015-February 29,2016;
p. 36 Extracts from Housing shortage growing by 40 homes a day, NZ building consents
fall 7.2pc in December, reflecting drop in apartments and Why does New Zealand have
a housing shortage problem now bow bad is it; **p. 4** Adapted from 9 Niche Marketing
Examples; **p. 92** www.nibusinessinfo.co.uk; **p. 287** From Inside scoop: Nestlé doubles its
largest quality assurance center to fight for confectionery safety **p. 100** From Adapted from
Part-time employment rate. OECD; **p. 252** From Adapted from Peter Koven, First Quantum
Minerals has overcome worst of liquidity problems, executives say; **p. 203** Extract from www.
support-finance.co.uk. Used with permission; **Pages 76, 79** from www.statista.com; **p. 23**
From strategictoolkits; **p. 23** Extract from http://strategictoolkits.com/strategic-concepts/
perceptual-map/; **p. 32** Extract from Sustrans.org.uk. Used with permission; **p. 138** www.
telegraph.co.uk; **p. 6** Based on Australia's online grocery market set to double, The Daily
Telegraph; **p. 40** Adapted from New tracer technology brings cost savings to unconventional
well stimulation, Brent Crude Oil performance and An Economic Perfect Storm Is Causing
Oil Prices to Drop to New Lows; **p. 171** From TRADING ECONOMICS; **pages 295, 296,
307** www.trad ngeconomics.com; **p. 285** Extract from Toyota (GB) PLC. Reproduced w.th
permission from Toyota (GB) PLC; **p. 71** www.volkswagen.co.uk; **p. 87** Extract from uSwitch.
com. Used with permission; **p. 130** Extract from xperthr. Used with permission; **p. 49** From
Adapted from What German households pay for power. **p. 1** Adapted from The World Bank,
China's domestic travel boom brings rush of start-up airlines, jet orders and Ranking of
China's Busiest Airports in 2015; **p. 3** Graph from The World Bank, Used with permission;

Every effort has been made to trace the copyright holders and we apologies in advance
for any unintentional omissions. We would be pleased to insert the appropriate
acknowledgement in any subsequent edition of this publication.

CONTENTS

COURSE STRUCTURE	IV
ABOUT THIS BOOK	VI
ASSESSMENT OVERVIEW	VIII
UNIT 1: MARKETING AND PEOPLE	2
UNIT 2: MANAGING BUSINESS ACTIVITIES	165
INDEX	325

UNIT 1: MARKETING AND PEOPLE

MEETING CUSTOMER NEEDS 2

1. THE MARKET 3
2. MARKET RESEARCH 11
3. MARKET POSITIONING 20

THE MARKET 30

4. DEMAND 31
5. SUPPLY 36
6. MARKETS 41
7. PRICE ELASTICITY OF DEMAND (PED) 46
8. INCOME ELASTICITY OF DEMAND (YED) 52

MARKETING MIX AND STRATEGY 56

9. MARKETING OBJECTIVES AND STRATEGY 57
10. PRODUCT/SERVICE DESIGN 68
11. PROMOTION AND BRANDING 74
12. PRICING STRATEGIES 83
13. DISTRIBUTION 89

MANAGING PEOPLE 95

14. APPROACHES TO STAFFING 96
15. RECRUITMENT, SELECTION AND TRAINING 104
16. ORGANISATIONAL DESIGN 113
17. MOTIVATION IN THEORY AND PRACTICE 121
18. LEADERSHIP 132

ENTREPRENEURS AND LEADERS 140

19. ROLE OF AN ENTREPRENEUR 141
20. ENTREPRENEURIAL MOTIVES AND CHARACTERISTICS 149
21. BUSINESS OBJECTIVES 155
22. BUSINESS CHOICES 160

UNIT 2: MANAGING BUSINESS ACTIVITIES

PLANNING A BUSINESS AND RAISING FINANCE 165

23. PLANNING	166
24. INTERNAL FINANCE	172
25. EXTERNAL FINANCE	177
26. FORMS OF BUSINESS	184
27. FORMS OF BUSINESS: PLCs	193
28. LIABILITY	199

FINANCIAL PLANNING 205

29. SALES, REVENUE AND COSTS	206
30. SALES FORECASTING	213
31. BREAK-EVEN	221
32. CASH FLOW	226
33. BUDGETS	233

MANAGING FINANCE 240

34. PROFIT	241
35. LIQUIDITY	248
36. BUSINESS FAILURE	256

RESOURCE MANAGEMENT 263

37. PRODUCTION, PRODUCTIVITY AND EFFICIENCY	264
38. CAPACITY UTILISATION	274
39. INVENTORY CONTROL	279
40. QUALITY MANAGEMENT	286

EXTERNAL INFLUENCES 294

41. ECONOMIC INFLUENCES	295
42. LEGISLATION	308
43. THE COMPETITIVE ENVIRONMENT	319

INDEX	325

ABOUT THIS BOOK

This book is written for students following the Pearson Edexcel International Advanced Level (IAL) Business specification. It covers the first year of the International A level qualification as well as the full International AS level.

The book has been carefully structured to match the order of topics in the specification although teaching and learning can take place in any order, both in the classroom and in any independent learning. This book is organised into two units (Unit 1: Marketing and people and Unit 2: Managing business activities), each with five topic areas.

Each topic area is divided into chapters to break the content down into manageable chunks. Each chapter begins by listing the key learning objectives and includes a getting started activity to introduce the concepts. There is a mix of learning points and activities throughout including global case studies to show a range of businesses within real-life contexts. Checkpoint questions at the end of each chapter help assess understanding of the key learning objectives.

The content for Unit 1 is applicable for Paper 1 (Marketing and people) and the content for Unit 2 is applicable for Paper 2 (Managing business activities). Knowing how to apply learning to both of these papers will be critical for exam success. There are exam-style questions at the end of each chapter to provide opportunity for exam practice. Answers are provided in the online teaching resource pack.

Specification reference
The specification reference is given at the start of each chapter and in the running header.

Topic openers
Introduce each of the key topics in the specification.

Learning objectives
Each chapter starts with a list of key assessment objectives.

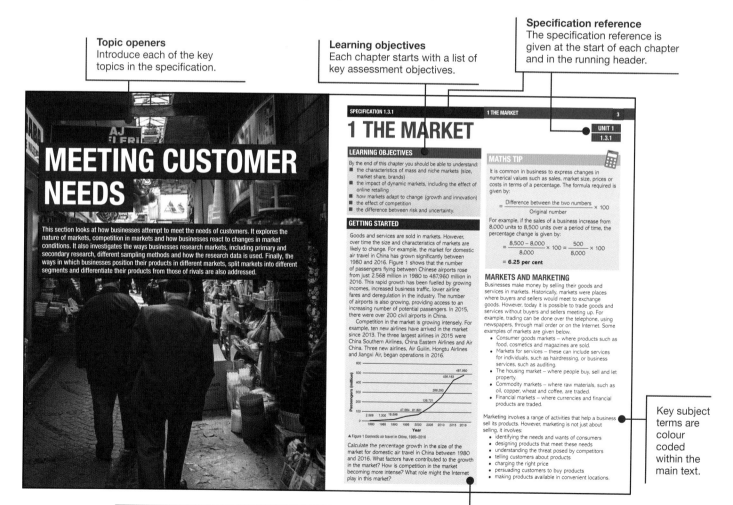

Key subject terms are colour coded within the main text.

Getting started
An activity to introduce the key concepts in each chapter. Questions are designed to stimulate discussion and use of prior knowledge. These can be tackled as individuals, pairs, groups or the whole class.

Activity
Each chapter includes activities to embed understanding through case studies and questions.

Skills
Relevant exam questions have been assigned key skills, allowing for a strong focus on particular academic qualities. These transferable skills are highly valued in further study and the workplace.

Thinking bigger
These sections provide opportunity to explore an aspect of business in more detail to deepen understanding.

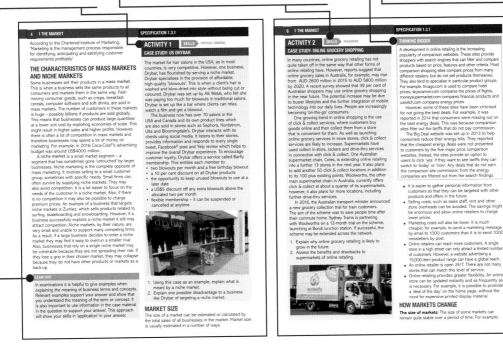

Exam hint
Tips give practical advice and guidance for exam preparation.

Checkpoint
Questions to check understanding of the key learning points in each chapter. These are NOT exam-style questions.

Exam practice
Exam-style questions are found at the end of each chapter. They are tailored to the Pearson Edexcel specification to allow for practice and development of exam writing technique. They also allow for practice responding to the command words used in the exams.

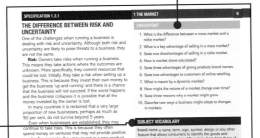

Subject vocabulary
An alphabetical list of all the subject terms in each chapter with clear definitions for EAL learners. Please note: A collated glossary is available on the ActiveBook.

ASSESSMENT OVERVIEW

The following tables give an overview of the assessment for this course. You should study this information closely to help ensure that you are fully prepared for this course and know exactly what to expect in each part of the assessment.

PAPER 1	PERCENTAGE OF IAS	PERCENTAGE OF IAL	MARK	TIME	AVAILABILITY	STRUCTURE
MARKETING AND PEOPLE Written exam paper Paper code WBS11/01 Externally set and marked by Pearson Edexcel Single tier of entry Calculators can be used	50%	25%	80	2 hours	January, June and October First assessment: January 2019	There will be three sections, A, B and C. Students must answer all questions. Section A: short- and extended-response questions based on sources (30 marks) Section B: same as Section A but different sources (30 marks) Section C: one 20-mark essay question, based on one or more sources (20 marks)

PAPER 2	PERCENTAGE	PERCENTAGE OF IAL	MARK	TIME	AVAILABILITY	STRUCTURE
MANAGING BUSINESS ACTIVITIES Written exam paper Paper code WBS12/01 Externally set and marked by Pearson Edexcel Single tier of entry	50%	25%	80	2 hours	January, June and October First assessment: June 2019	There will be three sections, A, B and C. Students must answer all questions. Section A: short- and extended-response questions based on sources (30 marks) Section B: same as Section A but different sources (30 marks) Section C: one 20-mark essay question, based on one or more sources (20 marks)

ASSESSMENT OBJECTIVES AND WEIGHTINGS

ASSESSMENT OBJECTIVE	DESCRIPTION	% IN IAS	% IN IA2	% IN IAL
AO1	Demonstrate knowledge and understanding of terms, concepts, theories, methods and models	27.5	20	23.8
AO2	Apply knowledge and understanding to various business contexts to show how individuals and organisations are affected by and respond to issues	25	22.5	23.8
AO3	Analyse business issues, showing an understanding of the causes, costs and consequences for individuals and organisations	27.5	30	28.8
AO4	Evaluate evidence to make informed judgements and propose evidence-based solutions to business issues	20	27.5	23.8

Note: Totals have been rounded either up or down.

RELATIONSHIP OF ASSESSMENT OBJECTIVES TO UNITS

UNIT NUMBER	ASSESSMENT OBJECTIVE			
	AO1	AO2	AO3	AO4
Unit 1	13.75%	12.5%	13.75%	10%
Unit 2	13.75%	12.5%	13.75%	10%
Total for International Advanced Subsidiary	27.5%	25%	27.5%	20%

Note: Totals have been rounded either up or down.

UNIT NUMBER	ASSESSMENT OBJECTIVE			
	AO1	AO2	AO3	AO4
Unit 1	6.9%	6.3%	6.9%	5%
Unit 2	6.9%	6.3%	6.9%	5%
Total for International Advanced Level	13.8%	12.6%	13.8%	10%

RELATIONSHIP OF ASSESSMENT OBJECTIVES TO COMMAND WORDS

COMMAND WORD	NUMBER OF MARKS	MARK SCHEME	ASSESSMENT OBJECTIVES
Define	2	Points based	AO1
Calculate	4	Points based	AO1, AO2, AO3
Construct	4	Points based	AO1, AO2, AO3
Explain	4	Points based	AO1, AO2, AO3
Analyse	6	Points based	AO1, AO2, AO3
Discuss	8	Levels based	AO1, AO2, AO3, AO4
Assess	10 (Units 1 and 2) 12 (Units 3 and 4)	Levels based	AO1, AO2, AO3, AO4
Evaluate	20	Levels based	AO1, AO2, AO3, AO4

MEETING CUSTOMER NEEDS

This section looks at how businesses attempt to meet the needs of customers. It explores the nature of markets, competition in markets and how businesses react to changes in market conditions. It also investigates the ways businesses research markets, including primary and secondary research, different sampling methods and how the research data is used. Finally, the ways in which businesses position their products in different markets, split markets into different segments and differentiate their products from those of rivals are also addressed.

1 THE MARKET

LEARNING OBJECTIVES

By the end of this chapter you should be able to understand:
- the characteristics of mass and niche markets (size, market share, brands)
- the impact of dynamic markets, including the effect of online retailing
- how markets adapt to change (growth and innovation)
- the effect of competition
- the difference between risk and uncertainty.

GETTING STARTED

Goods and services are sold in markets. However, over time the size and characteristics of markets are likely to change. For example, the market for domestic air travel in China has grown significantly between 1980 and 2016. Figure 1 shows that the number of passengers flying between Chinese airports rose from just 2.568 million in 1980 to 487,960 million in 2016. This rapid growth has been fuelled by growing incomes, increased business traffic, lower airline fares and deregulation in the industry. The number of airports is also growing, providing access to an increasing number of potential passengers. In 2015, there were over 200 civil airports in China.

Competition in the market is growing intensely. For example, ten new airlines have arrived in the market since 2013. The three largest airlines in 2015 were China Southern Airlines, China Eastern Airlines and Air China. Three new airlines, Air Guilin, Hongtu Airlines and Jiangxi Air, began operations in 2016.

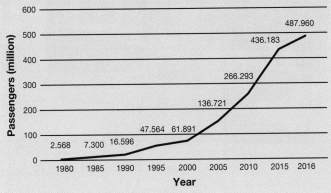

▲ Figure 1 Domestic air travel in China, 1985–2016

Calculate the percentage growth in the size of the market for domestic air travel in China between 1980 and 2016. What factors have contributed to the growth in the market? How is competition in the market becoming more intense? What role might the Internet play in this market?

MATHS TIP

It is common in business to express changes in numerical values such as sales, market size, prices or costs in terms of a percentage. The formula required is given by:

$$= \frac{\text{Difference between the two numbers}}{\text{Original number}} \times 100$$

For example, if the sales of a business increase from 8,000 units to 8,500 units over a period of time, the percentage change is given by:

$$= \frac{8,500 - 8,000}{8,000} \times 100 = \frac{500}{8,000} \times 100$$

$$= \textbf{6.25 per cent}$$

MARKETS AND MARKETING

Businesses make money by selling their goods and services in markets. Historically, markets were places where buyers and sellers would meet to exchange goods. However, today it is possible to trade goods and services without buyers and sellers meeting up. For example, trading can be done over the telephone, using newspapers, through mail order or on the Internet. Some examples of markets are given below.

- Consumer goods markets – where products such as food, cosmetics and magazines are sold.
- Markets for services – these can include services for individuals, such as hairdressing, or business services, such as auditing.
- The housing market – where people buy, sell and let property.
- Commodity markets – where raw materials, such as oil, copper, wheat and coffee, are traded.
- Financial markets – where currencies and financial products are traded.

Marketing involves a range of activities that help a business sell its products. However, marketing is not just about selling, it involves:
- identifying the needs and wants of consumers
- designing products that meet these needs
- understanding the threat posed by competitors
- telling customers about products
- charging the right price
- persuading customers to buy products
- making products available in convenient locations.

According to the Chartered Institute of Marketing, 'Marketing is the management process responsible for identifying, anticipating and satisfying customer requirements profitably'.

THE CHARACTERISTICS OF MASS MARKETS AND NICHE MARKETS

Some businesses sell their products in a **mass market**. This is when a business sells the same products to all consumers and markets them in the same way. Fast-moving consumer goods, such as crisps, breakfast cereals, computer software and soft drinks, are sold in mass markets. The number of customers in these markets is huge – possibly billions if products are sold globally. This means that businesses can produce large quantities at a lower unit cost by exploiting economies of scale. This might result in higher sales and higher profits. However, there is often a lot of competition in mass markets and therefore businesses may spend a lot of money on marketing. For example, in 2016 Coca-Cola®'s advertising budget was around US$4000 million.

A **niche market** is a small market segment – a segment that has sometimes gone 'untouched' by larger businesses. Niche marketing is the complete opposite of mass marketing. It involves selling to a small customer group, sometimes with specific needs. Small firms can often survive by supplying niche markets. They may also avoid competition. It is a lot easier to focus on the needs of the customer in a niche market. Also, if there is no competition it may also be possible to charge premium prices. An example of a business that targets niche markets is Zumiez, which sells products related to surfing, skateboarding and snowboarding. However, if a business successfully exploits a niche market it still may attract competition. Niche markets, by their nature, are very small and unable to support many competing firms. As a result, if a large business decides to enter a niche market they may find it easy to overrun a smaller rival. Also, businesses that rely on a single niche market may be vulnerable because they are not spreading their risk. If they lose a grip in their chosen market, they may collapse because they do not have other products or markets as a back-up.

ACTIVITY 1   SKILLS CRITICAL THINKING

CASE STUDY: US DRYBAR

The market for hair salons in the USA, as in most countries, is very competitive. However, one business, Drybar, has flourished by serving a niche market. Drybar specialises in the provision of affordable, high-quality 'blowouts'. This is when a client's hair is washed and blow-dried into style without being cut or coloured. Drybar was set up by Alli Webb, who felt she was paying too much for blowouts in traditional salons. Drybar is set up like a bar where clients can relax, watch a film and get a blowout.

The business now has over 70 salons in the USA and Canada and its own product lines which are also sold in stores such as Sephora, Nordstrom, Ulta and Bloomingdale's. Drybar interacts with its clients using social media. It listens to their stories, provides information and responds to every single tweet, Facebook® post and Yelp review which helps to improve the overall Drybar experience. To encourage customer loyalty, Drybar offers a service called Barfly membership. This entitles each member to:

- two blowouts per month and a free birthday blowout
- a 10 per cent discount on all Drybar products
- the opportunity to keep unused blowouts to use at a later date
- a US$5 discount off any extra blowouts above the allocated two per month
- flexible membership – it can be suspended or cancelled at anytime.

1. Using this case as an example, explain what is meant by a niche market.
2. Explain one possible disadvantage to a business like Drybar of targeting a niche market.

MARKET SIZE

The size of a market can be estimated or calculated by the total sales of all businesses in the market. Market size is usually estimated in a number of ways.

Value: This is the total amount spent by customers buying products. For example, in 2014 the value of the global fast food market (burgers/sandwiches, chicken, pasta/pizza, Asian/Latin American food, seafood and others) was approximately US$495,000 million. It was expected to reach approximately US$645,000 million by 2020.

Volume: This is the physical quantity of products that are produced and sold. For example, in 'Getting started', the market size for domestic air travel in China is measured by the number of passengers carried per year. This was 487,960 million in 2016. Some estimates of volume are based on the number or percentage of users, subscribers or viewers. This is often the case in markets for services, such as the number of mobile phone users, the number of television viewers or the percentage of households with digital television.

Different markets are likely to differ in size. For example, the sale of savoury snacks in 1 year is likely to be much smaller than the sales of footwear in the same year in a country.

MARKET SHARE

Market share or market penetration is the term used to describe the proportion of a particular market that is held by a business, a product, a brand or a number of businesses or products. Market share is shown as a percentage. The market share of a business can be calculated as:

$$\frac{\text{Sales of a business}}{\text{Total sales in the market}} \times 100\%$$

Why might the measurement of market share be important? It might indicate a business that is a market leader. This could influence other companies to follow the leader or influence the leader to maintain its position. It might influence the strategy or objectives of a business. A business that has a small market share may set a target of increasing its share by 5 per cent over a period of time. It may also be an indication of the success or failure of a business or its strategy.

Figure 2 shows the global market shares of smartphone suppliers. It shows, for example, that Samsung is the market leader with a 23.2 per cent share. It also shows that the top five producers have more than half of the entire market to themselves.

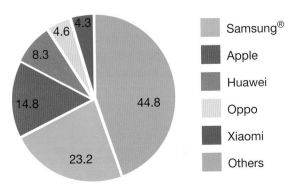

% Market share

- Samsung®
- Apple
- Huawei
- Oppo
- Xiaomi
- Others

▲ Figure 2 Global market shares of smartphone suppliers, 2016Q1

BRANDS

Many businesses try to establish themselves in markets by giving their products a **brand name**. Products are given brand names to distinguish them from other products in the market. Branding is particularly important in mass markets where lots of products are competing for a share of the market. Examples of common brand names include Google®, BBC, Toyota, Nike® and Apple®. Branding might be used to:

- differentiate the product from those of rivals
- create customer loyalty
- help product recognition
- develop an image
- charge a premium price when the brand becomes strong.

Branding is discussed in more detail in Chapter 10.

DYNAMIC MARKETS

Most markets do not remain the same over time – they tend to be dynamic, which means they are likely to change. They may grow, shrink, fragment, emerge or completely disappear. For example, in the majority of countries there is no longer a market for cassettes. Most people download audio material such as music from the Internet.

Dynamic markets can have a huge impact on businesses. A failure to adapt in a dynamic market can lead to the collapse of a business. For example, when digital photography emerged in the 1980s, Kodak® (the camera company) continued to rely on sales of film cameras. Eventually, the market for these types of cameras collapsed and Kodak went into **liquidation**. Those businesses that can adapt to changes in dynamic markets are more likely to survive in the long term. The changing nature of markets is discussed in more detail later.

ONLINE RETAILING

One of the biggest changes to occur in the marketing of products has been the development of **online retailing** or **e-tailing**. This is a popular branch of **e-commerce** that has emerged along with the development of the Internet. It involves shoppers ordering goods online and taking delivery at home. There are specialist e-tailers such as Amazon® and Alibaba® – retail 'giants' that sell a huge range of goods online. However, many retailers, both large and small, now have online services. Growth in online retailing is rapid and expected to continue into the future. Businesses may enjoy a number of benefits from offering online retail services.

- Retailers can market their goods to people who prefer to shop from home or who find it difficult to get to traditional shops. For example, people who do not enjoy the physical shopping experience, people too busy to go shopping and people with health conditions or disabilities that make physical shopping difficult.

ACTIVITY 2 · SKILLS · REASONING

CASE STUDY: ONLINE GROCERY SHOPPING

In many countries, online grocery retailing has not quite taken off in the same way that other forms of online retailing have. However, reports suggest that online grocery sales in Australia, for example, may rise from AUD 2600 million in 2015 to AUD 5800 million by 2020. A recent survey showed that 39 per cent of Australian shoppers may use online grocery shopping in the near future. The potential increase may be due to busier lifestyles and the further integration of mobile technology into our daily lives. People are increasingly becoming 'on-the-go' consumers.

One growing trend in online shopping is the use of click & collect services, where customers buy goods online and then collect them from a store that is convenient for them. As well as launching online grocery services in more stores, click & collect services are likely to increase. Supermarkets have used collect in-store, lockers and drive-thru services in connection with click & collect. One Australian supermarket chain, Coles, is extending online retailing into a further 13 stores in the next year. It also plans to add another 50 click & collect locations in addition to its 100 plus existing points. Woolworths, the other main supermarket chain in Australia, currently offers click & collect at about a quarter of its supermarkets, however, it also plans for more locations, including further drive-thru services.

In 2016, the Australian transport minister announced a new grocery collection trial for train customers. The aim of the scheme was to save people time after their commute home. Sydney Trains is partnering with Woolworths on a 12-month trial on the scheme, launching at Bondi Junction station. If successful, the scheme may be extended across the network.

1. Explain why online grocery retailing is likely to grow in the future.
2. Assess the benefits and drawbacks to supermarkets of online retailing.

THINKING BIGGER

A development in online retailing is the increasing popularity of comparison websites. These sites provide shoppers with search engines that can filter and compare products based on price, features and other criteria. Most comparison shopping sites compare prices from many different retailers, but do not sell products themselves. They also tend to specialise in particular product groups. For example, trivago.com is used to compare hotel prices, skyscanner.com compares the prices of flights, moneysupermarket.com compares financial products and uswitch.com compares energy prices.

However, some of these sites have been criticised for not giving the best deals. For example, it was reported in 2014 that consumers were missing out on the best energy deals. This was because comparison sites filter out the tariffs that do not pay commission.

The Big Deal website was set up in 2013 to help consumers reduce their energy bills. They reported that the cheapest energy deals were not presented to customers by the five major price comparison websites. Instead, the sites provide an option to users to click 'yes' if they want to see tariffs they can switch to 'today' or 'now'. Any deals that do not earn the comparison site commission from the energy companies are filtered out from the search findings.

- It is easier to gather personal information from customers so that they can be targeted with other products and offers in the future.
- Selling costs, such as sales staff, rent and other store overheads can be avoided. The savings might be enormous and allow online retailers to charge lower prices.
- Marketing costs will also be lower. It is much cheaper, for example, to send a marketing message by email to 1000 customers than it is to send 1000 newsletters by post.
- Online retailers can reach more customers. A single store in a high street can only attract a limited number of customers. However, a website advertising a 15,000-item product range can have a global reach.
- An online retailer is open 24/7. There are not many stores that can match this level of service.
- Online retailing provides greater flexibility. An online store can be updated instantly and as frequently as is necessary. For example, it is possible to promote a 'deal of the day' on the home page, without the need for expensive printed display material.

HOW MARKETS CHANGE

The size of markets: The size of some markets can remain quite stable over a period of time. For example, the size of the milk market in the UK probably hasn't changed much for many years. This is because consumption of milk is fairly constant.

However, the majority of markets are likely to grow. For example, *The Future of Global Packaging to 2018* reports that the global packaging market stood at US$799,000 million in 2012, increasing by 1 per cent over 2011 with sales projected to increase by 3 per cent. Some forecasters reckoned growth to 2018 would reach 4 per cent per year, with sales reaching over US$1 trillion. Factors driving growth in the packaging market include increasing urbanisation, investment in construction and housing, development of retail chains, and the expanding cosmetics and healthcare sectors in the emerging economies.

Some markets are in decline. For example, dial-up Internet services are gradually being withdrawn in many contries. They are being replaced by the much faster broadband services. Markets often decline because the need for a product ceases to exist. In the case of coal, other fuels, such as oil, gas, nuclear and renewable sources are now preferred by households and industry.

The nature of markets: Many markets are in a state of flux. This means that the structure and nature of the market is subject to constant change. It is also possible for consumer spending patterns to change. For example, significant changes are taking place in Indian markets. Shopping in India has become more social and often involves the whole family. Shopping events occur more frequently and immediate gratification is becoming more important. Traditionally the purchase of a house and a car took priority. However, today more Indian consumers want to buy holidays abroad and many are prepared to spend increasing amounts of money on 'comfort'. Another change is the desire to buy more 'upmarket' brands. Social media is influencing consumer behaviour as people attempt to match the spending habits of their peers.

New markets: While it is possible for some markets to completely disappear, new markets are always developing. One big source of new markets is from the development of 'emerging economies'. These include the BRIC (Brazil, Russia, India and China) countries and other developing nations, such as Mexico, Thailand, Indonesia and some South American countries. New markets also appear when completely new products are launched. In the 1970s no one had a mobile phone. In the 1980s no one had a smartphone. In the 1990s no one had a flat-screen television. In the 2000s few people had e-books. These are all examples of brand-new markets.

INNOVATION AND MARKET GROWTH

Markets can grow over time – some rapidly, some more slowly. Growth in existing markets and new markets may occur for the following reasons.

Economic growth: Global living standards tend to rise over time. This means that the world's population has more money to spend. As a result businesses can supply more of their output to growing global markets. Also, as people get wealthier they are likely to demand different types of goods. For example, the markets for holidays, electronic goods, cars, air travel, cosmetics, furniture and luxury goods will grow.

Innovation: Businesses can grow their markets through the process of innovation. They can create new wants and needs and meet them with new products. A lot of innovation emerges through technological research and development. The arrival of smartphones, tablets, the Internet, 3D printing, driverless cars, wearable technology and space travel have all created brand-new markets that did not exist before the technological breakthroughs. However, innovation can take other forms. Businesses can use clever marketing techniques to develop new wants. They can supply their products in new locations, for instance, supermarkets offering a click & collect service at stations. New businesses can cash in on the inadequacies of others. For example, since the '**credit crunch**' in 2008, new businesses have been set up to compete with banks. Crowd funding and peer-to-peer websites have started to provide **unsecured loans**. At the moment their market shares are relatively small. But if they prove successful the established banks will have to match these new innovations.

Social changes: Changes in society can have a big impact on markets. For example, the decline in the number of marriages, an increase in the proportion of working women and the growth in the number of one-parent families have increased the market size for childcare and housing.

Changes in legislation: New laws can affect markets. For example, environmental legislation has helped to stimulate growth in renewable energies and 'green goods'. Tighter laws relating to **payday lending** has resulted in many firms leaving the market. A ban on tobacco advertising in some countries might have reduced the market size for cigarettes.

Demographic changes: Changes in the structure of the population can affect the size of markets. In most countries the population is ageing. This will help a lot of markets to grow because populations get bigger. But there will also be an increase in the markets for specialist holidays for the elderly, healthcare, care homes and mobility aids.

ADAPTING TO CHANGE

If businesses do not adapt to market changes, they are likely to lose market share. At worst they could collapse. In 2017 it was reported that Microsoft® was losing market share. In September 2016 Microsoft's key product, Windows® 10, lost 0.46 per cent of its share and again in February 2017 it lost 0.11 per cent. These are not dramatic changes but could be a cause for concern if they become consistent. To help retain its share Microsoft is adding new features to Windows 10 in a bundle called Creators Update. This will enhance the experience for users, particularly those that use systems for gaming.

Flexibility: Businesses need to be prepared for change. One way is to develop a culture of flexibility within an organisation.

A business might need flexible working practices, machinery and equipment, pricing and staff. This could mean that staff have to be trained in a variety of skills and be prepared to change the tasks they undertake in the workplace. This might help businesses to serve customers more effectively when changes occur. For example, if customers want access to the business during the evening, then staff might have to work shifts. If businesses have flexible operations it will be a lot easier for them to adapt to market changes.

Market research: Businesses must keep in touch with developments in the market. One way to do this is to undertake regular market research. This might be aimed at current customers or potential customers. Firms need to be aware of any changes in customer needs or tastes. Communication with customers and potential customers should be an ongoing process if firms want to keep completely up to date. Market research is discussed in Chapter 2.

Investment: Those businesses that invest in new product development are likely to survive for longer in the market. Although research and development are expensive, a failure to innovate could be costly. A unique new version of a product or a brand could lift sales and help win a larger share of the market. In the car industry, firms spend very large sums of money on product development. BMW has enjoyed a larger slice of the small car market by extending the range of its Minis. Investment might also be needed in training and new flexible machinery.

Continuous improvement in the increasingly competitive environment: Businesses need to make continual improvements in all aspects of their operations. For example, if they can improve efficiency, costs will be lower and prices can be held or reduced. If customer service is excellent, customers are more likely to return. If new product ideas are encouraged, they may gain a competitive edge. A culture of continuous improvement can help businesses be more adaptable in the market.

Develop a niche: If a market is in decline and a business is unable to diversify, it may survive by serving a niche. A niche strategy is appropriate if groups of loyal customers can be served profitably. For example, Harley-Davidson survived by leaving most of the motorcycle market to the Japanese. They sold highly powerful 'hogs' to a small segment of motorcycle enthusiasts. As a result they became quite profitable and survived. Generally,

if firms cannot adapt quickly to the changing needs of customers, they will lose out to rivals that do adapt.

HOW COMPETITION AFFECTS THE MARKET

Competition is the rivalry that exists between businesses in a market. It would be rare for a business to operate in a market where there was absolutely no competition. The existence of competition will have an impact on both businesses and consumers in the market.

Businesses: Competition puts businesses under some pressure. It means that they have to encourage customers to buy their products in preference to those of rivals. They will use a range of methods to attract customers. These methods include:

- lowering prices
- making their products appear different to those of rivals
- offering better quality products
- using more powerful or attractive advertising or promotions
- offering 'extras', such as high-quality customer service.

All of these methods cost money and generally reduce the amount of profit a business can make. However, businesses have to use such methods in order to survive in the market.

Because competition makes running a business more challenging and reduces the profit potential, owners and managers might try to reduce competition in the market. One way of doing this is to take over their rivals. This might be achieved by purchasing a rival in the market. Alternatively, they might try to create obstacles that make it difficult for others to enter the market. For example, they may spend huge amounts of money on advertising, which potential entrants might struggle to match. It is generally the larger businesses in the market that are able to reduce competition in this way. However, there is a range of legislation that prevents businesses restricting competition using practices that are considered unfair.

Consumers: Consumers will generally benefit from competition in markets. In markets where there are lots of businesses competing with each other, there will be more choice. Most people enjoy having lots of choice because it makes their life more interesting. For example, when people buy a car they can choose from a huge range of different models, styles, colours and endless variations in specifications. Consumers may also enjoy better-quality products and lower prices.

In the absence of competition consumers might be exploited. A business with little or no competition might raise prices and restrict choice. They will lack the incentive to innovate. For example, they are unlikely to invest money to develop new products. Consequently, one of the roles of a government is to ensure that competition exists in markets.

THE DIFFERENCE BETWEEN RISK AND UNCERTAINTY

One of the challenges when running a business is dealing with risk and uncertainty. Although both risk and uncertainty are likely to pose threats to a business, they are not the same.

Risk: Owners take risks when running a business. This means they take actions where the outcomes are unknown. More specifically, they commit resources that could be lost. Initially, they take a risk when setting up a business. This is because they invest their own money to get the business 'up and running' and there is a chance that the business will not succeed. If the worst happens and the business collapses it is possible that all the money invested by the owner is lost.

In many countries it is reckoned that a very large proportion of new businesses, perhaps as much as 90 per cent, do not survive beyond 5 years.

Even when businesses are established, they may continue to take risks. This is because they often spend money on ventures that may not provide positive results. For example, they may invest in a new product, which subsequently fails in the market. If the product is withdrawn, most of the money spent on development and launch will be lost.

In 2014 Amazon, the online retailer, launched a mobile phone called the Amazon Fire Phone. It failed in the market and the price was reduced very quickly from US$199 to just US$0.99. It was reported that Amazon lost US$170 million as a result.

Uncertainty: The markets in which businesses operate are often subject to external influences. This means that events that are completely beyond the control of businesses can have an impact in the market, which can have financial consequences. For example:

- a new competitor might enter the market with a superior product
- consumer tastes might change as a result of a new social trend
- the government might introduce a new policy or piece of legislation
- some new technology might be invented
- there may be a natural disaster, such as a flood
- the economy might go into recession.

Unfortunately, such influences are very difficult to predict. This means that businesses have to operate all of the time in an environment of uncertainty.

However, the consequences of uncertainty are not always negative. For example, new technologies can provide new opportunities. The introduction of the Internet has resulted in an enormous range of new business opportunities. Generally though, businesses do not like uncertainty. Decision making becomes more difficult, particularly when investing for the future.

SUBJECT VOCABULARY

brand name a name, term, sign, symbol, design or any other feature that allows consumers to identify the goods and services of a business and to differentiate them from those of competitors.

credit crunch a time when borrowing money becomes difficult because banks reduce the amount they lend and charge high interest rates.

e-commerce the use of electronic systems to sell goods and services.

EV a motor vehicle that can be recharged from an external source of electricity, such as wall sockets, and the electricity stored in the rechargeable battery packs drives or contributes to drive the wheels. A PEV is an plug-in electric vehicle.

liquidation the act of closing a company by selling the things that belong to it, in order to pay its debts.

market a set of arrangements that allows buyers and sellers to communicate and trade in a particular range of goods and services.

marketing a management process involved in identifying, anticipating and satisfying consumer requirements profitably.

market share the proportion of total sales in a particular market for which one or more businesses or brands are responsible. It is expressed as a percentage and can be calculated by value or volume.

mass market a very large market in which products with mass appeal are targeted.

niche market a smaller market, usually within a large market or industry.

online retailing or e-tailing the retailing of goods online.

payday lending an amount of money that is lent for a short period of time, usually at a high rate of interest and because someone needs money until they get paid again from their job.

unsecured loan a loan where there are no assets to which the lender has a right if the borrower does not make repayments.

EXAM PRACTICE

GLOBAL EV MARKET

SKILLS ANALYSIS, INTERPRETATION, REASONING

Growing concerns about the environment, and agreements by many countries in the world to cut carbon emissions, have helped to encourage sales of electric vehicles (EVs) and hybrids. A hybrid vehicle is one that uses two or more power sources. These vehicles are now beginning to grab market share from traditional petrol and diesel models.

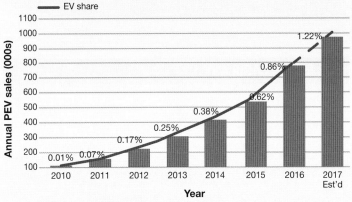

▲ Figure 3 Global sales of EVs, 2010 and 2017

Figure 3 shows that global sales of EVs in 2016 was 774,000 units. This was 42 per cent higher than for 2015. Sales of EVs grew 20 times faster than the overall vehicle market, however, this was only 0.86 per cent of the total market for vehicles. By the end of 2016, the number of EVs on the road passed 2 million. Of these 61 per cent were pure EVs and 39 per cent were hybrids. As Figure 4 shows, China is currently the most important market. It also plays a leading role in the manufacturing of EVs.

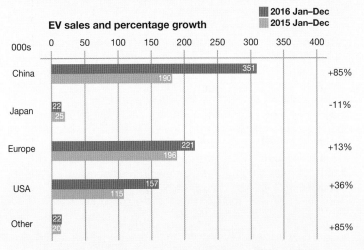

▲ Figure 4 EV sales and growth rates in a selection of regions, 2015 and 2016

Although EVs only have a very small market share at the moment, the sector is developing rapidly. One of the barriers to growth is the uncertainty about supporting infrastructure – stations that provide facilities for recharging batteries. However, locations for charging have increased at least tenfold and the number of available grid-charged models has increased from 70 to 130 since 2013. Also, the cost of batteries has fallen by 50 per cent in recent years and renewable sources are now roughly the same cost as fossil fuels in electricity generation.

Many governments around the world have also introduced financial incentives to encourage the purchase of EVs.

Q

(a) Define market share. **(2 marks)**
(b) Explain one reason why the global car market is likely to grow in the next 5 years. **(4 marks)**
(c) Discuss how a car manufacturer might adapt to changes in the market. **(8 marks)**
(d) Assess the factors that might affect the growth of the EV market in the future. **(10 marks)**

2 MARKET RESEARCH

LEARNING OBJECTIVES

By the end of this chapter you should be able to understand:

- the primary and secondary market research data (qualitative and quantitative) used to identify and anticipate customer needs and wants, quantifying likely demand and gaining insight into consumer behaviour
- methods of primary market research: surveys/questionnaires, focus groups/consumer panels, face-to-face/telephone interviews and product trials/test marketing
- methods of secondary market research: websites/social media, newspapers/magazines/television/radio, reports and databases
- sampling methods: random, quota and stratified.

GETTING STARTED

In 2017, Alok Hossain decided to set up a Bangladeshi takeaway food service in Lagos, Portugal. Before he started trading he gathered information about the market for takeaway food in the town. He spent a lot of time finding out about competitors. He found out about the:

- number and location of takeaway restaurants in Lagos
- menus and prices charged
- opening times
- advertising and promotions used
- additional services offered, such as delivery
- speed of service
- types of customers who bought Bangladeshi food.

The information gathered by Alok was very helpful. For example, he found that one of the main criticisms of current takeaway services was the slow speed of service. When Alok opened Chittagong Paradise his speed of service was a unique selling point.

Why would it have been a mistake for Alok not to carry out market research? Alok used primary or field research, what does this mean? Is market research expensive? What might be the limitations of Alok's research?

MARKET RESEARCH

Market research involves gathering, presenting and analysing information about the marketing and consumption of goods and services. Businesses spend money on market research because it helps to reduce the risk of failure. Products that are well researched are more likely to be successful. Market research data can be used for the following specific purposes.

Identify and anticipate customer needs and wants: Businesses will benefit if they can clarify the specific needs and wants of consumers. In order to design products that are likely to sell, they need to identify as precisely as possible the product features that people desire. For example, a car manufacturer will need to find out which product features are important to potential customers. Examples include:

- body design and style
- colour
- interior design and style
- economy
- ease of maintenance
- how long it will last
- performance (e.g. acceleration and top speed).

The data that market researchers gather need to be as comprehensive as possible so that all the needs and wants are identified. This data will be qualitative. This is explained later in this chapter.

Quantify likely demand: It is important to find out how much of a product a business might expect to sell in a market. This data will be quantitative. This is discussed in detail later in this chapter. One reason for this is to help determine whether or not a particular product is going to be commercially viable. If market research finds that demand is inadequate, a business might cancel the launch of a product. This could save the business a lot of money. This is one of the reasons why businesses carry out research.

Assuming that demand is adequate, a business will need to know how much it should produce. Once demand has been quantified a business can plan production of the product. This means that it can start to organise the resources that will be needed for production and draw up production schedules. For example, it might need to recruit more staff to work in the factory and work with different departments to ensure that the necessary resources can be acquired.

Gain an insight into consumer behaviour: Some market research is aimed at analysing consumer behaviour. Businesses might be more successful if they can identify and understand patterns of consumer behaviour. For example, a holiday company selling package (organised by travel agents) holidays abroad might use market research to find out:

- when consumers book their holidays
- when consumers are most likely to go on holiday
- the number of holidays people take each year
- which methods consumers use to book their holidays, e.g. online or travel agent
- how much money people spend on holiday
- whether customers take out holiday insurance
- how people travel to the airport.

Getting an insight into how people behave will help a business to meet customer needs more effectively. This is qualitative data and might also help them to identify new opportunities. Businesses can use a number of different methods to gather market research data. Some of these methods are explained in detail below.

PRIMARY RESEARCH

Primary research or field research involves collecting primary data. This is information that did not exist before the research began. In other words, it has to be collected by the researcher. It can either be carried out by a business itself or by a market research agency. Because of the high costs of using the services of a market research agency, many small businesses choose to conduct market research themselves.

Most primary information is gathered by asking consumers questions or by monitoring their behaviour. The most accurate way to do this would be to question or observe all consumers of a particular product (known as the population). However, in all but a few instances this would be either impractical to carry out or expensive. It is usual to carry out a survey of a sample of people who are thought to be representative of the total market.

METHODS OF PRIMARY RESEARCH

Some of the main methods of gathering data are discussed briefly below.

Questionnaires/surveys: A questionnaire is a list of written questions. They are very common in market research and are used to record the views and opinions of respondents. A good questionnaire will have the following elements.

- **Have a balance of *open* and *closed* questions.** Closed questions allow respondents a limited range of responses. An example would be 'How many times have you flown with Emirates® this year?'. The answers to closed questions are easier to analyse and represent numerically. Open questions let people say whatever they want. They do not have to choose from a list of responses. Open questions are best used if there are a large number of possible responses. An example would be 'How would you improve the quality of cabin service provided by Emirates?'.
- **Contain clear and simple questions.** Questions must be clear avoiding the use of jargon, poor grammar and bad spelling.
- **Not contain leading questions.** Leading questions are those that 'suggest' a certain answer. They should be avoided because otherwise the results will be unreliable.
- **Not be too long.** If questionnaires are too long people will not give up their time to answer them.

Questionnaires can be used in different situations. Two examples are outlined below.

- **Postal surveys.** Questionnaires are sent to people and they are asked to complete them in their own time. They may be more convenient for people but the vast majority of questionnaires are never returned. This means that resources are wasted.
- **Online surveys.** An increasing number of businesses are using online surveys to gather information from customers. These are likely to be cheap because they avoid printing and postage costs. Some businesses send consumers links to online surveys after they have made a purchase. These allow businesses to gather quick feedback from customers, which might help to identify strengths and weaknesses in their quality of service. Booking.com and Amazon are two examples of companies that use this approach. Also, in some countries, there are online surveys that pay cash to respondents if they complete questionnaires. These are used to gather information for a variety of different businesses.

Focus groups or consumer panels: If a business wants very detailed information from customers it might use focus groups or consumer panels. A focus group is where a number of customers are invited to attend a discussion organised by market researchers. The group must be representative of the whole population and be prepared to answer detailed questions. This is a relatively cost-effective method of collecting information but the group may be a little small. Consumer panels are similar to focus groups except that groups of customers are asked for feedback over a period of time. This approach allows businesses to see how consumers react to changes in their products.

Face-to-face/telephone interviews: Businesses may conduct face-to-face interviews in the street. For example, an interviewer might approach pedestrians, ask them a few questions and record the answers on a clipboard. The advantage is that questions can be explained if a respondent is confused. It may be possible to collect more detailed information. However, many people do not like being approached in the street. Another approach is to interview people over the telephone. This is likely to be cheaper than questioning people in the street. Also, people from a wide geographical area can be covered. However, some people do not like being telephoned

by businesses – especially if they have not made an appointment.

Product trials/test marketing: Some businesses use product trials to get feedback from customers. This is where consumers are encouraged to examine, use or test a product before it is launched fully into the market. This enables businesses to make late adjustments to the product, if necessary, based on the feedback they gather. In some cases, consumers might be offered cash for trying out products and providing feedback. A similar approach is called test marketing. This involves selling a new product in a restricted geographical area to test it before a wider launch. After a period of time feedback is gathered from customers. The feedback is used to make modifications to the product before the final launch across the whole market. This reduces the risk of failure.

Advantages	Disadvantages
Data can be collected that directly applies to the issue being researched. Secondary data will be data collected for another purpose.	It can be expensive to collect and may take longer than desk research.
The business that initially collects the data will be the only organisation with access to it. It can be used to gain marketing advantages over rival firms.	The sample taken may not represent the views of all the population.
Secondary data may be unavailable in a certain area.	If the research method is flawed, the findings will also be flawed. For example, a badly worded questionnaire may not provide the data a business requires.

▲ Table 1 Advantages and disadvantages of primary or field research

ACTIVITY 1　　SKILLS　ANALYSIS, REASONING

CASE STUDY: ONLINE SURVEYS

Some businesses use online surveys to gather data. This involves providing a link to a questionnaire on a company website and inviting people to complete it. An online questionnaire can be completed quickly and responses can often be analysed immediately. Survey costs are low because there are no printing and posting charges. Online surveys can be interactive and may be fun to complete. They can also be accessed 24/7 and be completed when it is convenient. However, there are problems. The sample of respondents may not be representative. This is because online surveys are only presented to Internet users. The views of others may not be

taken into account even though they may be potential customers.

Some businesses are keen to find out what customers think of their websites. They might use an online survey similar to the one shown in Figure 1.

1. Give one reason why it might be important to find out what people think of a business website.
2. Explain whether an online survey would benefit a company selling to: (a) customers in isolated areas (b) less-developed countries, such as Ethiopia, Bhutan and Haiti.
3. Discuss the advantages and disadvantages of online surveys.

Website survey

Thank you for using our website. We'd like to ask you some questions about your experience so that we can improve

We would like your feedback about the content on our site. How satisfied are you with the content?

○ Very dissatisfied ○ Dissatisfied ○ Neutral ○ Satisfied
○ Very satisfied

Please tell us how our site compares with similar sites for each of the items below If you did not experience an item, please select "N/A".

	Much worse	Worse	About the same	Better	Much better	N/A
Overall organisation/ navigation	○ 1	○ 2	○ 3	○ 4	○ 5	○ -
Home page content	○ 1	○ 2	○ 3	○ 4	○ 5	○ -
Product information	○ 1	○ 2	○ 3	○ 4	○ 5	○ -
Ease of finding how to contact us	○ 1	○ 2	○ 3	○ 4	○ 5	○ -
Downloading information	○ 1	○ 2	○ 3	○ 4	○ 5	○ -

How likely are you to recommend our site to others?

○ Definitely not ○ Unlikely ○ Neutral ○ May be likely
○ Very likely

What prompted you to visit our site today? Please select all that apply.

☐ Comparison shopping
☐ Interested in purchasing products/services
☐ Looking for contact information
☐ Looking for technical support
☐ Other, please specify

How did you find our site? Please select all that apply.

☐ Recommended by others
☐ Link from email our site sent you
☐ Link from another website
☐ Link from marketing leaflet
☐ Search engine results
☐ Other, please specify

How frequently do you visit our site?

○ First choice ○ Daily ○ A few times per week
○ A few times per month ○ Once per month ○ Less frequently than once per month

The next questions will only be used to group your answers with others like yourself.

Please tell us how you access the Internet. Check all that apply.

☐ Home   ☐ Cafe
☐ Work   ☐ Mobile phone
☐ College   ☐ Computer tablet (e.g. iPad(R))
☐ Library   ☐ Other, please specify

How long do you spend on the Internet each day? Select a choice.

○ 1-2 hours ○ 3-4 hours ○ More than 8 hours

Please indicate your gender.

○ Male ○ Female

Please select the category that includes your age.

○ 18-30 ○ 31-55 ○ 56 or older

Which one of the following ranges includes your total yearly household income before taxes?

○ up to £28,000 ○ over £28,000
○ Prefer not to answer

(Submit) Back

▲ Figure 1 An example of a website survey

SECONDARY RESEARCH

Secondary research or desk research involves the collection of secondary data. This is information that already exists in some form. It can be internal data, from records within the business, or external data, from sources outside the business.

METHODS OF SECONDARY RESEARCH

Websites: A business can carry out secondary research by gathering data from the websites of rivals. By analysing the websites of competitors, a wide range of information can be gathered very easily and cheaply. For example, information about prices charged, product ranges, delivery terms, payment terms, store locations, details of special offers and useful links that might provide even more information. A business might also use comparison websites to identify the cheapest suppliers in the market.

Social media: Few businesses can afford to neglect the role social media can play in marketing. An increasing number of businesses make use of social media platforms such as Facebook, Twitter®, YouTube®, blogs and coupon sites. Social media can provide a cost-effective and in-depth tool for gaining insights into a firm's customers, market, brand appearance and other important market research aspects.

For example, most social media platforms offer numerous ways to analyse trends and conduct market research. By simply searching the latest posts and popular terms, it is possible to gain insight into emerging trends and see what customers are talking about in real-time. One example of this is conducting hashtag searches on Twitter. By setting up a few searches with hashtags (#) related to a specific brand, industry or product, instant notifications (alerts) can be received when customers, clients or competitors use key terms.

One of the biggest weaknesses to most marketing research methods is that they are driven by questions. To obtain the proper information, you must first know what to ask. At the same time, simply changing the words of a question can result in drastically different answers. This means that market research is only as good as the questions used. With the broad scope and interactive nature of social media, information is gained through interaction and observation. Instead of leading the discussions, businesses can simply observe or join in as an equal. This can result in a variety of answers and discoveries that might have remained hidden using other research methods.

Table 2 summarises the advantages of using social media for market research.

Broad reach	It can reach millions of people all around the world.
Ability to target	Social media allows specific groups of people to be targeted.
Free or low cost	The use of social media may be free for businesses and paid options are usually cheap.
Personal	It allows communication on a personal basis with individual customers and groups.
Fast	Information can be collected very quickly from large numbers of people.
Easy	High-level IT skills and complex equipment are not needed.

▲ Table 2 The advantages of using social media for market research

Newspapers/magazines: Some businesses may be able to use written information printed in newspapers and magazines as a source of market research data. For example, a small business might use a local newspaper to help assess the strength of competition in a market. This might be done by analysing the small ads placed by rival firms.

Some magazines carry out surveys among their readership, which might be useful. For example, a survey that explores the way readers spend their leisure time might provide useful information for a business operating a fitness centre.

Trade journals, which are publications produced by businesses or industries, can be a major source for marketing data and intelligence for the industries and markets they cover. They regularly publish special issues that may include, for example: industry outlook; year in review; product sales and market shares; buyer's guides; and other statistics.

Television/radio: Programmes broadcast on television and radio may provide useful data for some businesses. For example, documentaries about business, industry, the economy and people's behaviour might be helpful. There may be some specialist channels that can provide very specific information. For example, shopping channels might be used to help analyse the products of competitors. Also, a business might be able to analyse the adverts used on television and radio to help gather information about rival products and marketing methods.

Reports: The reports published by a wide range of organisations might be used to gather secondary data. In many countries the government is likely to publish data that could be used by businesses. For example, statistical reports may be available free of charge to any business and contain information such as the:

- relative sizes of the primary, secondary and tertiary sector
- number of people in different age groups in a country
- income levels in different regions or countries
- spending patterns in different regions or countries
- value of output in different industries
- methods of transport used by people travelling to work.

Organisations, such as the EU, the World Bank, the World Trade Organization and the International Monetary Fund, also publish a wide range of regular reports that can be accessed by businesses.

DATABASES

A **database** allows a great deal of data to be stored. Every business that uses computers will compile and use databases. The information is set up so that it can be updated and recalled when needed. Table 3 shows part of a database of a finance company which gives details about their clients. The collection of common data is called a file. A file consists of a set of related records. In Table 3 all the information on Jane Brown, for example, is a record. The information on each record is listed under headings known as fields, e.g. name, address, age, occupation, income each year. A good database will have the following facilities:

- be user definable (having a function or meaning that can be specified and varied by a user)
- file-searching facility for finding specified information from a file, e.g. identifying all clients with an income over £33,000. It is usually possible to search on more than one criterion, e.g. all females with an income over £33,000

- file-sorting facility for rearranging data in another order, e.g. arranging the file in Table 3 in ascending order of income
- calculations on fields within records for inclusion in reports.

In the world of business and commerce there is actually a market for information held on databases. It is possible to buy banks of information from market researchers who have compiled databases over the years. Names and addresses of potential customers would be information well worth purchasing if it were legally available. The storage of personal data on a computer in the UK is influenced by the Data Protection Act. Any company or institution wishing to store personal data on a computer system must register with the Data Protection Office. Individuals have a right under the Act to request details of information held on them.

Surname	First name	Address	Town	Age	Occupation	Income p.a.
Adams	John	14 Stanley St	Bristol	39	Bricklayer	£32,000
Appaswamy	Krishen	2 Virginia St	Cardiff	23	Welder	£26,000
Atkins	Robert	25 Liverpool Rd	Cardiff	42	Teacher	£32,000
Biddle	Ron	34 Bedford Rd	Bath	58	Civil servant	£35,000
Brown	Jane	111 Bold St	Newport	25	Solicitor	£41,000

▲ Table 3 An extract from a simple database

Advantages	Disadvantages
It is relatively easy, quick and cheap to collect, especially if the sources that exist are known. This makes it very useful for smaller businesses.	Data is not always in a form that a particular business would want because it has been collected for another purpose. Adapting it may take time and become expensive.
Several sources may be used. This allows the data to be checked and verified.	Data may be out of date and not relevant, especially in fast-changing markets.
Historical data may be used which can show a trend over time.	Researchers must be aware of bias. For example, company reports and accounts may show figures in the best possible light to satisfy shareholders.
It can be used before carrying out primary research, which helps to establish the most useful questions to be asked in questionnaires.	There may have been problems with the research. For example, the footnotes to research may state that the sample used was too small and that the results may be inaccurate as a result.

▲ Table 4 Advantages and disadvantages of secondary or desk research

QUANTITATIVE AND QUALITATIVE RESEARCH

Data collected through desk and field research can be either quantitative or qualitative in nature.

Qualitative research involves the collection of data about attitudes, beliefs and intentions. Focus groups and interviews are common methods used to collect qualitative data. An example of qualitative research could be face-to-face interviews with 100 purchasers (buyers) of new Land Rover Discoveries to find out why they prefer this product to similar four-wheel drive vehicles sold by other car manufacturers. The information collected through qualitative research is usually regarded as being open to a high degree of interpretation. This means that there are often disagreements within businesses about the significance and importance of qualitative research data.

Quantitative research involves the collection of data that can be measured. In practice this usually means the collection of statistical data such as sales figures and market share. Surveys and the use of government publications are common methods of collecting quantitative research data. An example of quantitative research would be a survey of four-wheel drive vehicle owners in Bavaria to establish where they live, their ages, occupations, incomes and gender. The information collected through quantitative research is usually regarded as being open to less interpretation than that collected through qualitative research.

ACTIVITY 2   SKILLS   CRITICAL THINKING, ANALYSIS, INTERPRETATION, INNOVATION

CASE STUDY: TEKKONG AND VIRTUAL REALITY

TekKong, a technology company based in Hong Kong, China, has developed a new virtual reality (VR) headset that it hopes to launch in 2018. A VR headset is a device used to deliver VR experiences for three-dimensional (3D) simulations, computer games and other applications, such as movies. They may be used in the development of training methods, engineering design process, business environments and audience engagement (involvement), such as VR gaming, sports and events. VR headsets are also widely used by medical students when training for surgery. TekKong decided to develop the product after some desk research was carried out in 2016 to assess the size of the market and the strength of the competition.

Figure 2 shows the market sizes for four different types of wearable technology in 2016 and 2020. According to online research, 2016 saw significant fragmentation in the VR hardware market, with many new devices and platforms launching. Appearing alongside Google Cardboard were new platforms Google Daydream, Samsung Gear VR, Oculus Rift, PlayStation® VR and Steam® VR.

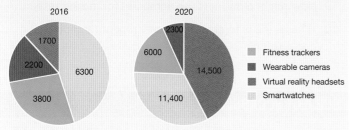

▲ Figure 2 Market sizes of four types of wearable technology (US$ million), 2016 and 2020 (estimated)

1. Define desk research.
2. Figure 2 is an example of quantitative data.
   (a) What does this mean?
   (b) Describe **one** advantage of gathering quantitative data.
3. Based on the data in Figure 2, discuss **one** possible reason why TekKong decided to develop a VR headset.

SAMPLING METHODS

Ideally, when carrying out a survey, information could be gathered from every single member in the target population. The target population includes all those people whose views a business wants to explore. The target population may be individual consumers, households or other businesses, for example. However, this may take too long and cost too much money. To overcome this problem businesses collect information from a sample of people in the population. A sample is a much smaller group. However, it is important that the behaviour and views of the sample are representative of all those in the population.

The sample size will affect the accuracy of the information gathered. Large samples will be more representative of the population and therefore more useful to a business. However, using larger samples is more expensive so there is a trade-off between cost and the level of accuracy required. It might be argued that

a sample size of at least 10 per cent of the population would be needed for a survey to be meaningful.

There are different types of sample and sampling methods that can be used by a business carrying out primary research.

Random sampling: Random sampling gives each member of a group an equal chance of being chosen. In other words, the sample is selected at random, rather like picking numbers out of a hat. Today computers can be used to produce a random list of numbers, which are then used as the basis for selecting a sample. However, it assumes that all members of the group are exactly the same, which is not always the case. A small sample chosen this way may not have the characteristics of the population. Therefore, a very large sample would have to be taken to ensure that it was representative. It would also be expensive for a business to draw up a list of the whole population and then to contact and interview them.

Quota sampling: Quota sampling involves the target population being segmented into a number of groups that share specific characteristics. These may be based on the age and gender of the population, for example. Interviewers are then given targets for the number of people out of each segment who they must interview. For example, an interviewer may be asked to interview 10 males between the ages of 18 and 25, or 15 females aged between 45 and 60. Once the target has been reached, no more people from that group are interviewed. The main advantage of this sampling method is that it is more cost effective than other methods. It is also useful where the proportions of the different groups within the population are known. However, results from quota sampling are not statistically representative of the population and are not chosen randomly.

Stratified sampling: This method of sampling is also random. However, unlike the method described above, stratified sampling is where the sample is divided into segments or strata based on previous knowledge about how the population is divided up. For example, a business may be interested in how employment status affected the demand for a food product. It might divide the population into different income groups, such as higher managerial and professional occupations, small employers and self-employed workers. A random sample could then be chosen from each of these groups, making sure that there were the same proportions of the sample in each category as in the population as a whole. Therefore, in this example, if the population had 10 per cent of small employers, the sample must also have 10 per cent. Stratified sampling is a popular method because it makes the sample more representative of the whole group.

ACTIVITY 3

SKILLS CRITICAL THINKING, REASONING, COMMUNICATION

CASE STUDY: BASEL INTERNATIONAL

Basel International is a multinational pharmaceutical company based in Basel, Switzerland. In 2017, 74 per cent of the company's products were aimed at the male market. The board of directors felt that this was a weakness and therefore commissioned a market research agency to carry out a worldwide study into female health. The board planned to use the results to identify gaps in the market for future product development.

The agency set about conducting a two-phase survey. In the first phase, 20,000 interviews were conducted with target respondents in 20 different countries. The agency used a combination of telephone and online surveys to gather information. In the second phase, 5 per cent of the initial respondents were chosen at random for a second interview. These interviews were conducted over the telephone and a greater proportion of open questions were used.

The research methods used meant that the same questions were put to all respondents and answers were collected in the same manner.

Random sampling is used by the market research agency in this case.

1. (a) Define random sampling.
   (b) Why are samples used in market research?
   (c) Describe **one** disadvantage of using random sampling.
2. On behalf of Basel International, information was gathered from 20,000 females in 20 different countries. Suggest why it interviewed (a) females only; (b) respondents in 20 different countries rather than one country only and (c) 20,000 people rather than 1000 or 1 million.
3. (a) What is the difference between open and closed questions in a survey?
   (b) Describe one advantage to Basel International of using open questions.

CHECKPOINT

1. How might market research reduce the risk in business?
2. State three advantages of primary research.
3. What is desk research?
4. State four sources of data for secondary research.
5. What is meant by quantitative market research?
6. Why might qualitative data be open to different interpretations?
7. How might a business use social media to conduct market research?
8. Give three advantages of using online surveys.
9. How might a business use databases for market research?
10. What is the difference between a random sample and a quota sample?

SUBJECT VOCABULARY

consumer panels groups of customers are asked for feedback about products over a period of time.
database an organised collection of data stored electronically with instant access, searching and sorting facilities.
focus groups a number of customers are invited to attend a discussion about a product run by market researchers.
market research the collection, presentation and analysis of information relating to the marketing and consumption of goods and services.
primary research or field research the gathering of 'new' information that does not already exist.
qualitative research the collection of data about attitudes, beliefs and intentions.
quantitative research the collection of data that can be quantified.
quota sampling respondents are selected in a non-random manner in the same proportion as they exist in the whole population.
random sampling respondents are selected for interview at random.
respondents people or organisations that answer questions in a survey.
sample a small group of people that must represent a proportion of a total market when carrying out market research.
secondary research or desk research the collection of data that is already in existence.
stratified sampling a method of quota sampling in which respondents are chosen at random.
target population the total number of consumers in a given group.

EXAM PRACTICE

MARKET RESEARCH ON 'CLICK & COLLECT' ORDERS

SKILLS ANALYSIS, INTERPRETATION, CRITICAL THINKING, REASONING, INNOVATION

Mintel is the world's leading market intelligence agency. It provides a wide range of services in the field of market research. For example, it carries out primary research, analyses market data and market trends, and produces specialist market research reports for its clients. Some of Mintel's reports can be purchased online and can cost up to £2500. The research data below about click & collect orders was gathered by Mintel in 2014.

- Click & collect orders made up 15 per cent of all Internet retail sales of goods in 2014. The collection rate was much higher for non-grocery orders than groceries.
- In 2014, online retail sales were expected to contribute up to 11.6 per cent of all retail sales. This means, in turn, that click & collect orders would make up 1.7 per cent of all retail sales in 2014.
- The survey estimated that in 2015, 17 per cent of all Internet retail sales (or 2.2 per cent of all retail sales) would be collected by customers. In September 2014, Transport for London reported that it had processed 10,000 orders at its click & collect stations in the first 10 months of operation.
- Thirty-five per cent of UK consumers had used click & collect services in the previous year and 64 per cent said that they shopped online more now because retailers offer click & collect services. Furthermore, 58 per cent said that click & collect encouraged them to visit stores more frequently.
- Sixty per cent of UK consumers only used click & collect for smaller items that were easy to carry, but 53 per cent said they would like drive-through points that offered click & collect for a number of retailers – suggesting opportunities to extend click & collect to heavier or bulkier items.

- New click-and-collect fashion facilities are likely to drive up online sales. In the survey, 80 per cent of consumers agreed that when shopping online it is difficult to tell if clothes will fit – consumers aged under 35 see this as the main issue.
- Fifty per cent of consumers (rising to 57 per cent of women) said the annoyance of returning goods through the post was one of the main barriers to buying clothes online. Thirty-one per cent of consumers preferred to be able to return their online order to an actual store – and 23 per cent of UK consumers said that an option to deliver to a store to try on before purchasing would encourage them to buy from one online retailer over another.

Source: adapted from www.mintel.com

 Q

(a) Define primary research. **(2 marks)**
(b) Explain one benefit of using qualitative market research. **(4 marks)**
(c) Explain one way in which the data in the Mintel report might be used by retailers. **(4 marks)**
(d) Assess the usefulness of market research data, like the above information, to retailers. **(10 marks)**

3 MARKET POSITIONING

LEARNING OBJECTIVES

By the end of this chapter you should be able to understand:
- product and market orientation
- market mapping
- market segmentation
- competitive advantage of a product or service
- the purpose of product differentiation
- adding value to products/services.

GETTING STARTED

The market for automobiles is very competitive. Consider the market for the cars below.

To what extent are the two cars the same or different? What might be the target markets for these two products? How might the manufacturers differentiate the two products? How might one of the manufacturers try to gain a competitive edge over their rival?

PRODUCT AND MARKET ORIENTATION

Some businesses are said to be relatively **product orientated** or **market orientated**.

Product orientation: Many businesses in the past, and some today, could be described as product orientated. This means that the business focuses on the production process and the product itself. It puts most of its effort into developing and making products that it believes consumers want and which will sell well.

In the past, businesses producing radios and televisions could be said to have been relatively product orientated. It was their novelty and the technical 'wonder' of the product that sold them. There were few companies to compete against each other, and there was a growing domestic market. There were also few overseas competitors. The product sold itself. Some industries today are still said to be product orientated.

The machine-tool industry, which produces machines used in the production of other goods, has to produce a final product that exactly matches a technical specification. However, because of increased competition, such firms are being forced to take consumers' needs into account. The technical specification to which a machine-tool business produces might be influenced by what customers want, for example.

Product-orientated businesses thus place their emphasis on developing a technically sound product, producing that product and then selling it. Contact with the consumer comes largely at this final stage. There will always be a place for product orientation. A great deal of pure research, for example, with no regard to consumers' needs, still takes place in industry, as it does in the development of pharmaceuticals.

Market orientation: A business that is market orientated is one that continually identifies, reviews and analyses consumers' needs. It is led by the market. A business is much more likely to be engaged in effective marketing if it is market orientated. Henry Ford was one of the first industrialists to adopt a market-orientated approach. When the Ford Motor Company produced the Model T, it did not just design a car, produce it as cheaply as possible, and then try to sell it to the public. Instead, in advance of production, Ford identified the price at which he believed he could sell large numbers of Model Ts. His starting point was the market and the Model T became one of the first 'mass-market' products.

This illustrates the market-orientated approach – consumers are central to a firm's decision making. Sony is one of many modern businesses that has taken a market-orientated approach. The iPhone® 6 by Apple is an example of a product being developed in response to the wishes of consumers.

A more market-orientated business may have several advantages over one which is more product orientated.
- It can respond more quickly to changes in the market because of its use of market information.
- It will be in a stronger position to meet the challenge of new competition entering the market.
- It will be more able to anticipate market changes.
- It will be more confident that the launch of a new product will be a success.

What effect will taking a market-orientated approach have on a business? It must:

- consult the consumer continuously (market research)
- design the product according to the wishes of the consumer
- produce the product in the quantities that consumers want to buy
- distribute the product according to the buying habits and delivery requirements of the consumer
- set the price of the product at a level that the consumer is prepared to pay.

The business must produce the right product at the right price and in the right place, and it must let the consumer know that it is available. This is known as the marketing mix. The adoption of a market-orientated approach will not always guarantee success. The failure rate for new products, even when launched by high-profile companies, is high. In grocery it is reckoned that the failure rate is between 80 and 94 per cent. One recent example of failure was Kellogg's® Breakfast Mates. This was a box containing cereal, milk (that did not need refrigeration) and a spoon. One reason why it failed was because people do not normally like to eat cereal without cold milk. Also, the adverts for Breakfast Mates showed the product being eaten by children while their parents were asleep. Unfortunately though, the packaging was not child friendly. Whether a business places great emphasis on the product or on the market will depend on a number of factors.

The nature of the product: Where a firm operates in an industry at the edge of new innovation, such as bio-technology, pharmaceuticals or electronics, it must innovate to survive. Although a firm may try to anticipate consumer demand, research is often 'pure' research, i.e. the researcher does not have a specific end product in mind.

Policy decisions: A business will have certain objectives. When these are set in terms of technical quality or safety, the emphasis is likely to be on production. When objectives are set in terms of market share or turnover, the emphasis is likely to be on marketing.

The views of those in control: An accountant or a managing director may place emphasis on factors such as cash flow and profit forecasts, a production engineer may give technical quality control and research a high priority and a marketing person may be particularly concerned with market research and consumer relations.

The nature and size of the market: If production costs are very high, then a company is likely to be market orientated. Only by being so can a company ensure it meets consumers' needs and avoid unsold goods and possible losses.

The degree of competition: A company faced with a lack of competition may devote fewer resources to research with little concern about a loss of market share.

Businesses in competitive markets are likely to spend more on marketing for fear of losing their share of the market.

The distinction between product and market orientation can be seen as a spectrum, as in Figure 1. Most business are somewhere along the spectrum. For example, supermarkets may be more market orientated and a copper mining company more product orientated.

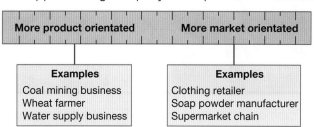

▲ Figure 1 Product versus market orientation

ACTIVITY 1   SKILLS   ANALYSIS, INTERPRETATION, CRITICAL THINKING, REASONING

CASE STUDY: SUN PHARMACEUTICAL INDUSTRIES

Sun Pharmaceutical Industries is the largest pharmaceuticals company in India. It focuses on three important areas of healthcare: cardiovascular and metabolic disease (CVMD); oncology; and respiratory, inflammation and autoimmunity (RIA).

The company employs over 50,000 people worldwide and manufactures products in 45 sites in many different countries. It is committed to ensuring a reliable supply of medicines where and when they are needed. In 2016, its total sales revenue was Rs 282,697 million.

Sun Pharmaceuticals has around 2000 research scientists working in several R&D centres around the world. Most centres are equipped with up-to-date technologies specifically designed for research. Their scientists have expertise in developing generics, difficult-to-make highly technical products, active pharmaceutical ingredients, novel drug delivery systems and new chemical entities. Figure 2 shows the amount of money Sun Pharmaceuticals has invested in R&D since 2011.

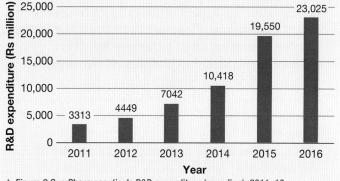

▲ Figure 2 Sun Pharmaceuticals R&D expenditure (spending), 2011–16

1. Comment on the pattern of R&D expenditure shown in Figure 2.
2. Explain one benefit to Sun Pharmaceuticals of being product orientated.
3. To what extent is Sun Pharmaceuticals product orientated?

MARKET POSITIONING

Market positioning is concerned with the perceptions consumers have about products. To simplify the choice from a vast range of products, consumers categorise them according to a range of factors. Such factors include the quality, status and value for money of products. It is the categories into which consumers place products that define their 'position'.

Consumers often position a business's products in relation to those of its competitors. This can be in the form of 'pecking order' or product ladder. Firms will plan marketing activities to shape consumer perceptions and therefore achieve a desired position. Some approaches that a business might use to position its products are outlined below.

- **The benefits offered by the product.** For example, in the automobile market, some manufacturers emphasise safety, others the quality of work and style, and yet more value for money.
- **The unique selling point.** The unique selling point or unique selling proposition (USP) of the product. This is the key aspect of the product or service that sets it apart from those of competitors. For example, some shampoos claim to remove flaky skin.
- **The characteristics/qualities of the product.** This is a common method used to position products. For example, the slogan 'M&Ms melt in your mouth, not in your hand' emphasises clearly a quality of this sweet.
- **The origin of the product.** In the market for cheese, the names of many products are derived from where they were originally manufactured.

Examples might be Lancashire, Port Salut, Edam, Gorgonzola and Camembert.
- **The classification name of the product.** The name of a product may be used to position a product in the market. This positioning strategy tends to take a leadership position in the overall market. Statements with the general message of 'we are the best in our field' are common. For example, Beanz Meanz Heinz.

As markets change in response to shifting consumer demand, some businesses find they need to **reposition** their products. This usually involves changing their target market, the features of the product or the image of the product that distinguishes it from those of rivals. For example, cleaning products originally designed for washing babies' nappies faced a sharp fall in demand when throwaway nappies were introduced. However, some companies successfully repositioned their brand for a new use – being an ideal washing powder for tough stains.

MARKET MAPPING

The positioning of a brand is influenced by customer perceptions rather than by those of businesses. For example, a business may feel its brand is a high-quality, upmarket product. But if customers see it as low quality and downmarket, it is their views that will influence sales.

So, if a business wants to find out where its brand is positioned in the market, it might carry out market research. This will help it to understand how customers see the brand in relation to others in the market.

A business may also wish to launch a new brand. Having decided the target market, market research might show what characteristics the brand must have to succeed in that market. It could reveal the price that customers are prepared to pay. It could also suggest what sort of promotional support will be needed. For example, will a national television advertising campaign be used? Will promotion to retailers be a better strategy?

The results of market research can be displayed on **market or perceptual maps** (sometimes also called positioning maps). An example is shown in Figure 3. This illustrates a perceptual map for a sample of motor cars.

The use of market maps can have its limitations. For example, perceptual maps are two dimensional, which means that only two product qualities can be analysed on the same map. They can also be more relevant for individual brands, and less helpful for a corporate brand image. The information needed to plot the maps can be expensive to obtain, requiring the use of primary market research. There may also be a difference between consumers' perception of the brand's benefits and the actual benefits.

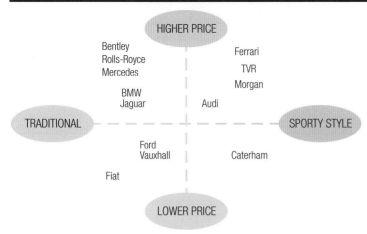

▲ Figure 3 A perceptual map for cars

Finally, perceptual maps need not come from a detailed study. There are also intuitive maps (also called judgemental maps or consensus maps) that are created by marketers based on their understanding of their industry. Management uses its best judgement. It is not certain how valuable this type of map is. Often they just give the appearance of reliability to management's preconceptions (presumptions).

ACTIVITY 2   SKILLS   ANALYSIS, CRITICAL THINKING, INTERPRETATION

CASE STUDY: ATHLETIC FOOTWEAR

A perceptual map provides a visual picture of how customers see different competitors

▲ Figure 4 A perceptual map for athletic footwear

Figure 4 shows a perceptual map for athletic footwear.
1. How might a Chinese sports shoe manufacturer use the map in Figure 4?
2. Describe **one** drawback of the Chinese sports shoe manufacturer using the perceptual map in Figure 4.
3. Assess the position of The North Face brand compared to that of Adidas using the perceptual map in Figure 4.

From time to time there may be a need to reposition an entire company, rather than just a product line. Reasons for repositioning an entire company might be to deal with a damaged image, to differentiate the company from rivals, to clarify the company's position, to create more business opportunities or to increase the value of the company. In 2015, Kia®, the South Korean car manufacturer used an advertising campaign involving television, print, digital and social media in an effort to reposition its brand. Historically, Kia had a reputation for 'affordable cars'. However, according to Kia, the new campaign had a 'premium feel'. It was designed to emphasise Kia's quality, reliability, design and technology and therefore repositioning it as a 'value brand'. Using the word premium in the adverts suggests that Kia's new brand won't be all about price.

Repositioning a company is an enormous task. It involves more than a marketing challenge. It requires making hard decisions about how a market is shifting and how a firm's competitors will react. Often these decisions must be made without the benefit of sufficient information. Positioning is also difficult to measure because customer perception of a product may not have been tested using quantitative techniques.

MARKET SEGMENTATION

Markets can be divided into different sections or **market segments**. Each segment is made up of consumers that have similar needs. Businesses recognise this and target particular market segments with their products.
- Some businesses concentrate on producing one product for one particular segment, for example, luxury cars targeted at a very wealthy market segment in the car market.
- Some businesses produce a range of different products and target them at several different segments.
- Some businesses aim their products at nearly all consumers. For example, large food manufacturers are likely to target their brands at everyone.

However, by dividing markets into segments businesses can more easily supply products that meet customers' needs.

wages and salaries go up people may decide to spend more money going out to restaurants, they may take an extra holiday or they may buy a new car. These are all **normal goods** – goods for which demand will rise when income rises. Most goods in the economy are normal goods; however, a minority are **inferior goods**. This means that demand for them will actually fall when incomes rise. Supermarket 'own-label' brands or public transport can be examples of inferior goods. For example, consumers who generally buy supermarket own-label detergent may switch to a more expensive brand, such as Persil® when their incomes rise. Therefore demand for the supermarket own-label brand will fall.

In Figure 2, if consumer incomes rise, the demand for skiing holidays would also probably rise causing a shift in the demand curve from D to D_1.

Fashions, tastes and preferences: Over a period of time, demand patterns change because of changes in consumer tastes and fashion. For example, the growth in demand for four-wheel drive cars in many countries is not because an increasing number of people need to drive off-road but because increasing numbers of drivers find them appealing. The clothes industry in particular is influenced strongly by changes in fashion. In many countries there are buying seasons for clothes – many clothes items bought in one season would not be in demand in later seasons because they will have gone out of fashion.

In recent years there has been a surge in the demand for coffee in India, traditionally a tea-drinking nation. This has been driven largely by the growth in a café culture in the country. Cafés are particularly appealing to young people. A coffee house is not only a place to buy different types of coffee, but also a much-needed urban space. A café offers a neutral meeting place that allows youngsters to get together in a comfortable environment that is neither a home nor a workplace.

Marketing, advertising and branding: Businesses try to influence demand for their products through advertising and other forms of promotion. If goods are heavily advertised demand for them is likely to increase. This helps to explain the huge amounts of money that some businesses are prepared to spend on advertising. For example, Procter & Gamble, the giant US multinational, spent US$7243 million on global advertising in 2016.

Businesses also use branding to influence demand. By giving products a name, term, symbol or any other sign, to distinguish them from those of competitors, businesses can develop brand recognition and increase sales. They do this by investing heavily in positioning, promoting and advertising to make the brand strong. Branding is discussed in Chapter 11. In Figure 2,

if businesses selling skiing holidays increase spending on advertising and branding, demand will probably increase from D to D_1.

Demographics: As population grows there will be an increase in demand for nearly all goods and services. However, demand is also affected by the structure of the population as well as its size.

- The age distribution of a population is the numbers of people that fall into different age groups. For example, in many countries there has been growth in the number of people aged over 60. This will have an effect on demand patterns. For example, as the population gets older there will be more demand for goods such as retirement homes, specialist holidays for the elderly and healthcare. In Figure 2, if there was an increase in the 18 to 40 age group, there might be an increase in the demand for skiing holidays. This would shift the demand curve from D to D_1.
- There are slightly more women than men overall in many countries. In the older age groups the number of women compared to men increases. Consequently, the gender distribution of the population is likely to affect demand patterns. For example, there will be a greater demand for women's clothes than men's clothes.
- Geographical distribution can also affect demand. Increasingly, in most developed and developing countries more and more people live in urban areas. As a result demand for schools and hospitals in these areas, for example, will be higher than in rural areas.
- Other factors can affect the structure of the population, such as the nature of households. For example, in some parts of the world there has been a growth in the number of one-person households. This trend increases the demand for single accommodation. Many countries have ethnic groups in their population structure. If these ethnic groups grow in size there is also likely to be an increase in demand for products associated with their culture.

Also, there are likely to be changes in the size and structure of populations over time. For example, if the birth rate or immigration rises they will increase the size and structure of the population. For many years the population of Australia has grown rapidly. Immigration has contributed significantly to this growth. In 2017, Australia had a population of around 24 million and about one-quarter of these people were from overseas. As a consequence many businesses have been established to serve this large body of immigrants. For example, there are huge numbers of ethnic restaurants in many of Australia's towns and cities.

External shocks: Factors beyond the control of businesses can have an impact on the demand for products. Some key examples are outlined below.

- **Competition.** If a strong new competitor enters the market for the first time, demand is likely to fall for the original firm's product. For example, it is possible that Sky may be negatively affected following BT winning the right to broadcast Barclays Premier League football for the first time in 2014.
- **Government.** A government can influence demand in a number of ways. Raising taxes, for instance, could decrease demand for many products because spending power would be restricted. New laws can affect demand. For example, legal measures designed to increase competition in the market for gas and electricity might result in a fall in demand for the existing operators in the market.
- **Economic climate.** If the economy is growing, demand for most goods and services will tend to rise. In contrast, during a recession, demand for non-essential goods such as skiing holidays is likely to fall. This would be represented by a shift from D to D_2 in Figure 2.
- **Social and environmental factors.** Demand for some goods might be affected by changes in society. For example, there has been a huge increase in demand for social media. New social websites have emerged as a major means of communication. This has helped to increase the demand for mobile phones, apps, tablets, smartphones and related services. Concerns about global warming have changed consumers' attitudes towards goods and services that raise carbon emissions. For example, there has been a significant increase in demand for electric cars and hybrids (cars which run on both petrol and electricity).

Seasonality: Some goods and services have seasonal demand. This means that demand rises at particular times of the year. For example, in the many countries with a mild climate demand for garden furniture rises in late spring when the weather starts to improve. Similarly, demand for warm clothing, such as coats and wool jumpers, rises in the late autumn when the weather turns colder. Demand is also influenced by calendar events, such as Christmas, Easter, Ramadan, the Chinese New Year, Diwali in India, Thanksgiving Day in the USA, Mother's Day, St Valentine's Day and Halloween.

EXAM HINT

When drawing demand curves to help illustrate answers in examinations, it is acceptable to draw straight lines. Remember the price is always on the vertical axis and quantity on the horizontal axis.

CHECKPOINT

1. What is the relationship between price and the quantity demanded?

2. Give two examples of goods that are close substitutes.

3. If the price of a product rises what will happen to demand for a complementary good?

4. What might happen to the demand for furniture if incomes fall?

5. If a business increases its spending on advertising, how will this affect the position of the demand curve?

6. How might demand be affected by a change in the structure of the population caused by an increase in immigration?

7. Give three examples of external shocks that might affect demand.

8. What might affect the demand for ice cream?

SUBJECT VOCABULARY

complementary goods goods that are purchased together because they are consumed together.
demand the quantity of a product bought at a given price over a given period of time.
demand curve a line drawn on a graph that shows how much of a product will be bought at different prices.
inferior goods goods for which demand will fall if income rises *or* rise if income falls.
normal goods goods for which demand will rise if income rises *or* fall if income falls.
substitute (goods) goods that can be bought as an alternative to others, but perform the same function.

EXAM PRACTICE

GLOBAL CARE GROUP

SKILLS ANALYSIS
INTERPRETATION

Global Care Group is an Australian not-for-profit organisation that has been caring for elderly and disabled people for over 20 years. The organisation is run by a voluntary, elected board of management, members of which are selected based on their commitment and achievements in the aged-care sector. The organisation focuses on providing premium care and not maximising (prioritising) profit.

Global Care's first move into the sector was in 1991 when it opened Morrison Lodge Midland. However, the group now offers a wide range of care services for the elderly including retirement living, day care and community care in the Wheatbelt and Midland region in Western Australia. Morrison Lodge can accommodate over 70 residents and has purpose-built facilities to cater for a variety of elderly people with different needs. Close to the lodge there is a day care centre, Hamersley House, and independent living village, Struckman Mews. Together, these centres create a comfortable community where friendships are formed and people can get access to high-quality care services.

Global Care Group also operate two other centres – Balladong Lodge and Balladong Country Estate in York. These centres offer high-quality living environments for the elderly in a peaceful country setting. Here, residents can enjoy independence and freedom in the knowledge that care services are immediately available if needed.

More recently, Global Care Group bought some land next to the Northam Country Club in Northam. This will be used to create a new retirement village for the elderly, called Northam Country Estate. Houses in the village will be custom built and residents will have access to the country club facilities, a shared vegetable garden, golf course and many interactive activities. The idea is that residents will live independently but share a similar lifestyle with like-minded people.

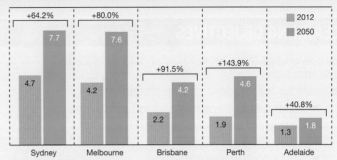

▲ Figure 4 Expected city populations in Australia in 2050 (million)

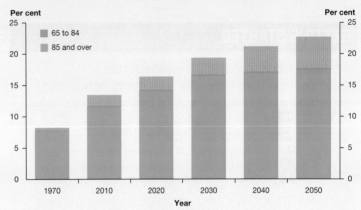

▲ Figure 5 The proportion of the population that is 65 or older in Australia, 1970–2050

Q

(a) Draw a diagram showing the likely effect on the demand for Global Care Group's services in the future. **(4 marks)**

(b) Discuss how the information shown in Figures 4 and 5 might affect demand patterns in Australia. **(8 marks)**

(c) Assess the impact that external factors might have on the demand for services supplied by companies like Global Care Group. **(10 marks)**

5 SUPPLY

LEARNING OBJECTIVES

By the end of this chapter you should be able to understand:

- factors leading to a change in supply:
  - changes in the costs of production
  - introduction of new technology
  - indirect taxes
  - government subsidies
  - external shocks.

GETTING STARTED

At the beginning of 2017 it was reported in New Zealand that there was a shortage of houses. Based on estimates by the ANZ Bank, at least another 60,000 houses were needed to meet the needs of the population. It was also reported that the shortage was increasing by another 40 houses every single day. In October 2016, the government said it would help to increase the supply of housing by generating an extra 30,000 houses. However, immediately after this promise in November and December, the number of approvals for new houses fell by 9.6 per cent and 7.2 per cent, respectively.

The shortage in the supply of houses is causing house prices and rents to rise sharply and for many people housing is becoming unaffordable. The housing shortages are being caused by growing immigration and inadequate supply. The supply of new houses, particularly in Auckland, is being restricted by a lack of suitable land and an overworked building industry, which has been described as badly managed, disordered and dishonest. Some of the production costs associated with construction, such as land and labour are also high.

Give **two** reasons why the supply of houses in New Zealand is inadequate. How might the government encourage the construction industry to build more houses? Why do prices rise when supply is inadequate? Is it possible to increase the supply of houses quickly? Explain your answer.

SUPPLY

Supply is the amount of a product that suppliers will offer to the market at a given price. The higher the price of a particular product or service, the more that will be offered to the market. For example, the amount of button mushrooms supplied to a market in any given week may be as shown in Table 1.

These figures have been drawn on a graph in Figure 1, which shows the **supply curve** for button mushrooms. The supply curve slopes up from left to right. This is because at higher prices a greater quantity will be supplied to the market and at lower prices less will be supplied.

A change in price will cause a movement either up or down the supply curve. The curve will not change its position assuming that all other factors remain the same. There are a number of other factors that may affect supply other than price. Changes in these factors will cause the whole supply curve to shift.

Price per kg (£)	Quantity supplied (000 kg)
0.50	20
1.00	40
1.50	60
2.00	80
2.50	100

▲ Table 1 The supply schedule for button mushrooms

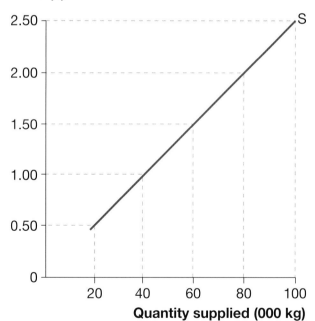

▲ Figure 1 The supply curve for button mushrooms

MATHS TIP

Most supply curves slope up from left to right, like the one in Figure 1. This reflects the direct relationship that exists between the price of the product and the quantity supplied. It shows that when price goes up, the quantity supplied also goes up. When the price goes down, the quantity supplied goes down.

In some circumstances the supply of a product or service may be fixed. If this is the case the supply curve will be vertical. Supply will be fixed if it is impossible for sellers to increase supply even when prices rise. The supply at venues such as cinemas, theatres and sports stadiums may be fixed. For example, the Camp Nou Stadium, home of FC Barcelona, currently holds 99,000 spectators. Even if the price of tickets were increased from €30 to, say, €100 no more seats could be supplied. However, there are plans to increase capacity to 105,000 in the near future. If this expansion goes ahead then supply will be fixed at the new level of 105,000 (see Figure 2).

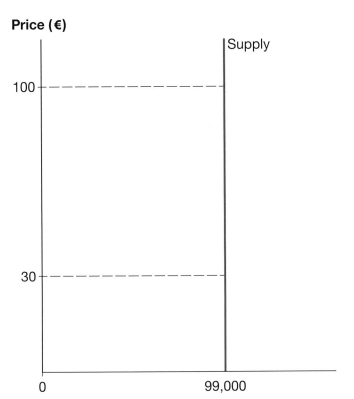

▲ Figure 2 Fixed supply – the capacity of the Camp Nou Stadium

FACTORS LEADING TO A CHANGE IN SUPPLY

The main determinant of supply is price. For most goods and services, when the market price rises suppliers are willing to supply more. This is because they are likely to make more profit at higher prices. However, a number of other factors can lead to a change in supply. Changes in these factors, which are outlined below, will actually shift the supply curve. This is different from a price change, which results in a movement along the supply curve.

Changes in the costs of production: The supply of any product is influenced by the costs of production, such

as wages, raw materials, energy, rent and machinery. If production costs rise, sellers are likely to reduce supply. This is because their profits will be reduced. For example, in 2013, Tata Chemicals shut its soda ash factory at Winnington in Northwich, UK. This factory had supplied soda ash for industries such as glass and soapmaking since 1874. The factory closed because it was being impacted by rising gas prices.

A rise in costs will cause the supply curve to shift to the left. This is shown in Figure 3. When costs rise, the whole supply curve will shift to the left, from S to S_2. At a price of P the quantity supplied in the market falls from Q to Q_2. If costs fall, supply will increase because production becomes more profitable. As a result the supply curve will shift to the right. This shows that more is supplied at every price. In Figure 3 the new supply curve would be S_1 and the amount supplied at P will rise from Q to Q_1.

The availability of resources will also affect supply. If there is a shortage in some of the factors of production, such as land, labour, raw materials or capital, it will make it difficult for producers to supply the market. For example, in some countries such as Germany, the USA and the Netherlands, there are shortages of skilled labour. In 2016, it was reported that shortages of workers with IT skills was worrying businesses, industry associations and government departments in Germany and the Netherlands. Germany had 43,000 vacancies for IT specialists while the Netherlands need at least another 15,000.

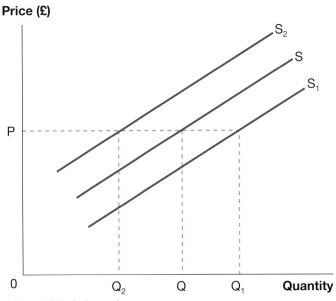

▲ Figure 3 Shifts in the supply curve

Introduction of new technology: As new technology becomes available many businesses will start to use it in their production processes. New technology is usually more efficient than older technology and will help to lower production costs, encouraging firms to offer more for sale. For example, Agricool, a French business, has developed technology that allows strawberries to be grown in containers. It grows fruit on the vertical surfaces of containers and each one can produce more than 4000 strawberries. The system also uses 90 per cent less water, renewable electricity and it aims to optimise the growing conditions, such as nutrition levels, watering and LED lighting. The air absorbed from outside is also cleaned to reduce air pollution inside the container.

ACTIVITY 1

SKILLS ANALYSIS, CRITICAL THINKING, PERSONAL AND SOCIAL RESPONSIBILITY

CASE STUDY: FARMBOTS

According to farmers and governments around the world, farming might be changed by the increasing number of 'farmbots' (farming machines) used in agriculture. The development of the machines aims to raise efficiency and complete complex tasks that have not been possible with the large-scale agricultural machinery of the past. For example, a 'lettuce bot' (shown in the photograph) can remove unwanted plants from the base of young lettuce plants. A 'farmbot' can look after vines, moving through the vineyards. Other bots are under development to remotely check crops for their growth, how dry they are and signs of disease. Drone technology (the use of aircraft controlled from a distance) is also being adapted for use on farms. For example, in South America, drones are being used for the supervision of animals and to monitor crops, and in Japan smaller models are designed to spray insect poison on crops.

However, there are doubts about how likely it is that new robot technology will become successful. Emma Hockridge, head of policy at the Soil Association, UK, has said: 'The potential use of robots on farms has been discussed for years, but we haven't yet seen anything practical close to reaching the market.'

While the prospect of replacing seasonal workers with robots may be attractive for farm bosses looking to integrate into bigger units, farm workers may be less keen. Even fans of the technology think that it will probably be decades before farmbots are used

commercially. The head of engineering at Harper Adams University, UK, Professor Simon Blackmore, said that his vision was for 'farming with robots in 2050', by which time he believes this should be practical.

Source: Based on UK farming conference hears how 'farmbots' will bring efficiencies and benefits and an end to back-breaking tasks. https://www.theguardian.com/environment/2014/jan/09/robots-farm-future

1. Explain one impact that the introduction of farmbots might have on agriculture.
2. Draw a diagram and analyse the effect that the introduction of farmbots might have on the supply of food.

The company reckons it can produce 120 times more fruit than on the same size of a piece of farmland.

The introduction of new technology will shift the supply curve to the right, from S to S_1 in Figure 3. The amount supplied in the market at price P will rise from Q to Q_1.

Indirect taxes: Indirect taxes are taxes imposed by the government on spending. Value added tax (VAT) and excise duties, such as those placed on petrol and tobacco, are examples of indirect taxes. Such taxes have an effect on supply. When they are imposed or increased, the supply curve will shift to the left, from S to S_2 in Figure 3. This is because indirect taxes represent a cost to firms. If indirect taxes are reduced, the supply curve will shift to the right, from S to S_1 in Figure 3. This is because costs are lower and firms will be encouraged to supply more in the market.

Following the introduction of an indirect tax, the burden is likely to be shared between the consumer and the producer. The size of the price increase faced by consumers will depend largely on the price elasticity of demand (this is discussed in Chapter 7). If an indirect tax is imposed and demand is relatively inelastic, the consumer will have to pay more of the tax.

In recent years a number of governments have increased VAT to raise money to help cut debt. For example, Greece increased VAT to 24 per cent in June 2016. Greece originally raised its standard VAT rate twice in 2010, from 19 per cent to 23 per cent.

Government subsidies: Sometimes the government may give money to businesses in the form of a grant. This is called a **subsidy**. Subsidies may be given to firms to try and encourage them to produce a particular product. For example, in common with many countries around the world, the government in Estonia has given fairly generous subsides to the producers of renewable energies. Estonia reached its 2020 EU target of 25 per cent of renewable energy in gross final energy consumption early in 2011. This was helped by government subsidies for biomass (organic matter used for fuel) and wind power generation and the extensive use of biomass (for heating).

If the government grants a subsidy on a product the effect is to increase its supply. This is because subsidies help to reduce production costs. As a result the supply curve will shift to the right, from S to S_1 in Figure 3.

External shocks: Factors beyond the control of businesses can have an impact on the supply of products. Some examples are outlined below.

- **World events.** Global events can have an impact on the supply of some products. For example, in recent years, some areas of the Middle East have experienced political instability. Consequently, when the situation becomes hostile, supplies of oil are threatened and the price rises. This is because a significant proportion of the global oil supply comes from this region.

  In 2008, the global financial crisis led to a 'credit crunch'. This meant that many firms were unable to borrow the money they needed to trade and invest for the future. As a result some businesses collapsed and others were unable to grow.

- **Weather.** The supply of agricultural products in particular can be affected by the weather. Good growing conditions will result in high crop production and increased supply. However, bad weather, such as a long period without rain, can reduce crop production severely and cause shortages. In 2014, there were larger than usual crops of wheat in Europe and the Black Sea region due to favourable growing conditions. The increase in the global supply of wheat helped to reduce prices.

  Bad weather, such as snow storms, can disrupt the supply of many goods in the short term, for instance by restricting the distribution of goods due to closed roads, railway lines and airports.

- **Government.** Government economic policies can have an impact on supply. For example, if central banks increase interest rates (in order to meet a government inflation target), this could increase business costs for firms with debt. Borrowing to invest might also be discouraged.

  Government laws can have an impact on supply. For example, if the government passes laws to make a particular market more competitive, then supply in that market is likely to increase as new entrants join the market.

- **Price of related goods.** In some markets supply can be affected by price changes of related goods. For example, if a farmer producing mainly potatoes sees that the price of carrots and cabbage are rising

in the marketplace, their response might be to grow more carrots and cabbage next season instead of potatoes. As a consequence the supply of potatoes could fall.

CHECKPOINT

1. Describe the relationship between price and the quantity supplied in a market.

2. What is fixed supply?

3. What might happen to the supply of laptop computers if wages of production workers rose significantly?

4. How might a fall in gold prices affect the supply of gold wedding rings?

5. What impact does the introduction of new technology have on the supply of goods and services?

6. What would happen to the supply curve for gardening services if VAT was increased?

7. Why is the supply of a product or service likely to increase if the government grants producers a subsidy?

8. How can government legislation affect supply?

9. State two external shocks that might affect the global supply of rice.

SUBJECT VOCABULARY

subsidy a grant given to producers, usually to encourage production of a certain product.
supply the amount of a product that suppliers make available to the market at any given price in a given period of time.
supply curve a line drawn on a graph that shows how much of a product sellers are willing to supply at different prices.

EXAM PRACTICE

GLOBAL OIL SUPPLY

SKILLS ANALYSIS, INTERPRETATION, REASONING, CRITICAL THINKING

In 2014/15, the global price of oil fell quite sharply. Figure 4 shows that it fell from over US$100 in 2014 to under US$30 for a period in 2016. Although the price has recovered since 2016, at US$50 it is still only one-half of what it was in 2014.

The fall in the price was caused to a significant extent by a global increase in supply. One of the reasons for this was because OPEC (a global cartel of major oil-producing countries including Saudi Arabia, Qatar, Iraq, Venezuela, Algeria, Nigeria, UAE and several others) failed to cut the production of oil, which led to oversupply. In the past, members of OPEC have been able to form agreements that restrict oil production and therefore limit global supply. This has driven up the price. More recently such agreements have not been made. OPEC members supply around 80 per cent of the world's oil.

Supply has also increased because Iran, a major world producer, has been allowed to sell more oil in the market. Iran was subject to sanctions from world powers that prevented it from selling oil. However, the sanctions were lifted recently when Iran reduced its development of nuclear facilities.

The supply of oil has also increased due to the discovery of new sources. In recent years the USA has started to extract oil from shale (a type of rock) using a process called fracking. For example, in 2017 the Energy Information Administration reported that crude (raw) oil storage in the USA rose to 8.2 million barrels (containers) from the previous week – four times higher than expected. US oil production is now growing at around 9.1 million barrels a day, the highest level in more than a year. Another state, Russia, has also been steadily supplying more oil to the market for around 20 years.

Finally, the fall in the price of oil may not have been caused entirely by an increase in supply. Global demand for oil has also weakened. The financial crisis, which started a world recession in 2008, reduced demand and the decrease in the growth of the Chinese economy in recent years also had an impact.

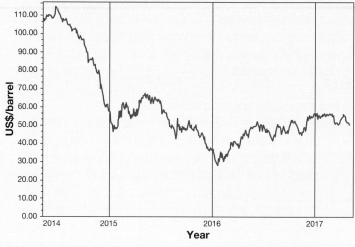

▲ Figure 4 Global oil price, 2014–17

Q

(a) Define supply. **(2 marks)**

(b) Explain the possible effects of the fall in the price of oil on (i) oil exploration companies and (ii) haulage contractors (transportation companies). **(4 marks)**

In recent years new technology in oil production such as tracer technology (used to measure flows in reservoirs and assess the economic viability of oil wells has helped to reduce costs.

(c) Draw a diagram to show the effect on the supply of oil when new technology in the oil industry is adopted. **(4 marks)**

(d) Assess the possible factors that have increased the global supply of oil in recent years. **(10 marks)**

6 MARKETS

LEARNING OBJECTIVES

By the end of this chapter you should be able to understand:
■ the interaction of demand and supply
■ how to draw and interpret demand and supply diagrams to show the causes and consequences of changes in demand and supply.

GETTING STARTED

The prices of some goods change slowly over time; others are more volatile. For example, the prices of some fresh produce rose sharply at the beginning of 2017 due to poor growing conditions in Spain and Italy. The supply of products like lettuces, aubergines, tomatoes and peppers was limited and prices rose by between 25 and 40 per cent. One supplier said that a combination of poor growing conditions had been created by flooding, cold weather and poor light levels. The price of flowers can increase greatly in the few days before Mother's Day. On Christmas Day and New Year's Eve it is common for taxi drivers to double their prices. In general, prices are determined by the interaction of demand and supply.

What market factor do you think has the most influence on the price of fresh produce such as lettuces and peppers? Why does the price of flowers rise by so much in the run up to Mother's Day? Why can't taxi drivers double their prices all year round?

THE INTERACTION OF DEMAND AND SUPPLY

In any market the price is set where the wishes of consumers are matched exactly with those of producers. This price, called the **equilibrium price**, is where supply and demand are equal. The way in which the forces of supply and demand determine prices in a market can be shown graphically. Figure 1 shows the supply and demand curves for mushrooms. Here the equilibrium price is £1.50. At this price consumers want to buy 60,000 kg and producers want to sell 60,000 kg. There is no other price where this happens. For example, if the price were £2, sellers would want to supply 80,000 kg. However, at this price, buyers only demand 40,000 kg because the price is too high.

The equilibrium price is also known as the **market clearing price**. This is because the amount supplied in the market is completely bought up by consumers. There are no buyers left without goods and there are no sellers left with unsold stock. The market is cleared.

Figure 1 also shows the **total revenue or total expenditure** at the equilibrium price. Total revenue is the

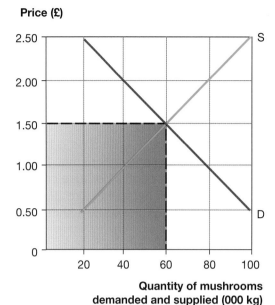

Price (£)

▲ Figure 1 The demand for and supply of mushrooms

ACTIVITY 1

SKILLS ▶ INTERPRETATION, PROBLEM SOLVING

CASE STUDY: FEEDING LIVESTOCK

During the summer months, particularly in countries with mild climates, livestock, such as cows and horses, are left in fields and eat grass. However, in the winter many of them are housed under cover and need to be fed. The market for large, round hay bales (a kind of livestock feed) is represented by the supply and demand curves shown in Figure 2.

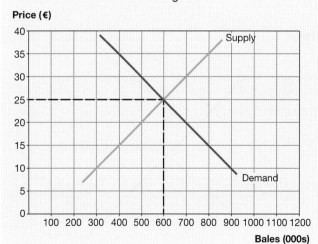

▲ Figure 2 The market for large, round hay bales

1. State the equilibrium price and quantity.
2. Using this diagram, explain what is meant by equilibrium price.
3. What is the value of total revenue at the equilibrium price?

amount of money generated from the sale of output. It is calculated by multiplying price and quantity.

Total revenue (TR) = Price (P) × Quantity (Q)

In Figure 1, total revenue at the equilibrium price of £1.50 is:

$$TR = P \times Q = £1.50 \times 60{,}000 = £90{,}000$$

There are many different factors that can cause a change in supply or demand. When such changes occur the supply and demand curves will shift. As a result there will be a change in the equilibrium price.

CHANGES IN DEMAND

If demand increases, price will rise. This is because producers react to rising consumer demand by putting up their prices. They can do this because customers want the product in higher numbers. In Figure 3(a), an increase in demand for a product is shown by a shift in the

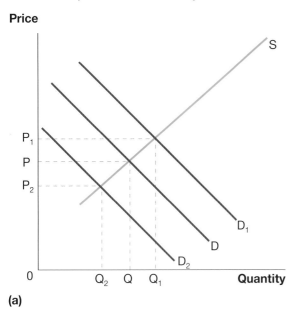

(a)

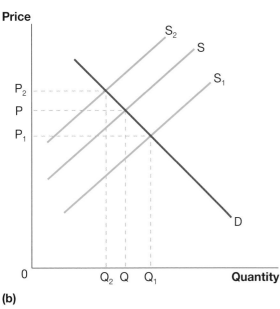

(b)

▲ Figure 3 The effect on equilibrium price of a change in demand and supply

demand curve to the right, from D to D_1. This changes the equilibrium price because supply and demand are now equal at a different point. The price is forced up from P to P_1 and the amount sold in the market has gone up from Q to Q_1.

ACTIVITY 2 — SKILLS — INTERPRETATION

CASE STUDY: COLD QUEENSLAND

In 2015, an unusual weather system hit eastern Australia. A very cold spell saw temperatures drop sharply. As a result, in Queensland, the demand for gas-fired outdoor heaters rose as shown in Figure 4. In particular, restaurant and café owners invested in the heaters so that customers could continue their practice of dining and drinking outside.

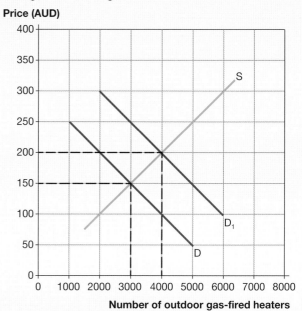

▲ Figure 4 The market for gas-fired heaters in Queensland, Australia

1. Explain the shift in the demand curve from D to D_1.
2. What has happened to the equilibrium price and quantity as a result of the shift in demand?

If demand were to fall, the opposite would happen. This is because producers are forced to lower their prices. Otherwise they would be left with too much unsold stock. They are forced to do this because customers are wanting much less of the product. The demand curve would shift to the left from D to D_2 and the price would fall to P_2. The amount traded in the market would fall from Q to Q_2.

CHANGES IN SUPPLY

A change in supply will also affect equilibrium price. For example, if supply increases the price will fall. In Figure 3(b), an increase in supply for the product is shown by a shift in the supply curve to the right, from S to S_1. This changes equilibrium price because supply and demand are now equal at a different point. The price is forced down from P to P_1 and the amount sold on the market has gone up from Q to Q_1. If supply were to fall, the opposite would happen. The supply curve would shift to the left from S to S_2, price would rise from P to P_2 and the amount traded in the market would fall from Q to Q_2.

WORKED EXAMPLE

Figure 5 shows the market for accommodation in a Spanish city. The equilibrium price per room is currently €60. What might happen to the price of rooms if some new hotels open up?

The arrival of new hotels in the city would increase the supply of rooms available. This would shift the supply curve to the right from S to S_1. As a result the equilibrium price per room is forced down from €60 to €40. The equilibrium number of rooms let rises from 20,000 to 25,000.

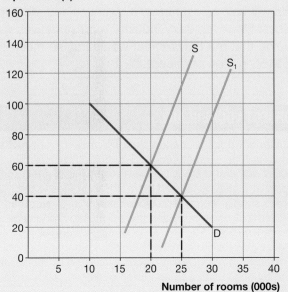

▲ Figure 5 The market for accommodation in a Spanish city

CHANGES IN DEMAND AND SUPPLY TOGETHER

It is possible for both demand and supply to change at the same time in a market. For example, demand might increase and supply decrease at the same time. This is shown in Figure 6. The original equilibrium price is P where S = D. The increase in demand is represented by a shift to the right from D to D_1. The decrease in supply is represented by a shift to the left from S to S_1. The new equilibrium price, where $D_1 = S_1$, is P_1. The price is higher and the amount sold in the market has fallen from Q to Q_1.

Note that it would be possible to redraw the diagram to show that, although the price will be higher, the quantity sold could also be higher. To do this it would be necessary to make the increase in demand greater than the decrease in supply. When there is a change in both demand and supply, it is not possible to show exactly what will happen to price and quantity unless it is known precisely by how much supply and demand shift.

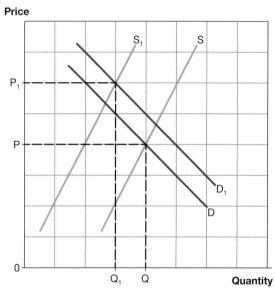

▲ Figure 6 A change in demand and supply

DISEQUILIBRIUM IN THE MARKET

If the price in a particular market is not set at the point where supply and demand are equal, there will be disequilibrium in the market. Two situations might occur.

Excess demand: If the price charged in a market is below the equilibrium price, demand and supply will not be equal. In Figure 7 the equilibrium price for button mushrooms is £1.50. At this price, supply and demand are both 60,000 kg. However, if the price is set lower, say at £0.50 per kg, the market is not in equilibrium. At this lower price demand is 100,000 kg and supply is only 20,000 kg. There is **excess demand**, which means there is a shortage of goods in the market. In this case there is a shortage of 80,000 kg (100,000 − 20,000).

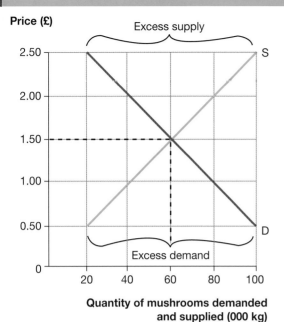

▲ Figure 7 The excess demand for and excess supply of button mushrooms

Excess supply: If the price charged is set above the equilibrium price, again, demand and supply are not equal. In Figure 7, if the price is set higher, say at £2.50, demand is only 20,000 kg while supply is 100,000 kg. This time there is **excess supply**, which means that goods would remain unsold. In this case, the quantity of unsold goods is 80,000 kg (100,000 − 20,000).

EXAM HINT

When drawing supply and demand curves you need to remember that demand curves always slope down from left to right and supply curves slope up from left to right (unless supply is fixed). You also need to remember to label the axes correctly. Marks may be awarded in examinations for labelling axes correctly and showing clearly the units measured.

CHECKPOINT

1. How are the prices of goods and services determined?

2. What is equilibrium price?

3. What will happen to the equilibrium price if there is a fall in demand?

4. What will happen to the equilibrium price if there is a fall in supply?

5. What is meant by fixed supply?

6. What would cause excess demand in a market?

7. What will happen to the equilibrium price if there is both an increase in demand and a fall in supply?

THINKING BIGGER

In 2016, there was a massive quantity of unsold cheese in the USA. The cheese 'mountain', as these food surpluses are sometimes called, is an example of excess supply. In recent years the supply of cheese has been greater than demand. As a result, stocks in the USA have built up to over 1200 million pounds (544,311 tonnes). This is shown in Figure 8. Increased milk stocks, growing dairy imports from Europe and a change in consumption patterns have all contributed to the market disequilibrium.

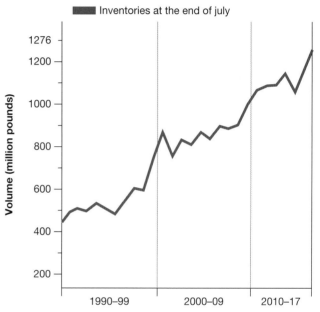

▲ Figure 8 The US cheese 'mountain', 1999–2017

To help reduce the excess supply the US Department of Agriculture is planning to buy US$20 million of cheese and distribute it to food banks nationwide. This will help boost farmer's revenues and stem their losses. However, dairy industry representatives were hoping that the government would buy as much as US$150 million of cheese.

SUBJECT VOCABULARY

equilibrium price or **market clearing price** the price where supply and demand are equal.
excess demand the position where demand is greater than supply at a given price and there are shortages in the market.
excess supply the position where supply is greater than demand at a given price and there are unsold goods in the market.
total revenue or **total expenditure** the amount of revenue generated from the sale of goods calculated by multiplying price by quantity in a given period of time.

EXAM PRACTICE

THE MARKET FOR ELECTRICITY IN KENYA

SKILLS ANALYSIS, INTERPRETATION, CRITICAL THINKING

Government officials in Kenya have been struggling to match the demand for electricity in the country with supply. A few years ago the Kenyan government began an ambitious plan to connect an increasing proportion of its population to the electricity network. In 2013, only 27 per cent of the population was connected. However, 4 years later, this had risen to 55 per cent and by 2020 the government hopes to achieve 'universal access', where 95 per cent of Kenyan households will have a supply. This is impressive when you consider it took the USA 33 years to achieve universal access. Access to electricity is very important in African states such as Kenya. It helps to improve educational standards, employment levels and agricultural productivity.

The government planned to increase power capacity from 1600 MW (mega-watts) in 2013 to 6600 MW in 3 years. However, demand for electricity has not grown by as much as it was predicted to do so by the government. In 2017, maximum power demand was 1620 MW. According to the Kenyan government this was expected to grow to 4755 MW by 2020. Some of the increase in demand was expected to come from the development of the Kenyan railway system when it became fully operational. Growth in the manufacturing sector and possible exports of electricity to neighbouring African nations were also predicted. However, after a German consultant was employed to estimate the nation's total demand, the reality was somewhat different. The government had clearly overestimated future demand. According to the consultant, which surveyed manufacturers and other large power users, Kenya's

maximum power demand will grow 72 per cent to 2259 MW by 2020 from the current 1620 MW.

Unfortunately, the manufacturing sector, the biggest user of electricity in Kenya, has performed poorly in recent years. A number of larger companies such as tyre maker Sameer, battery maker Eveready® and confectionery producer Cadbury®, have actually ceased production in Kenya. The sector has declined by an average of 10 per cent per annum in the last 10 years or so. Demand from domestic producers is still quite low despite the improvements in electricity access. Also, exports of electricity have not met expectations. This option has been held back by the lack of low-capacity transmission lines.

In order to better balance the demand for, and supply of, electricity the government has cancelled some of the new power generation projects. For example, plans have been dropped to construct a 700 MW natural gas power plant near Mombasa. Also, electricity retailer Kenya Power has expressed an interest in developing a street lighting programme across the country.

Q

(a) Explain how prices are determined in markets.
(4 marks)

(b) Using a demand and supply diagram, illustrate the impact on the market for electricity in Kenya resulting from the increase in capacity funded by the government. **(4 marks)**

(c) There is currently an excess supply of electricity in Kenya.
(i) Use a demand and supply diagram to show what is meant by excess supply. **(4 marks)**
(ii) Explain how this excess supply has occurred. **(4 marks)**

(d) Evaluate whether or not the excess supply of electricity will continue in Kenya. **(20 marks)**

7 PRICE ELASTICITY OF DEMAND (PED)

LEARNING OBJECTIVES

By the end of this chapter you should be able to:
- calculate price elasticity of demand
- interpret numerical values of price elasticity of demand
- understand the factors influencing price elasticity of demand
- understand the significance of price elasticity of demand to businesses in terms of implications of pricing
- calculate and interpret the relationship between price elasticity of demand and total revenue.

GETTING STARTED

The Abbasi brothers run a traditional Pakistani tea stall in Islamabad. The business has been in the family for 65 years and is located in a busy city centre street. It has served the family well, generating several thousand rupees profit each week. However, in the last 18 months the business has struggled due to the emerging 'coffee scene' in the city. Café chains, such as Coffee Republic and Gloria Jeans Coffees, have opened branches in Islamabad and the Abbasi brothers have seen sales and revenue fall. In order to restore revenue levels they decided to increase their prices from Rs 10 to Rs 12 per cup. As a result sales fell from 3200 to 2400 cups per week.

Calculate the total revenue the business earned (price x quantity sold) before the increase in price. Now calculate the revenue it earned after it increased price. Was the price increase a wise move for the business? Do you think the same would happen to any business that raised its price by 20 per cent?

WHAT IS PRICE ELASTICITY OF DEMAND?

For some goods a price change will result in a large change in demand and for others a smaller change. Figure 1 helps to illustrate this. Two demand curves (D_A and D_B) are shown with different slopes representing two different products: A and B. The demand curve for product A is steep and the demand curve for product B is flatter. At a price of £10, demand for both products is 100 units. However, when the price falls to £6 demand increases by different amounts for each product. Demand for product A only increases slightly to 120 units. But for product B demand increases a lot more to 200 units. Demand for product B is more **responsive** to the price change. This relationship that exists between the responsiveness of demand and a change in price is called **price elasticity of demand**.

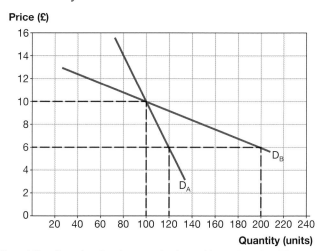

▲ Figure 1 The effect of a price change on the demand for products A and B

PRICE INELASTIC DEMAND

In Figure 1, for product A, the price change resulted in a less than proportionate change in demand. This means that the change in demand was not as big as the change in price. Price fell by 40 per cent (from £10 to £6) but demand only increased by 20 per cent (from 100 units to 120 units). When this happens economists say that the product has **price inelastic demand** or that demand is price inelastic. A minority of goods, such as petrol, have price inelastic demand.

PRICE ELASTIC DEMAND

In Figure 1, for product B, the price change resulted in a more than proportionate change in demand. This means that the change in demand was greater than the change in price. Price fell by 40 per cent (from £10 to £6) while demand increased by 100 per cent (from 100 units to 200 units). When this happens economists say that the product has **price elastic demand** or that demand is price elastic. Goods with elastic demand are more responsive to price changes. Most goods have price elastic demand.

CALCULATION OF PRICE ELASTICITY OF DEMAND

It is possible to calculate the price elasticity of demand of a product using the formula shown below.

$$\text{Price elasticity of demand} = \frac{\text{Percentage change in quantity demanded}}{\text{Percentage change in price}}$$

MATHS TIP

In the formula for elasticity calculation you need to work out percentage changes. The method below can be used.

Percentage change =

$$= \frac{\text{Difference between the two numbers}}{\text{Original number}} \times 100$$

The percentage change in the quantity demanded for product A is:

Percentage change =

$$= \frac{(120 - 100) \times 100}{100} = \frac{20 \times 100}{100} = 20\%$$

WORKED EXAMPLE

For product A in Figure 1, the price elasticity of demand would be:

$$= \frac{20\%}{-40\%} = -0.5$$

For product B in Figure 1, the price elasticity of demand would be:

$$= \frac{100\%}{-40\%} = -2.5$$

MATHS TIP

There is a minus number in the calculation above because the price fell by 40 per cent (from £10 to £6). Since the price change was negative a minus sign must be shown. Whenever price or demand falls in the calculation, it is proper, and may be helpful, to show the minus sign.

INTERPRETATION OF NUMERICAL VALUES OF PRICE ELASTICITY OF DEMAND

The values calculated above show whether demand is price elastic or price inelastic.

- If the value of price elasticity is less than 1 (i.e. a fraction, such as 1/2, or a decimal, such as 0.5), demand is said to be price inelastic. Demand for product A in Figure 1 is price inelastic because price elasticity is −0.5.
- If the value of price elasticity is greater than 1, demand is said to be price elastic. Demand for product B in Figure 1 is price elastic because price elasticity is −2.5.
- Note that the minus sign is not used to determine whether goods are price elastic or price inelastic. It is enough to focus on the numerical value.

ACTIVITY 1　　SKILLS　　INTERPRETATION

CASE STUDY: CARBONATED DRINKS IN MEXICO

Mexicans consume more carbonated drinks, such as Coca-Cola or lemonade, per person than any other nation in the world. In 2016, one Mexican drinks company, Agrios, sold 2 million cans of Agrioslimón at a price of MXN 10. In 2017, Agrios reduced the price of Agrioslimón to try and win a larger share of the very competitive market. The price was reduced to MXN 8 and sales rose to 2.6 million cans.

1. Calculate the price elasticity of demand for Agrioslimón.
2. State whether demand is price elastic or price inelastic.

THE FACTORS INFLUENCING PRICE ELASTICITY OF DEMAND

The value of price elasticity of demand for a product is mainly determined by the ease with which customers can switch to other similar substitute products. A number of factors are likely to determine this.

- **Time.** Price elasticity of demand tends to fall the longer the time period. This is mainly because consumers and businesses are more likely to turn to substitutes in the long term. For example, the demand for fuel oil is highly price inelastic in the short term. If the price of petrol goes up 20 per cent in a week, the fall in quantity demanded is likely to be only a few per cent. This is because car owners have to use their cars to get to work or to go shopping. But over a 10-year period, car owners will tend to buy more fuel-efficient cars. Businesses that use oil to heat their properties may start to use gas. Homeowners with oil-fired central heating systems might look for ways to stop heat escaping their houses to cut running costs or change to gas-powered heating systems. As a result, demand for oil in the long run is likely to be price elastic.

- **Competition for the same product.** Some businesses face highly price elastic demand for their products. This is because they are in very competitive markets, where their product is either identical (i.e. a perfect substitute) or little different from those produced by other businesses. Farmers, for example, when selling wheat or potatoes are in this position. If they push their prices above the market price, they will not be able to sell their crop. Customers will simply buy elsewhere at the lower market price.

- **Branding.** Some products are branded. The stronger the branding, the less substitutes are acceptable to customers. For example, many buyers of Kellogg's Corn Flakes do not see supermarket own-label brands as good substitutes for Kellogg's. They will often pay 50 per cent more to buy Kellogg's rather than another brand. Successful branding therefore reduces the price elasticity of demand for the product.

- **The proportion of income spent on a product.** For inexpensive products, where the proportion of a consumer's income spent on the transaction is very small, demand is likely to be price inelastic. For example, if the price of a box of matches rises by 20 per cent from £0.10 to £0.12, the fall in demand is likely to be a lot less than 20 per cent because the amounts of money involved are 'trivial'. In contrast, the demand for products where the proportion of a consumer's income spent on the transaction is much larger is likely to be price elastic. For example, if the price of a car rises by 20 per cent from £20,000

to £24,000, there is likely to be a more than proportionate fall in demand (i.e. greater than 20 per cent). This is because the increase in price of £4000 is likely to stop a significant number of consumers from purchasing the product. £4000 will represent a large proportion of many consumer's incomes.

- **Product types vs the product of an individual business.** Most products are made and sold by a number of different businesses. Petrol, for example, is processed and sold by companies such as Shell, Esso and Total. The major supermarkets also sell petrol, which they have bought from independent producers. The demand for petrol is price inelastic in the short term. But the demand for Shell petrol or Esso petrol is price elastic. This is because petrol has no real substitutes in the short term. But Esso petrol is a very good substitute for Shell petrol. In general, a product category like petrol, carpets or haircuts has a much lower price elasticity of demand than products within that category made by individual businesses.

However strong the branding and however little the competition that an individual product faces, it is still likely that a business will sell at a price where demand is price elastic. To understand why, consider a product which has price inelastic demand. As explained above, raising the price of the product would increase sales revenue. It would also reduce sales and costs of production would fall. So profits would rise. A business trying to make as much profit as possible should therefore continue raising price until demand is price elastic.

If demand is price elastic, raising price leads to a fall in sales revenue, but also a fall in costs because less is sold. At the profit-maximising point, any further increase in price would see the fall in sales revenue being greater than the fall in costs.

This would suggest that even strongly branded goods, such as Coca-Cola or McDonald's® meals, have a price elasticity of demand greater than one at the price at which they are sold. It also suggests that luxury brands, such as Chanel® or Gucci®, also have price elastic demand at their current price.

PRICE ELASTICITY OF DEMAND AND PRICING

A business may consider price elasticity of demand when setting the prices of its products. For a minority of products demand is price inelastic. This means that if a business raises its price there will be a less than proportionate fall in demand. For example, if a business (selling a product that is price inelastic) raises price by 10 per cent, demand might fall by, say, 7 per cent. This suggests that raising price when selling products with inelastic demand would be a good strategy.

Since 2006 in Germany, the price of electricity has risen significantly. Figure 2 shows that the price has gone up by around 50 per cent over the time period (although prices have stabilised in recent years). However, there is no evidence to suggest that demand has fallen by a significant amount. This suggests that demand for electricity is price inelastic and energy suppliers can raise prices without suffering any significant fall in demand.

If goods have price elastic demand, a price change will result in a more than proportionate change in demand. For example, if a business selling a product that is price elastic raises the price by 10 per cent, demand might fall by, say, 18 per cent. This suggests that raising the price when selling products with price elastic demand would not be a good strategy. However, if the business lowers the price, demand will rise by a larger proportion than the price cut. This might help to explain the success of low-cost supermarkets, such as Aldi and Lidl. Their sales have risen significantly, probably due to charging lower prices in a highly competitive market.

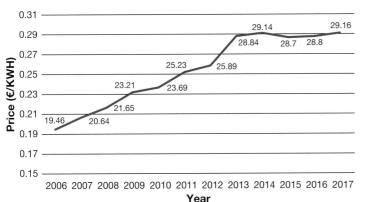

▲ Figure 2 Average electricity price in Germany, 2006–17

PRICE ELASTICITY OF DEMAND AND TOTAL REVENUE

When a business changes its price there will be a change in demand and therefore a change in total revenue. It would be useful for a business to know what effect a particular price change might have on total revenue. The value of price elasticity can help here. In Figure 1, the demand for product A is price inelastic and the demand for product B is price elastic. At the price of £10 the demand for both products is 100 units. However, when the price falls demand for product A rises to 120 units while the demand for B rises to 200 units. The different effects on total revenue for each product are outlined below.

For product A: When the price falls from £10 to £6 there is an increase in demand from 100 units to 120 units. This means that total revenue will change. This is shown by the following calculations.

When *P* = £10 *TR* = £10 × 100 = £1000
When *P* = £6 *TR* = £6 × 120 = £720

The price reduction from £10 to £6 has resulted in a £280 fall in total revenue (£1000 – £720). This shows that when demand is inelastic, a price cut will cause total revenue to fall. The opposite will happen if the price is increased. If demand is inelastic, a price increase will cause total revenue to rise.

For product B: When the price falls from £10 to £6, demand rises from 100 units to 200 units. The effect on total revenue is calculated below.

When *P* = £10 *TR* = £10 × 100 = £1000
When *P* = £6 *TR* = £6 × 200 = £1200

This time, for product B, the price reduction has resulted in a £200 increase in revenue from £1000 to £1200. This shows that when demand is price elastic, a price cut will result in an increase in total revenue. The opposite will happen if the price is increased. If demand is price elastic, a price increase will cause total revenue to fall. The effect of price changes on total revenue for different price elasticities is summarised in Table 1.

Price elasticity	Value of elasticity	Price change	Effect on TR
Inelastic	< 1	Decrease	Fall
Inelastic	< 1	Increase	Rise
Elastic	> 1	Decrease	Rise
Elastic	> 1	Increase	Fall

▲ Table 1 The effect of price changes on total revenue when demand is elastic and inelastic

To conclude, if businesses know the value of price elasticity for their products, they can predict the effect on total revenue of any price changes they make. They will know, for example, that if demand for their product is elastic, a price reduction will increase total revenue. This might help to explain why many rail companies charge lower prices for off-peak rail travel. By lowering the price more travellers are attracted and revenue rises. Demand during the off-peak period must be price elastic.

ACTIVITY 2   SKILLS   INTERPRETATION, PROBLEM SOLVING, CRITICAL THINKING

CASE STUDY: IBADAN PIZZAS

Rita Okobi runs a pizza takeaway restaurant called Ibadan Pizzas in the large city of Ibadan, Nigeria. The market for pizzas is growing but she faces competition from global brands such as Domino's®. However, she has traded profitably for a few years. She provides excellent customer service and uses a combination of flour and other grains to make the bases which gives them a distinctive taste.

In 2016, she wondered if she could increase her sales by charging less than her rivals. For example, a medium cheese pizza from Domino's costs about NGN 3000. Cheryl currently charges NGN 2600 for an equivalent product. She is considering a price cut to NGN 1950 to make the price difference more significant. Cheryl has done some research and reckons that the price elasticity of demand for her pizzas is about –2. In 2017, Cheryl sold 10,000 cheese pizzas.

1. Calculate the number of pizzas Rita would expect to sell in 2017 if she cut the price to NGN 1950.
2. Calculate the change in total revenue resulting from the price change above.
3. Assess whether Rita's decision to cut price might be successful.

THINKING BIGGER

When using price elasticity of demand to help make pricing decisions, businesses need to be aware of some possible drawbacks with the concept. The main problem is the origin of elasticity values. A business might estimate the value of price elasticity by measuring the effect on sales of previous price changes. For example, if a business cut the price by 12 per cent 4 years ago and demand rose by 18 per cent, price elasticity would be –1.5. However, this data is historic; what happened 4 years ago may not happen again in the future.

Another way of estimating elasticity values is to carry out market research to find out how consumers will react to price changes in the future. This would give more up-to-date values, but there could be problems with the accuracy of the data collected by market researchers. For example, the sample may not be representative or consumers might not behave in the way they said they would. Consequently, imperfect data would be flawed. Businesses need to be aware, therefore, that elasticity values may not be entirely accurate.

CHECKPOINT

1. What is elasticity of demand?

2. Give two examples of products that might have inelastic demand.

3. What is the formula for calculating price elasticity of demand?

4. The price of a product is increased by 8 per cent; as a result demand falls by 12 per cent. Calculate price elasticity of demand.

5. The price elasticity of demand for a product is –0.67. What will happen to total revenue if price is reduced?

6. The price elasticity of demand for a product is –2.7. What will happen to total revenue if price is raised?

7. State two factors that affect the price elasticity of demand for a product.

SUBJECT VOCABULARY

price elastic demand a change in price results in a greater change in demand.
price elasticity of demand the responsiveness of demand to a change in price.
price inelastic demand a change in price results in a proportionately smaller change in demand.

EXAM PRACTICE

ROBBAT ENGINEERING

SKILLS   ANALYSIS, INTERPRETATION, CRITICAL THINKING

Robbat Engineering operate from a factory in Kuala Lumpur, Malaysia, manufacturing components and spare parts for farm vehicles. The work undertaken by the company is quite specialised and it was thought that few rivals operate in the same market. At the end of 2016 the company had to make some modifications to two of the components, A and C. This was to comply with some new health and safety specifications. As a result the owner decided to raise the price of these two components by 20 per cent in 2017. Some financial information for three components made by Robbat Engineering is shown in Table 2.

Q

(a) Define the term 'elastic demand'. **(2 marks)**

(b) Explain **one** factor that might affect the price elasticity of demand. **(4 marks)**

(c) Calculate the expected change in revenue generated by product A in 2017 if the price is increased by 20 per cent. **(4 marks)**

(d) Evaluate whether or not the price changes made by Robbat Engineering will benefit the business. **(20 marks)**

	Price	Sales	PED
Component A	MYR 50	100,000	−0.8
Component B	MYR 35	150,000	−1.1
Component C	MYR 25	300,000	−1.2

▲ Table 2 Financial information and price elasticity of demand (PED) for three products, 2016

8 INCOME ELASTICITY OF DEMAND (YED)

LEARNING OBJECTIVES

By the end of this chapter you should be able to:
■ calculate income elasticity of demand
■ understand normal and inferior goods
■ interpret numerical values of income elasticity of demand
■ understand the factors influencing income elasticity of demand
■ understand the significance of income elasticity of demand to businesses.

GETTING STARTED

The demand for some products can be affected by changes in income. However, for some other products changes in income will have very little impact on demand.

Look at the two photographs below.

How do you think changes in income will affect demand for the two products? What would you expect to happen to the demand for luxury goods in the next 20 years? Can you think of any goods for which demand might actually fall if incomes rose? What might explain this fall in demand?

WHAT IS INCOME ELASTICITY OF DEMAND?

One of the main factors that can change the demand for products is the amount of income consumers have to spend. **Income elasticity of demand** measures the responsiveness of demand to a change in income.

Consider two products: A and B. If incomes rise by 10 per cent and demand for product A rises by 25 per cent, the change in demand is proportionately greater than the change in income. Economists would say that demand for product A is **income elastic**. Demand for many goods and services is income elastic. Examples might include cars, fashion accessories, entertainment, holidays and a wide range of luxury goods.

In contrast, if demand for product B only rose by 5 per cent, economists would say that demand for product B is **income inelastic**. This is because the percentage increase (or change) in demand is proportionately less than the percentage increase (or change) in income. Demand for some goods and services may be income inelastic. Examples are likely to be essential goods, such as milk, food in general and heating fuel.

CALCULATION OF INCOME ELASTICITY OF DEMAND

It is possible to calculate the income elasticity of demand for a product using the formula:

$$\text{Income elasticity of demand} = \frac{\text{Percentage change in quantity demanded}}{\text{Percentage change in income}}$$

WORKED EXAMPLE

For product A in the earlier example, income elasticity of demand would be:

$$\frac{25\%}{10\%} = \mathbf{2.5}$$

For product B in the earlier example, income elasticity of demand would be:

$$\frac{5\%}{10\%} = \mathbf{0.5}$$

NORMAL AND INFERIOR GOODS

The value of income elasticity can also show whether goods are **normal goods** or **inferior goods**. For normal goods, where an increase in income results in an increase in demand, the value of income elasticity will be positive (+).

Products A and B above are both normal goods because income elasticity is positive in both cases. For inferior goods, where, for example, an increase in income results in a decrease in demand, the value of income elasticity will be negative (–). Some examples are shown in Table 1.

Good	Income elasticity	Elastic or inelastic	Type of product	The effect of a 10% increase in income
Product W	0.6	Inelastic	Normal	Demand would increase by 6%
Product X	−2.4	Elastic	Inferior	Demand would fall by 24%
Product Y	1.9	Elastic	Normal	Demand would rise by 19%
Product Z	−0.8	Inelastic	Inferior	Demand would fall by 8%

▲ Table 1 Some examples of goods with different income elasticities of demand

INTERPRETATION OF THE NUMERICAL VALUES OF INCOME ELASTICITY OF DEMAND

The values calculated above show whether demand is income elastic or income inelastic.

- If the value of income elasticity is greater than 1, demand is said to be income elastic. Demand for product A is income elastic because income elasticity is 2.5. This means that the change in demand is proportionately greater than the change in income.
- If the value of income elasticity of demand is less than 1, demand is said to be income inelastic. Demand for product B is income inelastic because income elasticity is 0.5. This means that the change in demand is proportionately less than the change in income.

MATHS TIP

Always show the positive (+) and negative (–) signs when performing elasticity calculations. If you leave a negative sign out, you could end up getting a wrong answer. The signs also tell you whether the product is normal or inferior.

ACTIVITY 1   SKILLS   PROBLEM SOLVING, CRITICAL THINKING

CASE STUDY: DAR ES SALAAM PAPER

Dar Es Salaam Paper sell standard A4 paper to a wide variety of stationers, other retailers and office equipment suppliers. In 2016/17, incomes rose by 2 per cent; as a result, demand for paper rose from 2,000,000 reams to 2,030,000 reams.

1. Calculate the income elasticity of demand for paper in this case.
2. Explain whether (a) demand for paper in this case is income elastic or income inelastic and (b) whether paper is a normal good or an inferior good.

THE FACTORS INFLUENCING INCOME ELASTICITY OF DEMAND

The main factor affecting income elasticity of demand is whether or not goods are necessities or luxuries.

Necessities: These are basic goods that consumers need to buy. Examples include food in general, electricity and water. Demand for these types of goods will be income inelastic. Another example of a product which has income inelastic demand is cigarettes. A study in Ukraine a number of years ago found that the income elasticity of demand for cigarettes was 0.06. It could be argued that cigarettes are a necessity once people become addicted to them.

Luxuries: These are goods that consumers like to buy if they can afford them. Spending on these types of goods is **discretionary**, which means that customers can choose whether or not to make these purchases. Demand for these goods is income elastic. Examples include air travel, satellite television, fashion accessories, and many goods and services in the leisure and tourism industry. It is also argued that the demand for imported goods is income elastic. It has been found that as developing nations become better off, their demand for imports rises significantly.

The price of a product relative to incomes: This can also influence income elasticity. Demand for products that are relatively cheap, such as pencils, will tend to be income inelastic. However, demand for expensive items, such as houses, will be income elastic.

THE SIGNIFICANCE OF INCOME ELASTICITY OF DEMAND TO BUSINESSES

Businesses may be interested in income elasticity of demand because changes in income in the economy can affect the demand for their products.

Businesses selling goods with high income elasticity: The demand for goods that are very sensitive to changes in income (i.e. highly income elastic) is often cyclical. This means that when the economy is growing, demand for these types of goods, such as air travel, restaurants and luxury goods, is also growing. But when the economy falls into recession, demand also falls. This can cause difficulties for such businesses. During a recession they may lay off workers and postpone or cancel investment projects. Predicting demand for goods that are influenced by the business cycle can be quite difficult. The business cycle is discussed in Chapter 41.

Businesses selling goods with low income elasticity: Demand for goods that are income inelastic tends to be more stable during the different phases in the business cycle. For example, farmers are much less affected by income changes because demand for many food products is fairly stable. This makes production planning and investment decisions a little easier. In countries where economic growth is steady, over a period of time the demand for inferior goods and normal necessities tends to decline. It could be argued that businesses operating in these sectors should attempt to diversify into goods with higher income elasticity of demand in the long run.

Production planning: If businesses know the income elasticity of demand for their products they can respond to predicted changes in incomes. Businesses that produce goods that have income elastic demand will expect changes in income to affect demand. So if incomes are expected to rise in the future they can plan ahead, making sure they have enough capacity, for example. Whereas, if a recession is expected, these businesses would plan to cut output. This is because incomes are likely to fall during a recession. In 2008, as a result of the global recession, car manufacturers started to cut their output. For example, it was widely reported that Honda, the Japanese car manufacturer, stopped production in some factories around the world in 2009. In contrast, producers of inferior goods might start to increase capacity if they believed a recession was coming. When incomes fall, demand for inferior goods, such as those sold by low-cost supermarkets, starts to rise.

Product switching: Some manufacturers have flexible resources and can switch from the production of one product to another. For example, a manufacturer of plastic products may be able to switch from the production of plastic household goods to plastic toys. A predicted rise in incomes may encourage such a business to make more plastic toys if demand for them was income elastic.

CHECKPOINT

1. What does it mean when a product is described as 'income elastic'?

2. Give two examples of goods that might be income inelastic.

3. What is the formula for calculating income elasticity of demand?

4. If incomes rise by 12 per cent and demand rises by 20 per cent, what is income elasticity of demand?

5. A product has income elasticity of −0.9. Is this good normal or inferior?

6. State two factors that might affect income elasticity of demand.

7. Why are imports believed to be income elastic?

8. State two implications of income elasticity for businesses.

SUBJECT VOCABULARY

discretionary expenditure non-essential spending or spending that is not automatic.
income elastic the percentage change in demand for a product is proportionately greater than the percentage change in income.
income elasticity of demand where the responsiveness of demand to a change in income.
income inelastic where the percentage change in demand is proportionately less than the percentage change in income.
inferior goods goods for which demand will fall if income rises or rise if income falls.
normal goods goods for which demand will rise if income rises or fall if income falls.

EXAM PRACTICE

CHINESE OUTBOUND TOURISM

SKILLS ANALYSIS, INTERPRETATION, CRITICAL THINKING

In recent years the Chinese economy has grown significantly (Figure 1). Many people have benefited from the growth in manufacturing and a significant proportion of China's population has become wealthier. As a result the number of Chinese people taking holidays abroad has increased dramatically. Figure 2 shows the growth in the number of Chinese people crossing borders for holidays between 2010 and 2015.

In 2016, the most popular destination for Chinese tourists was Hong Kong Special Administrative Region. More than 35 million Chinese tourists visited the region. Other popular destinations included Thailand, South Korea, Japan and the USA.

Q

(a) Define the term income elasticity of demand.
(2 marks)

(b) Calculate the income elasticity of demand for foreign holidays in China between 2010 and 2015. **(4 marks)**

(c) Explain why an overseas holiday to China is classified as a normal good. **(4 marks)**

(d) Analyse **two** factors that might influence income elasticity of demand. **(6 marks)**

(e) Assess how useful income elasticity might be for a business selling holidays to Chinese tourists.
(10 marks)

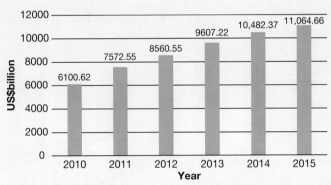

▲ Figure 1 Chinese GDP, 2010–15

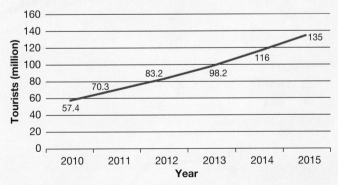

▲ Figure 2 Chinese outbound tourism, 2010–15

MARKETING MIX AND STRATEGY

This section covers the importance of marketing in business. It looks at different marketing objectives, such as increasing market share and brand building, and the different marketing strategies that businesses might use. It also looks at the different elements in the marketing mix – product, promotion, pricing and place (the 4 Ps). This includes the design of products and how elements of the design mix reflect changes in social trends, types of promotion and branding and how businesses might build a brand, different pricing strategies and the factors that might influence the choice of pricing strategy and, finally, the different distribution channels used by businesses.

9 MARKETING OBJECTIVES AND STRATEGY

LEARNING OBJECTIVES

By the end of this chapter you should be able to understand:

- marketing objectives: increase market share, increase revenue and build a brand
- the product life cycle and extension strategies
- the Boston matrix and the product portfolio
- the concept of the marketing mix
- marketing strategies appropriate for different types of market: mass markets, niche markets, business to business (B2B) and business to consumer (B2C)
- consumer behaviour – how businesses develop customer loyalty.

GETTING STARTED

Karrandore is a large holiday company based in Santiago, Chile. It offers a very wide range of different holiday experiences for many different consumer groups. It is a stable and profitable company but one of its products is currently in decline. This is a product called Patagonia Cruises. It involves a 6-day trip on a cruise ship between Punta Arenas, Chile, and Ushuaia, Argentina. Passengers get to explore the heart of Patagonia's scenic beauty. They visit scenic coastline in search of whales and wildlife, and explore on guided tours given by an expert. Figure 1 shows sales figures for Patagonia tours from 2010 to 2017.

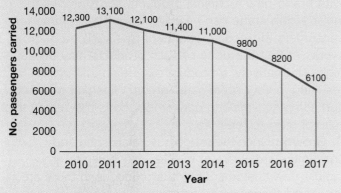

▲ Figure 1 Sales for Patagonia Cruises, 2010–17

After a senior management meeting, where the withdrawal of Patagonia Cruises was discussed, it was decided to extend the life of the product. The company has agreed to invest CLP 9000 million to upgrade the cruise ship and advertise a new and improved service. The service will include luxury cabins and improved restaurant facilities for all passengers. The objective is to relaunch the product and raise sales to 15,000 by 2020.

Discuss possible reasons why Karrandore decided not to withdraw Patagonia Cruises? What is Karrandore's marketing objective in this case? Would you describe Patagonia Cruises as a mass-market product or a niche-market product? Explain your answer. How might Karrandore develop some customer loyalty for its products?

MARKETING OBJECTIVES

The marketing activities of a business are likely to be more effective if there are clear **marketing objectives**. These are the goals that a business is trying to achieve through its marketing. Although the general role of marketing is to help sell products, it is possible to identify specific marketing objectives. These objectives may differ between different business organisations. It is also likely that the marketing objectives of a particular business will vary over time to match its changing marketing needs. Three key marketing objectives might include the following.

Increase market share: Businesses often want to gain a larger share in the market. This is because having a larger market share is likely to give a business a competitive edge. As market share grows, a business will have to produce more output. As a result it may exploit economies of scale, which will help to lower costs. For example, a business may get better prices from suppliers because they are buying larger volumes of resources. If a business can grow a large enough share it may also have some influence on the prices charged in the market.

To win a larger market share a business may have to invest in an advertising campaign or adjust its pricing strategy, for example. This is discussed in Chapters 11 and 12, respectively. Increasing market share is an important marketing objective for many businesses.

Increase revenue: Businesses often introduce specific marketing activities in order to boost their revenues. If revenues are higher it is likely that profits will also be higher. If a business sets out to increase revenue, there are a number of marketing activities that could be used to achieve this objective. For example, it could invest in an online advertising campaign, sponsor an international sporting event, reduce its price or widen its distribution. These activities are discussed in Chapters 11, 12 and 13, respectively.

Build a brand: Many businesses want to establish the name of their company or their products. They can do this by giving products brand names. For example, the brand name Samsung, the South Korean electronics manufacturer, is likely to be recognised by many people worldwide. Strong brands can generate huge returns for a business, so building a brand over a period of time is important for many – particularly those in highly competitive markets. If a business aims to build a brand it may exploit a unique selling point, invest heavily in television advertising or use social media to achieve this specific marketing objective. This is discussed in detail in Chapter 11.

Finally, a business is more likely to achieve its marketing objectives if they are SMART. This means that they should be specific, measurable, agreed, realistic and time specific. An example of a SMART marketing objective might be to increase market share from 17 per cent to 20 per cent within 2 years. SMART objectives are discussed in Chapter 21.

THE PRODUCT LIFE CYCLE

Product is one part of the marketing mix. For marketing to be effective, a business must be aware of its **product life cycle**. The product life cycle shows the different stages that a product passes through over time and the sales that can be expected at each stage. By considering product life cycles, businesses can plan for the future.

Most products pass through six stages – development, introduction, growth, maturity/saturation and decline. These are illustrated in Figure 2.

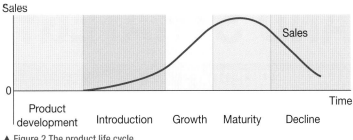

▲ Figure 2 The product life cycle

Development: During the development stage the product is being researched and designed. Suitable ideas must be investigated, developed and tested. If an idea is considered worth pursuing then a prototype or model of the product might be produced. A decision will then be made about whether or not to launch the product. A large number of new products never progress beyond this stage and will fail. This is because businesses are often reluctant to take risks associated with new products. During the development stage it is likely that the business will spend to develop the product and costs will be high. As there will be no sales at this stage, the business will initially be spending but receiving no revenue.

Introduction: At the start of this stage the product will be launched. As the product is new to the market, initial sales are likely to be slow. Costs are incurred when the product is launched. It may be necessary to build a new production line or plant, and the firm will have to meet promotion and distribution costs. A business is also likely to spend on promotion to make consumers aware of the new product. Therefore, it is likely that the product will still not be profitable. Prices may be set high to cover promotion costs. But they may also be set low in order to break into the market. Few outlets may stock products at this stage. The length of this stage will vary according to the product. With brand-new technical products, for example, the introduction stage can be quite long. It takes time for consumers to become confident that such products 'work'. At first the price of such products may be quite high. Alternatively, a product can be an instant hit resulting in very rapid sales growth. Fashion products and some fast-moving consumer goods may enjoy this type of start to their life.

Growth: Once the product is established and consumers are aware of it, sales may begin to grow rapidly, new customers buy the product and there are repeat purchases. Unit costs may fall as production increases. The product then becomes profitable. If it is a new product and there is a rapid growth in sales, competitors may launch their own versions. This can lead to a slowdown of the rise in sales. Businesses may need to consider their prices and promotion. For example, a high price charged initially may need to be lowered, or promotion may need to increase to encourage brand loyalty.

Maturity and saturation: At some stage the growth in sales will end. The product has become established with a stable market share at this point. Sales will have reached their highest point and competitors will have entered the market to take advantage of profits. As more firms enter the market, it will become saturated. Some businesses will be forced out of the market, as there are too many firms competing for consumers. During the maturity and saturation stages of the product life cycle, many businesses use extension strategies to extend the life of their products. These are discussed below.

Decline: For the majority of products, sales will eventually decline. This is usually due to changing consumer tastes, new technology or the introduction of new products. The product will lose its appeal to customers. At some stage it will be withdrawn or sold to another business. It may still be possible to make a profit if a high price can be charged and little is spent on promotion or other costs.

EXTENSION STRATEGIES

Extension strategies, ways to prolong the life of a product before it starts to decline, are popular with businesses. This is because the costs of product development are high and extension strategies help a product to generate more cash. Two general approaches are often used. One is to make some adjustments to the product; the second is to invest in promotion.

Product adjustments: Many companies try to prolong the life of the product by 'freshening' it up. This might involve making improvements, updating the product, repackaging the product or extending the range.

- Updating is quite a common approach for technical products and certain types of consumer durables. For example, in the car industry firms are keen to bring out updated versions of their successful models. An example is shown in Activity 1 on the next page.
- Some businesses add value to their products by making improvements. For example, computer manufacturers bring out new machines that are faster, have more memory, look more stylish and have more functions than previous versions. In the service industry, banks offer new accounts with extra services, such as travel insurance, breakdown cover and mobile phone insurance.
- Another common approach is to extend the product range. Crisp manufacturers have used this method

in the past by bringing out new flavours. However, a wide range of industries can adopt this approach. For example, CK International, a producer of waste compaction equipment based in Northern Ireland, extended its product range in 2017. It launched the CK300VX baler. This new design is ideal for volume reduction of medium quantities of plastic and cardboard and can produce up to 300 kg bale of cardboard, making it possible to gain revenue on bales.

- Some businesses give the impression that the product has been modified by changing the packaging. For example, many soft drinks manufacturers sell their brands in cans, glass bottles and different-sized plastic bottles. In the music industry, record companies often release albums that re-use hits from a number of previously released albums. The new album is supported with a new cover.

Promotion: Some businesses prefer to leave the product unchanged but give a boost to falling sales by investing in promotion campaigns.

- One approach is to find new uses for a product. For example, WD-40® was first developed in 1953 to protect metal corrosion by displacing water. Today it has multiple advertised uses, such as removing dirt, cleaning bike chains and displacing water in car engines.
- Some businesses try to find new markets for their products. For example, a local business might start to serve a larger region. A regional business might try to market its products nationally. A business with a national market might begin to export its products. Many Western business are looking to sell their existing products in growing overseas markets, such as India and China.
- Investment in a advertising campaign can sometimes boost sales. A big advertising campaign on television, for example, can get people interested in a product again.
- Another approach is to encourage more frequent use of the product. An example of this might be cereal manufacturers persuading people to eat cereals for supper as well as for breakfast.

The effect that an extension strategy can have on a product life cycle is shown in Figure 3. As the market becomes saturated and sales begin to fall, the decline in sales is delayed by the use of an extension strategy. It would be sensible for a business to extend the life of a mature product before sales start to decline. Firms that can predict falling sales from market forecasts may attempt to use extension strategies before the decline takes place – that is at the maturity stage.

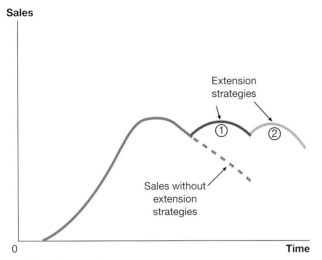

▲ Figure 3 Extension strategies

ACTIVITY 1 SKILLS ANALYSIS

CASE STUDY: GOLF GTI

The Golf GTI is produced by Volkswagen (VW), the German-based multinational car manufacturer. The Mk I GTI was launched at the Frankfurt Motor Show in 1975. The model could reach 60 mph (95 kpm) in 9 seconds. Designed with the emphasis on fun, it used colourful fabrics and an golf-ball-shaped gearstick. To extend the life of the model a further six versions were introduced, as outlined below.

- **1984** The Mk II GTI was launched with a new body structure, a 1781 cc engine and new styling to appeal to a new generation of drivers.
- **1987** The Mk III GTI had a new 2.0-litre eight-valve engine and a redesigned body that made the vehicle more efficient. This reduced the 0–60 mph (0–95 kpm) time to 8.3 seconds.
- **1998** The Mk IV GTI had improved safety features and updated styling. In 2002 the fastest and most powerful GTI produced to date was released for the 25th Anniversary Edition.
- **2004** Launched at the Paris Motor Show, the Mk V GTI was the most powerful GTI yet produced. The vehicle had other upgrades to make the driving experience quieter, smoother and safer.
- **2009** Mk VI GTI won the 'Best Hot Hatch' award at the Auto Express Awards. Testers complimented the sharp handling, impressive features and excellent comfort, and called it the best Golf to date.
- **2012** The Golf GTI Mk VII was launched with a lighter but stronger base. This was the most fuel-efficient GTI to date, and was capable of 0–62 mph (0–100 kpm) in 6.5 seconds.

VW plan to bring out an updated seventh version of the Golf GTI in 2018. The GTI range will have slightly

updated front and rear fenders and a tweaked cabin. The infotainment system will feature a super slick touch screen (with Apple CarPlay® and Android™ Auto). It has been described as not laggy, not slow but all very dependable and Golf-ish.

Source: Based on https://www.cnet.com/roadshow/auto/2018-volkswagen-golf/preview/

1. What is meant by an extension strategy?
2. Explain one way in which VW extended the life of the Golf GTI.
3. Explain one advantage to VW of using an extension strategy.

BOSTON MATRIX AND THE PRODUCT PORTFOLIO

Product life cycle analysis shows businesses that sales of products eventually decline. A well-organised business with one or more products will attempt to phase out old products and introduce new ones. This is known as managing the **product portfolio** or product mix.

The product portfolio: The product portfolio will be made up of **product lines**. A product line is a group of products which are similar. For example, televisions are a product line including flat screen, HD widescreen and portable televisions. With a constant launch of new products, a business can make sure gaps are not created as products reach the end of their life.

Figure 4 shows how a business can manage its product portfolio. Say that a business over a particular time period aims to launch three products. By organising their launch at regular intervals, there is never a gap in the market. As one product is declining, another is growing and further launches are planned. At point (i), as sales of product X are growing, product Y has just been launched. This means that at point (ii), when sales of product X have started to decline, sales of product Y are growing and product Z has just been launched.

This simple example shows only three products. In practice, a business may have many products. It would hope that existing products remain in 'maturity' for a long period. The profit from these mature products would be used to 'subsidise' the launch of new products. New products would be costly at first, and would make no profit for the business.

Examples of businesses that have successfully managed their product portfolios are sweet manufacturers. Companies such as Nestlé® produce a wide range of products, including KitKat®, Milkybar® and Yorkie®, and constantly look to launch new products.

The Boston matrix: One problem for firms when planning their product portfolios is that it is very difficult in practice to tell what stage of the life cycle a product is at. Also, there is no standard lifetime for products. For example, young people's fashion clothing has life cycles which can be predicted with some certainty. Other products are less reliable. Who, for example, could have predicted the lengthy life cycles of products such as the VW Beetle, or the short life cycle of products such as the Sinclair C5 – a sort of electric 'mini-car' introduced in the 1980s?

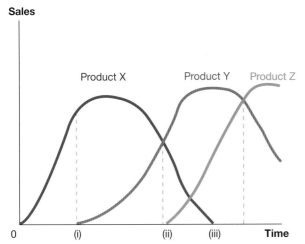

▲ Figure 4 Managing the product portfolio

A useful technique for allowing firms to analyse their product portfolios is the Product Portfolio Matrix developed by the Boston Consulting Group. It is sometimes called the Boston matrix or the Growth Share Matrix. This is shown in Figure 5. Products are categorised according to two criteria.

- **Market growth.** How fast is the market for the product growing? The market may be declining or it may be expanding. Sales of a product in a fast expanding market have a better chance of growing than a product in a mature or declining market.
- **Relative market share.** How strong is the product within its market? Is it a market leader that other products follow? Is it a product that is 12th in terms of sales? To measure this the market share of a product is compared with the strongest rival product. For example, if product X had a market share of 10 per cent and the market leader had 40 per cent, then the relative market share of product X is 0.25 (10 per cent ÷ 40 per cent). If product Y is a market leader with 50 per cent market share and the next most important product had a market share of 25 per cent, the relative market share of product Y is 2.0 (50 per cent ÷ 25 per cent).

Using these criteria the products of a business can be placed into one of four categories on the Boston matrix.

Stars: A star is a product with a high market growth and a relatively high market share. Stars are valuable to businesses. The product will be in a strong position in its

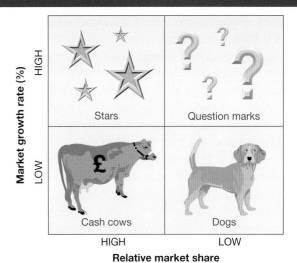

▲ Figure 5 The Boston matrix
Source: adapted from The BCG Portfolio Matrix from the Product Portfolio Matrix, © 1970, The Boston Consulting Group (BCG)

market as it has a high market share and the business can take advantage of a fast-growing market. A star is already likely to be profitable as it has a relatively high market share. But a business will need to invest in the product to cope with a growing market and growing sales. This could mean investing in new production facilities or promotion to protect the product from competition. **Net cash flow** may be nearly zero. This is because although profits will be high, bringing money in, investment spending will also be high, leading to outflows.

Cash cows: A cash cow is a product with a relatively high market share. It is therefore well positioned in the market and likely to be profitable. But the market it is in will have weak growth. So there will be little chance of increasing sales and profits in future. There will be little need for investment. With slow growth in sales there should be little need for new premises, for example. Cash cows have strong positive net cash flow. Money coming into the business from profits will not be taken out via investment.

Question marks: Question marks, sometimes known as problem children or wildcats, are products with a relatively low market share in a fast-growing market. This can be a problem for a business because it is unclear what should be done with these products. If a product is performing weakly it is unlikely to be profitable. But as it is in a fast-growing market, there is potential to turn it into a star. Net cash flow is likely to be zero or negative. Weak relative market share means that it will not be profitable. But investment will be needed to cope with expanding sales in a fast-growing market.

Dogs: These are products with a relatively low market share in a market with low growth. Dogs have poor prospects for future sales and profits. They may generate some positive net cash flow because they will need little investment but may earn some profit. But if they make little or no profit, net cash flow may be zero or even negative.

Businesses can make use of the Boston matrix to manage their product portfolios.

Balancing product lines: Businesses must ensure that their product portfolios do not contain too many items within each category. Naturally, they do not want lots of dogs, but they should also avoid having too many stars and question marks. Products on the top of the Boston matrix are in the early stages of the product life cycle and are in growing markets. But the cost of developing and promoting them will not yet have been recovered. This will use up resources. Balancing these with cash cows will mean that the positive net cash flow from the cash cows can be used to support products in a growing market. The development cost of cash cows is likely to have already been recovered and promotional costs should be low relative to sales. This does not mean though that a business would want lots of cash cows and few question marks and stars. This is because many of the stars and perhaps some question marks might become the cash cows of the future.

Taking appropriate decisions: Products in different categories in the matrix may require different approaches.

- Stars have great future potential. They are future cash cows. A business will need to build the brand of these products so that sales increase and competition is fought off successfully.
- Cash cows might be milked for cash, which can then be used to develop other products. Or the business may decide to spend just enough on promotion and development to maintain sales and market share, known as holding.
- For question marks a business has choices. It can build the brand, hoping to turn it into a star, harvest the product by raising price and cutting promotion so that profits are increased, or divest itself of the product, withdrawing it or selling it because it is not making a profit.
- Dogs may be divested if they are not making a profit or in some cases harvested.

Helsinki-based CheezyBix manufactures a range of cheesy snacks in Finland. The business currently has four products in its portfolio. They are shown in Figure 6. CheezyBix, a product first launched in 1987, brings in about 65 per cent of the company's revenue. It has a high market share and it is still growing.

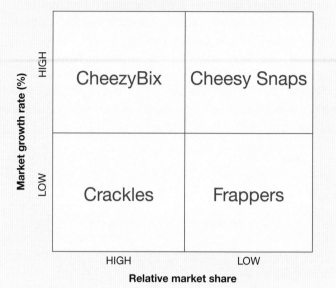

▲ Figure 6 CheezyBix product portfolio

1. Explain how you would categorise the position of Crackles in the Boston matrix using Figure 6.
2. Explain one way in which CheezyBix might use the information in Figure 6.

THE CONCEPT OF 'MARKETING MIX'

In order to market its products effectively a business must consider its **marketing mix**. The marketing mix refers to those elements of a firm's marketing strategy that are designed to meet the needs of its customers. The marketing mix emphasises four particular elements often referred to as the 4 Ps – product, price, promotion and place. To meet customer needs and to create an effective marketing mix, businesses must produce the right product, at the right price, make it available in the right place and ensure that customers are aware of its existence through effective promotion.

Product: It is important that products meet customer needs. This means that businesses must address a number of features relating to the product.

- **How consumers use the product.** A ladies shoe manufacturer, for example, will understand that customers will need different footwear for going to work and for attending a dinner party.
- **The appearance of a product.** Businesses need to consider the different colours, sizes, shapes and styles when designing products. For example, many businesses try to differentiate their products by making them look more attractive than those of rivals. For some goods, such as cars, clothes and jewellery, this might be very important to consumers.
- **Financial factors.** Businesses need to develop products that customers can afford to buy. There is no point in developing an attractive and highly

comfortable armchair if it costs US$20,000. Customers want value for money and they may also take into account the quality of after-sales service before they make a purchase.

- **The product's life cycle.** Earlier in this chapter it was shown that sales for a product rise at first and then eventually fall. A business must decide whether to allow a product to decline or try to refresh it in some way. In 'Getting started', Karrandore decided not to withdraw Patagonia Cruises. Instead, the company invested in an upgraded service to improve the declining product.
- **A product's unique selling point (USP).** This is the aspect or feature of the product which distinguishes it from that of a rival. If a business can develop a USP it may gain a competitive edge in the market.

Price: The pricing policy of a business is often a reflection of the market at which it is aiming. Prices will not always be set at the level which will maximise sales or short-term profits. For example, a business may charge a high price because it is aiming to sell to consumers who regard the product as exclusive rather than because production costs are high. However, for most products, costs are a very important influence on price. Pricing is discussed in Chapter 12.

Promotion: Customers must be given information about products and encouraged to buy them. Businesses can choose from a wide range of different promotional methods. They can advertise on television, online or in newspapers and magazines, for example. Alternatively, they may decide to use sponsorship, coupons, free gifts, competitions or some other method that suits their product and customer target group. Promotion is discussed in Chapter 11.

Place: Products must be made available at convenient locations at times when customers want to buy them. This means that a business has to make decisions about the way in which products will be physically distributed, i.e. by rail, road, sea or air. It also means taking into account how the product is sold. Increasingly businesses are selling their products online rather than from physical outlets such as shops.

MARKETING STRATEGIES

A **marketing strategy** is a set of plans that aim to achieve a specific marketing objective. For example, a local company that rents cars might aim to become the market leader in the region. Its strategy to achieve this objective might be to:

- improve the quality of customer service by delivering cars to people's homes
- contact all previous customers offering them a half-price deal

- offer a 3-day weekend rental for the price of 2 days
- invest £500 in a local newspaper advert
- donate a vehicle to a local community group to get some PR
- set up a website to promote the business and take online bookings.

This strategy involves all aspects of the marketing mix and a number of different promotional methods.

Strategies for mass markets: Some businesses sell products into mass markets. Such markets are huge, often global, and can have millions of potential customers. Procter & Gamble, Kraft Heinz, Kellogg's, Coca-Cola and General Motors are examples of businesses that sell into mass markets. Mass markets are usually very competitive because the rewards for success can be significant. A wide range of different marketing strategies can be used in a mass market, but some general similarities are as follows.

- **Product.** In a mass market there will be many products competing for customer attention. Most of these products will be very close substitutes for each other. The most successful businesses are likely to be those that can differentiate their product in some way. Developing a USP will help a business's product 'stand out from the pack'. If a business is unable to differentiate its product it will have to rely on other elements in the marketing mix to compensate.
- **Price.** The prices charged by businesses in a mass market are likely to be very similar. All businesses in the market are likely to fear a price war because they usually reduce revenue for every competitor. This helps to explain why businesses are happy to charge the 'going rate' in the market. Price leadership is common in mass markets where the dominant business, perhaps the one with the lowest unit costs, sets the price and everyone else follows.
- **Promotion.** In the absence of price competition, firms look to non-price competition to help gain an edge. This means they are prepared to invest heavily in advertising and promotion because it is such an important part of the marketing mix in mass markets. An overwhelming majority of television adverts are placed by businesses selling into mass markets. Perhaps less than 5 per cent of those that see the adverts will buy the product. However, 5 per cent of several million is a significant number.
- **Place.** Businesses serving mass markets will often use multiple channels to distribute their goods. Businesses selling fast-moving consumer goods will target supermarkets, wholesalers, independents and any other outlet that is suited to their particular product. Some manufacturers pay supermarkets

to display their goods in prominent places – at eye level or at the end of aisles, for example. The Internet is used increasingly by businesses to sell goods and services in mass markets. All banks, for instance, offer online bank accounts and an increasing number of supermarkets offer online shopping and delivery or 'click & collect' services. The Internet has allowed small businesses and other independents to have access to mass markets. For example, a small glove manufacturer based in, say, Gothenburg in Sweden could distribute its products to individual customers anywhere in the world.

Strategies for niche markets: Customers in niche markets have very particular needs, which are sometimes neglected by larger firms. Consequently, there is a gap in the market for a business that is prepared to produce goods or services for this small customer group. Businesses selling to niche markets will use different marketing strategies from those selling into mass markets.

- **Product.** In a niche market the product is likely to have quite significant differences from its rivals. For example, in the eating-out market there are around 420,000 restaurants in the UK. However, only four of these have been awarded three Michelin stars (the highest award possible for food quality and service). These four restaurants serve stunning food of the highest possible quality – very different from that served in the overwhelming majority of other restaurants. They cater for a particular niche – people who want to experience the very best food, perhaps just as a one-off, and are prepared to pay for it. In niche markets products will be designed carefully in order to meet the very specific needs of the customer group. Product will be a key element in the marketing mix.
- **Price.** Businesses selling in niche markets have more flexibility in their pricing. There is less competition in niche markets so higher prices can be charged without losing significant market share to rivals. Also, customers may be prepared to pay higher prices if their specific needs are being met effectively. For example, the prices charged by restaurants with three Michelin stars can be over £100 per person.
- **Promotion.** In niche markets promotion and advertising will tend to be more targeted. Since niche markets are smaller there is less need to use national media when advertising. Businesses need to identify their customer profile very accurately to ensure that advertising and promotion expenditure is not wasted. Adverts are likely to be placed in specialised publications. For example, yachts and chandlery (boat equipment

and accessories) are likely to be advertised in magazines such as *Yachting Monthly* and *Boating World*. Some manufacturers of golf clubs and golf accessories advertise on television, but only use specialised channels, such as the golf channel on Sky Sports.

- **Place.** Businesses selling into niche markets are often more selective when choosing distribution channels. They are more likely to use exclusive distributors or to handle distribution privately. They will also use the Internet if it is practical. One example is Blue Mountain coffee. This is a high-quality coffee grown exclusively in Jamaica, which can only be purchased from selected stores and online. It is marketed at around £24 per 227 g compared to around £3.50 or less for rival beans, which might be sold in supermarkets, for example.

STRATEGIES FOR BUSINESS-TO-BUSINESS (B2B) AND BUSINESS-TO-CONSUMER (B2C) MARKETS

Many businesses supply goods and services to other businesses. For example, JCB produces a wide range of machinery for use in the construction industry. It sells most of its products to construction companies and plant hire companies all over the world. The marketing strategies used by companies that sell to other businesses (B2B) are likely to be different from those discussed above, that sell to consumers (B2C). In B2B marketing, one approach is to distinguish between outbound and inbound marketing strategies.

Outbound marketing strategies: This involves directing marketing material at potential customers whether they are expecting it or not. This could include sending direct mail, email, marketing by telephone, sponsorship, targeted adverts in specialist publications or trade shows. However, there are some drawbacks using this approach. People are increasingly ignoring adverts. How many do people remember? Also, many people are annoyed by being contacted by phone and other similar marketing methods. Frequent or repeated use of these approaches could damage a brand's reputation. Many of the potential customers obtained using these methods are poor quality and waste resources when they do not lead to sales. It has also been reported that potential customers found through outbound marketing cost significantly more to acquire than leads found through inbound marketing.

Inbound marketing strategies: This involves attracting potential customers to websites when they are looking for suppliers or solutions to problems. Some of the common inbound marketing techniques are summarised in Table 1.

Method	Description
Blogging	Provide content on company blogs to help draw in potential customers
Social media marketing	Develop a following on social media, such as Twitter, LinkedIn and Facebook
Search engine optimisation	Increase website traffic by getting a high-ranking placement in searches
Free e-books	Offer useful, in-depth information for website visitors to download
Video marketing	Produce short and informative video clips for website visitors
Targeted email marketing	Send personalised emails targeted to people – for example, those who have downloaded a free e-book

▲ Table 1 Common inbound marketing techniques

The use of inbound methods also has challenges. For example, it requires effort and resources to build up enough useful content on websites to convert visitors into leads. Recruitment of experienced inbound marketers can be difficult, and it can be tricky to keep the strategy up to date with rapidly emerging trends.

Hybrid strategies: This involves a combination of both outbound and inbound methods. It is reckoned that inbound strategies take at least 6 months to generate results, so some outbound methods can be employed in the short term. Once inbound methods start to generate meaningful leads some of the less effective outbound methods can be dropped. This will help to reduce costs and create sustainable growth in market share.

EXAM HINT

You need to understand that marketing strategies can vary hugely. They depend on a wide range of factors, such as the nature of the product, the resources available to a company, the aim of the strategy, the size and nature of the market, corporate strategy and the creativity of employees. You would expect very different products to be marketed differently; for instance, the way healthcare and toys are marketed is likely to be very different. However, businesses in the same industry can also have different marketing strategies. Small businesses will use different approaches to multinationals because they have fewer resources. Some businesses may have similarities in their marketing strategies, but they will rarely be identical.

HOW BUSINESSES DEVELOP CUSTOMER LOYALTY

A business is likely to be more successful if it can persuade customers to keep returning. How can businesses develop customer loyalty?

Communication: A business must keep customers informed. In a mass market this might involve using national advertising campaigns to tell customers about new products. Some businesses may use reassuring adverts. These help to convince customers that they have made the right purchase. Some firms send out regular newsletters, usually by email, to keep customers up to date with company events. Regular communication helps to build a relationship between a business and a customer. If a bond can be formed customers are more likely to return.

Customer service: Customers are more likely to return to a business if they receive high-quality customer service. Employees who interact with customers must be professional, reliable and conduct themselves honestly and sincerely. Customer service can often be improved by dealing with matters more promptly, providing a more effective after-sales service or making the 'purchasing experience' a pleasant one. Some businesses provide customers with refreshments while they are conducting a transaction.

Customer incentives: Many businesses reward their customers if they keep returning. For example, cafe chains and supermarkets use loyalty or reward cards. These give customers discounts, cash vouchers or free goods as rewards for loyalty. The value of the rewards are usually linked directly to the amount spent by customers. In some countries these are in decline. However, a survey of 1,524 respondents in the top 10–15 per cent of earners split equally across China, Hong Kong Special Administrative Region and Singapore, found that 72 per cent of Chinese consumers 'regard themselves as engaged members of loyalty programmes'. The survey also found that 89 per cent of Chinese respondents and 87 per cent from Hong Kong Special Administrative Region agreed that a loyalty programme makes them want to spend more.

Personalisation: Some businesses try to deal with customers on a personal level. They may address individual customers by their name – perhaps in person or in letters. Some firms send customers birthday cards to help build relationships. However, dealing with a customer at a personal level is a lot easier for a smaller business than, say, a multinational.

Preferential treatment: Many people like the idea of receiving preferential treatment from a business. For example, many airlines have VIP lounges at airports where first class, business class or other select passengers can relax away from the loud and busy environment of normal airport business. The lounges usually offer free refreshments, free access to Wi-Fi, satellite television, comfortable seats and showers. The principle behind all this is that if a business can provide customers with preferential treatment they may return for more.

ACTIVITY 3   SKILLS ▷ PROBLEM SOLVING, ANALYSIS

CASE STUDY: CREDIT CARD CASHBACK DEALS

A number of banks offer their customers 'cashback deals' when using credit cards. This means that a credit card user can receive an amount of cash depending on how much is spent on the card. For example, American Express offered customers 5 per cent cashback if they spent up to £2000 in the first 3 months of a platinum card membership. After the initial 3 months customers could earn up to 1.25 per cent cashback, depending on how much they spent each month. If customers spent:

- between £0 and £3500, they got 0.5 per cent cashback
- between £3500 and £7500, they got 1 per cent cashback
- over £7500, they got 1.25 per cent cashback.

Provided customers spent a minimum of £3000 in a year, almost every pound spent using the card qualified for cashback. There was no annual fee charged on this level of membership (the Platinum Cashback Everyday Credit Card).

1. Calculate the amount of cashback a customer would be entitled to if £5000 is spent on the card in the ninth month of ownership.
2. Explain one way in which cashback cards might help to develop customer loyalty.

CHECKPOINT

1. Describe the first stage in the product life cycle.
2. What pricing strategy might be used in the launch stage of the product life cycle?
3. What happens to sales in the maturity stage of the product life cycle?
4. Why might some products decline very quickly?
5. Give three examples of possible extension strategies.
6. What is the difference between a product portfolio and a product line?
7. What is a question mark product in the Boston matrix?
8. How might businesses distribute their products in a mass market?
9. Why are prices likely to be higher in niche markets?
10. What is the difference between outbound and inbound B2B marketing?
11. Give three examples of inbound B2B marketing.
12. State three ways in which a business might develop customer loyalty.

SUBJECT VOCABULARY

Boston matrix a 2x2 matrix model that analyses a product portfolio according to the growth rate of the market and the relative market share of products within the market.
extension strategies methods used to prolong the life of a product.
marketing mix the mix of marketing elements used by a company, which are usually known as the 4Ps: product, price, place, and promotion.
marketing objectives goals that a business attempts to achieve through its marketing activities.
marketing strategy a set of plans that aim to achieve a specific marketing objective.
product lines a group of products that are very similar.
product portfolio the collection of products a business is currently marketing.
unique selling point the aspect or feature of the product that differentiates it from those of rivals.

EXAM PRACTICE

ENSCHEDE GRASSMAAIERS

SKILLS ANALYSIS, INTERPRETATION, CRITICAL THINKING, REASONING

In developed countries, most households with gardens have a lawnmower to cut their grass. Enschede Grassmaaiers, a Dutch company, manufacture ride-on mowers, which are purchased by the owners of properties with very large lawns, sports clubs and a few small farmers such as fruit growers. Enschede Grassmaaiers operate in a niche market. The company distributes its products through a small range of specialist dealers throughout most of the Netherlands. Established in 1980, sales grew steadily. However, in the last 10 years or so they have levelled out. Their main product, which accounts for 80 per cent of revenue, has reached the maturity stage in the product life cycle. Figure 7 shows sales levels of this product between 1980 and 2020.

The company directors believe that action is needed to extend the life of the product. There are fears that some of the very large manufacturers from overseas, such as Honda, might enter the market and drive them out of business. The company currently charges a premium price for its mowers. This is possible because an excellent after-sales service is available to all customers free of charge (excluding spare parts). The company has a breakdown support team which is on call 7 days a week. This means that customers can contact the company and organise a visit from the service team on the same day in the event of a breakdown. However, the lawnmowers are extremely well made. They are manufactured from high-quality materials and components and very rarely breakdown. The mowers often last for 20 years or more. The after-sales service facility helps to reassure customers when they first buy a ride-on lawnmower. They are happy to pay a premium price.

The directors of the company have organised a meeting to discuss the way forward and outline a clear marketing strategy for the main product. The company's goal is to extend the life of the product for another 20 years.

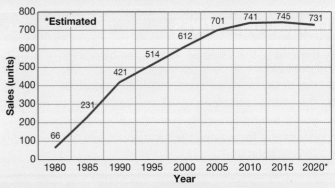

▲ Figure 7 Sales of Enschede Grassmaaiers' main product, 1980–2020

Q

(a) Explain what is meant by the marketing mix. **(4 marks)**

(b) Explain how a business like Enschede Grassmaaiers might benefit from having a specific marketing objective? **(4 marks)**

(c) Analyse **two** possible extension strategies that Enschede Grassmaaiers might consider. **(6 marks)**

(d) Assess how the marketing strategies of a business might differ for a business operating in a mass market. **(10 marks)**

10 PRODUCT/SERVICE DESIGN

LEARNING OBJECTIVES

By the end of this chapter you should be able to understand:

■ the design mix: function, aesthetics and cost
■ the changes in elements of the design mix to reflect social trends (concern over resource depletion, designing for waste minimisation, re-use and recycling, ethical sourcing).

GETTING STARTED

Look at the product in the image. Do you like the design? Explain your reasons. State three factors that might be important when designing a product like this. How might the design be affected by changes in social trends, such as health and safety issues, resource depletion and waste minimisation?

PRODUCT/SERVICE DESIGN

Many businesses are keen to bring new products and services to the market. New products and services help to generate more revenue and ensure that businesses remain competitive. The process of creating a new product or service is called **product design**. It involves the generation and development of ideas through a process that leads to new products/services.

Once a business has identified a need for a product, a design brief can be written. This will contain features about a product that the designers can use. For example, a business aiming to produce a new travel iron may write a design brief such as 'a new travel iron that is compact and possesses all the features of a full-sized model'. Designers can work from this design brief. When designing the new travel iron they may take into account:

- the shape and appearance of the iron
- whether it fits the intended need

- how easily and cost effectively it can be produced from the design
- the dimensions and preferred materials to be used
- the image it gives when displayed
- whether the design should create a 'corporate identity', saying something about the image of the company.

DESIGN MIX

When designing any product or service a number of key features have to be considered. These features may be referred to as the **design mix** and are summarised in Figure 1.

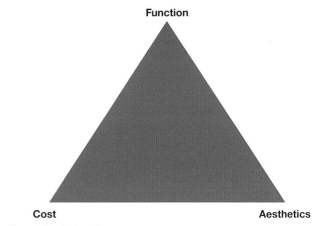

▲ Figure 1 The design mix

Function: A product must be fit for purpose, which means that it must be capable of doing the job that it is sold to do. For example, a waterproof jacket must not let in rain. It must also be reliable and work every time the customer uses it. Product design is also important for services as well as goods. For example, an Internet service provider must provide a reliable and safe connection. The manufacturers of many **consumer durables** offer long warranties to show that they have confidence in the reliability and durability of their products. Products that are not fit for purpose are also likely to be returned, which will add to business costs.

Products and services should also be convenient and easy for the customer to use. People will get frustrated if they cannot download an app quickly or understand how to construct flat-pack furniture from a set of instructions. Technical products and machinery often need maintenance, so these products should be designed so that maintenance can be carried out easily. However, if there is adequate competition in the market this might not be an issue. Consumers can find another supplier if they are unhappy with the level of convenience offered by a particular business.

Some products are designed with **ergonomics** in mind. This means that they are designed so that people can interact with them safely and without using unnecessary effort. Figure 2 shows how a workstation might be ergonomically designed to ensure that a person at work is entirely comfortable.

If a business can design a product or service with superior functionality, it may be used as a unique selling point, or USP. Most people recognise that Volvo emphasise the safety of their cars. This is their USP.

Designers must also ensure that new products or services are safe. Safety is particularly important if children, the elderly or pregnant women use the products. Safety issues could include ensuring that products do not contain poisons or dangerous materials, such as toxic paint. If potentially dangerous features are necessary, such as a sharp edge on a power tool, then it is important to design the product to provide adequate protection.

ACTIVITY 1   SKILLS   ANALYSIS, PERSONAL AND SOCIAL RESPONSIBILITY

CASE STUDY: ERGONOMIC WORKSTATIONS

An office supplies company has produced a new ergonomically designed computer workstation. Figure 2 shows how it has taken into account the needs of users.

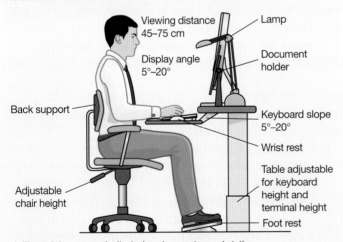

▲ Figure 2 An ergonomically designed computer workstation

1. Explain what is meant by an ergonomically designed product.
2. Explain the possible benefits to a business of using ergonomically designed workstations.

Aesthetics: Products and services should stimulate people's senses in addition to performing a function. This is the product or service's aesthetic appeal. Designers must consider elements of a product, such as its size,

appearance, shape, smell or taste, or the presentation of a service, because it has an impact on the choices that consumers make. For example, some companies choose designs that use more expensive materials to add to the aesthetic appeal of a product, because a product that appeals to the senses may sell better. Someone may buy a luxury car because they like the smell of leather seats or the appearance of wooden components, and the atmosphere that these features create, rather than because of its fuel economy or speed.

As the cost of resources and manufacturing comes down over time, aesthetics is likely to become more important in the design mix. Product and service design has changed dramatically in recent years, as computers, vehicles, mobile phones and music players have become more compact and more powerful. Many consumers prefer smaller and more portable products that are more user-friendly.

Cost/economic manufacture: A well-designed product or service is more likely to be economically viable. This means that a business should be able to produce and sell the product or service at a profit. Therefore, designers will need to select materials and processes that minimise costs. For example, it was reported that Apple wanted to use curved glass for early iPhone models. However, the prototypes were too expensive to manufacture, so they were abandoned. In the airline industry, new routes must be cost effective if they are to be introduced. Businesses often have to reach a compromise between design and cost. If costs are high, products or services may be dropped altogether.

ACTIVITY 2   SKILLS   INTERPRETATION, REASONING

CASE STUDY: THE DESIGN MIX

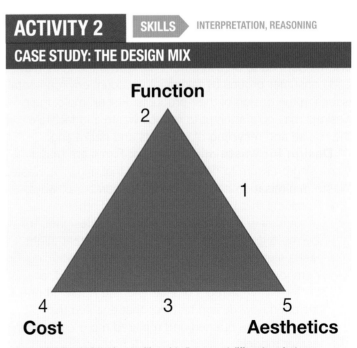

▲ Figure 3 The design mix – positions 1 to 5 represent different products

1. Match the following products with the positions (1 to 5) shown on the triangle which best represent the design mix in Figure 3. Each of the positions suggests which aspect of the mix may be relatively more important for particular products. (a) designer shoes, (b) a sports car, (c) a life assurance policy, (d) a dining room table, (e) a smartphone.
2. Explain how cost might affect the design of a package holiday.

THE DESIGN MIX AND SOCIAL TRENDS

Product designers need to be aware of changes in social trends. For example, people have become increasingly aware about the effects their lifestyles have on the environment. Worries about global warming, **resource depletion** and pollution have encouraged many to adopt more environmentally friendly lifestyles. Businesses have also responded to pressure from the government, media and consumer groups by taking into account environmental issues in the design of their products. For example, their designs may now attempt to reduce waste and facilitate the re-use and **recycling** of products and packaging.

Design for waste minimisation: Firms are under increasing pressure to design products that minimise waste. **Waste minimisation** can take place in a number of ways.

- Products that use a lot of energy and other resources in manufacturing should be designed to be more durable by designing products that might last a lifetime. This could be achieved by including components in a design that can be replaced, or better still, repaired. For example, the Apple iPhone 6 included new design features that enabled the product to be opened and repaired more easily than earlier models.

- Products could be designed to be smaller and lighter. This will help to save the amount of material used in production. Resources used in handling, packaging and transport will also be reduced. Examples of this include laptops, tablet computers, smartphones, digital cameras, music systems and flat-screen televisions.

- Designers could be discouraged from designing single-use, disposable products. Products such as disposable razors, plastic spoons, cardboard plates and paper cups can be replaced with durable equivalents. There is probably a lot more scope here for businesses to make improvements. At the moment, the amount of packaging used by businesses and thrown away by customers is considerable.

- In the restaurant industry, dishes and menus could be designed to reduce food waste, such as meat offcuts.

Although there are clear benefits of designing products that reduce waste, many businesses have not embraced the idea. For example, many products are discarded because they are considered 'out of date'. In the fashion industry, for example, clothes and accessories are often worn for a limited period of time only. They are discarded even though they are still functional. This is because fashions change and businesses can make money by selling consumers 'new season' collections. At the moment this is unlikely to change. There would need to be a radical change in social trends for people to change their behaviour.

Design for re-use: Resources can be saved if products are designed so that they can be re-used. For example, mobile phones are designed to last for years but are thought to have an average first use of around 18 months, so it is important that their component parts can be re-used to prevent waste.

- Businesses could be encouraged to design packaging which can be re-used. In the past, fizzy drinks were sold in returnable bottles. Customers would return their empty bottles and get a refund. The empty bottles would then be returned to the supplier, washed and re-used. Many countries around the world, such as Holland and Germany, still give customers money for returning their empty bottles.

- Another approach is to design products so that components can be easily re-used. For example, Philips designed a new light bulb that was easier to take to pieces than previous light bulbs, so that the component parts could be re-used.

Design for recycling: Businesses are making increasing use of recycled materials in their designs.

- Some businesses are adapting their production methods so that newly designed products can be produced using recycled materials. For example, carpet manufacturers are developing ways of using their old carpets in the production of new ones. Glass manufacturers have long used recycled glass in the production of new glass.
- Some businesses specialise in the sole use of recycled materials in their manufacture. For example, the Reefer Sail Company makes its products from recycled materials, including boat and windsurf sails and kites, as well as from sail makers' roll ends and offcuts. Its product range includes deck chairs, cushions, buckets, bags and children's toys.
- Some firms make use of waste discarded by other businesses in their designs. For example, Yübe is a storage system built with panels made from sugar cane waste. The Yübe frames, which can be arranged in multiple ways, are made of a combination of sugar cane fibre, recycled plastic and bamboo.
- In the media, it may be possible to recycle material to save time and effort. For example, the same news stories might be adapted and used in several different formats. They might appear in print, online, as television broadcasts, as radio broadcasts and as podcasts.

Ethical sourcing: In order to reflect social trends, some businesses use ethically sourced resources in their designs. **Ethical sourcing** means that businesses only use materials, components and services from suppliers that respect the environment, treat their workforce well by paying them a fair wage and providing a safe working environment, and generally trade with honesty. For example, a clothes designer might insist that their collections are not manufactured by overseas businesses that use child labour in their factories.

In 2016, a US retailer called BJ's Wholesale Club, joined a boycott on cotton from Uzbekistan. The company discovered that cotton production in Uzbek involved the use of forced labour. According to a press release, 'The Uzbek government forces over 1 million citizens to labour in the country's cotton fields each year. The government shuts down universities and public offices for months at a time, mobilises the country's students, teachers, and civil servants, and sends them to the cotton fields every autumn.'

ACTIVITY 3   SKILLS   ANALYSIS, INTERPRETATION, PERSONAL AND SOCIAL RESPONSIBILITY

CASE STUDY: DELL™

Dell, the Texan computer company, has responded positively to social trends by designing products and production process that are sensitive to the needs of the environment. Dell claims that it considers the environment at every stage of the product life cycle.

- Dell believes that all materials are valuable and waste should be eliminated.
- The company uses environmentally friendly materials, such as recycled plastics, and exceeds legal requirements when selecting 'safe' materials for production.
- Between 2015 and 2016 Dell reduced the average energy used to build each item in its product portfolio by around 16 per cent. Since 2012 the reduction has been 42.8 per cent.
- The use of glues and adhesives, which are not easily recycled, have been replaced with new 'snap-fits' and other substitutes.
- Dell uses a closed-loop plastics supply chain. This means that it repeatedly recycles and re-uses materials over and over again.
- Dell tries to use reputable third-party eco-labels such as ENERGY STAR, EPEAT and the 80 PLUS Program, when searching for technology to use in its organisation.

1. Explain how Dell is reduces waste through its design process.
2. Explain how Dell's approach reflects social trends.

▲ A plastic recycling plant

Although some businesses try to adopt an ethical approach to supplying products, it could be argued that the majority are still focused on lowering costs. For example, the cheap 'value brands' in supermarkets are still very popular. Perhaps this is because people are more concerned with getting products for the lowest possible price. They may have little regard for ethically sourced products.

BENEFITS OF ADAPTING PRODUCT DESIGNS TO CHANGES IN SOCIAL TRENDS

Although businesses may have to make an effort to reflect social trends in their designs, which could possibly increase costs, there are likely to be some lucrative benefits.

- If businesses can reduce waste they will use fewer resources. This will result in lower costs and higher profits.

- If designs reflect social trends, products are likely to be more popular and sell in larger quantities. This will raise revenue and improve profits.
- Some businesses use their design features as a USP. This will help to market their products more effectively. For example, Ecover™ produces household cleaners made from plant and mineral materials. Avoiding the use of chemicals is environmentally friendly, and it is also their USP.
- Businesses that adopt some of the emerging design features relating to social trends are more likely to be viewed as good corporate citizens. Many businesses attempt to emphasise corporate social responsibility in their marketing strategy. By doing this they aim to raise sales revenue and profit. They may also avoid criticism for trading unethically.

CHECKPOINT

1. State two examples of products where aesthetics is particularly important in the design mix.

2. State two examples of products where functionality is of prime importance in the design mix.

3. Give one way in which the government might affect the design of products.

4. State three examples of products that are likely to be ergonomically designed.

5. State two benefits to consumers of designs that reflect changes in social trends.

6. State two benefits to businesses of designs that reflect changes in social trends.

7. How might ethical sourcing affect the design of clothing?

SUBJECT VOCABULARY

consumer durables goods that can be used repeatedly over a period of time, such as cars and household appliances.
design mix the range of features that are important when designing a product.
ergonomics the study of how people interact with their environment and the equipment they use – often in the workplace.
ethical sourcing using materials, components and services from suppliers that respect the environment, treat their workforce well and generally trade with integrity.
product design the process of creating a new product or service.
recycling making use of materials that have been discarded as waste.
resource depletion the using up of natural resources.
waste minimisation reducing the quantity of resources that are discarded in the production process.

EXAM PRACTICE

STANLEY MODULAR

SKILLS ANALYSIS, INTERPRETATION, ADAPTABILITY

The construction sector generates millions of tonnes of waste every year in most countries. This includes building materials, such as nails, electrical wire, steel and waste from site preparation such as tree stumps and the remains of demolished structures. Some construction waste can be dangerous, as it can contain lead, asbestos or other dangerous substances, and this sort of waste needs to be disposed of carefully.

Construction companies have come under increasing pressure to reduce this waste. A construction firm in New Zealand, Stanley Modular, is committed to reducing waste and has come up with some effective designs. Stanley constructs schools and homes in New Zealand using a limited set of standard components. Wall, ceiling and floor panels are constructed in a factory and then transported to the building site. Almost all of the work is done in the factory, with just a small proportion done on site.

Constructing the panels in a factory cuts down the amount of waste on site, and the management of waste and materials becomes easier as they are all in one place, making it easier to collect and sort the waste.

Almost all the materials used by Stanley Modular end up in their completed buildings, because the parts of each building are created to fit the exact size of the finished structure. The small amount of excess is mostly recycled, with a tiny proportion discarded. Keeping the amount of waste to these levels requires more employees to actively work on waste management, as the factory environment has to be strictly controlled to ensure that waste is kept to a minimum.

Waste is minimised in a wide range of areas.

- **Transportation.** A Stanley Modular house can be transported to site on a single truck, with flat-pack panels on the front, roofing on the back and a 4-metre trailer containing the bathroom components. More complex parts of the building process require more trips, but far fewer than would be required on a traditional building site.
- **Materials.** In a typical build, 1200 kg of wood is wasted – Stanley Modular only waste around 10 per cent of this. Reductions in waste have been found when all gun nails use standard nail strips, which prevents operators from mixing up nail types, resulting in rework. The use of computer numerical control (CNC) machinery maximises the usable material from pieces of wood and metal.
- **Time wastage.** Stanley Modular save a lot of time in their operations. They estimate that modular building is up to a third faster than traditional construction. The use of CNC machinery is also 50 per cent faster than machinery controlled by hand.

Stanley Modular continually explore ways to decrease the impact of construction on the environment. Their projects show how a well-designed prefabricated building system can minimise waste, improve productivity and speed up construction projects.

Source: adapted from www.branz.co.nz/REBRI

Q

(a) Explain how designs that reduce waste benefit Stanley Modular. **(4 marks)**
(b) Explain the aspects of the traditional design mix that might be important to Stanley Modular. **(4 marks)**
(c) Assess the benefits to Stanley Modular of adapting its designs to reflect changes in social trends.

(10 marks)

11 PROMOTION AND BRANDING

LEARNING OBJECTIVES

By the end of this chapter you should be able to understand:
- types of promotion
- types of branding
- the benefits of strong branding: added value, ability to charge premium prices and reduced price elasticity of demand
- ways to build a brand: unique selling points (USPs)/ differentiation, advertising, sponsorship and the use of social media
- changes in branding and promotion to reflect social trends: viral marketing, social media and emotional branding.

GETTING STARTED

According to Zenith, the ROI Agency, in 2017 businesses will spend more on Internet advertising than on television advertising for the first time ever. In 2017, global spending on Internet advertising was US$205,000 million. This compares with US$192,000 million on television. Figure 1 shows how global advertising expenditure is allocated between different advertising media in 2017.

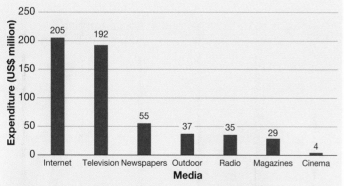

▲ Figure 1 Predicted global advertising expenditure by media, 2017

According to the predictions, how much in total will be spent on global advertising in 2017? Why do businesses spend so much on advertising? What might explain the changes in spending by businesses on newspaper and Internet advertising? What other methods might a business use to promote its products?

WHAT IS PROMOTION?

An important element in the marketing mix is **promotion**. This involves businesses drawing attention to their products, services or companies. Generally, businesses use promotion to obtain and keep customers. However, promotion is also likely to be used to achieve some specific aims.
- Tell consumers about a new product.
- Remind customers about an existing product.
- Reach a target audience that is spread over a wide area.
- Reassure customers about products.
- Show consumers that rival products are not as good.
- Improve or develop the image of the business.

ABOVE-THE-LINE PROMOTION

Above-the-line promotion involves **advertising** in the media. Businesses pay television companies or newspapers, for example, to have their adverts broadcast or printed. Advertising may be placed into different categories.
- **Informative advertising.** This means that the adverts are designed to increase consumer awareness of products. They may give clear information about the features of a product, for example. The classified advertisements in newspapers are examples of informative advertising.
- **Persuasive advertising.** Some advertising is designed to put pressure on consumers to buy a product. Persuasive advertisements often try to convince consumers to buy a particular brand rather than that of a competitor. They are often designed to appeal to people's emotions, such as fear and pity. Persuasive adverts may also appeal to people's respect for authority and fascination with celebrity. A lot of television and cinema adverts are persuasive.
- **Reassuring advertising.** This advertising is aimed at existing customers. It is designed to be comforting and suggest to consumers that they were 'right' to buy a particular product and that they should continue to do so. Businesses selling financial services may use this approach to reassure people that their money is 'safe'.

Table 1 shows the advantages and disadvantages of the main advertising media.

Media	Advantages	Disadvantages
Television	Huge audiences can be reached The use of products can be demonstrated Sound and movement can be used Scope for targeting groups with digital television	Very expensive Message may be short lived Some viewers avoid television ads Delay between seeing ads and shopping
Newspapers and magazines	National and local coverage Reader can look back Ads can be linked to articles and features Vouchers can be used Scope for targeting with specialist magazines Relatively cheap	No movement or sound Individual ads may be lost in a 'sea of ads'
Cinema	Big impact with a big screen Can be used for local and national advertising Specific age groups can be targeted Sound and movement can be used	Limited audience Message may only be seen once Message is short lived
Radio	Sound can be used Minority audiences allow targeting Cheap production Can target youngsters	Not visual May be ignored May lack impact Can be annoying or disrupting to listen to
Posters and billboards	Can produce national campaigns Seen repeatedly Good for short sharp messages Large posters can have big impact	Posters can be deliberatively damaged by vandals Only limited information can be shown Difficult to evaluate effectiveness
Internet	Can be updated regularly Can be targeted Hits and response can be measured Can be sent to mobile devices For goods available online, there is no delay between seeing ads and shopping for the product online	Some ads such as pop-up ads are irritating Possible technical problems

▲ Table 1 The advantages and disadvantages of selected advertising media

ACTIVITY 1   SKILLS   ANALYSIS, CRITICAL THINKING, ETHICS, PERSONAL AND SOCIAL RESPONSIBILITY

CASE STUDY: WORLD WIDE FUND FOR NATURE

The World Wide Fund for Nature (WWF) is the largest independent conservation organisation in the world. Its mission is to create a world where people and wildlife can exist together. One of the ways in which the organisation tries to influence people's behaviour towards wildlife is to use poster campaigns. The poster shown was used by the WWF to raise awareness about global warming and the impact it might have on the planet.

1. Define above-the-line promotion.
2. Explain **one** advantage of using posters as an advertising media.
3. Assess to what extent the advert in this poster is meant to be persuasive.

BELOW-THE-LINE PROMOTION

Below-the-line promotion refers to any form of promotion that does not involve advertising. It can take many forms.

Sales promotions: Incentives used to encourage people to buy products are called **sales promotions**. They are used to boost sales in the hope that if new customers are attracted they will continue to buy the product. They might be used to break into a new market. They may also be used to reward loyal customers and allow businesses to measure the impact of promotion, by counting the number of returned coupons, for example.

- **Free gifts.** Businesses might give free gifts to customers when they buy the product; for example, computer companies often give away free software.
- **Coupons.** Money-off vouchers can be used by businesses to attract customers. They may be attached to products, appear in newspaper adverts, or delivered to homes.
- **Loyalty cards.** Some businesses reward customers according to how much they spend. Points are collected and then exchanged for cash, vouchers or free goods. Loyalty cards are popular with supermarkets, credit card companies and stores.
- **Competitions.** People may be allowed free entry into a competition when they buy a particular product. An attractive prize is offered to the winners.
- **BOGOF offers.** BOGOF stands for 'buy one, get one free'. These offers are popular with many businesses, such as supermarkets, transport services and restaurants.
- **Money-off deals.** Businesses may offer customers discounts such as '30 per cent off' or 'an extra 20 per cent free'. These are similar to BOGOF deals and are used by a range of suppliers.

Public relations: Some businesses communicate with stakeholders using **public relations** (PR). The main purpose of PR is to increase sales by improving the image of the business. A number of approaches might be used by businesses to attract publicity.

- **Press releases.** Some information about the business may be presented to the media. This might be used to write an article or feature in a television programme. For example, a business might announce that it is to create 2000 new jobs. Such positive news would be of interest to the media and they might want full details.
- **Press conferences.** This is where representatives meet with the media and present information in person. This allows for questioning and other feedback. The press might be invited to a product launch, for example.
- **Sponsorship.** Sponsorship is when businesses attract publicity by linking their brands with events, particularly

CASE STUDY: SPORTS SPONSORSHIP

Sport has attracted funding from sponsors for many years. High-profile sporting events, such as the FIFA World Cup, the Wimbledon Tennis Championships, the Olympic Games, the Open Golf Championship and many others, raise considerable sums from a wide variety of different sponsors. In 2017, global sponsorship spending is expected to be US\$62,800 million. This is 4.5 per cent higher than in 2016 when it was US\$60,100 million. The majority of this was spent on sport.

Rolex, the luxury watchmaker, spends a lot of money on promoting its products. In 2014, it was reported to have spent US\$56.37 million on advertising. It is also reported to be the most active sports sponsor. Sponsors like Rolex benefit from having their name and logo 'splashed' everywhere at an event. For example, Rolex were one of the official partners of the US Open Golf Championship, which was broadcast around the world – this represents a massive potential audience.

1. Define sponsorship.
2. Explain the advantages of sponsorship to a company like Rolex.

sporting events, television programmes and films. For example, Amazon, Vodafone, Ceat, Vivo and Yamaha® Motorcycles were some of the companies making financial contributions to the Indian Premier League in return for publicity at events in 2017. They were the sponsors. The sponsoring of television programmes is also popular. For example, in China, for several seasons Unilever has sponsored Televisa's localised version of the series *Ugly Betty*. The main advantage of sports sponsorship is that brand names are shown globally on the television without having to pay the owners of television companies.

- **Donations.** Donations to charities and the local community might be used by businesses to improve their image. A large donation from a business is likely to be reported in the media, which is good publicity.

The main advantage of PR to businesses is that it is often a cheap method of promotion. Some businesses have been known to deliberately seek bad publicity by being controversial. This can raise the profile of a business very quickly, sometimes at no cost.

Merchandising and packaging: Some businesses may arrange the point of sale so that it is interesting and eye-catching, and likely to encourage sales. This is called merchandising. Some examples are outlined below.

- **Product layout.** The layout of products in a store is often planned very carefully to encourage shoppers to follow particular routes and look at certain products. Products that stores want you to buy are placed at prominent locations, such as at the end of shelves and at eye level.
- **Display material.** Posters, leaflets and other materials may be used to display certain products with the aim of persuading customers to buy. Lighting and other special effects can improve the shopping environment. Window displays are considered important by retailers as they can draw in customers.
- **Stock.** Businesses must keep shelves well stocked because empty shelves create a bad impression. Also, if items are out of stock customers may shop elsewhere.

Direct mailing: This is where businesses mail out leaflets or letters to households. Sometimes personal letters are used. They may contain information about new products or details of price changes, for example. Increasingly, email and text messages (often called spam) are being used to contact consumers rather than the postal system. The development of sophisticated computer systems and use of customer databases has resulted in more personalised marketing.

Direct selling or personal selling: This might involve a 'sales rep' calling at households or businesses hoping to sell products. It could also be a telephone call from a call centre where sales staff are employed to sell over the telephone. One advantage of this approach is that the features of the product can be discussed. However, people are often irritated by this approach because the callers have not been invited.

Exhibitions and trade fairs: Some businesses attend trade fairs or exhibitions to promote their products. Businesses set up a stand and promote their products face to face. Trade fairs can be attended by commercial buyers or consumers, or both. The China Sports Show, the largest

and most influential sporting goods exhibition in the Asia-Pacific region, is held every year in Shanghai. In Dubai, the World Travel Catering & Onboard Services Expo is a trade fair for services for airports and the airline catering industry. It is aimed at manufacturers from home and abroad. There are certain advantages of this method of promotion.

- Products can be tested out on consumers before a full launch.
- Some exhibitions are overseas and can be used to break into foreign markets.
- Products can be physically demonstrated and questions answered.
- Exhibitions often attract the media.
- Customers can speak to business owners or senior personnel face to face.

CHOOSING METHODS OF PROMOTION

Many businesses use a range of different promotional methods. However, these must be co-ordinated so that they support each other. Small businesses often have limited budgets so careful consideration is needed when choosing a method of promotion.

What affects the choice of promotion?

- **Cost.** Not all businesses can afford to advertise on television and in national newspapers so they have to find other more cost effective, and often more appropriate, means.
- **Market type.** Local businesses often rely on adverts in local newspapers and listings in business phone directories. In contrast, businesses aiming their products at mass markets are more likely to use television and national newspapers, or specialist magazines.
- **Product type.** Certain products are better suited to certain methods of promotion. For example, a car manufacturer is not likely to use sales promotions such as coupons, BOGOF deals or loyalty cards, preferring television and cinema advertising, and billboards. Similarly, supermarkets are unlikely to use personal selling.
- **Stage in the product life cycle.** It is common for promotional methods to change as a product gets older. For example, PR is often used at the launch of a product, but when the product matures other methods will be used.
- **Competitors' promotions.** It is common for businesses to copy successful methods of promotion used by rivals. Once one business comes up with a successful promotion, others soon bring out their own versions.
- **Legal factors.** In many countries laws designed to protect consumers can affect the method and style of promotion. For example, in the EU tobacco products cannot be advertised on television.

TYPES OF BRANDING

The aim of many businesses is to build a powerful brand. Branding involves giving a product a name, sign, symbol or logo, design or any feature that allows consumers to instantly recognise the product and differentiate it from those of competitors.

Brands can come in a number of forms.

- **Manufacturer brands.** Manufacturer brands are brands created by the producers of goods and services. The goods or services bear the producer's name. Examples might be Kellogg's Corn Flakes, Gillette® razors or Dell™ computers. The manufacturers are involved in the production, distribution, promotion and pricing decisions of these products.
- **Own-label brands.** Own-label brands (also known as distributor or private brands) are products which are manufactured for wholesalers or retailers by other businesses. But the wholesalers and retailers sell the products under their own name. One example of a product containing the retailer's name is French supermarket chain, Carrefour's Cola Classic or Nilgiris private label pasta (an Indian supermarket brand). Sometimes the retailer will create its own brand name, for example F&F clothes sold at Tesco. These products allow a retailer to buy from the cheapest manufacturer, reducing its cost. It will hope to promote its own products effectively to shoppers in its outlets.
- **Generic brands.** Some generic brands are products that only contain the name of the actual product category rather than the company or product name. Examples are aluminium foil, carrots or aspirin. These products are usually sold at lower prices than branded products. They tend to account for a small percentage of all sales.

THE BENEFITS OF STRONG BRANDING

If a business can establish a strong brand it will enjoy a number of benefits.

Added value: A strong brand may add value to a product in the eyes of customers. For example, if a business can capture a desirable image that is reflected in the brand, it is likely to have a competitive edge. It could be argued that perfume manufacturers are able to do this. They may use powerful television adverts that feature celebrities using the product. Some adverts suggest that if you buy a particular brand you will belong to a group of elegant and sophisticated consumers, similar to those featured in adverts. Such adverts may offer consumers glamour, confidence and style. This approach can add value for some consumers.

Ability to charge premium prices: Products with strong brands can be priced higher than those of competitors. This is because of the customer loyalty that has been built up over a period of time. People are less likely to switch to cheaper brands if they have developed the habit of buying a 'favourite' brand. Kraft Heinz, the food processing company, generally charges higher prices for its canned and bottled products because they are perceived to be 'superior' to those of rival brands.

Reduced price elasticity of demand: The strength of a brand may be reflected in the price elasticity of demand for a product (price elasticity of demand is explained in Chapter 7).

Firms would prefer their brands to be inelastic in demand. This means that a price increase will have less impact on demand. For example, if a product has price elasticity of demand of −1.5, a 10 per cent increase in price will result in a 15 per cent fall in demand. However, if demand is inelastic at say, −0.9, a 10 per cent increase in price will reduce demand by just 9 per cent. Consequently, with a strong brand and a more inelastic demand curve, price increases are more viable.

WAYS TO BUILD A BRAND

Different companies may use different methods in an effort to build a brand.

Exploiting a unique selling point: One of the best ways to build a brand is to develop a unique selling point (USP) for a product. If a product has a USP it is much easier to differentiate the brand and make it 'stand out from the pack'. Some companies develop USPs by incorporating special features in their designs. Another approach is to make promises to customers. For example, some companies offer to give customers their money back if they are not satisfied. Producers of luxury goods, such as Prada or Gucci, use the fact that they are only affordable to a few, select customers as their USP.

Advertising: Advertising may be used in different ways. A business might use advertising to introduce a new brand. If the brand becomes popular and established, advertising is likely to continue in order to remind consumers that 'it is still out there'. Advertising spreads the word about a brand, and the more people who are familiar with the brand the greater the firm's market power. Advertising also reassures customers. An important element of advertising is pride. Advertising may be a source of pride for customers who have chosen the brand. The importance of advertising to help build brands is reflected in the amount of money spent by businesses on advertising. In 2013, over US$500,000 million was spent worldwide. Table 2 shows the top ten global advertisers in 2016.

	Company	Ad spend (US$ million)
1	Pampers® (ranked 50th most valuable brand)	8300
2	Gillette (28th)	8300
3	L'Oréal (34th)	8200
4	Chevrolet (59th)	5100
5	Louis Vuitton (19th)	4400
6	Ford (35th)	4300
7	Coca-Cola (4th)	4000
8	Amazon (12th)	3800
9	Sony (76th)	3700
10	AT&T (13th)	3600

▲ Table 2 Top ten global advertisers in 2016
Source: Global Advertising Market – Statistics & Facts. Statista Inc.

Sponsorship: Some companies favour the use of sponsorship to help build their brands. Many argue that sponsorship is a cheaper method of promotion than advertising – although many companies use both. The majority of sponsorship spending is in sport. Companies sponsor both national and international sporting events. For example, Banco Santander currently sponsors the Spanish La Liga. Sponsorship helps to:

- raise brand awareness, create preference and develop brand loyalty
- create positive PR and raise corporate awareness
- build brand positioning by linking the product to attractive images at events
- support other promotional campaigns
- create emotional commitment to the brand
- promote good relations with customers because sponsors often provide corporate hospitality at events.

Using social media: An increasing number of businesses are switching marketing resources into social media. Social media can be used in more than one way. For example, a business can place its adverts in strategic places on sites such as Facebook, Twitter, Instagram and Google+. The use of social media often allows businesses to focus more easily on particular customer groups. Social media also helps businesses to get to know their customers better and enables them to communicate with them more effectively. Social media may help to increase trust in a business or brand. Seeing that a particular business is active on social media helps customers to develop trust. A social media presence may suggest that a business cares about its customers. For example, if anything goes wrong customers will feel more secure if they know that it is easy for them to make contact and raise their issues.

A large and increasing number of businesses use social media to help build their brands. For example, Kentucky Fried Chicken (KFC®) used a social media campaign to attract more young female customers.

It created a widely shared ad featuring the comedian Jenny Bede suggesting reasons for eating unhealthy food.

Building a brand is an ongoing process. Even companies with extremely strong brands, continually invest in advertising and promotional campaigns to support and reinforce their brands.

CHANGES IN BRANDING AND PROMOTION TO REFLECT SOCIAL TRENDS

Businesses are under constant pressure to keep up to date with trends, patterns, fashions and new technology. This pressure extends to the methods they use to promote and brand their products. For example, since the rise of the Internet, most firms have set up their own business websites. These are used to provide information, promote products and in some cases to sell goods directly to customers. Some other very recent developments are outlined below.

Viral marketing: Communication using the Internet has provided the opportunity for **viral marketing**. This involves any strategy that encourages people to pass on messages to others about a product or a business electronically. It creates the potential for rapid growth in the exposure of a message. Like a virus, these strategies exploit the process of rapid multiplication that results from people sending messages to family, friends and colleagues, who then send them on again. Not only can people send text relating to a marketing message, but they also can send images, such as photographs and video clips. One example of a successful viral marketing campaign was produced by Volvo. It featured a video clip of Jean-Claude Van Damme doing the splits between two Volvo trucks as they were being driven along a road. The clip was used to demonstrate the stability and precision of Volvo's steering system. The video had been seen over 76 million times at the time of writing.

Social media: A survey of marketing leaders in 2017 showed they devoted around 10.5 per cent of their marketing budgets to social media – a figure that continues to rise (see Figure 2). Using social media,

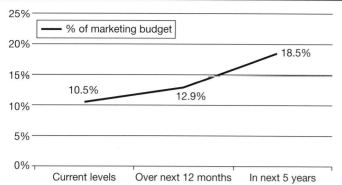

▲ Figure 2 Mean percentage of marketing budget spent on social media
Source: *The CMO Survey – Highlights and Insights Report*, Figure 5.1, February 2017

such as Facebook and Twitter, to help build a brand is important but many businesses go further. An increasing number are developing their own social networks, which are linked to the main platforms. Some analysts suggest that, while Facebook is a good platform to use to find customers and raise brand awareness, most people who 'like' a brand page on Facebook never visit it again. In comparison, some companies create their own social networks. Virgin Atlantic is one example of a business that has developed its own social platform.

Emotional branding: Emotional branding refers to the practice of using the emotions of a consumer to build a brand. It is designed to appeal to a customer's emotion, human need, or a perceived ambition. The aim of emotional marketing is to develop a relationship between a consumer and a brand. Businesses try to develop in their customers the emotional attachment that football supporters have with their chosen clubs. The overwhelming majority of football supporters all over the world could not switch their support to another club even when theirs is performing badly – the bond is just too strong. Emotional branding is also based on the idea that people's actions are driven more by emotion than reason.

One example of a business that has used emotional branding effectively is Apple. Apple has found a way to connect with its customers and create with them a powerful bond. They achieved this by connecting with younger people in particular and creating a 'cool' product image. The Apple brand has associated itself with design innovation; the release of a new Apple product is an event and people will queue for hours. They have created an emotional attachment with their customers, one which is not defined by commerce.

ACTIVITY 3   SKILLS   ANALYSIS, CRITICAL THINKING, CREATIVITY, INNOVATION

CASE STUDY: BLOGGING

One established social trend that has had an impact on marketing in business is blogging. Blogging involves sharing opinions, information, observations and other content online. Bloggers usually write regular articles, perhaps in a diary form, to express their views and provide updates on a very wide range of topics. One popular and large part of blogging is fashion blogging.

In China, fashion bloggers are having an increasing influence on the fashion industry. It is important for businesses in China to know about fashion bloggers because their views can influence what consumers buy. There are a number of high-profile fashion bloggers in the country including Fang Yimin, or 'Li Beika/Becky', as she is known to her fans. Consumers read her blogs for fashion and shopping tips and by mid-2016 she had over 700,000 followers. She writes about clothes and fashion accessories sold by well-known luxury brands and those available from little known high-quality independents. Li's background is in journalism – current affairs and politics. Although she has no real work experience or training in the fashion industry, she has developed the ability to identify trends in the industry, understand what readers like and dislike and what writing styles attract interest. The target audience of Li's WeChat blog is women of upper to middle-income class.

Every day Li advises readers where and how they should spend their money. Li has an excellent reputation for spotting fashion trends and knowing outlets from where products can be purchased. In one of her blogs, Li recommended an Italian handbag fashion brand. It was only known to few and only available in one store which was in south-west China. As a result of her blog, the brand saw very rapid sales growth. So far, Li has worked with brands like Gucci, Chanel, Jo Malone and many others.

1. Explain the potential role played by fashion bloggers in business.
2. Assess the benefits to businesses in the Chinese fashion industry of using social media in this way.

CHECKPOINT

1. State six examples of advertising media.
2. What is meant by below-the-line media?
3. What is direct mailing?
4. State four aims of promotion.
5. Identify four different methods of sales promotion.
6. State three different types of branding.
7. State two benefits of sponsorship.
8. Why can strong brands charge premium prices?
9. How might a business use social media as a promotional aid?
10. Why are businesses spending more money on social media to promote products?
11. What is emotional branding?
12. Why might viral marketing benefit a business?

SUBJECT VOCABULARY

above-the-line promotion placing adverts using the media.

advertising communication between a business and its customers where images are placed in the media to encourage the purchase of products.

below-the-line promotion any promotion that does not involve using the media.

emotional branding the practice of using the emotions of a consumer to build a brand.

generic brands products that only contain the name of the product category rather than the company or product name.

manufacturer brands brands created by the producers of goods or services.

merchandising a promotion specifically at the point of sale of a product.

own-label, distributor or private brands products that are manufactured for wholesalers or retailers by other businesses.

point of sale any point where a consumer buys a product.

promotion an attempt to obtain and retain customers by drawing their attention to a firm or its products.

public relations an organisation's attempt to communicate with interested parties.

sales promotions methods of promoting products in the short term to boost sales.

sponsorship making a financial contribution to an event in return for publicity.

viral marketing any strategy that encourages people to pass on messages to others about a product or a business electronically.

EXAM PRACTICE

PROCTER & GAMBLE (P&G)

SKILLS ANALYSIS, INTERPRETATION, CRITICAL THINKING, ADAPTABILITY

Procter & Gamble (P&G) is a large US multinational. It manufactures and sells cleaning agents, personal care and hygiene products. The corporation has four key divisions:

- Global Beauty
- Global Baby, Feminine and Family Care
- Global Fabric and Home Care
- Global Health and Grooming.

Some of its globally recognised brands include Ambi Pur®, Ariel®, Bounty®, Charmin®, Crest®, Dawn®, Downy®, Fairy®, Febreze®, Gain®, Gillette, Head & Shoulders®, Lenor® and Olay®. These brands are powerful and valuable and their products are purchased by around 5000 million people worldwide. P&G has 23 multimillion-dollar brands worth between US$1000 million to US$10,000 million each. Many of P&G's brands are positioned at the 'top end' of the market. Much of the company's marketing is designed to show quality in the products which allows P&G to charge higher prices than many of its rivals. In 2015, P&G enjoyed sales revenue of US$76,280 million and a profit for the year of over US$7000 million.

P&G invests heavily in advertising. In 2013, P&G spent more on advertising than any other company in the world. In 2016, it also benefited from one of its adverts 'going viral'. At the beginning of the year P&G invested in a new television advert to promote Ariel, one of its cleaning products, in India. The 2-minute advert, referred to as 'sharetheload', features the challenges faced by a young Indian women attempting to balance the demands of raising a family with developing a career. The advert critically explores India's traditional male-dominated society. In the clip the visiting father is seen apologising to his adult daughter (by composing a letter in his head) for failing to help with the chores. The father also apologises for her husband's seemingly naïve role reinforcing the idea that a woman's place is in the home – where her work is never done.

When the father returns home to his wife the film shows him emptying his suitcase, and much to his wife's shock, placing his dirty laundry into the washing machine. The advert ends with the lines: 'Why is laundry only a mother's job?' and 'Dads #ShareTheLoad'.

The 'sharetheload' advert went viral in India as soon as it was first broadcast. It was produced by BBDO Mumbai and won a Glass Lion, which is a special prize for adverts that address issues of gender inequality, at the Cannes Film Festival.

▲ Dads helping sharing the load

Q

(a) Define viral marketing. **(2 marks)**

(b) Explain **one** way in which P&G might have benefited from its Ariel advert that 'went viral'. **(4 marks)**

(c) Explain how P&G differentiates many of its brands. **(4 marks)**

(d) Assess the benefits to P&G of having very strong brands. **(10 marks)**

12 PRICING STRATEGIES

LEARNING OBJECTIVES

By the end of this chapter you should be able to understand:

- types of pricing strategy: cost plus (mark-up on unit cost), price skimming, penetration, predatory, competitive and psychological
- factors that determine the most appropriate pricing strategy for a particular situation: number of USPs/amount of differentiation, price elasticity of demand, level of competition in the business environment, strength of brand, stage in the product life cycle, costs and the need to make a profit
- changes in pricing to reflect social trends: online sales and price comparison sites.

GETTING STARTED

Lower Sackville Farm

Mark and Rosemary Valentine run Lower Sackville Farm in Nova Scotia, Canada. The dairy farm produces milk that is sold for CAD 10.58 per litre. Mark and Rosemary are 'price takers', which means they have no control over the price they get for their milk. In 2016, Lower Sackville Farm made a modest profit. Their total costs were CAD 1,220,000 and total revenue was CAD 1,251,500.

Zong (China Mobile Pakistan)

Chinese-owned Zong is a mobile telecommunications operator based in Islamabad, Pakistan. The company began trading in Pakistan in 2008 and is currently the second largest operator in the country. When it entered the market it offered many services at relatively low prices. However, at a later date prices were increased. For example, in 2017, the prices of some MBB packages were increased significantly. These are shown in the Table 1.

Package	Old price (PKR)	New price (PKR)
50 GB	2000	2500
10 GB	3800	4000
150 GB	5000	8000
200 GB	6000	10,000

▲ Table 1 MMB package prices, 2017

What would happen if Mark and Rosemary tried to increase the price of their milk to CAD 13.00 per litre? Calculate the percentage increase in the price of Zong's 150 GB package. Comment on the size of the increase. Why do you think Zong charged a low price originally? How might price elasticity of demand influence the price set by a business?

PRICING STRATEGIES

A strategy is a set of plans designed to meet objectives. **Pricing strategy** is part of the marketing strategy of the business. Other strategies, such as product and distribution strategy, also make up a marketing strategy. Marketing strategy is then part of the corporate strategy of the business. Other strategies include production and financial strategy.

Pricing strategy is therefore a set of plans about pricing, which help a business to achieve its marketing and corporate objectives. For example, a corporate objective might be to double in size over the next 5 years. A marketing objective to achieve this might be to take the products of the business 'upmarket'. The pricing strategy developed from this could be to increase the average price of the products made by the business.

- Some pricing strategies can be used for new products, such as market skimming or penetration pricing (these strategies will be discussed on the next page).
- Some strategies may be more suitable for existing products.

COST PLUS PRICING

Businesses have to set prices that generate a profit. One method that ensures that all costs are covered is **cost plus pricing**. It involves adding a **mark-up** to **unit costs**. The mark-up is usually a percentage of the unit cost. This method is common with retailers. However, one of the drawbacks of this method is that it ignores market conditions. For example, the mark-up used by a business may be far too high in relation to the prices of rival products. This might result in low sales. Another problem is that it may be difficult to identify precisely all the costs associated with the production of a particular product – particularly for multi-product businesses.

WORKED EXAMPLE

The unit cost to a manufacturer of making a plastic rowing boat is £80. The manufacturer adds a mark-up of 25 per cent to get the price. Therefore the price of the boat is:

Price = unit cost + (mark-up × unit cost)

£80 + (25% × £80) = £80 + £20 = **£100**

ACTIVITY 1

CASE STUDY: BANGLADESHI STREET FOOD

Raihan Mahmud sells street food from a stall that is located close to the busy railway station in Sylhet, Bangladesh. He offers customers a variety of snacks but his three best sellers are singara, fish somosa and poori bhaji. He buys most of his produce from a local supplier every day and the costs of his three best sellers are:

- singara – BDT 10
- fish samosa – BDT 12
- poori bhaji – BDT 8.

Raihan uses cost plus pricing to set the price of his snacks. He adds a 50 per cent mark-up. Raihan is happy with this profit margin and hopes one day to open a shop where he can make his own snacks to sell.

One busy day in May 2017, Raihan sold 80 singara, 100 fish samosa and 70 poori bhaji.

1. (a) Calculate the prices charged by Raihan for his three best sellers.
   (b) Calculate the total profit (before overheads) made by Raihan from these sales.
2. Explain **one** possible disadvantage to businesses of using cost plus pricing.

MATHS TIP

It may be necessary to calculate the percentage mark-up. This is the difference between unit cost and price, expressed as a percentage of the unit cost. For example, if unit cost is £40 and price is £70, the percentage mark-up is 75 per cent (£70 – £40 = £30, 30/40 × 100 = 75%).

PRICE SKIMMING

Some businesses may launch a product into a market charging a high price for a limited time period. This is called **skimming or creaming**. The aim of this strategy is to generate high levels of revenue with a new product before competitors arrive, and exploit the popularity of a new product while it is unique.

This method is common with technical products. For example, when laptop computers were first introduced they were over £1000. However, they can now be purchased for less than £200 in many countries. Pharmaceutical companies also use this method. They sell new drugs for high prices when they are first launched. However, when a patent (a licence that prevents competition for a number of years) runs out, competition emerges and prices fall. Charging a high price initially helps such companies recover high development costs.

An advantage of skimming is that high prices are charged in a market where there are people who are prepared to pay them. This helps to maximise revenue. As the price is lowered, other customer groups are drawn into the market. The higher, initial revenues help a business to recover the cost of research and development. The higher price also helps to make a product appear more prestigious. However, skimming can only be used if demand is price inelastic. Skimming might also attract competitors into the market.

PENETRATION PRICING

Sometimes a business will introduce a new product and charge a low price for a limited period. This is called **penetration pricing**. The aim of this strategy is to develop a secure initial position in the market from which further progress can be made. Businesses using this strategy hope that customers are attracted by the low price, and then carry on buying it when the price rises. One approach is to offer products at a very cheap rate for a trial period – sometimes as low as half price or even free. Another is to offer the first one or few items free, or at a low price, such as driving lessons. Such a strategy is sometimes called an introductory offer. Penetration pricing has a number of benefits.

- It is particularly beneficial when products are targeted at middle- or low-income consumer groups. This is because such groups are more likely to be responsive to low-price introductory offers.
- It can grow sales of new product lines very quickly. Usually, the lower the introductory offer the faster the growth in sales.
- Fast growth in sales may allow a business to lower production costs by exploiting economies of scale.
- This strategy can put pressure on rivals. They may have to lower their prices or make an effort to differentiate their products. Either way financial pressure is applied.

Businesses using this strategy are better placed if they have lower costs. They must also resist the temptation of extending such offers for too long. If consumers become accustomed to low prices they may be lost when the introductory offer expires as they are not prepared to pay the higher price.

Penetration pricing is used by a variety of industries. For example, sports clubs to attract members, and satellite broadcasters to attract subscribers and driving schools (businesses that teach people how to drive a motor car) to attract learners.

ACTIVITY 2 — SKILLS ANALYSIS, REASONING

CASE STUDY: PLAYSTATION 3

Sony launched PlayStation 3 at a price of US$599 (60 GB Model) in 2006 but eventually dropped the price to US$299 in 2009. This pricing strategy is common with technological goods, such as gaming machines. When Sony launched PlayStation 4 it was priced at US$399 and near the end of the first year it had sold around 14 million units worldwide. Many gaming enthusiasts were waiting for the price to fall before buying their own. However, it was reported in November 2014 that a price cut was not planned for the short term.

1. Explain the pricing strategy used by Sony in this case.
2. Assess the advantages and disadvantages of the pricing strategy used by businesses like Sony.

PREDATORY PRICING

Predatory pricing or destroyer pricing aims to eliminate competitors from the market. It involves charging a very low price for a period of time until one or more rivals leave the market. In many countries some forms of predatory pricing are illegal. This is when a business is selling a product below the cost of production with the deliberate aim of forcing a competitor out of the market. This practice is illegal because in the long term it can lead to a lack of competition in a market. As a result, if all firms have left the market except for the predator, the price is likely to be raised beyond the initial level.

Such low-price strategies are allowed if low-cost businesses are prepared to endure low profit margins for extended periods of time. They can also be used to sell stocks that would otherwise remain unsold or as a means of breaking into a new market.

In 2016, Ola, India's largest ride-hailing app, accused Uber, a fierce competitor, of predatory pricing. The founder of Ola suggested that the Indian government could do the same as the Chinese government and impose regulations preventing such operators from setting prices below cost.

COMPETITIVE PRICING

Some businesses take a very close look at what their rivals are charging when setting their prices. This approach is called competitive pricing and is likely to be used by businesses operating in a fiercely competitive market. One approach is to charge the same price as competitors. The advantage of this strategy is that a price war is likely to be avoided. It is considered to be a safe pricing strategy. Another approach is for the market leader to set the price and all others follow. This is called price leadership. Price leaders are usually the dominant firms in the market. They may have developed their dominance through being a low-cost operator or perhaps by building a strong brand over a period of time.

PSYCHOLOGICAL PRICING

One common pricing strategy is to set the price slightly below a round figure – charging US$99.99 instead of US$100. This is called psychological pricing. Consumers are 'tricked' into thinking that US$99.99 is significantly cheaper than US$100. Of course it is not but this psychological effect often works for businesses. This approach targets consumers who are looking for bargains. It is not likely to be used by businesses selling 'upmarket' products.

ACTIVITY 3 — SKILLS INTEPRETATION, REASONING

CASE STUDY: PETROL PRICING

1. Explain the pricing strategy used by the petrol station in the image.
2. Explain one reason why such a pricing strategy might be so popular with businesses such as petrol stations.

You should avoid confusing penetration pricing with predatory pricing. Both of these pricing strategies involve charging a low price. However, penetration pricing involves charging a low price for a short time in order to break into a new market. Predatory pricing involves trying to eliminate rivals in the market. Penetration pricing is legal, but predatory pricing may be illegal. This is likely to be the case if a business is selling a product below cost price for a period of time with the deliberate aim of driving out a rival.

FACTORS THAT DETERMINE THE MOST APPROPRIATE PRICING STRATEGY FOR A PARTICULAR SITUATION

Setting the right price is an important marketing decision for businesses. A number of factors have to be taken into account before the price is set.

Differentiation and USP: A business can generally charge a higher price if its product has a USP or is sufficiently differentiated from those of its rivals. This is because many consumers are prepared to pay more for products with some individuality or additional features. For example, restaurants can differentiate their service if they offer innovative dishes, in a uniquely interesting and comfortable environment with warm and friendly customer service. As a result they may be able to charge higher prices.

Price elasticity of demand: If the demand for a firm's products is price inelastic, there will be scope for price increases. For example, if price elasticity was −0.8, a business could raise its price by 10 per cent and demand would only fall by 8 per cent. As a result, total revenue would rise. Some utility companies, such as those supplying gas, electricity and water, have been able to raise prices quite significantly in recent years without any serious negative impact on demand. This is because demand for these services is price inelastic. In contrast, if a firm's product is price elastic, it may benefit from price cuts. For example, if price elasticity was −2.7, a 10 per cent reduction in price would result in a 27 per cent increase in demand. This would increase total revenue. Many low-cost supermarkets around the world have benefited from this strategy. See Chapter 7 for detailed information about price elasticity of demand.

Amount of competition: The amount of competition in a market will have a big influence on pricing. If there is very little competition in the market, a business can charge much higher prices because consumers cannot switch to a rival. For example, a grocery shop in an isolated village in the Scottish Highlands, UK, may be able to charge much higher prices because there is no other shop nearby. In contrast, in highly competitive markets, firms are not generally able to charge higher prices. In some cases, firms might be price takers. This means they have to charge the market price. This is often the case for farmers who sell their produce in national or international commodity markets.

In competitive markets, businesses are likely to use competition-based pricing strategies. Many will prefer to charge the 'going rate' price, i.e. the same or very similar price to those of competitors. This will help to avoid price wars. If a firm has some power in a competitive market it may become the price leader. In this situation all other firms are likely to be content just copying or following the leader.

Strength of the brand: A business with a strong brand can generally charge a higher price than those with weaker brands. One of the reasons why companies like Coca-Cola and Unilever spend so much money on supporting their brands, with advertising for example, is so they are able to charge higher prices. Companies with strong brands are in a better position to use price skimming when introducing new products. They might also consider predatory pricing to discourage other companies from entering into the market.

Stage in the product life cycle: Products pass through a number of stages over their lifetime. Life for a product begins with its development and, for many products, ends when they are withdrawn from the market. The level of sales that can be expected in each stage over this time period is called the product life cycle. This is discussed in detail in Chapter 9.

As a product passes through the different stages of this cycle, a business may adjust the price charged. For example, when a product is first launched a business might use penetration pricing to try and get established in the market. Later, when sales start to grow, the price can be increased. As the product matures, prices might be reduced a little in order to remain competitive. Alternatively, a business may use price skimming when the product is launched. This approach might be used if the product is new and has few, if any, rivals. Later, when rivals copy the product or bring out versions of their own, prices are likely to gradually decrease.

Costs and the need to make a profit: In the long term, price must cover all the costs of production and generate a profit. This might explain why many businesses use cost plus pricing. Once the unit cost of a product has been calculated, a business knows that if it adds mark-up a profit will be made. However, customers do not care about costs, they care about value for money. It is possible to under-price a product and not maximise potential revenue using this approach. Businesses need to consider the value of their products in addition to costs if they are to extract the most from consumers.

CHANGES IN PRICING TO REFLECT SOCIAL TRENDS

It is possible for social trends to have an impact on pricing strategies. For example, it could be argued that today's consumers are more aware and better informed than ever before. As a result they may challenge the prices charged by businesses. They may negotiate prices or spend more time searching for bargains. They may also be less tied to particular brands and consider instead the views and experiences of friends and colleagues posted on social media sites.

Online sales: Businesses are having to adapt to selling goods online. Many businesses use traditional pricing strategies, such as cost plus pricing. However, for others, selling goods online has provided opportunities for new pricing strategies.

Dynamic pricing: Often used in the travel industry. For example, in the airline industry prices are flexible and different passengers can pay different fares depending on the day of the week, time of day and number of days before the flight. For airlines, there are dynamic pricing factors in different components, such as how many seats a flight has, departure time and average cancellations on similar flights. Dynamic pricing is also used in the hotel industry, entertainment and retail. The aim of dynamic pricing is to maximise revenue and profits by filling capacity such as stadiums, flights or other products with limited sales quantities.

Auction sites: Avabid, eBay® and Serukuru, for instance, sell goods to the customer who offers the highest price. This allows sellers to get the best possible price for goods. However, the seller has to pay a fee for the use of the site. One other advantage of this method of pricing is that online auction platforms create a sense that it is important to act quickly. Consumers fear missing a bargain if they wait too long. This helps to encourage more sales.

Personalised pricing: Involves the use of data relating to a specific online shopper, such as purchase history, browsing history, demographic data, hardware and operating system used, to set a unique price for that shopper. This data could come from a retailer's own database, be enhanced by a third party or be offered up by the user's own computer, tablet or mobile phone. The advantage of this method to businesses is that they can charge higher prices to those customers who are prepared to pay more. It has been reported that Amazon has tried this method of pricing.

Subscription pricing: Usually involves charging customers a regular monthly fee for the use of a service or access to a specific product range. This is not a new concept, but it lends itself well to online shopping. Online magazines and newspapers; software providers, such as Adobe® Systems; music streaming services such as Spotify®; gaming sites, such as PlayStation Plus; fashion retailers, such as ASOS Premier; and television and film providers, such as Netflix®, are examples of businesses that use subscription pricing. The main advantage is that customers are tied into long-term agreements with businesses. Although customers have the right to cancel subscriptions, many do not. This is an attractive proposition. It helps to improve cash flow and removes some of the uncertainty about future sales levels.

Price comparison sites: Many online shoppers make use of comparison websites. The sites simply compare the prices of goods and services from a range of suppliers. Some sites are general, but an increasing number are specialists. For example, trivago® provides a comparison of hotel prices, KAYAK the prices of flights, Carrentals the prices of car hire, uSwitch® energy prices and Mobile Checker for mobile phone prices. Comparison sites are useful for consumers because they may be able to identify the cheapest deals available. These sites might also be used by people who prefer not to shop online. They may check out prices online and then go to the store that is offering the best deal.

Consumers should understand that no two price-comparison websites are likely to give exactly the same results – even if you provide them with identical information. This is because they may provide prices from different providers, depending on which companies they have access to.

CHECKPOINT

1. In competitive markets some firms are price takers. What does this mean?

2. What is the main disadvantage of cost plus pricing?

3. If a product costs £500 and sells for £600, what is the percentage mark-up?

4. When is a business likely to use penetration pricing?

5. What is likely to happen to price as a product nears the end of its life in the product life cycle?

6. State two advantages of skimming.

7. How can firms avoid a price war in a highly competitive market?

8. What is the aim of predatory pricing?

9. How might price comparison sites benefit consumers?

10. What is meant by dynamic pricing?

SUBJECT VOCABULARY

competitive pricing pricing strategies based on the prices charged by rivals.

cost plus pricing adding a percentage (the mark-up) to the costs of producing a product to get the price.

mark-up the percentage added to unit cost that makes a profit for a business when setting the price.

penetration pricing setting a low price when launching a new product in order to get established in the market.

predatory or destroyer pricing setting a low price forcing rivals out of business.

pricing strategy the pricing policies or methods used by a business when deciding what to charge for its products.

psychological pricing setting the price slightly below a round figure.

skimming or creaming setting a high price initially and then lowering it later.

unit costs the same as average cost (total cost divided by output).

EXAM PRACTICE

ADOBE®

SKILLS ANALYSIS, INTERPRETATION, CRITICAL THINKING, ADAPTABILITY

Adobe Systems is a multinational software provider based in California, USA, and is probably best known for creating Photoshop®, Acrobat®, InDesign® and Dreamweaver®. In 2013, Adobe announced that subscription pricing would be introduced. Before the new pricing system, customers paid a single fee for Adobe's Creative Suite® (many of its applications integrated to one product) and had permanent access. However, from June 2013, a monthly fee was required to continue to access programs individually or as a suite of programs through Adobe's Creative Cloud®. Although individual Creative Suite products were still available, there were no further upgrades outside Creative Cloud.

The announcements from Adobe stated that improvements to Creative Cloud from June 2013 would be released on a regular basis as features rolled out. The subscription system would no longer be limited by a traditional upgrade cycle that meant that customers waited for new features. Development of Creative Suite was frozen at version 6, with no improvements or new features, though bug fixes were available. Before June 2013, it cost over £1500 for the version of Creative Suite 6, with 16 programs such as Dreamweaver, Photoshop, Illustrator®, Adobe Premiere® and Adobe Audition®.

Customers were only able to access updates and changes to Creative Suite applications by subscription to Adobe's Creative Cloud, a web-based system that gave access to all of Adobe's software. It also provided an online storage system and project management tools. The cost for UK customers to access all programs in the Creative Cloud was £47 a month, if they agreed this payment for at least a year.

Some Adobe customers preferred the company's traditional sales approach. However, it was widely reported that by the end of 2014 there were over 3 million subscribers to Creative Cloud, and feedback that the satisfaction level was high.

In 2011, Microsoft introduced Office 365, a subscription version of Office applications plus other productivity programs. Adobe's introduction of a subscription pricing strategy in 2013 reflected a growing trend for large software firms to adopt a subscription pricing strategy. Feedback on customer satisfaction indicated that more customers were comfortable, as part of this trend, in paying for an online service.

(a) Define subscription pricing. **(2 marks)**

(b) Explain one reason why Adobe switched to subscription pricing. **(4 marks)**

(c) Discuss the success of Adobe's subscription pricing strategy. **(8 marks)**

(d) Evaluate whether subscription pricing or cost plus pricing would be the most suitable pricing strategy for Adobe. **(20 marks)**

13 DISTRIBUTION

LEARNING OBJECTIVES

By the end of this chapter you should be able to understand:
- distribution channels: four stage, three stage and two stage
- changes in distribution methods.

GETTING STARTED

Cadbury
Cadbury is a well-known confectionery (sweets and chocolates) manufacturer. It is owned by Mondelēz International (a large Chinese multinational) and is famous for its brands, including the Cadbury's Creme Egg®, Cadbury's Roses®, Cadbury's Flake® and Cadbury's Dairy Milk®. Cadbury sells its products in as many outlets as possible, for instance convenience stores, sweet shops, supermarkets, petrol stations, cinemas, sports venues and vending machines.

Ghanaian farmers
In Ghana a lot of fresh produce such as fruit and vegetables are grown on small, independent farms. Many farmers sell their produce directly to consumers in local markets. However, producers of organic goods in Ghana have struggled to find suitable outlets for their crops. They were often restricted to setting up stalls in international school markets where they were permitted to sell their goods to parents and staff. However, this was only until recently when a specialist market was set up. The Accra Green Market was established to allow small growers, using sustainable agriculture practices, to sell their organic produce to the wider local community. This was Ghana's first ever market for locally grown, sustainable organic produce. In what ways are these businesses selling products to customers? Do you think Cadbury sells to online shoppers via a website? Explain a reason for your answer. What might be the advantages to producers of organic goods in Ghana of selling in a specialist market?

▲ Farmers selling produce in a market in Accra, Ghana

DISTRIBUTION

One important marketing activity is the **distribution** of products, which refers to the location where consumers can buy products from. If businesses cannot get products in the right place at the right time they are not likely to be successful. If products are not available in convenient locations consumers may not have the time to search for them. For example, if motorway service stations were located 2 or 3 miles (3 or 5 km) from the motorway, they might struggle to survive. Food producers would have limited sales if they did not make groceries available in supermarkets.

DISTRIBUTION CHANNELS

The route taken by a product from the producer to the customer is called a **distribution channel**. Businesses can choose from a number of different distribution channels. Some of the main channels used for consumer goods are shown in Figure 1.

Some products use a four-stage channel of distribution. This involves the use of wholesalers and retailers when transferring products from producers to

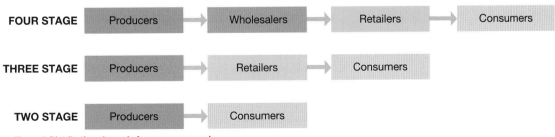

| FOUR STAGE | Producers | → | Wholesalers | → | Retailers | → | Consumers |

| THREE STAGE | Producers | → | Retailers | → | Consumers |

| TWO STAGE | Producers | → | Consumers |

▲ Figure 1 Distribution channels for consumer goods

consumers. Producers of fast-moving consumer goods such as potato crisps and breakfast cereals, for example, might use this method. A simpler method is to use a three-stage channel of distribution. This is where retailers take products from producers and sell them to consumers. Clothes producers and travel companies, for example, might use this approach. Finally, the most straightforward distribution channel involves producers selling their products directly to consumers. This is a two-stage distribution channel and an example would be a producer selling online.

WHOLESALING

The four-stage channel of distribution involves the use of **wholesalers**. Wholesalers usually buy from manufacturers and sell to retailers. Wholesalers may break bulk, repack goods, redistribute smaller quantities, store goods and provide delivery services. A wholesaler stocks goods produced by many manufacturers. Therefore retailers get to select from a wide range of products.

RETAILING

Both the four-stage and three-stage distribution channels use **retailers**. These are businesses that buy goods and sell them straight to consumers. They provide a number of services.

- They buy large quantities from manufacturers and wholesalers, and sell small quantities to customers. This is called **breaking-bulk**.
- They sell in locations that are convenient to consumers. Most supermarkets, for example, are conveniently located and have ample parking space.
- They may add value to products by providing other services. These might include help with packing or delivery, repair services, information about products, warranties and wrapping products as gifts. Table 1 summarises the main forms of retail outlet used around the world.

Consumer behaviour varies in different countries. As a result, the demand for the different types of retail outlet will vary. For example, in rural India and many African countries, a lot of retailing is undertaken by small traders in markets and other similar locations. In many well developed countries such as the USA, Australia, Germany and Canada, large stores, supermarkets and chainstores are popular. In Italy, where the retail sector is highly fragmented, consumers prefer to shop at smaller convenience stores. Also, in Italy there are regional differences. Table 2 shows the number of hypermarkets, supermarkets and independents in the three main regions of the country. For example, in the south of Italy, where the population is less dense, there are considerably fewer hypermarkets.

Retailer	Description
Independents	Mainly small shops, though some can be quite large, such as convenience stores, grocers and specialists (e.g. jewellers).
Supermarkets	Large chain stores selling up to 20,000 lines, including food and non-food products, e.g. Mercardo in Spain and Carrefour in France.
Department stores	Large stores divided into separate departments, such as mens clothes, electricals and cosmetics.
Multiples	Chains of stores selling common goods, e.g. Croma and Big Bazaar in India and Casa Ideas and Mall Sport in Chile.
Online retailers	Wide-ranging, from giants such as Amazon and Alibaba selling many goods, to small independents.
Superstores	Sometimes called hypermarkets – very large stores selling a wide variety of goods, often very cheaply.
Kiosks/street vendors	Small outlets, usually specialists, selling limited ranges in airports, stations, malls, etc.
Market traders	Usually small businesses selling from market stalls in streets, squares and market halls – can be temporary or permanent.

▲ Table 1 Common types of retail outlet around the world

	North	Central	South
Hypermarkets	519	158	148
Supermarkets	3631	1960	2701
Smaller stores	8022	4842	7384

▲ Table 2 Composition of shops, Italy

TWO-STAGE DISTRIBUTION

Some producers market their products directly to consumers. For example, many services are sold directly – banks, solicitors, hairdressers, dentists, plumbers, restaurants and taxis, for instance, do not normally use intermediaries. Some manufacturers may use **direct selling** as well. This can take a number of forms; for example, Avon uses door-to-door agents to sell its cosmetics. Other methods include the following.

- **The Internet.** A rapidly growing number of retailers sell their products online. Some manufacturers also have their own websites. Online distribution is discussed in more detail later in the unit.
- **Direct mail.** This is where suppliers send promotions through the post direct to customers inviting them to buy products. The utilities industry (water, electricity and gas, for example) spent £11.9 million on direct mail in 2010, while almost 25 per cent of all direct mail is sent by financial services companies.

ACTIVITY 1   SKILLS   ANALYSIS, REASONING

CASE STUDY: DRESSMAKING IN FAISALABAD

Mansoor Aslam employs five skilled dressmakers in his small factory in Faisalabad, Pakistan. The business, which makes beautiful handmade dresses, has a limited product line but has been trading for 30 years. The family business is profitable and is currently managed by Mansoor's eldest son, Islam. He is ambitious and wants to pursue growth. Most of the dresses are distributed to independent retailers in and around Faisalabad, with a few of them in Lahore. However, the business has a contract to supply a small chainstore in the north of Pakistan. Islam wants to widen the distribution network. He thinks that contracts with department stores and one or two larger chainstores would be a good short-term target. In the future Islam also thinks that he should look into online selling. However, at the moment the product line is too small to justify the investment needed to set up an online selling operation.

1. What is the difference between a department store and a chainstore?
2. Explain why distribution through multiples might be more profitable for Mansoor Aslam's business than independent retailers.

- **Door-to-door selling.** This is where salespeople visit households directly, inviting people to buy products or services. Energy providers have used this method to try and persuade customers to change their supplier. However, after complaints about the tactics used by some of the door-to-door sellers in the UK, and the growth of comparison websites, the practice has been stopped by most energy providers. It is likely that this method of distribution is in decline.
- **Mail order catalogues.** This is where catalogues are distributed to customers who may buy the products illustrated – sometimes on credit. Traditionally people would fill in an order form and post it back to the company. Examples include nznature and NZBulbs in New Zealand, Ashro in the USA and 3Suisses in France. However, many mail order companies also offer online ordering.
- **Direct response adverts.** Some businesses place adverts in newspapers, magazines or on television inviting people to buy goods and services. For example, local service providers, such as cleaners, gardeners, tutors, builders, child carers and many other traders offer their services in this way.
- **Shopping parties.** Representatives organise parties and invite people to attend for an enjoyable social occasion while having the opportunity to buy products such as jewellery, cosmetics, kitchenware and fashion accessories.
- **Telephone selling.** Although many people do not welcome telephone calls from businesses trying to sell them goods and services, the practice is still widespread. In some countries, suppliers of insurance, home improvements, legal services (to help you make claims from the mis-selling of financial products, for example), energy-saving improvements and energy providers are often associated with this method of distribution. A development in telephone selling (sometimes called telemarketing) is the use of 'robocalls'. This is where an automated telephone call delivers a message. The message usually invites people to press a number on the phone to continue the conversation.

The main advantage of direct selling is that intermediaries are not required, so producers are able to make more profit. Producers can also reach customers who do not like going to shops. The main drawback is that with some methods people cannot physically see the products until they have been purchased. Also, some people object to direct mail, door-to-door salespeople and unwanted telephone calls.

AGENTS OR BROKERS

Some producers using four- or three-stage channels of distribution may use **agents or brokers** in the distribution process to link buyers and sellers. They are used in a variety of markets. For example, travel agents sell holidays and flights for holiday companies, airlines and tour operators. Estate agents sell properties on behalf of vendors. Agents are also used to sell insurance, life insurance and other financial products. Manufacturers may also use agents when exporting. Agents can reduce the risk of selling overseas because they have knowledge of the country and the market.

ACTIVITY 2   SKILLS   ANALYSIS, CRITICAL THINKING

CASE STUDY: AGENTS

The use of agents when selling goods overseas is common. Agents know the foreign market and can introduce a business to overseas customers. They are paid a commission for any sales made, ranging between 2.5 per cent and 15 per cent. When a business exports for the first time it may lack the experience and confidence to 'go it alone'. For example, a European company trying to enter the Chinese market is likely to face a number of obstacles. The use of an agent may reduce the risk of exporting and provide a number of specific advantages.

- The costs of recruiting, training and paying specialist staff for sales overseas are avoided.
- An agent is likely to have a network of contacts that can be exploited immediately. Such contacts would take time to develop when 'going it alone'.
- Agents may be preferred to distributors because the seller then has more control over matters such as prices, display and brand image.
- Agents have the experience and knowledge needed to sell in places where culture, trading practices, commercial laws and other customs are different from those in most European countries.

Despite the advantages of using agents when selling overseas there may be some drawbacks. For example, shipping and other related costs may not be met by an agent. After-sales service may be difficult to provide and the amount of control over marketing and brand image will be less than it would be if selling abroad independently.

Source: adapted from www.nibusinessinfo.co.uk

1. Explain one motive for using an agent when selling overseas.
2. Assess the advantages of using agents when trying to penetrate overseas markets.

CHOOSING THE APPROPRIATE DISTRIBUTION CHANNEL

The channels of distribution chosen by a business will depend on a number of factors. It should also be noted that many businesses use a combination of different

channels. This will help to widen the distribution network and reach a larger number of potential customers.

The nature of the product: Different types of products may require different distribution channels. Some examples are given below.

- Most services are sold directly to consumers. It might not be appropriate for window cleaners, gardeners and hairdressers, for example, to use intermediaries. This is because unlike goods, services cannot be held in stock.
- Fast-moving consumer goods like breakfast cereals, confectionery, crisps and toilet paper cannot be sold directly by manufacturers to consumers. This is because such goods could not be sold effectively by manufacturers in single units. Wholesalers and retailers are used because they break bulk.
- Businesses producing high-quality 'exclusive' products, such as perfume and designer clothes, will choose their outlets very carefully. The image of their products is important, so they are not likely to use supermarkets, for example.
- Products that need explanation or demonstration, such as technical products or complex financial products might need to be sold by expert salespeople or specialists.

Cost: Businesses will normally choose the cheapest distribution channels. They also prefer direct channels. This is because if intermediaries are used they will take a share of the profit. Large supermarkets will try to buy direct from manufacturers as they can bulk buy and get lower prices. Independents are more likely to buy from wholesalers and will have to charge higher prices as a result. Many producers now sell direct to consumers from their websites. This helps to keep costs down.

The market: Producers selling to mass markets are likely to use intermediaries. In contrast, businesses targeting smaller markets are more likely to target customers directly. For example, a building contractor in a small town will deal directly with customers. Producers selling in overseas markets are likely to use agents because they know the market better. Businesses selling goods to other businesses are likely to use more direct channels.

Control: For some producers it is important to have complete control over distribution. For example, producers of exclusive products do not want to see them being sold in less prestigious outlets as this might damage their image. Some products, such as heating systems, require expert installation and need to comply with health and safety legislation. Producers of such products might prefer to handle installation themselves and deal directly with customers. They can then ensure safe installation more easily.

CHANGES IN DISTRIBUTION METHODS

The way in which goods and services are sold is subject to change. Many of these changes reflect technological developments and social trends. Here are some examples:

- a huge growth in online shopping (this is discussed below)
- the building of large US-style shopping malls
- sellers using call centres to sell products, such as financial services
- supermarkets extending their product ranges and opening hours
- shopping becoming more of a leisure activity for many people
- a growth in the use of television shopping channels.

Online distribution: The most important new trend is probably the development of online distribution. It is often called e-commerce because it involves the use of electronic systems to sell goods and services. There are two main types.

- **Business to consumers (B2C).** This is the selling of goods and services by businesses directly to consumers. Most web-based retailing involves ordering goods online and taking delivery at home or work. However, new 'click & collect' services are being developed where people order goods online and then pick them up from a store or a central hub. In London, tube stations are being used as sites for hubs. In Spain, Amazon has teamed up with Spain's national postal service. It uses around 2400 Correos post offices as pick-up points for click & collect customers. Most large retailers now have online services. Other examples of B2C e-commerce include:
  - tickets for air, rail and coach travel
  - tickets for sports fixtures, cinemas and attractions
  - holidays, weekend breaks and hotel rooms
  - access to online music and film broadcasts
  - a wide range of goods on eBay and other auction sites.
- **Business to business (B2B).** This involves businesses selling to other businesses online. Businesses can also use specialist software to purchase resources. The software helps to find the cheapest supplier and carries out all the paperwork. The benefits to consumers and businesses of online distribution are summarised in Tables 3 and 4, respectively.

• It is cheaper because online retailers often have lower costs
• Consumers can shop 24/7
• There is generally a huge amount of choice
• People can shop from anywhere if they have access to the Internet

▲ Table 3 Benefits to consumers of online distribution

• Online retailers may not have to meet the costs of operating stores
• Lower start-up costs – both fixed and variable costs are lower
• Lower costs when processing transactions – many systems are automated
• Less paper is needed for documents, such as invoices and receipts
• Payments can be made and received online using credit cards or PayPal®
• B2C businesses can offer goods to a much wider market – e.g. global
• Businesses can serve their customers 24/7
• Businesses have more choice of where to locate their operations

▲ Table 4 Benefits to businesses of online distribution

Despite the advantages to both consumers and businesses of online distribution, there are some drawbacks for businesses. They face increasing competition, since selling online is a relatively cheap method of distribution. As it can be organised from any location in the world, at any time of the day, businesses will face more competition from overseas. There is also a lack of human contact, which might not suit some customers, and there is heavy dependence on delivery services where online retailers often lack control on the quality of delivery. There may also be technical problems online. For example, websites can crash or be attacked by viruses, and Internet connections can be unreliable. Another drawback is that some people do not have access to the Internet or may not use credit cards. This would result in lost customers. Finally, there is also a security risk as computer hackers might gain access to sensitive information.

Additional drawbacks for consumers include not being able to physically inspect goods before purchase and the risk of a poor after-sales service. In addition, fake businesses may be more difficult to identify online and people may have problems taking delivery of goods, for instance if they are at work all day.

ACTIVITY 3   SKILLS   ANALYSIS, PROBLEM SOLVING

CASE STUDY: POLISH ONLINE RETAIL

In common with most countries around the world the pace of growth in online shopping in Poland has been fast. For example, between 2014 and 2016 the value of the online retail market in Poland is expected to grow from PLN 27.4 billion to PLN 38.1 billion. (The 2016 figure is a forecast).

1. Calculate the percentage change in online retail spending between 2014 and 2016.
2. Explain one reason that might account for the change in online spending in Poland.
3. Assess the advantages to Polish businesses of online distribution.

because they are anxious about learning new production techniques or may fear losing their jobs as work processes are taken over by machines.

- **Flexible working.** Employers prefer to employ a flexible workforce because it helps to manage production more effectively and keeps costs down. However, some of the methods used to develop more flexibility, such as zero-hours contracts, can be unpopular with employees.
- **Work conditions.** Employees may want better conditions or facilities from employers, such as the provision of care facilities for workers' children. However, employers may consider such things inappropriate or too expensive.

The relationship that exists between employers and employees can be shaped using two approaches. They are both often concerned with finding resolutions to the areas of conflict outlined above.

Individual approach: An increasing number of employers develop relationships with employees at an individual level. This means that terms of employment and disagreements are settled through negotiation between an individual employee and a representative of the employer. In a small business the employer representative is likely to be the owner. In a large business it could be a manager – perhaps from the human resources department.

This approach means that individuals will negotiate wages, holiday and other benefits, hours of work and other terms of employment, directly with the employer. If an employee has a work-related dispute, it also has to be raised and discussed with their employer. For example, if an employee feels that more training is required, they would have to make a case and present it individually.

With an individual approach, pay and other conditions may vary between employees. Those individuals with good negotiating skills may get a 'better deal'. This might be a source of conflict in itself. Many would argue that individual bargaining in this way favours the employer. In a large firm the bargaining skills of most individuals would not match those of an experienced and trained human resources manager. Many employees would prefer to be represented by an equally skilled and trained body – perhaps collectively.

Collective bargaining: The alternative to individual bargaining is **collective bargaining**. This involves determining wages, conditions of work and other terms of employment through a negotiation process between employers and employee representatives, such as **trade union** representatives. Trade unions represent the views of their members and try to negotiate in their interests. One individual in a large company employing, say, 10,000 staff, would have little or no influence in determining

wages and conditions. A representative body, such as a trade union, however, would have more strength and influence to negotiate for its membership. Without such a bargaining process, employers and managers would be able to set wages and conditions without taking into account the interests of employees.

For collective bargaining to take place:
- employees must be free to join representative bodies, such as trade unions
- employers must recognise such bodies as the legal representatives of workers and agree to negotiate with them
- such bodies must be independent of employers and the state
- bodies should negotiate honestly in their members' interests
- employers and employees should accept negotiated agreements without having to use the law to enforce them.

Bargaining between employers and employee representatives has often led to conflict in the past. A failure to reach agreement may result in **industrial action**. The worst that can happen is that workers go on strike. In 2017, air traffic controllers in France went on strike. Workers from the UNSA union withdrew their labour in Brest, Bordeaux and Aix-en-Provence airports as part of their 4-day strike. The dispute was over working hours and conditions.

Industrial action like this can damage the employer, employees and customers. When the air traffic controllers went on strike hundreds of flights were cancelled or subject to delay, airlines lost revenue, passengers were inconvenienced and workers lost pay. Table 1 summarises the possible advantages and disadvantages of collective bargaining.

Advantages	Disadvantages
• Agreements are transparent and legally enforceable	• Negotiations can result in more bureaucracy and take longer
• May be more cost effective to have just one set of negotiations	• The views of individuals are not always reflected by unions
• Rules and terms are more likely to be respected by both parties	• Negotiation costs can be high and are usually met by businesses
• Outcomes may be fairer because power between both sides is equalised	• A failure to agree can have serious consequences, e.g. strike action
• Unfair treatment of individual who are bullied or 'favourites' of their managers may be avoided	• Owners may feel their freedom to manage is compromised
• Employee representatives are democratically elected	

▲ Table 1 The possible advantages and disadvantages of collective bargaining

THINKING BIGGER

Trade unions are organisations of workers who join together to further their own interests in the workplace. They tend to represent groups of workers with different skills and needs. It is important for employees to have their voice heard at work – they need representation – because individual workers find it difficult to stand up for themselves. When trying to exercise their rights against a large multinational, for example, they need a more powerful authority to represent them. Trade unions can provide this authority.

If workers join a trade union they will have to pay an annual membership fee. In return they get a number of benefits. Trade unions:

- represent workers by negotiating with employers on their behalf. They employ skilled negotiators to get the best possible deal for workers. They press for higher pay, better working conditions, improved health and safety, and they fight against redundancies

- have a legal network that will represent individual members in cases such as discrimination and unfair dismissal. The cost to workers of legal representation would be huge without their support

- act as a pressure group to influence business decision making in general

- provide other benefits such as access to cheap insurance, discounts on loans for houses and travel, social facilities and support when times are hard

- play a key role in industrial relations at work. For example, they communicate the views of workers when big changes are about to take place, such as the introduction of new technology.

ACTIVITY 3   SKILLS   ANALYSIS, INTERPRETATION, NEGOTIATION

CASE STUDY: SOUTH AFRICAN CABIN CREW STRIKE

In April 2017, cabin crew workers employed by South African Airways (SAA) went on strike for 1 day. As a result SAA was forced to cancel 28 domestic flights, three regional flights and one international flight. Cabin crew workers were demanding that their meal allowances on international flights be increased from US$130 (ZAR 1699) to US$170 (ZAR 2217). The workers claimed that they needed the increase to pay for meals when they get to destinations where the living conditions are not the same as those in South Africa. The strike was well supported with around 80 per cent of South African Cabin Crew Association (SACCA) members joining in.

However, striking workers returned to work the next day after SAA obtained a ruling by the Labour Court, which agreed that the industrial action did not comply with the law. A spokesperson for SAA said after the court hearing, 'We are inviting SACCA back to the negotiating table as soon as possible and would like parties to have open minds when deliberating and considering options. It is in the interests of all parties to find lasting solutions to the issues in dispute. We remain confident that a final solution to this matter will be found in the coming days.'

1. What has led to the breakdown in the employer/employee relationship in this case?
2. Discuss the possible disadvantages to SAA of collective bargaining.

CHECKPOINT

1. State three employee needs.
2. What is the main disadvantage of treating staff like costs?
3. State two advantages of multiskilling to a business.
4. What is the difference between part-time and temporary staff?
5. What are the advantages to a business of using more home workers?
6. Give one motive for outsourcing jobs.
7. What is the difference between dismissal and redundancy?
8. State two advantages of collective bargaining to a business.
9. Why might employees prefer not to negotiate their pay and conditions individually?
10. What are the benefits of a positive relationship between employees and employers?

SUBJECT VOCABULARY

collective bargaining a method of determining conditions of work and terms of employment through negotiations between employers and employee representatives.

flexible workforce a workforce that can respond, in quantity and type, to changes in market demand.

home workers people who undertake their regular work from home.

industrial action disruptive measures taken by workers to apply pressure on employers when disagreements cannot be resolved.

multiskilling the process of increasing the skills of employees.

outsourcing getting other people or businesses to undertake work that was originally done in-house.

trade unions organisations of workers that exist to promote the interests of their members.

zero-hours contract a contract that does not guarantee any particular number of hours' work.

EXAM PRACTICE

SCHLOSS POWER TOOLS

SKILLS ANALYSIS, INTERPRETATION, CRITICAL THINKING

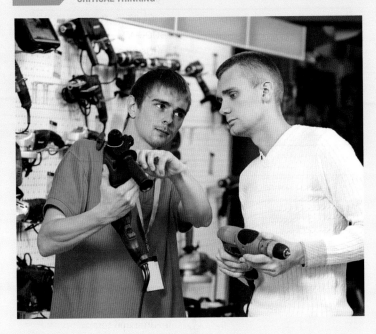

Austrian-based Schloss Power Tools makes a range of power tools for the construction industry and DIY enthusiasts, who enjoy repairing or upgrading their own homes. It has a reputation for high-quality, long-lasting products and good after-sales service. Its products are distributed through large DIY stores, independents and, increasingly, online. In 2009, Schloss Power Tools was hit hard by the recession. Demand for its products fell sharply as the construction industry went into decline and people spent less on DIY. As a result the business had to make 20 of its production and back-room office staff redundant.

After making small losses for 3 years between 2009 and 2012, the directors decided that some changes were needed to make the business more competitive. It was felt that the workforce needed to be more flexible. The proposals included the following.

- Training production staff in all aspects of production so that they could be moved from one task to another easily.
- Introducing flexible working hours in the office so that the business could answer customer calls from 7.00 a.m. to 8.00 p.m.
- Employing more temporary staff to help deal with high levels of demand in the spring and summer months. Temporary staff also give more flexibility if there is another fall in demand.
- Outsourcing the production of some components to a Chinese supplier to save €1.5 million per year. This would result in the loss of 12 more jobs.

The directors expected a negative reaction from the workforce when the proposals were announced. Therefore it was agreed that wages would have to be increased by the CPI (cost of living) plus 1 per cent for the next 3 years.

Q

(a) Define redundancy. **(2 marks)**

(b) Explain one advantage to workers at Schloss Power Tools of multiskilling. **(4 marks)**

(c) Explain one possible drawback to Schloss Power Tools of outsourcing the production of some components. **(4 marks)**

(d) Evaluate whether (i) training production staff or (ii) employing more temporary workers would have the most impact on improving worker flexibility. **(20 marks)**

15 RECRUITMENT, SELECTION AND TRAINING

LEARNING OBJECTIVES

By the end of this chapter you should be able to understand:
- recruitment and selection processes: internal versus external recruitment
- costs of recruitment, selection and training
- types of training: induction, on the job and off the job.

GETTING STARTED

Elena Bonetti has just landed a €50,000 a year job at a major marketing agency in Turin, Italy. Her job title will be Head of Creative Design. She saw the job advertised online and was invited to an interview within 2 weeks. Part of her job when she starts is to recruit three up-and-coming creative designers. She will also be responsible for providing them with on-the-job training.

Why might the marketing agency use the Internet to recruit staff like Elena? What costs might the business have incurred when recruiting Elena? Explain how Elena might recruit three new creative designers. What do you think is meant by on-the-job training?

RECRUITMENT

When businesses hire new employees they need to attract and appoint the best people – those with the right skills and appropriate experience. This is called recruitment and selection. In a very small business recruitment might be undertaken informally – a chat between a business owner and someone who is searching for a job. In a large business, the human resources department is likely to be responsible for employing staff, following a lengthy, formal recruitment process, as explained below.

A business may need new staff because:
- the business is expanding and more labour is needed
- people are leaving and they need to be replaced
- positions have become vacant due to promotion
- people are required for a given period to cover temporary staff absence, due to maternity or paternity leave, for example.

STAGES IN THE RECRUITMENT AND SELECTION PROCESS

The recruitment process may be broken down into a number of stages, as shown in Figure 1.

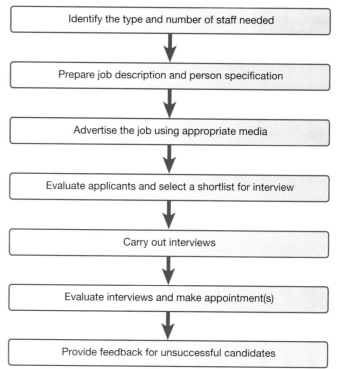

▲ Figure 1 Stages in the recruitment process

- The first stage is to identify the number and type of staff that need to be recruited. The overall business plan will help provide this information. For example, if the business is planning to expand, larger numbers of applicants will need to be attracted. A business may also need to choose between full-time, part-time, temporary and permanent workers.
- The right people are more likely to be selected if a **job description** and **person specification** are drawn up. These are explained on the next page.
- Advertising costs money, so businesses must place job advertisements in media where they are likely to attract sufficient interest from the 'right' sort of applicants. For example, a hospital would not use a national newspaper to advertise jobs for porters; a local newspaper or a jobcentre would be more suitable. Whereas, a vacancy for a senior manager is an important position and a business would want to attract interest from a wide area. Therefore a national newspaper would be appropriate.
- Job applications can be made on standard forms shared with applicants who respond to an advert. Some applicants might write letters and include a **curriculum vitae (CV)**. This is a document that

contains personal details, qualifications, experience, names of referees, hobbies and reasons why the person is suitable for the job. A business must sort through all the applications and might draw up a shortlist. This is because it is not normally possible to interview every single applicant. Also, some applicants will be unsuitable.

- Shortlisted applicants may then be invited for an interview. This is where interviewers can find out more about the applicants by asking questions. It also gives candidates the opportunity to provide more detailed information and ask questions about the job and the business. Interviewing is often best done by people who are experienced or have been trained in interviewing. For many jobs interviews are carried out by more than one person. This provides an opportunity for a discussion about the performance of candidates in their interviews.
- After the interviews the interviewers must decide who to appoint. In many cases, interviewees are told the outcome of the interview by post at a later date. This gives the business more time to evaluate the performance of the candidates. A business might also check references before making a final decision.
- The recruitment process ends when a job offer has been made and accepted. It is also polite to provide feedback to the unsuccessful candidates.

An increasing number of businesses are using online recruitment methods. People can submit application forms online and in some cases might be asked to complete an online test. For example, the retailer Next uses online testing.

The main advantage of online recruitment is that people can apply for jobs at any time and their application details can be stored by a business until they are needed. Online recruitment is also a cheap alternative to traditional methods.

JOB DESCRIPTION

A job description states the title of a job and outlines the tasks, duties and responsibilities associated with that job. If a new job is created, a new job description may have to be prepared. If a business is replacing someone who is leaving, the job description may be the same. However, when someone leaves a post the job description may be updated.

The main purpose of a job description is to show clearly what is expected of an employee. Extracts from it are likely to be used in a job advert. It might also be used during appraisal to see how well an employee has performed in relation to what was expected of them. Figure 2 shows an example of a job description.

PERSON SPECIFICATION

A person specification provides details of the qualifications, experience, skills, attitudes and any other characteristics that would be expected of a person appointed to do a particular job. It is used to assess applicants when sorting through the applications. Applications that do not match the person specification can be ignored. It is common to state on the specification whether a particular requirement is 'essential' or 'desirable'. An example of a person specification is shown in Figure 3. The style of both job descriptions and person specifications is likely to vary between different businesses according to their specific needs.

Job title
Cabin crew member.
Function
Perform ground and air duties that the company may reasonably require. Ground duties apply to any area of work connected to aircraft operational requirements.
Other duties, including boardroom functions and publicity, are voluntary.

Cabin crew must also:
- be familiar and comply with company policy and procedures
- provide a high standard of cabin service and perform their duties thoroughly and carefully at all times
- not behave in any way that reflects badly upon the company or harms its reputation.

Pay and expenses
Salary will be £17,000 per annum.
Payment will be 1 month in arrears, paid directly into the employee's bank account.
Expenses will be paid as set out in the current contract.
If flights are cancelled, you will be entitled to a reporting allowance as set out in the current contract.

Work time
You are required to work 20 days in every 28-day period.
Days and hours will vary according to the company's requirements.
Details of rest periods and flight time limitations are set out in the staff manual.

▲ Figure 2 A job description for a cabin crew assistant for an airline

	Essential/Desirable
Aptitudes/skills/abilities	
Able to take a flexible approach to working conditions and a changing working environment	E
Self-motivated and enthusiastic	E
Ability to work on own initiative	D
Work effectively as part of a team	D
Qualifications/knowledge and experience	
4 GCSEs grade 4 or above	E
Able to use computer software	E
Good written and spoken communication skills	E
Able to solve problems effectively	E
Planning and organisational skills	D
Experience of working in a manufacturing environment	D

▲ Figure 3 A person specification for an administrative assistant in an engineering plant

ACTIVITY 1 — SKILLS — ANALYSIS

CASE STUDY: JOB DESCRIPTION

Job title
Accounts Assistant
Grade 1

General role
To join the accounting team in the recording of financial transactions and the generation of financial information.

Responsibilities
- Matching, batching and coding of invoices.
- Investigating aged debtor services.
- Allocating cost codes.
- Matching invoices to purchase orders.
- Arranging payments through cheque runs, BACS or CHAPs.
- Allocating items of expenditure to cost centres.
- Potentially dealing with internal expenses.

Salary
US$24,500–29,000 p.a. depending on experience.

Hours and conditions of work
- 35 hours per week
- 8.30 a.m.–4.30 p.m.
- 21 days annual holiday

▲ Figure 4 Job description for an accounts clerk

1. Explain what is meant by a job description, illustrating your answer with examples from Figure 4.

INTERNAL AND EXTERNAL RECRUITMENT

Internal recruitment is recruitment from within the business. An employee may be chosen to be offered a post. Or the business may advertise internally, asking employees to apply for the vacancy. The advertisement may be sent round via email and posted on a noticeboard. Larger organisations may have regular newsletters devoted to internal vacancies, or notices may be put in the company magazine or on the company website. Internal recruitment has a number of advantages compared to external recruitment.

- It is often cheaper because no adverts have to be placed and paid for at commercial rates.
- Internal recruits might already be familiar with the procedures and working environment of the business. They may, therefore, need less induction training and be more productive in their first year of employment.
- The qualities, abilities and potential of the candidates should be better known to the employer. It is often difficult to predict exactly how an external recruit will perform in a particular work environment.

- Regular internal recruiting can motivate staff. They might see a career progression with their employer. Even for those who are not seeking promotion, internal recruitment suggests that the employer is looking after existing staff.

External recruitment is when someone is appointed from outside the business. External recruitment has two main advantages over internal recruitment.

- The employer may want someone with new and different ideas to those already working in the business. Bringing in experience of working in different organisations can often be helpful in keeping a business competitive.
- External recruitment might attract a larger number of applicants than internal recruitment. The employer then has more choice of whom to appoint.

External recruitment requires the employer to communicate with potential employees. Ideally, every person who is suitable and who might consider the job should apply. That way, the employer will have the maximum number of candidates from which to choose. There are a number of ways in which an employer can do this.

Word of mouth: A common method of hearing about a job is through word of mouth. This means a person hearing about a job from someone else, often someone who works in the place of employment. For example, a person might hear about a vacancy for a hospital porter from their next-door neighbour who works as a nurse in a local hospital.

Direct application: Many jobseekers send their details to employers for whom they would like to work just in case they have a vacancy. An employer might then use these to recruit if a vacancy arises.

Advertising: The employer may place advertisements in local or national newspapers, and specialist magazines and journals. The Internet is another medium for job advertisements. Advertisements may appear on a company website. Advertisements on a board or window on the employer's premises can also be successful. Advertisements are sometimes costly. But they can reach a wide number of potential applicants. People wanting to change their job are likely to seek out advertisements.

Private employment agencies: The business may employ a private employment agency to find candidates. Private employment agencies are probably best known for finding temporary workers (temps). However, many also specialise in finding permanent staff. At the top end of the range, private employment agencies tend to call themselves executive agencies. They specialise in recruiting company executives and finding jobs for executives seeking a change or who have been made redundant. Using an employment agency should take much of the work out of the recruitment process for the employer. But it can be costly because the employment agency charges a fee. Private employment agencies have a website where specialist workers can look for jobs or advertise their services.

Headhunting: For some posts, such as chief executive of a company, it may be possible to headhunt a candidate. This is where the agency draws up a list of people they think would be suitable for a job. Having cleared the list with the organisation making the appointment, the agency will approach those on the list and discuss the possibility of them taking the job. Some will say no. Others will indicate that, if the terms were right, they might take the job. A final selection is then made and one person is offered the job. Nobody has formally applied or been interviewed. Headhunting works best where there is only a limited number of people who potentially could take on the post and where the agency knows about most of those people.

Jobcentres: Businesses can advertise vacancies through jobcentres run by the government. Jobcentres are often used by the unemployed and vacancies tend to pay less than the average wage. So a cleaner's post is more likely to be advertised in a jobcentre than a chief executive's post. For a business, this is a relatively cheap way of advertising, but it is not suitable for many vacancies.

Government-funded training schemes: Some businesses take on trainees from government-funded training schemes in some countries. For example, for the period 2015–16, an apprenticeship grant was made available to employers in the UK through the Skills Funding Agency, sponsored by the Department for Business, Innovation and Skills. This grant was set up to fund businesses that could not otherwise afford to employ apprentices, targeting those aged 16–24.

THINKING BIGGER

Both large and small businesses make use of online recruitment. A number of online tools can be used by businesses, such as Internet job boards, applicant tracking systems, CV databases, and online testing and assessments. Such tools can be used to identify and sort applicants, assess personalities and assess applicants to see if qualified candidates match the company's values and culture. Some recruitment software providers combine all of these technologies into a simple-to-use package. Software can also be adapted to meet the needs of individual businesses.

One of the main advantages of online recruitment is that applicants can be drawn from a much wider area – global if necessary, 24 hours a day. Specialists

may be attracted by positions with niche industries that are targeted by some online job boards. Employers may also post job advertisements on the websites of many professional associations. This can attract candidates who may not actively be looking for employment, as well as attracting candidates with specific skills.

The cost of using the Internet to recruit staff is very low compared with other methods. It has been reported that the costs of posting jobs and/or searching for candidates online can be up to 90 per cent lower than the costs of using conventional methods. Recruiting online reaches a broad audience with reduced human interaction. It also reduces cost and time through the use of automated selection tools, electronic recording of files, and less demand on storage. The pressure on employee time for maintaining and administering selection procedures is also reduced.

ACTIVITY 2 | SKILLS | ANALYSIS

CASE STUDY: JOB ADVERTISEMENT

The advertisement in Figure 5 was placed by a large multinational company with a big operation in Qatar. The corporation wants to attract some staff to work in a newly opened fitness centre, which is located at one of its key sites near Doha.

EMPLOYMENT OPPORTUNITY

The Aspire Park Fitness Centre exclusive fitness facility is looking for:

FULL-TIME AND PART-TIME FITNESS COACHES

Applicants must have:

- A recognised qualification for fitness instruction
- A desire to help others achieve their goals
- A passion for fitness

Excellent benefits are included with this opportunity.

Please send in CV and cover letter to:

The manager
Aspire Park Fitness Centre
1664 Al Waab St
Doha

▲ Figure 5 Recruitment advertisement from a local newspaper

1. Explain one benefit of using external recruitment for the Aspire Park Fitness Centre
2. Discuss the suitability of using a local newspaper to advertise the job shown above.

COSTS OF RECRUITMENT, SELECTION AND TRAINING

At each stage in the recruitment process shown in Figure 1, a business will incur costs. These costs can be significant and underline the importance of employing an effective recruitment process to attract and retain high-quality staff. According to a report carried out by *Oxford Economics*, the cost of replacing a single member of staff in the UK can be as much as £30,614. There are two elements to this cost – lost output while a replacement is found and inducted, and the process costs of recruiting and selecting a new worker. Generally, recruitment costs will tend to rise directly in relation to the level of the post. Some of the main costs incurred are outlined below.

Recruitment and selection costs: Costs are incurred throughout the whole recruitment and selection process.

- The human resources department will incur costs when identifying the number and type of staff required. For a single post the cost might be quite small, but if, for example, a chain store is opening a new branch, and requires, say, 80 new recruits, the task is significant and will require more time and planning. If a manufacturer is expanding production in a new plant and requires 1500 new staff, then the task is even more costly, because of the complex arrangements needed.
- Some administrative costs will be incurred when checking and updating job descriptions and person specifications. These costs will be higher if the nature of the jobs have changed or if the jobs are newly created.
- Jobs will have to be advertised. If internal recruitment is being used, such costs will be quite low since internal communication systems will be used. However, if external recruitment is being used there will be a cost.
- Time will be spent handling and sorting applications. Some adverts can attract thousands of applications – particularly when unemployment is high. This cost can be miminised by designing a job advert that attracts a small number of perfectly suitable candidates and actively discourages unsuitable ones. However, this can be a challenging task. The aim of this sorting process is to compile a shortlist of candidates to interview. Further costs are incurred if interviewees are contacted by post or phone.
- The interviewing process can also be expensive for a business. It is likely to involve some highly paid senior staff. While these people are involved in the interview process, they are not undertaking their normal tasks; this can have a financial impact. Some businesses use two or even three rounds of interviews when selecting staff. Interviews can require candidates to sit tests or undertake personality assessments – these activities will also incur costs. Documents need to be photocopied and circulated, rooms booked, interviewees welcomed and briefed, refreshments provided and interview staff co-ordinated.
- After the interviews have taken place the performance of interviewees will have to be evaluated. The more people involved in the interview process, the higher the cost. Finally, the selection is made, unsuccessful candidates are given feedback and the successful candidate receives a formal job offer. There may be some official procedures to complete, which might also add to the cost.
- Sometimes the new person recruited will negotiate a higher salary or better benefits than the outgoing person they are replacing, again adding to the business's costs.

Training costs: Costs can be so high that businesses can be reluctant to invest heavily in training. Some training costs are essential and have to be met by a business. For example, employees often have to be trained in health and safety by law. Examples of training costs are outlined below.

- **Training courses and other resources.** Businesses will have to pay training providers if they use external training. Even internal training can be expensive if specialist training staff and equipment is needed.
- **Loss of output.** If workers are involved in off-the-job training they will not be producing anything. This will result in lower output levels. Even if workers are trained on the job, there may be a loss of output due to mistakes and slow work associated with the fact people are learning.
- **Employees leaving.** Businesses are likely to get very frustrated if employees leave and join a rival company after they have invested in training them. Some businesses actually prefer to recruit workers that have already been trained by others to avoid such losses.

TRAINING

Training is the process of increasing the knowledge and skills of workers so that they are better able to perform their jobs. The objectives of training differ from business to business but they include:

- making workers more productive by teaching them more effective ways of working
- giving workers the skills they need to use new equipment or technology
- educating workers in new methods of working, such as shifting from production line methods to cell methods
- making workers more flexible so that they are able to do more than one job role
- preparing workers to move into a different job role within the business, which could be a new job at a similar level or a promotion
- improving standards of work in order to improve quality
- implementing health and safety at work policies
- increasing job satisfaction and motivation, because training should help workers feel more confident in what they are doing and they should gain self-esteem
- assisting in recruiting and retaining high-quality staff, attracted by the quality of training offered.

Sometimes, individual employees request training or undertake training without the financial or time support of their employers. For example, a manager may take an MBA (masters of business administration) university course in her own time. More frequently, training is provided by the employer. The need for training is sometimes identified in the appraisal process.

INDUCTION TRAINING

Many businesses put on training for people starting a job. This is known as **induction training**. It is designed to help new employees settle quickly into the business and their jobs. Exactly what is offered differs from business to business and job to job. For example, a small business might simply allocate another worker to look after the new employee for a day to 'show them the ropes'. A young person just out of university might have 1-year-long induction programme to a large company. They might spend time in a number of departments, as well as being given more general training about the business. But most induction training attempts to introduce workers to the nature of the business and work practices, including health and safety issues.

ON-THE-JOB TRAINING

On-the-job training is training given in the workplace by the employer. There are many ways in which this could happen.

Learning from other workers: An employee might simply work next to another worker, watch that worker do a task and with their help repeat it.

Mentoring: This is where a more experienced employee is asked to provide advice and help to a less experienced worker. The less experienced worker can turn for help and advice to another more experienced worker at any time.

Job rotation: This is where a worker spends a period of time doing one job, then another period of time doing another job, and so on. Eventually they have received the broad experience needed to do a more specialist job.

Traditional apprenticeships: In the past, workers in traditional skilled trades, such as woodwork or engineering, would undertake training over, say, 3 to 5 years in an apprenticeship. This would involve a mix of training methods. When the business decided they had 'qualified' they would be employed as a full-time worker. Many of these schemes died out due to the cost for the business, the decline in traditional trades, mechanisation and the need for more flexible work practices.

Graduate training: Medium- to large-sized businesses may offer graduate training programmes. They are typically designed to offer those with university degrees either professional training, such as in accountancy or law, or managerial training.

Advantages	Disadvantages
• Output is being produced	• Output may be lost if workers make mistakes
• Relevant because trainees learn by actually doing the job	• May be stressful for the worker – particularly if working with others
• Cheaper than other forms of training	• Trainers may get frustrated if they are 'unpaid' trainers
• Can be easy to organise	• Could be a danger to others, e.g. surgeon or train driver

▲ Table 1 Advantages and disadvantages of on-the-job training

OFF-THE-JOB TRAINING

Off-the-job training is training which takes place away from the immediate workplace. It might take place at a company-owned training centre or at a college or university. For example, 16–25 year olds might go to college 1 day a week to do a catering course or an engineering course. A trainee accountant might have an intensive course at an accountancy college or attend night classes before taking professional exams. A graduate manager might do an MBA course at a business school in the evenings and at weekends.

Off-the-job training can provide courses which a business internally would be unable to provide. But it can be expensive, particularly if the business is paying not just for the course but also a salary for the time the employee is attending the course.

Advantages	Disadvantages
• Output is not affected if mistakes are made	• No output because employees do not contribute to work
• Workers' learning cannot be distracted by work	• Some off-the-job training is expensive if provided by specialists
• Training could take place outside work hours if necessary	• Some aspects of work cannot be taught off the job
• Customers and others are not put at risk	• Trainees may feel that some of the training is not relevant to them
	• It may take time to organise

▲ Table 2 Advantages and disadvantages of off-the-job training

BENEFITS OF TRAINING

Although it is expensive, a number of stakeholders will benefit from training.

- **Managers.** Managers will benefit because workers may be better motivated and more satisfied. This makes them more co-operative and easier to work with. They will be better at doing their job. Workers may also be more flexible which will help managers in their organisation. Providing training may also improve the image of the business and make it easier to attract and retain high-quality staff.

ACTIVITY 3   SKILLS   ANALYSIS, REASONING

CASE STUDY: HONDA

Honda, based in Tokyo, Japan, is a large multinational corporation that manufactures motorcycles, motor cars, aircraft and power equipment. The company offers a very wide range of career opportunities for people and has an established and successful apprenticeship programme. Young people joining the programme work alongside experienced staff, can earn money and also gain industry qualifications, skills and knowledge. The Honda Apprenticeship Programme has a reputation for delivering a quality training experience.

Honda has purpose-built technical training centres, with practical workshop areas and individual training rooms. Apprentices receive lots of support, using the latest technology, in a safe and supervised environment. The Honda Institute Centre of Excellence has classrooms, computer rooms, offices and a canteen. There is also a 'Wow Door'. This opens out onto a viewing gallery where you can see a huge space containing all the latest Honda products and technology, which is used solely for learning. Honda apprentices receive a personal development programme, which includes:

- training in first aid, fire equipment, safety, citizenship, health and well-being and equality and diversity
- the chance to drive and use nearly all of Honda's cars, motorcycles, off-road vehicles, go-karts, power equipment and boats
- visits to industry shows
- an introduction to the history and philosophy of Honda, its customers and its environmental policies
- the chance to develop self-confidence and communication skills.

Once young people graduate from the Honda Apprenticeship Programme there is a wide range of career paths to choose from. For example, graduates may choose to become a Honda Repair Technician or a department manager with responsibility for developing other people and providing Honda customers with first-class service. Alternatively, they might use their skills and knowledge to sell Honda products.

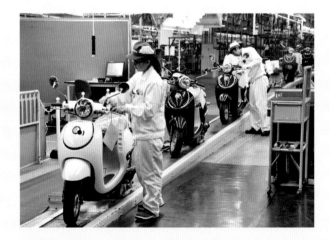

1. Describe **two** possible training costs that Honda might incur providing its apprenticeship programmes.
2. Explain **one** reason why some businesses may be reluctant to invest in training.
3. Honda apprentices receive a lot of off-the-job training. Assess the advantages and disadvantages of off-the-job training.

- **Owners.** Businesses will benefit from training if productivity is higher. This means that costs will be lower and the business might gain a competitive edge in the market. This should improve the financial performance of the business, with higher profits and higher rewards for the owners.
- **Employees.** If workers have been trained they will be able to do their jobs more effectively. This should reduce anxieties about their work and provide more job satisfaction. Employees will feel valued if their employer is paying for their training. They may also feel better motivated, less stressed out and enjoy more job satisfaction. They are likely to develop a range of skills that they can use in the future – to gain promotion or get a better job.

- **Customers.** If training improves quality and skills, then customers will benefit from better quality products and improvements in customer service following training, such as a better outcome when making complaints.

One example of a business that recognises the benefits of training is the retailer and owner of Waitrose, John Lewis Partnership (JLP). It offers their employees, who are addressed as partners, a wide range of training opportunities. For example, JLP have two apprentice training programmes – Retail Apprentice Scheme (Level 2) and Advanced Retail Apprentice Scheme (Level 3). Both schemes use a combination of on-the-job and off-the-job training methods. JLP also use online recruitment methods to help in their selection process.

CHECKPOINT

1. State three reasons why a business might need to recruit new staff.
2. Outline the different stages in the recruitment process.
3. What is the difference between internal and external recruitment?
4. Give one advantage of internal recruitment.
5. Give one drawback of external recruitment.
6. Give three examples of external recruitment.
7. State three specific costs of recruitment and selection.
8. What is the purpose of induction training?
9. State two disadvantages of on-the-job training.
10. Describe the possible benefits of training employees to be shareholders in a plc.

SUBJECT VOCABULARY

curriculum vitae (CV) a document that lists personal details, qualifications, work experience, referees and other information about the jobseeker.

external recruitment appointing workers from outside the business.

induction training training given to new employees when they first start a job.

internal recruitment appointing workers from inside the business.

job description a document that shows clearly the tasks, duties and responsibilities expected of a worker for a particular job.

off-the-job training training that takes place away from the work area.

on-the-job training training that takes place while doing the job.

person specification a personal profile of the type of person needed to do a particular job.

training a process that involves increasing the knowledge and skills of a worker to enable them to do their jobs more effectively.

EXAM PRACTICE

Milano Il Migliore (MIM)

SKILLS ANALYSIS
INTERPRETATION

Milano Il Migliore (MIM) is an Italian multinational retailer selling high-quality clothing and fashion accessories for women. It has 230 stores worldwide although the majority of them are in Europe. In 2017, the business generated revenue of €1980 million and made a profit of €327.3 million. The company employs over 20,000 people worldwide and uses online recruitment to attract some of its staff. Graduates can apply online for jobs in buying, merchandising and design.

The online recruitment process used by MIM is often extremely thorough, and can take several months to complete. There are usually three key stages, beginning with an online application.

1. Candidates have to complete an application form online. These are then reviewed and successful candidates are invited to complete a short test, which is also online.
2. If candidates do well on the test they are then invited to participate in a video interview, normally held via Skype™. These consist of a set of questions that all applicants are asked and often are competency-based questions. So, candidates might be asked to describe a time when they dealt with a difficult customer, for example. These interviews last around an hour and are conducted by a manager.
3. Once the interviews are over, candidates are then moved to the 'offline' stage of the process.

Candidates will be invited to group interviews at local stores where they will be assessed by at least two people. Activities such as role plays are used to assess suitability.

Many companies have their own training programme for graduates. The training and development provided by MIM is admired across the industry and is often adapted by other companies. Training at MIM starts with an introduction to the whole of the business, so that recruits understand the overall objective of the business before learning about their specific business area in detail. Recruits are paired up with more experienced staff members so that they have all the support they need. By offering numerous training opportunities and encouraging their recruits to learn from colleagues, MIM encourages promotion in less than 2 years.

Q

(a) Explain one reason why recruitment is such an important activity for MIM. **(4 marks)**
(b) Explain how MIM attempts to overcome the problem of recruiting sufficiently high-quality staff. **(4 marks)**
(c) Discuss the benefits of online recruitment to MIM. **(8 marks)**
(d) Assess the importance of training to a business like MIM. **(10 marks)**

16 ORGANISATIONAL DESIGN

UNIT 1
1.3.4

LEARNING OBJECTIVES

By the end of this chapter you should be able to understand:

- structure: hierarchy, chain of command, span of control, and centralised and decentralised
- types of structure: tall, flat and matrix
- impact of different organisational structures on business efficiency and employee motivation.

GETTING STARTED

The Ravi Chhetri Theatre is located in Hyderabad, India. It is one of the largest in the region and is used for staging productions and showing movies. It is privately owned and employs 26 local people. The staff are divided into four departments organised as follows (the figures in brackets represent the number of additional staff in each department).

General manager (2) Mithali is in charge of the whole operation. She meets every day with the departmental heads and is the public face of the organisation. She spends a lot of her time trying to raise funds – from organisations that support the arts, for example.

Booking and administration (5) Adnan is head of this department, which handles all the ticketing and booking arrangements. It also keeps financial records and works closely with the external accountant.

Theatre maintenance (8) Anuja is responsible for ensuring that the theatre is cleaned after every performance and maintaining what is an old building requiring significant repair and upgrading.

Production liaison (4) Amrinder and his small team are responsible for working with the groups of actors and production teams that put on plays and other events.

Marketing (2) Sandesh is in charge of promoting the theatre and its productions.

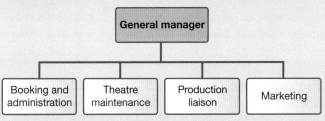

▲ Figure 1 Organisational chart for the Ravi Chhetri Theatre

Who is in control of the Ravi Chhetri Theatre? Describe briefly how staff are organised at the theatre. What is Adnan's role in the organisation? To whom is Amrinda accountable? What might be an advantage of drawing a chart to represent people in an organisation?

ORGANISATIONAL STRUCTURES

Each business has its own organisational structure or business structure. The structure is the way in which positions within the business are arranged. It is often know as the internal structure or **formal organisation** of the business.

The organisational structure of the business defines:

- the workforce roles of employees and their job titles
- the route through which decisions are made
- who is responsible and who is accountable to whom, and for what activities
- the relationship between positions in a business
- how employees communicate with each other and how information is passed on.

Different businesses tend to have different objectives, relationships and ways in which decisions are made. So they may have different structures. But there may also be some similarities. For example, small businesses are likely to have simple structures. Larger businesses are often divided into departments with managers.

Structure is important to all businesses. It helps them to divide work and co-ordinate activities to achieve objectives. But it may be more important for larger businesses. For example, a two-person bathroom installation business is likely to have fewer problems deciding 'who does what' than a business operating in many countries.

One method of organising a business is where managers put people together to work effectively based on their skills and abilities. The structure is 'built up' or it 'develops' as a result of the employees of the business. In contrast a structure could be created first, with all appropriate workforce roles outlined, and then people employed to fill them. It has been suggested that the entrepreneur Richard Branson worked out a complete organisation structure for his Virgin Atlantic airline before setting up the company, and then recruited the 102 people needed to fill all the positions.

HIERARCHY

Some businesses produce an **organisational chart**. These illustrate the structure of the business and the

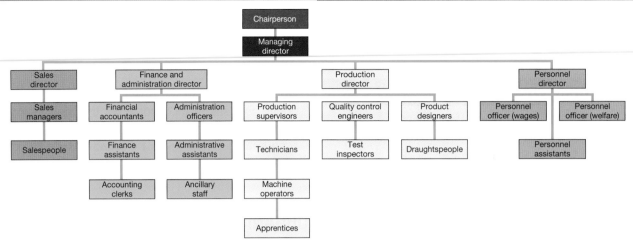

▲ Figure 2 A formal organisational chart for Able Engineering

workforce roles of people employed in the business. Organisational charts show:

- how the business is split into divisions or departments
- the roles of employees and their job titles
- who has responsibility
- to whom people are accountable
- communication channels
- the relationships between different positions in the business.

An organisation chart for Able Engineering, an engineering company, is shown in Figure 2. It is a traditional organisational chart and the person in charge, at the top of the hierarchy, is the chairperson, accountable to the shareholders. The hierarchical nature of the structure shows that employees have different levels of **authority** and **responsibility**. The chairperson at the top of the hierarchy has the most, while the apprentices, at the very bottom, have the least. The roles played by the different employees in an organisation are outlined below.

EMPLOYEE ROLES IN THE ORGANISATIONAL HIERARCHY

The positions in an organisation will have particular workloads and jobs allocated to them.

Directors: Directors are appointed to run the business on behalf of its owners. In smaller businesses, owners may also be directors. But in larger businesses owned by shareholders, for example, they may be different.

Directors are in overall charge of activities in an organisation. They meet, as the board of directors, to make major decisions that will affect the owners. Some directors, known as executive directors, will be involved in the running of a business. Non-executive directors may play little part in its running. The managing director (MD) will have overall responsibility for the organisation and have authority over specific directors, such as the finance or marketing director.

Managers: Managers are responsible for controlling or organising within the business. They often make day-to-day decisions about the running of the business. The sales manager, for example, would have responsibility for sales in the business and be responsible to the marketing director. Businesses often have departmental managers, such as the marketing, human resources, finance and production managers. There may also be regional managers, organising the business in areas of a country, or branch managers, organising particular branches or stores.

Team leaders: Team leaders are members of a team whose role is to resolve issues between team members and co-ordinate team efforts so that the team works effectively. A team leader may be part of a permanent cell production team or a team set up for a particular job, such as investigating staff motivation. A team leader may also take responsibility for representing the views of a team to the next higher reporting level, for example, to report the conclusions of a market research team.

Supervisors: Supervisors monitor and regulate the work in their assigned or delegated area, for example stock supervisor or payroll supervisor. Supervisors may be given some of the roles of managers, but at a lower level. Their roles in this case may be to hire, discipline, promote, punish or reward.

Professionals: These are positions for staff with high levels of qualifications and experience. The job roles are likely to involve a degree of decision making and responsibility for ensuring that tasks are carried out effectively to a high standard. Examples might include doctors, architects, stockbrokers, product designers, chefs and accountants.

Operatives: These are positions for skilled workers who are involved in the production process or service provision. They carry out the instructions of managers or supervisors. In their own area of activity they may have to ensure targets are met and tasks are carried out effectively. Examples of operatives in business might include staff in:

- production, for example, assembling a car or manufacturing furniture
- warehousing, for example, checking invoices against goods and ensuring effective deliveries
- IT, for example, giving technical support for machinery.

General staff: There are a variety of positions in business that are carried out by staff with non-specific skills. They follow instructions given by superiors to carry out particular tasks and are an essential part of the production process or service provision. Examples might include checkout staff and shelf fillers in supermarkets, cleaners and receptionists in offices. They might also include general jobs on a farm or building site, such as cleaning.

Although there may be similar job roles, there will be differences between organisations in the precise nature of these roles, relationships between various job roles, how they are managed and how decisions are made.

CHAIN OF COMMAND

The **hierarchy** in a business is the levels of management in a business, from the lowest to the highest rank. It shows the **chain of command** within the organisation – the way authority is organised. Orders pass down the levels and information passes up. Businesses must also consider the number of links or levels in the chain of command. R. Townsend, in his book *Up the Organisation*, estimated that each extra level of management in the hierarchy reduced the effectiveness of communication by about 25 per cent. No rules are laid down on the most effective number of links in the chain. However, businesses generally try to keep chains as short as possible.

SPAN OF CONTROL

The number of people, or **subordinates**, a person directly controls in a business is called the **span of control**. For example, if a production manager has ten subordinates, their span of control is ten. If a business has a *wide* span of control it means that a person controls relatively more subordinates. Someone with a *narrow* span of control controls fewer subordinates. If the span of control is greater than six, difficulties may arise. Henri Fayol, who developed a general theory of business administration in his 2001 work *Critical Evaluations in Business*

Management, argued that the span of control should be between three and six because:

- there should be tight managerial control from the top of the business
- there are physical and mental limitations to any single manager's ability to control people and activities.

The implications of wide and narrow spans of control are discussed in more detail below.

AUTHORITY AND RESPONSIBILITY

Employees in the hierarchy will have responsibility and authority. However, as we mentioned earlier these terms do not mean the same thing. Responsibility involves being accountable or being required to justify an action. So, for example, managers who are responsible for a department may be asked to justify poor performance to the board of directors. The human resources department may be responsible for employing workers. If a new worker was unable to do a particular job, they would be asked to explain why.

Authority, in contrast, is the ability to carry out the task. For example, it would make no sense asking an office worker to pay company debts if she did not have the authority to sign cheques. Employees at lower levels of the hierarchy have less responsibility and authority than those further up. However, it may be possible for a superior to delegate (pass down) authority to a subordinate, e.g. a manager to an office worker, but continue to have responsibility. Increasingly, businesses are realising the benefits of delegating both authority and responsibility.

ACTIVITY 1   SKILLS   ANALYSIS

CASE STUDY: CHATUCHAK TEXTILES

The textile and garment industry plays a significant role in Thailand's economic and social development. The textile industry in Thailand covers a wide variety of products; everything from hi-tech synthetic yarns to wool fabrics, cotton bed linens to technical textiles, and pajamas to high fashion. One manufacturer, Chatuchak Textiles, makes a range of clothing. Its factory, based in Chatuchak, Bangkok, has three production lines, where machinists are employed to operate the machines that make the clothes. Figure 3 shows part of the organisational chart.

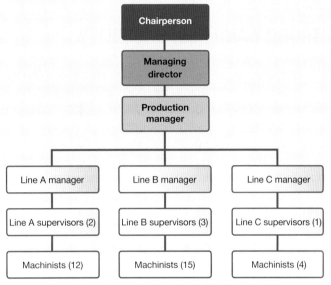

▲ Figure 3 Extract from the organisational chart of Chatuchak Textiles

1. What is the span of control for the manager of Line B?
2. Using Figure 3, describe the chain of command at Chatuchak Textiles, from the chairperson to the machinists working on all lines.
3. Explain one reason why the business might produce an organisational chart.

CENTRALISATION AND DECENTRALISATION

Centralisation and decentralisation refer to the extent to which authority is delegated in a business. If there was complete centralisation, subordinates would have no authority at all. Complete decentralisation would mean subordinates would have all the authority to take decisions. Some delegation may always be necessary in all firms because of the limits to the amount of work senior managers can carry out. Tasks that might be delegated include staff selection, quality control, customer relations, and purchasing and stock control. Even if authority is delegated to a subordinate, it is usual for the manager to continue to have responsibility.

In pyramid structures, subordinates often have little authority, with most decisions being taken at the top of the organisation. Some would argue that this form of organisation may not suit the various markets that a

growing and competitive business could face. Individuals close to consumers might be better placed to make decisions. Hence regional, divisional or, in some cases for multinational companies, national operations may become a 'business unit' with its own cost and profit centre. However, it would still remain accountable to the head office. The advantages of centralisation and decentralisation are shown in Table 1.

Advantages of centralisation	Advantages of decentralisation
• Senior management has more control of the business, e.g. budgets. • Procedures, such as ordering and purchasing, can be standardised throughout the organisation, leading to economies of scale and lower costs. • Senior managers can make decisions from the point of view of the business as a whole. Subordinates would tend to make decisions from the point of view of their department or section. This allows senior managers to maintain a balance between departments or sections. For example, if a company has only a limited amount of funds available to spend over the next few years, centralised management would be able to share the funds out between production, marketing, research and development, and fixed asset purchases in different departments, etc. • Senior managers should be more experienced and skilful in making decisions. In theory, centralised decisions by senior people should be of better quality than decentralised decisions made by others less experienced. • In times of crisis, a business may need strong leadership by a central group of senior managers. • Communication may improve if there are fewer decision makers.	• It empowers and motivates workers. • It reduces the stress and burdens of senior management. It also frees time for managers to concentrate on more important tasks. • It provides subordinates with greater job satisfaction by giving them more say in decision making, which affects their work. • Subordinates may have a better knowledge of 'local' conditions affecting their area of work. This should allow them to make more informed, well-judged choices. For example, salespeople may have more detailed knowledge of their customers and be able to advise them on purchases. • Delegation should allow greater flexibility and a quicker response to changes. If problems do not have to be referred to senior managers, decision making will be quicker. Since decisions are quicker, they are easier to change in the light of unforeseen circumstances which may arise. • By allowing delegated authority, management at middle and junior levels are prepared to take over higher positions. They are given the experience of decision making when carrying out delegated tasks. Delegation is therefore important for management development.

▲ Table 1 Advantages of centralisation and decentralisation

ACTIVITY 2
SKILLS ANALYSIS, CRITICAL THINKING

CASE STUDY: VMWARE INC.

VMware Inc., owned by Dell Technologies, provides cloud and virtualisation software and services. In 2016, after carrying out some research, the company published a report that suggested that the management of information technology (IT) in businesses was being decentralised. The survey, which questioned 200 IT decision makers and line managers, found that the decentralisation of IT was proving successful. For example, 56 per cent of respondents said that they were able to develop and launch new products more quickly. Sixty-three per cent said that there was more freedom in their organisations to drive innovation. The decentralisation of IT had also contributed to lower staff turnover. For example, 53 per cent of respondents said that employee satisfaction had improved.

However, some respondents said that decentralisation did have its drawbacks. For example, 63 per cent of business leaders said that it was leading to some IT resources being constructed more than once and 62 per cent said that accountability was becoming a problem. Also, 59 per cent said that in some cases unsecure solutions were being purchased.

Unsurprisingly, IT departments did not favour decentralisation. Seventy per cent of IT managers said that IT should be more centralised. Seventy-nine per cent argued that they should be in control of core functions like network security and compliance. Forty-six per cent said that IT disaster management was too important to be decentralised and 39 per cent said data storage should also be their responsibility.

Although businesses are looking to innovate, improve efficiency and find ways of competing in an increasingly dynamic business environment, it is important to embrace new methods of IT management cautiously. According to a spokesperson for VMware 'Too often, we're seeing this trend (decentralisation of IT) left unchecked and without adequate IT governance, meaning that organisations across Europe, the Middle East and Africa are driving up costs, compromising security and muddying the waters as to who does what, as they look to evolve.'

1. Define decentralisation. Use the example in this case to illustrate your answer.
2. Explain why IT departments are unlikely to support the decentralisation of IT.
3. Assess the possible impacts of the decentralisation of IT on businesses.

TYPES OF ORGANISATIONAL STRUCTURE

Organisational structures can vary between different businesses. This is because different businesses have different needs and possibly have different views about the way staff should be organised and controlled. Organisational structures may be flat, tall or matrix. Examples are shown in Figure 4 on the next page.

Tall structures: Figure 4a shows a tall structure. Here there is a long chain of command, but a narrow span of control. In this chart there are five levels in the hierarchy. Some advise that the number of levels should not exceed eight, the point at which the disadvantages of tall structures begin to outweigh the advantages.

Flat structures: A flat structure means there are fewer layers in the hierarchy. In Figure 4b the flat structure only has three layers in the hierarchy. The chain of command is short but the span of control is wide. This type of structure means that employees are free from strict, close control in the workplace. They have more freedom and responsibility.

Matrix structures: Matrix structures allow businesses to connect people with particular specialist skills, as shown in Figure 4c. They involve getting people together from different areas in the business to form a project team. Individuals within the team each have their own responsibility. Teams are not fixed, and can be made, altered or dissolved to suit the business need at the time. Matrix structures are often used to solve problems in a business – particularly problems that require a range of areas of expertise.

IMPLICATIONS OF DIFFERENT ORGANISATIONAL STRUCTURES

The different structures used by businesses to organise their workforces have advantages and disadvantages. The implications of each type are outlined below.

Tall structures: With tall structures the span of control can be small. This means that managers have more control over their subordinates. As a result employees can be more closely supervised. There is a clear management structure

(a) Tall structure

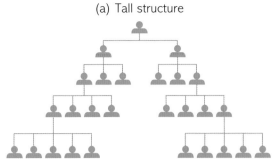

A long chain of command and a narrow span of control. A production department may look like this. One manager is helped by a few assistant managers, each responsible for supervisors. These supervisors are responsible for skilled workers, who are in charge of a group of semi-skilled workers. Close supervision is needed to make sure quality is maintained. This is sometimes referred to as a tall organisational structure.

(b) Flat structure

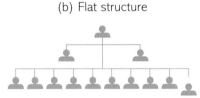

A short chain of command and a wide span of control. A higher or further education department may look like this, with a 'head' of department, a few senior staff and many teaching staff. Staff will want a degree of independence. This is sometimes referred to as a flat organisational structure.

(c) Matrix structure

The matrix structure here shows two specific business projects, X and Y, drawing people from four different departments – production, marketing, human resources and accounting.

▲ Figure 4 Tall, flat and matrix organisational structures

and a clear route for promotion. This might help to motivate staff. However, management costs will be higher since there are more managers. Communication through the whole structure can be poor because there is a long chain of command. Messages may get distorted as they get passed down through the different layers in the hierarchy. It might also slow down the decision-making process as approval may be needed at each level of management. Finally, close-quarters control may be disliked by some staff and they could become demotivated.

Flat structures: With flat structures, communication is better because the chain of command is generally shorter. Communication can be quicker and there is less potential for messages to be distorted. Management costs are lower because there are fewer layers of management. Decision making may be quicker because approval from several managerial layers is not required. Also, employees may be better motivated because they are less closely controlled. Indeed, in many flat structures employees are empowered. They have more responsibility for organising their work and may be allowed to solve their own problems. This can help to make their work more interesting. However, managers may lose control of the workforce because the span of control is too wide. As a result discipline may be lacking, which could have a negative impact on productivity. There could also be co-ordination problems if managers are responsible for too many subordinates. As a result they may become overworked.

Matrix structures: Managers often argue that this is the best way of organising people. This is because it is based on the expertise and skills of employees, and gives scope for people lower down the organisation to use their talents effectively. For example, a product manager looking into the possibility of developing a new product may draw on the expertise of employees with skills in design, research and development, marketing, costing, etc. In this way, a matrix structure can also operate within a business that has a bureaucratic structure.

The matrix model fits with some of the motivational theories discussed in Chapter 17, which view employees in a very positive light. It is suggested that this structure improves flexibility and the motivation of employees. However, the method often needs expensive support systems, such as extra administrative and office staff. There may also be problems with co-ordinating a team drawn from different departments and with the speed of decision making.

THINKING BIGGER

Delayering also involves a business reducing its staff. The cuts are directed at particular levels of a business, such as managerial posts. Many traditional organisational charts are hierarchical, with many layers of management. Delayering involves removing some of these layers. This gives a flatter structure. In the late 1980s, the average number of layers in a typical organisational structure was seven, although some were as high as 14. By the early 2000s this was reduced to less than five. The main advantage of delayering is the savings made from laying off expensive managers. It may also lead to better communication and a better motivated staff if they are **empowered** and allowed to make their own decisions.

However, remaining managers may become demotivated after delayering. Also staff may become overworked as they have to take on more tasks. Fewer layers may also mean less chance of promotion.

CHECKPOINT

1. Why do some businesses need a formal organisation?
2. State three benefits of drawing an organisational chart.
3. What is the advantage of a short chain of command?
4. What is the advantage of having a small span of control?
5. State two advantages of a centralised organisation.
6. State two benefits of decentralisation.
7. Give one disadvantage of a tall organisational structure.
8. Describe the benefits of using a matrix organisational structure.
9. How might motivation be affected by employing a flatter organisational structure?
10. How might communication be less effective in a tall organisational structure?

SUBJECT VOCABULARY

authority the right to command and make decisions.
centralisation a type of business organisation where major decisions are made at the centre or core of the organisation and then passed down the chain of command.
chain of command the way authority and power is organised in an organisation.
decentralisation a type of business organisation where decision making is pushed down the chain of command and away from the centre of the organisation.
delayering removing layers of management from the hierarchy of an organisation.
delegation the passing of authority further down the managerial hierarchy.
empowerment giving official authority to employees to make decisions and control their own work activities.
formal organisation the internal structure of a business as shown by an organisational chart.
hierarchy the order or levels of responsibility in an organisation, from the lowest to the highest.
organisational chart a diagram that shows the different job roles in a business and how they relate to each other.
responsibility the duty to complete a task.
span of control the number of people a person is directly responsible for in a business.
subordinates people in the hierarchy who work under the control of a senior worker.

EXAM PRACTICE

VALVE®

SKILLS   ANALYSIS, INTERPRETATION, PRODUCTIVITY, COMMUNICATION

Based in Bellevue, Washington, USA, Valve is a video game developer and digital distribution company. Some of its popular games include Half-Life®, Counter-Strike®, PortalTM, Day of Defeat®, Team Fortress®, Left 4 Dead, and Dota® 2. Valve is also famous for Steam, the innovative game platform that distributes and manages thousands of games directly to a global customer base of over 65 million people. This product has generated enormous revenues for Valve. In 2016, it was reported that 5245 new games were released on Steam.

In common with a number of technology businesses, Valve has a flat organisation. However, many would regard the organisation of this company as unusual. There are no managers and all staff have equal status. Employees can sit anywhere they like, work on whichever project they choose and even make decisions about their colleagues' salary. According to one Valve employee, D. J. Powers, he does not report to anyone and no one reports to him. He says, 'We're free to choose to work on whatever we think is interesting. People ask you questions about what you are working on. Staff are encouraged to be open and appreciate that they are interdependent.'

Employees at Valve are encouraged to move around the office and to interact with their work colleagues. In fact, furniture in the Valve offices is on wheels to make moving around easier. There are even instructions in the Valve staff handbook that show employees how to move their desks. This is shown in Figure 5. Powers, who has probably moved his desk ten times in 3 years, said, 'We form into teams based on the need to complete a feature or complete a game, and then we disperse into new teams... The ability to be able to pick up and move and be in another office in 20 minutes as opposed to a day-and-a-half is really attractive.'

Academics that have studied the effectiveness of flat organisations think that one of the main reasons why they work is because they encourage staff interaction – dialogue and information sharing. They also attract high-quality staff or 'elite performers', as one academic put it. However, Powers suggests that the structure works

because it was the way the organisation was originally designed. It has always been like this. He also says that it might be a mistake to try and introduce such a flat structure in an organisation that has traditionally been hierarchical.

Finally, Powers said, 'I think the fact that we're not managed by people and we're not managing people and you're able to formulate your own ideas and work with whoever it is to come up with a project or feature – that's empowering.'

Valve is a privately owned company so details about its revenues and profits are not widely distributed. However, it is reckoned that its most popular product, Steam, controls between 50 and 70 per cent of the US$4000 million downloadable PC games market. It has also been reported that Valve generates higher profits per employee than both Apple and Google.

Q

(a) Define a flat organisation structure. **(2 marks)**

(b) Evaluate whether or not Valve will benefit from having a flatter organisational structure. **(20 marks)**

17 MOTIVATION IN THEORY AND PRACTICE

LEARNING OBJECTIVES

By the end of this chapter you should be able to understand:

■ the importance of employee motivation to a business
■ motivation theories: Taylor (scientific management), Mayo (human relations theory), Maslow (hierarchy of needs) and Herzberg (two-factor theory)
■ financial incentives to improve employee performance: piecework, commission, bonus, profit share and performance-related pay
■ non-financial techniques to improve employee performance: delegation, consultation, empowerment, team working, flexible working, job enrichment, job rotation and job enlargement.

GETTING STARTED

Gladys Chickwelu works for a Nigerian financial services business selling private pensions. She is in charge of a small team of six sales staff. She receives a basic pay of NGN 3,800,000 a year, but gets 2 per cent per month commission based on the team's monthly sales. Last month the team sold NGN 400 million worth of policies. Gladys enjoys her job and is well motivated. She can choose her hours of work and gets up to 8 weeks holiday a year.

Calculate the amount of money that Gladys earned last month. How do you think her employer motivates sales staff in this case? What do you think would motivate you? What are the advantages to a business of teamworking?

THE IMPORTANCE OF MOTIVATION

Why is it important for a business to find out what satisfies the needs of its employees? It is argued that if an individual's needs are not satisfied, then that worker will not be motivated to work. Businesses have found that even if employees are satisfied with pay and conditions at work, they complain that their employer does not do a good job in motivating them. This applies to all levels, from the shop floor to the senior management. It appears in many companies that employers are not getting the full potential from their employees because they are not satisfying all of their employees' needs.

It is important for a business to motivate its employees. In the short term, a lack of motivation may lead to reduced effort and lack of commitment. If employees are watched closely, fear of wage cuts or redundancy may force them to maintain their effort even though they are not motivated. This is negative motivation.

In the long term, a lack of motivation may result in high levels of absenteeism, industrial disputes, and falling productivity and profit for a business. So it is argued that well-motivated employees will be productive, which should lead to greater efficiency and profits.

There are a number of motivational theories used in business.

TAYLOR'S THEORY OF SCIENTIFIC MANAGEMENT

Frederick W. Taylor set out a theory of **scientific management** in his book *The Principles of Scientific Management* in 1911. Many of the ideas of today's 'scientific management school' come from the work of Taylor.

The turn of the 20th century in the USA was a time of rapid expansion. Compared to today, the organisation of work in factory production was left much more in the hands of workers and their supervisors. Workers often brought their own tools and decisions about the speed of machines were left to operators. There were few training programmes to teach workers their jobs, and skills were gained simply by watching more experienced colleagues. Decisions about selection, rest periods and redundancies were frequently made by supervisors.

Taylor suggested that such arrangements were disorganised and inefficient. On the one hand, management did not understand the production process and allowed wasteful work practices to continue. Workers, on the other hand, left to their own devices, would do as little as possible. 'Soldiering' would also take place (working more slowly together so that management did not realise workers' potential) and workers would carry out tasks in ways they were used to rather than the most efficient way.

Taylor's scientific principles were designed to reduce inefficiency of workers and managers. This was to be achieved by 'objective laws' that management and workers could agree on, reducing conflict between them.

Neither party could argue against a system of work that was based on 'science'. Taylor believed his principles would create a partnership between manager and worker, based on an understanding of how jobs should be done and how workers are motivated.

Taylor's approach: How did Taylor discover what the 'best way' was of carrying out a task? Table 1 shows an illustration of Taylor's method. Taylor had a very simple view of what motivated people at work – money. He felt that workers should receive a 'fair day's pay for a fair day's work', and pay should be linked to output through piece rates. A worker who did not produce a 'fair day's work' would face a loss of earnings; exceeding the target would lead to a bonus. In 1899, Taylor's methods were used at the Bethlehem Steel Works in the USA, where they were responsible for raising pig iron production by almost 400 per cent per man per day. Taylor found the 'best way to do each job' and designed incentives to motivate workers.

Taylor's message for business is simple – allow workers to work and managers to manage based on scientific principles of work study. Many firms today still attempt to use Taylor's principles. In the 1990s, for example, some businesses introduced business process re-engineering (BPR). This is a management approach where organisations look at their business processes from a 'clean slate' perspective and determine how they can best construct these processes to improve how they conduct business. Taylor's approach is similar in that it advises businesses to find the best way of doing something to add value to the business.

- Pick a dozen skilled workers.
- Observe them at work and note down the elements and sequences adopted in their tasks.
- Time each element with a stopwatch.
- Eliminate any factors that appear to add nothing to the completion of the task.
- Choose the quickest method discovered and fit them in their sequence.
- Teach the worker this sequence; do not allow any change from the set procedure.
- Include time for rest and the result will be the 'quickest and best' method for the task. Because it is the best way, all workers selected to perform the task must adopt it and meet the time allowed.
- Supervise workers to ensure that these methods are carried out during the working day.

▲ Table 1 Taylor's method, designed to find out the 'best way' to carry out a task at work

Problems with Taylor's approach: There are a number of problems with Taylor's ideas. The notion of a 'quickest and best way' for all workers does not take into account individual differences. There is no guarantee that the 'best way' will suit everyone.

Taylor also viewed people at work more as machines, with financial needs, than as humans in a social setting. There is no doubt that money is an important motivator. Taylor overlooked that people also work for reasons other than money.

A survey in America by Robb and Myatt in 2004, for example, found that of the top ten factors motivating workers, the first three categories were a sense of achievement, having that achievement recognised and positive working relationships. This suggests there may be needs that must be met at work, which Taylor ignored, but were recognised in Maslow's ideas which came later.

MAYO'S THEORY OF HUMAN RELATIONS

Taylor's scientific management ideas may initially have seemed appealing to business. Some tried to introduce his ideas in the 1920s and 1930s, which led to workers taking industrial action. Others found that financial incentives did motivate workers, and still do today. However, what was becoming clear was that there were other factors that may affect workers' motivation.

The Hawthorne studies: Many of the ideas that are today known as the 'human relations school' grew out of experiments between 1927 and 1932 at the Hawthorne Plant of the Western Electric company in Chicago, USA. Initially these were based on 'scientific management' – the belief that workers' productivity was affected by work conditions, the skills of workers and financial incentives. Over the 5-year period, changes were made in incentive schemes, rest periods, hours of work, lighting and heating, and the effect on workers' productivity was measured. One example was a group of six women assembling telephone switches. It was found that whatever changes were made, including a return to the original conditions, output rose. This came to be known as the **Hawthorne effect**.

The study concluded that changes in conditions and financial rewards had little or no effect on productivity. Increases in output were mainly due to the stronger teams and better communication that workers in groups developed as they interacted and were motivated to work together. Workers were also motivated by the interest shown in their work by the researchers. This result was confirmed by further investigations in the Bank Wiring Observation where 14 men with different tasks were studied.

The work of Elton Mayo (and Roethlisberger and Dickson) in the 1930s, who reported on the Hawthorne studies, has led to what is known today as the human relations school. A business aiming to maximise productivity must make sure that the 'personal satisfactions' of workers are met for workers to be motivated. Management must also work and communicate with informal work groups, making sure that their goals fit in with the goals of the business. One way to do this is to allow such groups to be part of decision making. Workers are likely to be more committed to tasks that they have had some say in.

There are examples of these ideas being used in business. The Volvo plant in Uddevalla, Sweden, opened in 1989, was designed to allow workers to work in teams of eight to ten. Each team built a complete car and made decisions about production. Volvo found that absenteeism rates at Uddevalla averaged 8 per cent, compared to 25 per cent in their Gothenburg plant, which used a production line system. Other examples have been:

- Honda's plant in Swindon, UK, where 'teamwork' has been emphasised – there were no workers or directors, only 'associates'
- McDonald's picnics, parties and McBingo for their employees where they were made to feel part of the company
- Mary Kay's seminars in the USA, which were presented like the American Academy awards for company employees.

Problems: There are a number of criticisms of the human relations school.

- It assumes workers and management share the same goals. However, general agreement within a workplace may not always exist. For example, in the 1980s Rover tried to introduce a programme called 'Working with Pride'. It was an attempt to raise quality by gaining employee commitment. This would be achieved by greater communication with employees. The programme was not accepted throughout the company. As one manager stated: 'We've tried the face-to-face communications approach. It works to a degree, but we are not too good at the supervisory level... enthusiasm for the Working with Pride programme is proportionate to the level in the hierarchy. For supervisors it's often just seen as a gimmick...'
- It is assumed that communication between workers and management will break down 'barriers'. It could be argued, however, that the knowledge of directors' salaries or redundancies may lead to even more 'barriers' and dissatisfaction.
- It is biased towards management. Workers are 'tricked' into being productive by managers. It may also be seen as a way of reducing trade union power.

MASLOW'S HIERARCHY OF NEEDS

The first comprehensive attempt to classify needs was by Abraham Maslow in his book *Motivation and Personality*, published in 1954. **Maslow's hierarchy of needs** theory

consisted of two parts. The first concerned classification of needs. The second concerned how these classes are related to each other. Maslow suggested that 'classes' of needs could be placed into a hierarchy. The hierarchy is normally presented as a 'pyramid', with each level consisting of a certain class of needs. This is shown in Figure 1. The classes of needs were:

- physiological needs, e.g. wages high enough to meet weekly bills, good working conditions
- safety needs, e.g. job security, safe working conditions
- love and belonging, e.g. working with colleagues that support you at work, teamwork, communicating
- esteem needs, e.g. being given recognition for doing a job well
- self-actualisation, e.g. being promoted and given more responsibility, scope to develop and introduce new ideas, and take on challenging new job assignments.

Figure 1 can also be used to show the relationship between the different classes. Maslow argued that needs at the bottom of the pyramid are basic needs. They are concerned with survival. These needs must be satisfied before a person can move to the next level. For example, people are likely to be more concerned with basic needs, such as food, than anything else. At work an employee is unlikely to be concerned about acceptance from colleagues if he has not eaten for 6 hours. Once each level is satisfied, the needs at this level become less important. The exception is the top level of **self-actualisation**. This is the need to fulfil your potential. Maslow argued that although everyone is capable of this, in practice very few reach this level.

▲ Figure 1 Maslow's hierarchy of needs

Each level of needs is dependent on the levels below. Say an employee has been motivated at work by the opportunity to take responsibility, but finds they may lose their job. The whole system collapses, as the need to feed and provide for themselves and those who depend on then again becomes the most important need.

Maslow's ideas have great appeal for business. The message is clear – find out which level each individual is at and decide on suitable rewards. Unfortunately, the theory has problems when used in practice. Some levels do not appear to exist for certain individuals, while some rewards appear to fit into more than one class. Money, for example, needs to be used to purchase essential items, such as food, but it can also be seen as a status symbol or an indicator of personal worth. There is also a problem in deciding when a level has actually been 'satisfied'. There will always be exceptions to the rules Maslow outlined. A well-motivated designer may spend many hours on a creative design despite lack of sleep or food.

HERZBERG'S TWO-FACTOR THEORY

In 1966, Fredrick Herzberg attempted to find out what motivated people at work. He asked a group of professional engineers and accountants to describe incidents in their jobs which gave them strong feelings of satisfaction or dissatisfaction. He then asked them to describe the causes in each case.

Results: Herzberg divided the causes into two categories or factors. These are shown in Figure 2.

- **Motivators.** Motivators are the factors that give workers job satisfaction, such as recognition for their effort. Increasing these motivators is needed to give job satisfaction. This, it could be argued, will make workers more productive. A business that rewards its workforce for, say, achieving

a target is likely to motivate them to be more productive. However, this is not guaranteed, as other factors can also affect productivity.

- **Hygiene or maintenance factors.** Hygiene or maintenance factors are factors that can lead to workers being dissatisfied, such as pay or conditions. Improving hygiene factors should remove dissatisfaction. For example, better canteen facilities may make workers less dissatisfied about their environment. An improvement in hygiene factors alone is not likely to motivate an individual. But if they are not met, there could be a fall in productivity.

There is some similarity between Herzberg's and Maslow's ideas. They both point to needs that have to be satisfied for the employee to be motivated. Herzberg argues that only the higher levels of Maslow's hierarchy motivate workers.

Herzberg's ideas are often linked with job enrichment. This is where workers have their jobs 'expanded', so that they can experience more of the production process. This allows the workers to be more involved and motivated, and have a greater sense of achievement. Herzberg used his ideas in the development of administrative work. He selected a group of workers in a large corporation. Performance and job attitudes were low. Herzberg redesigned these jobs so that they were given more responsibility and recognition.

Problems: Herzberg's theory does seem to have some merits. Improving pay or conditions, for example, may remove dissatisfaction at first. Often, however, these things become taken for granted. It is likely that better conditions will be asked for in following years. Evidence of this can be seen in wage claims, which aim to be above the rate of inflation in some businesses every year. Job enrichment may also be expensive for many

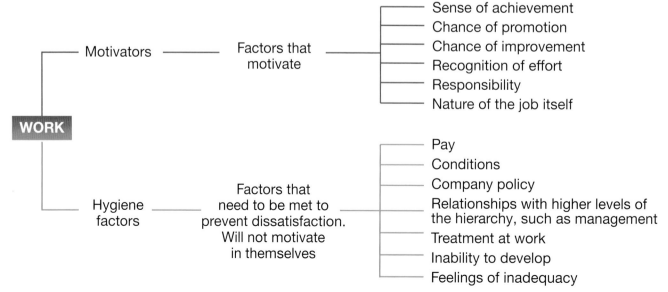

▲ Figure 2 Herzberg's two-factor theory

firms. In addition, it is likely that any benefits from job improvements will not be seen for a long time and that businesses will not be able to continue with such a policy in periods of recession.

Surveys that have tried to reproduce Herzberg's results have often failed. This may have been because different groups of workers have been examined and different techniques used. Also, there is a problem in relying too much on what people say they find satisfying or dissatisfying at work, as this is subjective. For example, if things go wrong at work individuals have a tendency to blame it on others or factors outside of their control. Whereas, if individuals feel happy and satisfied when they are at work then they tend to see it as their own doing.

ACTIVITY 1　　SKILLS　ANALYSIS

CASE STUDY: UJJIVAN FINANCIAL SERVICES

Ujjivan Financial Services, based in Bangalore, India, is a microfinance company that recently went public and is on its way to becoming a small finance bank. It began by offering financial help to the poor. However, the company now lends to groups or individuals that require funding for agricultural projects, education, home improvement, home purchases and purchases of livestock such as sheep or goats. Ujjivan serves over 2.77 million customers in India through 469 branches and employs 7786 people.

In 2016, the company was ranked third among the top 25 companies to work for in India by the Great Places to Work® Institute in partnership with *The Economic Times*. One of the main reasons why employees think it is a great place to work is because the work itself is interesting and satisfying. For example, one employee, Mantasha Mizaj a management associate, says that the best thing about working for Ujjivan is the excitement and energy that you get from working with such a young workforce, combined with the opportunity to work with experienced seniors. She also enjoys the meaningful social work that the job involves – it drives her enthusiasm to be part of Ujjivan.

Staff at Ujjivan enjoy a number of benefits. For example, all employees are offered the chance to buy esops (stock options for employees) depending on performance. Employees are also required to take 10 unbroken days of holiday each year – this is in addition to their casual leave. The company believes that staff need time in addition to regular leave to reconnect with themselves and their families. Female employees also have access to free childcare facilities. This helps new mothers when they return to work.

There are no job titles at Ujjivan and communication between all levels of staff is very good indeed. Samit Ghosh, the CEO and managing director, does not have a personal secretary and all staff are welcome to speak to him at any time. Ujjivan also recognises and rewards staff achievements. For example, an employee in Kerala won an award for designing a celebratory logo. The CEO understands the importance of a well-motivated workforce. He believes that customers can only be happy if the employees are happy. Ujjivan treats employees as important stakeholders.

1. Explain **one** reason why motivation is important to a business like Ujjivan.
2. Identify **two** of Herzberg's hygiene factors at Ujjivan.
3. Explain **one** factor that will help to motivate staff at Ujjivan according to Herzberg.

FINANCIAL METHODS TO IMPROVE STAFF PERFORMANCE

A number of theories have tried to explain the factors that motivate people at work. Some of these theories stress that money is the most important factor. The scientific approach, in particular, argues that workers respond to financial rewards. It is argued that such rewards are necessary to motivate a reluctant workforce. Employees see work as a means to an end. As a result they are far more likely to be interested in financial rewards. In contrast, the human relations view argues that workers are motivated by a variety of factors. An employee working in a car assembly plant, for example, may be highly motivated by working as part of a team.

Piecework: Piece rates are payments for each unit produced. They are an example of **payment by results**. For example, a fruit picker might be paid US$1.00 per kilogram of strawberries picked or a tractor driver might be paid US$3.50 per hectare of land ploughed. **Piece rates** were recommended by Frederick Taylor, founder of the scientific management school. He thought they were an ideal way to motivate workers. Workers who produced more were more highly paid. However, piece rates are only suitable for jobs where it is easy to identify the contribution of an individual worker. It would be difficult to design a piece rate system for, say, secretaries or managers. Piece rates have been criticised on health and safety grounds. They might encourage workers to take dangerous short cuts in a bid to reduce the amount of time taken for each item. Rushing production might also affect the quality of the product.

Commission: Commission is a payment system mainly used with white-collar workers. Commission, like piece

ACTIVITY 2 SKILLS ANALYSIS

CASE STUDY: PAID BY OUTPUT

Paying workers according to what they produce is common in a number of industries. One such industry is textiles. For example, people employed on machines to make garments are likely to be paid according to how many units they produce in a shift.

1. Explain the payment system used in this case.
2. Explain which motivational theory this payment system might be based on.
3. Explain one possible disadvantage of this method as a means of motivating machinists.

rates, is a payment for achieving a target. For example, car salespeople may get a commission of US$200 for each car they sell. Some white-collar workers are paid entirely on commission. A salesperson, for example, may be paid entirely on the basis of their sales record. Alternatively, a worker may be paid a basic salary and then receive commission on top. Commission-based pay systems are intended to 'incentivise' workers by tying in pay with output.

Bonus: Some firms make **bonus** payments to workers. Bonuses are paid in addition to the basic wage or salary. They are usually paid if targets are met. For example, machine operators may be paid a bonus if they reach a weekly production target. Bonuses can also be paid to groups of workers. For example, a sales team may get a bonus if the whole team meets a sales target.

The main advantage to businesses of bonus payments is that they are only paid if targets are met. This means that money is only paid if it has been earned. Bonus payments may help to motivate employees as they work to reach a target to earn their bonus. Finally, some businesses pay their staff loyalty bonuses. These are usually paid annually, often at the end of the year. Such bonuses are not necessarily linked to productivity. They are designed to reward workers for staying with the company.

Profit sharing: Some businesses have **profit sharing** schemes. In a company, profits would normally be distributed to shareholders. Profit sharing occurs when some of the profits made are distributed to workers as well as shareholders.

Profit sharing can motivate workers to achieve the objectives of the business. Shareholders want higher profits. So too do workers if they are to receive a share of them. Profit sharing therefore unites the goals of both owners and workers for extra money. Profit sharing can also be a way of showing staff that they are appreciated. In Maslow's hierarchy of needs, it may help satisfy the need for love and belonging.

However, most individual workers will have little or no control over how much profit their company makes. If they make extra effort to raise sales or reduce costs, the benefit of that extra effort will be shared between all the other workers. There is no link between individual effort and individual reward in profit sharing. Profit sharing is also unlikely to motivate financially if the amount received is fairly small.

One example of a company that uses profit-related pay is the Chinese telecoms giant, Huawei. This employee-owned organisation appears to reward staff generously. A few years ago the amount paid to employees' in salaries, bonuses and dividends was 2.8 times the company's annual net profit. Huawei hope to increase this ratio to 3:1 very soon.

Performance-related pay: Performance-related pay (PRP) is a pay system designed specifically to motivate staff. Introduced in the 1980s and 1990s, it is now used widely in a number of countries among white-collar workers, especially in the financial services industry, such as banking, and in the public sector.

PRP gives workers extra pay for achieving targets. The extra pay may be a fixed sum such as US$2000 or it could be a percentage of salary. Some PRP systems make distinctions between levels of achievement. For example, one worker may be rated 'excellent' and receive a 10 per cent bonus, another 'good' and receive a 5 per cent bonus, another 'satisfactory' and receive no bonus.

The targets are likely to be set through a system of appraisal. This is where the performance of individual staff is reviewed against a set of criteria. These criteria could include factors such as arriving for work on time, ability to get on with other workers, improving skills through training or achieving a particular task within the job. Staff are likely to have a performance appraisal interview where someone more senior, such as their line manager, conducts the appraisal.

PRP is widely used because it directly links performance with pay. According to the scientific management school, it should motivate workers to achieve the goals set for them by the organisation.

However, PRP and performance appraisal have been widely criticised for a number of reasons.

- The bonus may be too low to give workers an incentive to achieve their targets.
- Achieving the targets may have far more to do with the smooth running of machinery or technological systems, or how a group of workers perform than the performance of an individual. For example, a worker may set a goal of increasing forms processed by 5 per cent. But the number of forms she receives may depend on how many are processed by other members of her team or whether the printing machines are working smoothly. Where teamworking is an important management tool, it is likely to be better to give bonuses based on the output of a team rather than an individual.
- Targets may be difficult or even impossible to achieve in the eyes of workers. If this is the case, then they are unlikely to make any effort to achieve them.
- Few staff see appraisal as an independent objective procedure. Staff are quite likely to put their failure to achieve a grade in an appraisal interview down to the unfairness of the interviewer. This is particularly true when there are already problems in the relationship between, say, a worker and his or her boss. Staff who do achieve highly in appraisal interviews may be seen by others as 'favourites' of the interviewer.

Failure to receive a high enough grade in the appraisal process may act as a demotivator of staff. Instead of staff wanting to improve their performance, they may simply give up attempting to change their behaviour and attitudes. Failure to receive a PRP bonus could challenge the physiological needs of staff in Maslow's hierarchy of needs because it deprives them of money. It could also make them feel less 'loved' by the organisation, challenging their need for love and belonging. It will almost certainly knock their self-esteem.

ACTIVITY 3   SKILLS ▷ ANALYSIS

CASE STUDIES: PRP IN FOOTBALL

An increasing number of football clubs around the world are making more use of performance-related pay in their organisations. One reason for this is to avoid a situation where an expensive player ends up 'seeing out' his €50,000 per week contract by playing in the reserves or sitting on the substitute's bench. This might happen because he suddenly loses form or because the player was purchased by a manager who has now been replaced. Also, a new ruling by UEFA called Financial Fair Play means that clubs have to be more financially responsible and transparent. This has put pressure on clubs to lower their costs.

Football clubs are now reviewing their remuneration systems. There is a shift towards lower basic pay and a larger variable element linked to performance. In football there are two main approaches to determining performance-related pay. One is to reward players for team success – team bonuses for promotion or winning a trophy, for example. The problem with 'team rewards' is that not every player makes an equal contribution. Alternatively, individual incentives can be offered for certain contributions – individual bonuses, for goals scored, the number of 'assists' or the number of 'duals' won, for example. However, there is a problem here too. Historically, the analytical tools used to measure player performance lack sophistication, although they have improved in recent years. They are not able to reward players without affecting their conscious decision making during games. For example:

- goal bonuses encourage players to shoot instead of passing
- assist bonuses encourage players to pass instead of shooting
- rewarding pass-completion percentage means players will play too cautiously
- rewarding forward passes means they will take too many risks.

Generally, if players' incentives are linked to such shallow and one-dimensional measures of performance they will focus on the numbers and creativity in football will be stifled.

However, there is not likely to be a reverse of current remuneration trends. Also, the statistical analysis of player performance is improving. One British company, Opta Sports, leads the world in analysing live sports data. It gathers information from 35 different leagues around the world and monitors the games from a live video stream in locations such as London, Manchester, Munich, Madrid, Milan, Paris, Amsterdam, Montevideo and New York. Three analysts are employed per match. One covers the home team, one the away team and a third monitors quality control. For example, when a free-kick is hit into a defensive wall and play continues, the first two will carry on in their individual roles. However, the third person reviews their footage and assigns the block to a player in the wall. A spokesperson said, 'We measure passes by using a mouse over a grid of an overhead view of the pitch and hot keys… There are 16 different types of pass in our categorisation such as long ball, high ball and through-ball and we're very clear when it comes to differentiating the various classifications.'

One club that has embraced this level of sophistication in their pay structures is Liverpool FC. Liverpool CE, Ian Ayres, said that the club's Performance and Analysis team spend a lot of time analysing performance and structuring pay deals.

This means that when an offer is made to a player that includes performance-related elements, the data can be used, not just to show how much they can earn, but also show how achievable it is. Ayres also said that the system was working well for them and that the players were a 'happy bunch'.

1. What is performance-related pay?
2. Explain **one** reason why football clubs are introducing performance-related pay.
3. Explain **one** possible problem of using performance-related play to reward footballers.

NON-FINANCIAL METHODS TO IMPROVE STAFF PERFORMANCE

Financial rewards have often been used in the past by firms in an attempt to motivate employees to improve productivity. However, increasingly businesses have realised that:

- the chance to earn more money may not be an effective motivator
- financial incentive schemes are difficult to operate
- individual reward schemes may no longer be effective as production has become organised into group tasks
- other factors may be more important in motivating employees.

If other factors are more important than pay in motivating workers, it is important for firms to identify them. Only then can a business make sure its workforce is motivated.

Delegation: In some situations a manager may hand a more complex task to a subordinate. This is called delegation. The manager will still have responsibility, but authority is passed down the hierarchy. However, time can be saved if a subordinate completes the task. Sometimes delegation can motivate workers. This is because they feel they are being trusted to carry out more difficult work. Delegation is most likely to improve motivation if managers:

- only delegate when their workload is too high, otherwise subordinates may feel the delegation is unfair

- take time to explain the tasks carefully and be sure subordinates have the skills to complete them
- give subordinates complete authority to carry out the task and that colleagues are aware of the delegation
- do not interfere with delegated tasks
- provide the support and resources that are needed to carry out the delegated task.

Consultation: Staff often complain when changes are made and they are not consulted. For example, if a business introduced flexible working hours so that it could remain open 7 days a week without consulting staff, it is likely that the workforce would be displeased. If staff are consulted by employers when changes are proposed they are more likely to feel that their views are valued. This can improve motivation. Consultation has other advantages. Changes are less likely to be resisted if staff are consulted. It is also possible that employees may have ideas of their own that could benefit the business. Such ideas can only be expressed if there is a proper consultation process. However, some might argue that consultation takes too long and slows down the process of change. Also, some see consultation as a 'shallow' process where the views of workers are heard but then ignored.

Empowerment: Delegated decision making can be more successful if employees are empowered. Empowerment of employees involves a number of aspects.

- Recognising that employees are capable of doing more than they have in the past.
- Making employees feel trusted, so that they can carry out their jobs without constant checking.
- Giving employees control of decision making.
- Giving employees self-confidence.
- Recognising employees' achievements.
- Developing a work environment where employees are motivated and interested in their work.

Many businesses now recognise the need to empower employees. There are a number of advantages of this for a business and for employees.

- Employees may feel more motivated. They feel trusted and feel that businesses recognise their talents. This should improve productivity and benefit the business in the long term, for example by reducing absenteeism.
- Employees may find less stress in their work as they have greater control over their working lives. This could reduce illness and absenteeism.
- Decisions may be made by those most suited to make them. Also, employees may feel less frustrated that senior staff who are less equipped to make decisions are making them.
- There may be greater employee skills and personal development.
- Businesses may be able to make their organisations more efficient and delegate decision making.

- Workers may feel less frustrated by more senior staff making decisions which they feel may be incorrect.

However, empowerment is sometimes criticised as simply a means of cutting costs and removing layers from the business. Passing decision making down the hierarchy might allow a company to make managers redundant. Employees are given more work to do, but for the same pay. Some businesses argue that they want to empower workers, but in practice they are unable or unwilling to do this. For example, a manager may feel insecure about subordinates making decisions that might affect his position in the business. Feeling that they may 'make the wrong decision' might lead to constant interruptions which are counter-productive. A further problem is the cost involved to the business, such as the cost of training employees or changing the workplace.

Teamworking: The Swedish car firm Volvo is a well-known example of a company that has effectively introduced 'teamwork'. In both its plants at Kalmar and Uddevalla, it set up production in teams of eight to ten highly skilled workers. The teams decided between themselves how work was to be distributed and how to solve problems that arise. It is questionable whether these practices led to an increase in productivity, but the company firmly believed that this method of organisation was better than an assembly line system. Teamworking has a number of benefits.

- Productivity may be greater because of combined talents.
- People can specialise and draw on the skills and knowledge of others in the team.
- Increasingly businesses are finding that the abilities of teams are needed to solve difficult business problems.
- Responsibility is shared. People may be more prepared to take risks.
- Ideas may be created through group discussions.
- It allows flexible working.

However, in practice teamwork does not always produce the desired results. Part of the problem may lie in the way teams are organised. Members may fail to work well together for several reasons, from lack of a sense of humour to conflicting goals. Studies of teams in the USA have shown a number of problems with teamwork.

- Too much emphasis on harmony. Teams probably work best when there is room for disagreement. Hiding differences sometimes leads to vague or bland recommendations.
- Too much disagreement and argument. Tension can destroy team effectiveness.
- Poor preparation. It is important that team members prepare for meetings by focusing on the facts. Members should have a detailed knowledge of the issues at hand and all work with the same information.

- Too much emphasis on individualism. For example, teams may fail to deliver results if the emphasis of the company is placed on individualism.
- A feeling of powerlessness. To work well, teams must be able to influence decisions.
- The failure of senior management to work well together. This creates problems because team members may walk into meetings with different priorities.
- Unnecessary meetings. Teams should not try to do everything together. Too many meetings waste the team's time.
- Seeing teams as the solution for all problems. Some tasks are better accomplished by individuals, rather than groups.

Flexible working: Employing a flexible workforce has a number of benefits for a business. For example, it can cope with small changes in demand more easily and extend opening hours. However, flexible working may also help to motivate workers. This is most likely if staff can choose their hours of work, work from home or take lengthy periods of leave, for example. Flexible working is discussed in detail in Chapter 14.

Job enrichment: The idea of **job enrichment** came from Herzberg's two-factor theory. Job enrichment attempts to give employees greater responsibility by 'vertically' extending their role in the production process. An employee, for example, may be given responsibility for planning a task, quality control, work supervision, ordering materials and maintenance.

Job enrichment gives employees a 'challenge', which will develop their 'unused' skills and encourage them to be more productive. The aim is to make workers feel they have been rewarded for their contribution to the company. Employees will also be provided with varied tasks, which may possibly lead to future promotion. It is not, however, without problems. Workers who feel that they are unable to carry out the 'extra work', or who consider that they are forced into it, may not respond to incentives. In addition, it is unlikely that all workers will react the same to job enrichment. Trade unions sometimes argue that such practices are an attempt to reduce the labour force, and disputes about the payment for extra responsibilities may arise. In practice, job enrichment has been found to be most successful in administrative and technical positions.

Job rotation: **Job rotation** involves an employee changing jobs or tasks from time to time. This could mean, for example, a move to a different part of the production line to carry out a different task. Alternatively, an employee may be moved from the human resources to the marketing department where they have skills which are common to both. From an employee's point of view this should reduce boredom and enable a variety of skills and experience to be gained. An employer might also benefit from a more widely trained workforce.

Although job rotation may motivate a worker, it is possible that any gains in productivity may be offset by a fall in output as workers learn new jobs and take time to 'settle in'. Worker motivation is not guaranteed if the employee is simply switched from one boring job to another. In fact some workers do not like the uncertainty that job changes lead to and may become dissatisfied. Although used by firms such as Volkswagen in the past, where employees carried out a variety of production tasks, job rotation has declined in popularity.

Job enlargement: **Job enlargement** involves giving an employee more work to do of a similar nature. For example, instead of an employee putting wheels onto a bicycle he could be allowed to put the entire product together. It is argued that this variety prevents boredom with one repetitive task and encourages employees' satisfaction in their work, as they are completing the entire process. Job enlargement is more efficient if workers are organised in groups. Each worker can be trained to do all jobs in the group and job rotation can take place. Other forms of job enlargement include job rotation and job loading.

Critics of this method argue that it is simply giving a worker 'more of the same'. It is often called the problem of horizontal loading – instead of turning five screws the worker turns ten. In many businesses today such tasks are carried out more effectively by machines, where repetitive tasks can be completed quickly and efficiently without strain, boredom or dissatisfaction. It could even be argued that allowing employees to complete the entire process will reduce efficiency. This is because the fall in productivity from carrying out many tasks is greater than any productivity gains from increased worker satisfaction.

EXAM HINT

Do not confuse job enlargement with job enrichment. They are similar, but not the same. Remember that job enrichment 'vertically' extends the job by giving an employee greater responsibility. Job enlargement expands the job 'horizontally' by giving an employee 'more of the same'.

SUBJECT VOCABULARY

bonus a payment in addition to the basic wage for reaching targets or in recognition for service.
commission percentage payment on a sale made to the salesperson.
consultation listening to the views of employees before making key decisions that affect them.
delegation the passing of authority further down the managerial hierarchy.
empowerment giving official authority to employees to make decisions and control their own work activities.
Hawthorne effect the idea that workers are motivated by recognition given to them as a group.
hygiene or **maintenance factors (Herzberg's)** things at work that result in dissatisfaction.
job enlargement giving an employee more work to do of a similar nature; 'horizontally' extending their work role.
job enrichment giving employees greater responsibility and recognition by 'vertically' extending their work role.
job rotation the periodic changing of jobs or tasks.
Maslow's hierarchy of needs the order of people's needs starting with basic human requirements.
motivated the desire to take action to achieve a goal.
motivators (Herzberg's) things at work that result in satisfaction.
payment by results payment methods that reward workers for the quantity and quality of work they produce.
performance-related pay (PRP) a payment system designed for non-manual workers where pay increases are given if performance targets are met.
piece rates a payment system where employees are paid an agreed rate for every item produced.
profit sharing where workers are given a share of the profits, usually as part of their pay.
scientific management a theory that suggests there is a 'best way' to perform work tasks.
self-actualisation a level in Maslow's hierarchy where people realise their full potential.
teamworking organising people into working groups that have a common aim.

CHECKPOINT

1. State three reasons why it is important for a business to motivate staff.

2. What method of pay might Taylor recommend to help motivate staff?

3. What helps to motivate people at work according to Mayo?

4. What is meant by self-actualisation needs in Maslow's hierarchy of needs?

5. How might a business meet its workers' esteem needs?

6. What is the difference between piece rates and performance-related pay?

7. How might profit sharing motivate workers?

8. State two advantages of flexible working to employees.

9. Give two advantages of delegation as a means of motivating staff.

10. What is the difference between job enrichment and job enlargement?

11. How might job rotation help to motivate staff?

12. State two advantages of job enrichment to a business.

EXAM PRACTICE

KAPLINSKY MARINE

SKILLS ANALYSIS, INTERPRETATION, PROBLEM SOLVING

Poland has a history of exporting boats. One Polish boat-maker, Kaplinsky Marine, produces luxury yachts. The process of building a yacht is highly complex and requires specialised technical knowledge. Over many years of trading Kaplinsky Marine has developed a highly skilled and well-motivated workforce. The company has created a team of specialists, each highly qualified within their field and who work with shared passion, enthusiasm and commitment. In 2017, the company employed 340 staff and made a profit of PLN 35.5 million.

Arguably, key to its success, are the methods used to motivate staff and the way production is organised. All staff, after 2 years' service, receive profit-related pay. In addition to their basic annual salary, employees receive 0.05 per cent of the profit made by the business each year. This arrangement was agreed in 2011 after an employee vote showed 87 per cent support for its introduction. A lot of other attractive benefits can be enjoyed. For example, there is a non-contributory pension scheme (which the employer pays into even if the employee pays nothing), a free fitness centre and sports club, 21 days paid holiday and a free breakfast. The canteen also provides subsidised meals throughout the rest of the day.

The workforce is divided into teams of around 20. Each team concentrates on a specific process, task or business area. For example, they focus on design, hull-making, joinery, assembly, fitting, finishing, administration, marketing and finance. Despite using state-of-the art tools and machinery in production, boat-building is still very much a manual process. Every aspect of the boat – interior and exterior – is worked on by hand.

Every new employee recruited to a team undergoes a 6–12-month training period and is assigned to a mentor – an experienced member of staff with special responsibility for mentoring. The mentor system was introduced to improve training and enrich the jobs of experienced workers. They are sought-after roles and carry a special allowance.

Kaplinsky makes use of flexible working in its organisation. For example, it offers term-time only contracts for parents, 4-day per week contracts and unpaid long-term leave. It has also shortened the hours of some office-based staff in return for extending opening hours from 7.00 a.m. to 7.00 p.m. Office staff work from either 7.00 a.m. to 1.00 p.m. or 1.00 p.m. to 7.00 p.m. They are free to switch shifts to suit their personal needs provided the office is fully staffed for the 12-hour working day. Staff are also encouraged to switch teams and learn new skills – particularly in production.

In 2017, the HR department carried out an internal survey interviewing every member of the workforce. It was found that:

- 94 per cent felt that their employment at the company was secure
- 87 per cent felt valued by the company
- 93 per cent said the company provided opportunities to reach their full potential and learn new skills
- 88 per cent said that managers/team leaders were supportive and open
- 79 per cent of staff were happy with their remuneration and benefits.

Q

(a) (i) Define profit-related pay. **(2 marks)**
    (ii) Calculate the annual profit-related bonus per employee in 2017. **(4 marks)**

(b) Explain one possible drawback of profit-related pay. **(4 marks)**

(c) Explain how Kaplinsky Marine uses flexible working to help motivate its staff. **(4 marks)**

(d) Assess the extent to which Kaplinsky Marine meets the needs of employees as identified by Maslow. **(10 marks)**

18 LEADERSHIP

LEARNING OBJECTIVES

By the end of this chapter you should be able to understand:
- leadership: the distinction between management and leadership
- types of leadership style: autocratic, paternalistic, democratic and laissez-faire
- the difficulty of moving from entrepreneur to leader.

GETTING STARTED

Kim Dong-won worked for a South Korean toy manufacturer helping to make teddy bears and other soft toys. He disliked his job and spent at least 10 hours every week searching for another. The main problem was his boss. The managing director of the company was unpopular with everyone. He was rarely to be seen and did not know the names of the 21 staff that worked for him. In the last 15 weeks Mr Kim had spoken to him twice. On both occasions he called him Mr Lee and failed to listen to his answer after asking a question. All decisions were made by the managing director without consultation. Staff turnover at the company was 41 per cent and the working atmosphere was very negative.

Describe the approach to leadership used by the managing director in this case. Explain why this approach may not be working. What characteristics might it be useful for leaders to have? Does every person have the potential to lead?

THE DISTINCTION BETWEEN MANAGEMENT AND LEADERSHIP

Management has a number of functions. For example, managers, according to the management theorist Henri Fayol, should predict what will happen in the future, plan to achieve their objectives, organise resources, exercise command over staff lower down the hierarchy, co-ordinate day-to-day tasks and monitor how well objectives are being achieved. Peter Drucker, writing 40 years later, *The Practice of Management*, added to this list motivating and communicating with staff, and giving them training opportunities.

Some writers make no distinction between management and leadership in an organisation. Managers are leaders because of the roles they play. Others, however, suggest that leaders are not necessarily the same as managers.

Leaders may perform the same functions as managers. But in addition, they may do some or all of the following.
- Leaders can be visionaries, understanding where an organisation is at today and seeing the direction in which an organisation has to change to survive and grow.
- Leaders tend to be good at carrying through the process of change. Because they understand the starting point and the end point, they can chart a route from one to the other. Where others may see only chaos and think the organisation is taking the wrong road, the leader has the ability to see through the details and small setbacks which are a part of any change.
- Leaders are often excellent at motivating those around them, allowing them to perform at their best. They are particularly good at motivating others to change both themselves and the organisation.

It could be argued that, in large businesses, leaders create strategies while managers are responsible for implementing them. However, sometimes leaders do get involved in implementation because they appreciate that it is just as important to implement change as it is to create strategies. In small businesses, leaders often have the skills to both create and carry out a strategy.

THE CHARACTERISTICS OF LEADERS

One approach to finding out what makes good leaders is to identify the qualities, characteristics or traits that they should have (see Figure 1). A number of characteristics have been suggested.
- Effective leaders have a positive self-image, backed up with a genuine ability and realistic ambitions. This is shown in the confidence they have. An example might be Richard Branson, in his various innovative business activities. Leaders also appreciate their own strengths and weaknesses. It is argued that many managers fail to lead because they spend too much time focusing on short-term activity.
- Leaders need to be able to get to the 'core' of a problem and have the vision and commitment to suggest radical solutions. For example, after working at Apple for a period of time, Steve Jobs left in 1985. However, he returned in 1996 to help recover the company's successful position. Steve Jobs cut the number of Apple development projects from 350 to 10. He was then responsible for launching the iMac®, the iPod®, iTunes® and the iPhone. Jobs helped Apple's shares to rise by 9000 per cent.

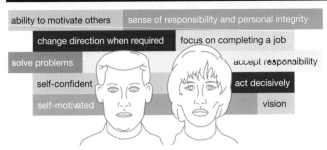

▲ Figure 1 Leadership traits

- Studies of leaders in business suggest that they are experts in particular fields and well read in everything else. They tend to be 'out of the ordinary', intelligent and excellent communicators. Examples might be Anita Roddick, the founder of Body Shop, or Bill Gates, the founder of Microsoft.
- Leaders are often creative and innovative. They tend to seek new solutions to problems, make sure that important things are done and try to improve standards.
- Leaders often have the ability to sense change and can respond to it. This is dealt with later in this chapter.

LEADERSHIP STYLES

Successful businesses often have very good leaders. However, the style of leadership adopted by individual leaders may be very different. Some of the most common leadership styles are outlined below.

Autocratic leadership: An autocratic leadership style is one where the manager sets objectives, allocates tasks and insists that instructions are obeyed. Therefore the group become dependent on him or her. The result of this style is that members of the group are often dissatisfied with the leader. This results in little teamwork, the need for high levels of supervision, and poor levels of motivation among employees.

Autocratic leadership may be needed in certain circumstances. For example, in the armed forces there may be a need to move troops quickly and for orders to be obeyed instantly.

Paternalistic leadership: Paternalistic leaders are similar to autocratic leaders. They make all the decisions and expect subordinates to obey these decisions. However, whereas an autocratic leader may be uninterested in the well-being of subordinates, a paternalistic leader places

---

ACTIVITY 1   SKILLS   LEADERSHIP, REASONING, CRITICAL THINKING

CASE STUDY: DA HINGGAN AIRLINES

Wen Ailing was appointed CEO of Da Hinggan Airlines, China, in 2010. The airline company was suffering difficulties given the success of competitors who were quicker at adapting to market trends. When Wen Ailing was appointed she identified that slow decision making was a key reason why this problem kept occurring. She felt that there were too many levels of management and too many people had to discuss and approve decisions before change could happen. To stop this being an issue, Ailing took rapid action and made 50 people redundant, removing an entire management layer and placing herself closer to key people in the organisation's structure.

Ailing could be described as an autocratic leader. She makes all the key decisions and when she passes these down to her management team, she expects them to be implemented without any question. Ailing has many of the qualities of a successful leader – she is ambitious and confident, and decisive and dominant. Furthermore, she is a dynamic leader and is popular with her shareholders, if not always with the staff members below her. Her popularity with shareholders might be due to how her decisiveness affects the revenue of the company. Figure 2 shows the substantial increase in revenue growth trends under Wen Ailing's leadership.

In 2013, a cloud of volcanic dust from an erupting volcano was heading towards the airline flightpaths. Following guidelines regarding air safety the government grounded all flights. Ailing felt that the closure was maintained for too long and started flying planes before the ban had been fully lifted, with no problems. The ban was lifted after this and Ailing proved herself a strong leader, willing to risk her personal reputation.

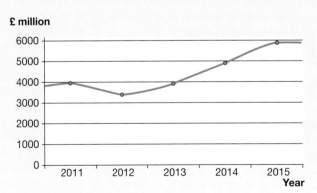

▲ Figure 2 Da Hinggan Airlines revenue, 2011–15

1. Assess the advantages and disadvantages to Da Hinggan Airlines of employing an autocratic leader.

a great deal of importance on their welfare. Historically, there have been a number of paternalistic leaders, such as Joseph Rowntree and George Cadbury, in the UK. Examples of their concern for employees included the building of new houses, which they could rent at low rates. As with autocratic leaders, paternalistic leaders do not give subordinates control over decision making.

Democratic leadership: A democratic leadership style encourages involvement in decision making. Democratic leadership styles can be persuasive or consultative.

- **Persuasive.** This is where a leader has already made a decision, but takes the time to persuade others that it is a good idea. For example, the owner of a business may decide to employ outside staff for certain jobs and persuade existing staff that this may ease their workload.
- **Consultative.** This is where a leader consults others about their views before making a decision. The decision will take into account these views. For example, the views of the marketing department about whether to launch a new range of products may be considered.

Democratic leadership styles need good communication skills. The leaders must be able to explain ideas clearly to employees and understand any feedback they receive.

It may mean, however, that decisions take a long time to be reached as lengthy consultation can take place.

It has been suggested that a democratic style of leadership can be more effective in business for a number of reasons.

- There has been increased public involvement in social and political life. Democratic management reflects this trend.
- Increasing income and educational standards means that people now expect greater freedom and a better quality of working life.
- Research suggests that this style is generally more effective. Managers are able to 'tap into' the ideas of people with knowledge and experience. This can lead to better decisions being made.
- People involved in the decision making process are likely to be more committed and motivated, to accept decisions reached with their help, to trust managers who make the decisions, and to volunteer new and creative ideas.

Laissez-faire leadership: A laissez-faire leadership style is more of a 'hands-off' approach to leadership. A laissez-faire leader provides others with the proper tools and resources needed, and then moves away. The leader gives little guidance and direction, and allows

ACTIVITY 2   SKILLS   LEADERSHIP, ANALYSIS

CASE STUDY: WARREN BUFFETT

Warren Buffett is one of the wealthiest individuals in the world. In 1964, he was appointed CEO of Berkshire Hathaway, now a US multinational holding company. The company owns businesses in a wide range of industrial sectors, such as confectionery, retail, railways, furniture, vacuum cleaners, jewellery and newspaper publishing, as well as several regional electric and gas utilities. In 2016, the business employed 367,000 people and generated US$223,604 million in revenue.

Warren Buffett is known internationally as an investment guru as a result of his success in buying businesses and watching them grow. His leadership style is widely reported as laissez-faire. He allows subsidiary heads lots of freedom. In his 2009 letter to shareholders he said, 'We tend to let our many subsidiaries operate on their own, without our supervising and monitoring them to any degree', and that most managers 'use the independence we grant them magnificently, rewarding our confidence by maintaining an owner-oriented attitude that is seldom found in huge organisations.'

Some people argue that a laissez-faire style of leadership results in low levels of productivity. However, in the case of Berkshire Hathaway it was widely reported to have worked well. This might be because Warren Buffett was effective in hiring talented and well-motivated people to run the various businesses. He also gave them complete independence and enough resources to enable them to meet company objectives. However, if these employees needed guidance or support, Warren was available for consultation. It was also widely reported that laissez-faire leadership worked well because each business had its own culture, and each person appointed by Warren understood the way that each particular business worked.

Source: adapted from www.berkshirehathaway.com

1. Explain the style of leadership used by Warren Buffett.
2. Explain one reason why this style of leadership has been successful at Berkshire Hathaway.
3. Assess the possible benefits to Berkshire Hathaway of this style of leadership.

others the freedom to make decisions. This leadership style can be effective when the group members are highly skilled, experienced, motivated and capable of working on their own. However, it is not ideal in many situations. This is particularly the case if others lack the experience or knowledge needed to complete the tasks or make decisions. Also, some people are not capable at setting their own deadlines or managing their own projects. Some people in the group may also lack the motivation needed to get certain tasks done on time. Such people usually need an 'extra push' from the leader. As a result deadlines may be missed, which could cost a business money.

MOVING FROM ENTREPRENEUR TO LEADER

If an entrepreneur sets up a business and it becomes successful, the role of the entrepreneur is likely to change as the business expands. Running a sole trader business with two employees and a turnover of £250,000 is different from the challenge of running a large plc with 59,000 employees and a turnover of £3600 million. The change in role stems from the need to deal with growth. For example, there is likely to be a growth in the:

- number of employees
- number and size of financial transactions
- number and size of customers
- amount of regulation
- quantity of resources used
- level and range of communication needed.

The transition from entrepreneur to leader is likely to require a number of changes in the way the business is run. This usually means that entrepreneurs have to adapt and perform different functions.

The need for formality: Small businesses can be run on an informal basis. This means that communication takes place without the need for regular structured meetings, detailed documentation or official communication channels. They employ just a few employees and communication between them can be ongoing as they are likely to be working in close proximity to each other. Decisions can be made swiftly because the entrepreneur is always at hand. However, in a large organisation, where the entrepreneur becomes a leader, there is a need for formality. Communication between thousands of employees requires systems and formal structures. The business is likely to be split up into departments or divisions. There will have to be formal communication channels that are recognised and approved by all staff. There will be a need for a formal organisational structure so that the business can be controlled and employees brought to account. The entrepreneur in a small business may become a chairperson or a senior executive in a large business.

The need for shared ownership: When businesses grow they need capital to fund expansion. To obtain funding it is sometimes necessary to invite new owners to contribute capital. For very large corporations this usually means selling shares and operating as a plc. Entrepreneurs begin their business life as sole owners, but often end up having to share ownership with others. Ownership is likely to be shared with financial institutions, such as pension funds and insurance companies, as well as an army of very small investors.

Greater responsibility to others: An entrepreneur running a small business is only likely to have responsibility for a small number of employees. However, when a business grows into a corporation the number of people employed could be tens of thousands or more. The livelihoods of these people will often rest on the decisions made by the leader. This is an enormous responsibility. A leader may also have responsibility to other stakeholders, such as shareholders, and a far larger number of suppliers and customers.

The need for motivation and inspiration: As the size of the business grows there is a need to focus more on the workforce. This is because there are a lot more people to manage. As entrepreneurs develop into leaders, there is a greater need for motivational skills. Some people are self-motivated but most people need encouragement and well-defined goals, which leaders have to provide. Workers are likely to look to the leader for support and inspiration. Leaders also have to develop the talents of others.

The need for strategy and vision: In a small business the owner is likely to be involved in production and other business functions, such as marketing, finance and administration. However, as the business expands, specialists undertake most of these tasks. The leader becomes more concerned with designing business strategies and providing a vision for the future direction of the company. However, there are exceptions to this. For example, television chef Jamie Oliver is the leader of a sizable catering and restaurant business but is still involved in cooking in various kitchens in his organisation. Some of the people who have made a success of the transition from entrepreneur to leader include Richard Branson (the Virgin brand), Michelle Mone (founder of Ultimo), Lord Sugar (computers), Deborah Meaden (holiday business) and Hilary Devey (logistics). They all began their careers with modest business start-ups and developed into successful leaders of large corporations.

THE DIFFICULTIES IN DEVELOPING FROM AN ENTREPRENEUR TO A LEADER

When dealing with the changes required in the transition from entrepreneur to leader, inevitably there will be difficulties.

Adapting the mindset: Entrepreneurs usually have a desire for greater control over their life, career and destiny. They want more autonomy and to do things in their own way. However, a different mindset is needed when the business expands. Leaders have to relinquish some control and learn to delegate and focus on different things. They have to believe that specialists will do a better job in certain fields and that they cannot do everything themselves. For some people this is very difficult. They may have doubts, fears and a lack of trust that could create a barrier to development.

Stress: Running a business is stressful. The livelihood of entrepreneurs and their families are dependent upon the success of the business. There is the constant worry that the business 'won't provide' and what will happen if the business collapses? One major cause of stress is the worry that debtors will fail to pay what they owe. However, if the business grows it is likely that it is being successful. But with growth comes more stress, as there is more at stake. The business may have borrowed money that must be repaid. There are more staff and more responsibilities, with an increased scope for conflict because more people are involved. Conflict is a common cause of stress in larger organisations. Some stakeholders have different needs that might cause conflict. For example, workers may want a wage increase but customers want stable or lower prices. The threat of a strike would cause stress in such cases.

Sharing ownership and control: Some entrepreneurs may struggle with a loss of control when the business expands. Inviting partners, business angels or shareholders to contribute capital means that business ownership is shared. It also means that future profits have to be shared. Some entrepreneurs may also find it difficult to share control and resent others influencing the shape and direction of a business that they set up from scratch. They may feel that their leadership is being undermined, which may cause conflict.

Trust: As entrepreneurs develop as leaders, they may have problems trusting people. As the business grows there is a need to delegate and employ specialists. Some leaders find it difficult to delegate and may become suspicious of new senior staff. Where specialists are appointed, the leader may feel that the specialists know more than them. The leader may feel threatened and concerned that they are being kept in the dark or manipulated. If leaders cannot trust the new owners and staff there may be problems because employees may question whether or not the leader trusts them.

Lack of leadership qualities: As entrepreneurs take on more leadership duties there may be concern that they lack the necessary leadership skills and qualities. These might include management, communication, problem solving, decision making and organisational skills. It is true that entrepreneurs also need these skills to be successful. However, once the business grows, these skills have to be applied on a different scale. The problems are likely to be larger, decisions more important and communication more complex. For example, in communication, entrepreneurs may have to give instructions to employees, discuss specifications with a customer and meet the accountant to finalise a tax return. A high-profile business leader may meet with other leaders and politicians in Germany, speak in more than one language, write reports for shareholders and give presentations to the media. Such demands may cause problems for some entrepreneurs as they develop into leaders.

OVERCOMING DIFFICULTIES

The changes required in the transition from entrepreneur to business leader are substantial. It is easy to see why many business owners are happy to remain small traders, maybe preferring a lifestyle business. However, despite the difficulties outlined above, some people do make the transition successfully. They learn to adapt and overcome the difficulties. They might use a number of methods, including those listed below.

Delegation and trust: A successful business leader must be comfortable with delegation. The delegation of tasks to specialists and experts will improve the performance of the business. A good leader will surround themselves with talented, honest and trustworthy people. Leaders can reduce the risk in recruitment if they employ a thorough and effective recruitment process. The ability to delegate and trust will reduce stress.

Earn respect: Many of the difficulties outlined above can be overcome if a leader can earn respect from all stakeholders. People will be more trustworthy, effective and flexible if they are treated well. This means meeting their needs at work, praising them when they excel, being fair but tough, open and honest. Respect might also be earned if the organisational culture is open, positive and accepted.

Maturity and experience: Some people are born leaders. They find leadership natural and have the charisma and leadership qualities needed to be successful. However, others may develop into good leaders. Through maturity, experience, drive and learning from mistakes, they can overcome any difficulties they may encounter. The transition from entrepreneur to corporate leader may be a lengthy one.

Education: Some of the leadership skills can be learned by attending specialist courses. There are countless courses designed to help business people improve management, negotiation, communication and decision-making skills. Additional languages can be taught, as can report writing and IT skills.

Reduce stress: Calm leaders are more likely to succeed than stressed leaders. Figure 3 summarises some of the measures that might be used to reduce stress.

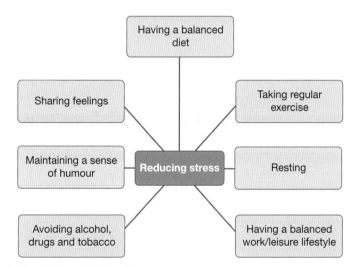

▲ Figure 3 Ways of reducing stress

CASE STUDY: MENOS DE 10S

Adriana Oliveros owns a large children's retail chain in Argentina called Menos de 10s (under 10s). She first demonstrated her entrepreneurial skills when running a baby-sitting agency while studying at college. Then, after working in a small store selling children's clothes in Rosario, she started buying very cheap housing in the city. She used the properties to provide student accommodation in Rosario. After 4 years she sold her property business for ARS 16 million.

Adriana then saw that the small store that she had previously worked in was for sale. She bought it and began building her chain – Menos de 10s. The store had been run down and needed a number of key changes to become profitable. She sourced a new and exciting product range from a number of countries in South-East Asia. She also employed young and flexible staff, who she motivated with her warm and enthusiastic brand of leadership. Adriana worked very hard opening two new shops per year for 3 years in Rosario and then six shops a year for 5 years across Argentina. Adriana is now a respected business person, the chief executive officer of Menos de 10s and has a reputation for retail development.

Adriana is now considered a highly competent leader. However, the transition from entrepreneur to leader was not without problems. Initially, she was overwhelmed by the extra responsibility. She also felt stressed out. However, she took a 4-week break about 7 years ago and realised that she needed to change her expectations of herself. She also developed some strategies for coping with stress.

1. Discuss **two** changes that might have occurred in Adriana's business role over the years.
2. Discuss **two** problems that Adriana encountered when making the transition to corporate leader.
3. Explain **two** possible methods of coping with stress.

THINKING BIGGER

The media often suggests that 'heroic' leaders are vital to making a successful business. Such leaders make things happen. They are heroes because they alone have the vision, personality and capability to bring things about in the business, either by themselves or through others. Although not denying that leaders have special qualities, it could be argued that focusing too much on leadership can create problems. For example, this approach may lead to the conclusion that a business without a heroic leader may not be able to function properly. Or it might suggest that the heroic leader is the most important thing to organisational effectiveness. It also perhaps devalues the role and importance of other employees.

There is evidence to suggest that effective businesses are those which are more concerned with the creativity of their products and organisational structures that enable those products to be produced and sold than those that rely heavily on leadership. It could be argued that the ability to teamwork, delegate and manage others effectively is more important in the daily workings of creative organisations than the qualities of heroic leadership, such as vision, command and personality.

Mainstream approaches to leadership also assume that there is agreement within organisations, i.e. that employees are generally happy to be at work and that leadership is about providing them with the direction to get the most out of them. Where there is conflict, this is often seen as being related to problems with an individual or about resistance to change. The possibility that there might be underlying conflicts associated with inequalities of wealth, status or power between leaders and subordinates is not considered. Critics argue that although businesses may appear to be based on consent, this is because leaders occupy positions in the hierarchy that enable them to suppress conflict or because subordinates have an understanding that obeying instructions is in their own 'best' interests. In other words, the absence of conflict is a consequence of dependence - subordinates depend on managers for terms and conditions, including keeping their jobs, promotion, future employment and references.

CHECKPOINT

1. What are the main differences between a leader and a manager?

2. State three different leadership traits.

3. Under what circumstances might an autocratic leadership style be particularly appropriate?

4. Some people argue that Sir Alex Ferguson (ex-manager of Manchester United) had an autocratic leadership style. To what extent do you agree with this?

5. State two disadvantages for a business of an autocratic leadership style.

6. What is the difference between an autocratic leader and a paternalistic leader?

7. What is the difference between persuasive and consultative democratic leadership?

8. State two disadvantages of democratic leadership.

9. State the main advantage of laissez-faire leadership.

10. State three ways in which the role of an entrepreneur might change as the business grows.

11. Why is there a need to introduce formality in businesses when they grow?

12. How might entrepreneurs have to adapt their mindset when developing into a leader?

SUBJECT VOCABULARY

autocratic leadership a leadership style where a manager makes all the decisions without consultation.
democratic leadership a leadership style where managers allow others to participate in decision making.
laissez-faire leadership a leadership style where employees are encouraged to make their own decisions, within certain limits.
paternalistic leadership a leadership style where the leader makes decisions but takes into account the welfare of employees.

EXAM PRACTICE

UPPSALA TRAVEL

SKILLS LEADERSHIP, INITIATIVE, ANALYSIS, INTERPRETATION, CRITICAL THINKING

Uppsala Travel based in Uppsala which is about 70 km from Stockholm, Sweden, organises specialist holidays for the 55+ age group. The company was the subject of a management buy-out in 2009 after the previous owners decided to abandon the business because of poor financial performance. The management team, led by Lotta Berglund, bought the indebted company for SEK 10. It had debts of SEK 11.7 million and was struggling due to the economic recession. The previous owners had run the business very badly. However, the new management team believed that they could manage the company much better. They aimed to counter earlier poor marketing decisions, weak leadership and to raise workforce motivation levels.

The management team raised SEK 5.5 million privately and persuaded a venture capitalist to invest a further SEK 16 million for 49 per cent of the company. Lotta Berglund was appointed CEO and some key changes were made. The company:

- redesigned its website. It was made more attractive and easier to use. The site also introduced a review system so that clients could describe their experiences and rate the company's performance
- carried out some market research to find out which types of holiday were most popular with the 55+ age group and which particular features were most important to them
- outsourced marketing to an agency with particular experience in the holiday industry
- introduced a new pay system to help motivate sales staff. The system organised sales people into three teams of eight and awarded a monthly team bonus linked to monthly sales. If teams performed well, each team member could earn up to an extra SEK 10,000 per month on top of their basic pay of SEK 150,000 per annum

- introduced an annual profit-related bonus for all staff, which was paid just before Christmas. In 2016 this amounted to SEK 33,000 each for the 50 staff employed by the company.

After a slow start the fortunes of the company started to change. Figure 4 shows the profit made from 2009 to 2016. Lotta led the company with confidence and verve. She had charm, was well liked by staff and led by example. All key decisions made by the business were discussed at management meetings. In the early days of the 'buy-out' some of these meetings were hard work and lasted for several hours – sometimes a whole day. At the end of the meetings the four senior managers and Lotta would vote on new company policies. Most of the votes were carried without opposition. Lotta also consulted staff and held voluntary meetings in work time to get their views and ideas. The new pay system introduced for sales staff was the idea of a sales assistant.

In 2016 the company made a record profit. The new website was starting to attract an increasing amount of visitors and bookings made via the website doubled in 2 years. The marketing agency was also producing good results – it was expert at placing ads that the target market would see. Finally, as the economy started to grow in 2016, consumer confidence improved and the holiday industry in general picked up. Demographics were also working in the company's favour. The proportion of people aged over 55 in Sweden is a fast-growing sector.

Profit (SEK million)

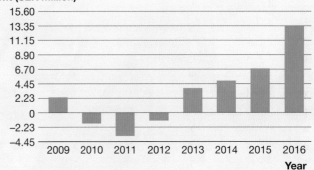

▲ Figure 4 Uppsala Travel profit after tax, 2009–2016

Q

(a) Explain one characteristic of an effective leader.
(4 marks)

(b) Explain one benefit to Uppsala Travel of Lotta's style of leadership. **(4 marks)**

(c) Evaluate whether the recent success of Uppsala Travel can be attributed to (i) Lotta's leadership or (ii) other factors. **(20 marks)**

ENTREPRENEURS AND LEADERS

In this final section of Unit 1 the role of entrepreneurs, such as risk-taking, organisation and business development, are explored, as are barriers to entrepreneurship, and the risk and uncertainty that exists in the business environment. The motives and characteristics of entrepreneurs are discussed as are the different business objectives, such as survival, profit maximisation and social objectives. Finally, the importance of opportunity cost in businesses is covered in connection with the choices businesses face and the possible trade-offs that might exist for them.

19 ROLE OF AN ENTREPRENEUR

LEARNING OBJECTIVES

By the end of this chapter you should be able to understand:

- creating and setting up a business
- running and expanding/developing a business
- innovation within a business (intrapreneurship)
- barriers to entrepreneurship
- anticipating risk and uncertainty in the business environment.

GETTING STARTED

Luisa Rosucci worked for a large US film producer for 10 years as a make-up artist. In 2011, she moved to Italy and immediately wanted to set up her own business. She considered starting a health farm, but thought that such an enterprise would cost too much to set up. After doing some market research, talking to a number of business people, and undertaking a great deal of planning, Luisa opened an 'upmarket' beauty salon in Napoli. She invested €20,000 of her own money and provided services such as hair-styling, make-up and skin treatments. The business was a success and by 2017 she employed 16 staff. The business was turning over €1.3 million per annum. Luisa now plans to develop a chain of beauty salons in Italy.

State four tasks that Luisa might have carried out before setting up her business. What resources might Luisa have needed before setting up her business? What role do entrepreneurs like Luisa play in their businesses? How might Luisa's role change if she starts to develop a chain of salons?

CREATING AND SETTING UP A BUSINESS

The role of entrepreneurs: Entrepreneurs are people who have a business idea and want to make money working for themselves. They are the owners of a business and without them the business would not exist. The roles played by entrepreneurs in business are summarised below.

- Entrepreneurs are innovators because they try to make money out of a business idea. Such ideas might come from spotting a gap in the market, a new invention or market research. However, many people set up a business by copying or adapting what another business does. Business ideas are discussed below.
- Entrepreneurs are responsible for organising other factors of production. They buy or hire resources, such as materials, labour and equipment. These resources are used to make or deliver products. Organising involves giving instructions, making arrangements and setting up systems.
- Since entrepreneurs are the owners they have to make all the key decisions. They may make decisions on how to raise finance, product design, choice of production method, prices, recruitment and wages.
- Entrepreneurs are risk takers. This is because they risk losing any money they put into the business if it fails. However, if the business is successful they will be rewarded with profit. The risks faced by entrepreneurs are discussed below.

Risks and rewards for entrepreneurs: In 2015, 581,000 new businesses were set up in the UK. This was expected to rise to over 600,000 in 2016. However, less than one-half of these were predicted to survive beyond 5 years. Starting up a new business offers the potential for high rewards. Some entrepreneurs, like Richard Branson, Stelios Haji-Ioannou and Martha Stewart, have become rich through developing their own businesses. Starting a new business also offers a chance for many people to do something different. If nothing else, it means working for yourself rather than for someone else.

However, being an entrepreneur is risky. The downside of success is business failure. If the business fails, it may leave debts to be paid off. The entrepreneur might have borrowed money to start the business or to finance growth. Getting back into a normal job may also be difficult, especially if the entrepreneur left a well-paid job to set up their business. The risk of failure is a major motivator for entrepreneurs to carry on and make a success of their enterprise even when faced with challenges.

Success and failure have an opportunity cost. The opportunity cost of an activity is the benefits lost from the next best alternative. For example, an entrepreneur who has just started up a business might have left a job earning €40,000 a year. Part of the opportunity cost of setting up the business would then be the benefits gained from earning €40,000 a year. They would only be part of the opportunity cost because the job would probably have had other benefits too, including the satisfaction from doing the job. For a successful entrepreneur, the opportunity cost of being an entrepreneur is likely to be lower than the benefits of owning a business. For an unsuccessful entrepreneur, the opportunity cost is likely to be higher. This is why the unsuccessful entrepreneur is likely to close the business and move on to something else.

Entrepreneurs and business ideas: Each year, hundreds of thousands of people set themselves up in business. Instead of working for someone else, they become the owner. Or, they move from owning one business to owning another business. If they are successful, they may start to own and set up a string of businesses. But how do most would-be entrepreneurs find a business idea? There are a number of ways.

Business experience: For most people starting a small business, the business idea comes from their existing job. A plumber might work for a plumbing company and decide to set up on her own. A marketing consultant working for an advertising agency sets up his own marketing agency. This is likely to be the most risk-free way of setting up a business because the would-be entrepreneur already has knowledge of the market.

Personal experience: Some people draw on their personal experience outside of work to find a business idea. Some turn a hobby into a job. An amateur cyclist might buy a cycle shop. A keen gardener might set up a gardening services business. Some use their customer experience to spot a gap in the market. A mother might find it difficult to find a baby product and so set up a business to make it.

Skills: Some entrepreneurs draw on their broad skills base to start a business. A person with an administration job might judge that they have good 'people skills' and decide to set up a business in selling. A plumber might judge that in his area electricians can charge more for their work. So he gets training as an electrician and sets himself up as a self-employed electrician.

Lifestyle choices: Some business areas attract people who want to make a lifestyle change. They might want to move to the country and invest in a small holding. They might always have wanted to run a caravan site so they buy a caravan site. Or they might be retiring from a full-time job but still want to carry on working on their own. So they invest a seaside hotel that only opens for part of the year.

Stages in setting up a business: The way an entrepreneur goes about setting up a business is important. It needs to be carried out in a structured way and carefully planned. The future success of a business might depend on the quality of work undertaken during

the setting-up process. One approach to setting up a business is summarised in Figure 1.

- **Idea.** A business cannot start without an entrepreneur having a business idea. The sources of ideas are discussed above.
- **Research.** The viability of a business idea has to be researched. This might involve carrying out market research and analysing the competition to decide whether the idea is likely to work. Other research might involve meeting people, such as bankers and business people, to get advice on setting up and running a business. It may also be possible to attend a course designed for new entrepreneurs.
- **Planning.** Planning is a very important stage in setting up a business. Business planning is discussed in Chapter 23.
- **Financing.** Entrepreneurs will provide some of the money needed to set up a business. Finance may also be needed when the business is 'up and running'. Entrepreneurs have to decide how much finance they will need and which sources they will use to obtain this. Sources of finance are discussed in Chapter 24 and 25.
- **Location.** The location an entrepreneur chooses will depend on the nature of the business. Some people, such as tradespeople or tutors, offer services to the local area. Others work from home and yet offer services nationally, such as website designers. Restaurants and shops may be located close to their target market customers. Manufacturers will have to decide whether their factories will be close to business customers and suppliers, or whether they will transport their products. Certain types of business activity may need planning permission. For example, to change the use of a building from a computer repair shop to a fast-food takeaway is likely to need planning permission. This could take many months to obtain.

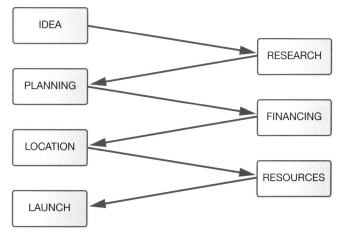

▲ Figure 1 Stages in setting up a business

- **Resources.** The business plan will contain a list of the resources needed to set up and run the business. For example, a dentist will need suitable premises, furniture, specialist dental equipment, a computer, uniforms, protective gear, and so on. Adverts might have to be placed to attract workers. Entrepreneurs will also have to find suppliers of materials, utilities and other day-to-day resources.
- **Launch.** This is an exciting time for an entrepreneur. It is when the business first starts trading. Some entrepreneurs organise an opening event. For example, a new restaurant might have a special opening night where guests are invited for a free meal. Special launches like this are designed to create good public relations (PR) with customers, so that people become aware of the new enterprise. Some entrepreneurs 'ease' themselves into their new business life by keeping their jobs for a while until the business gets established.

Although the information above suggests that setting up a business in an organised and systematic way will help to reduce the risk of failure, some entrepreneurs may omit many of these stages and set up anyway. Such people, driven by an entrepreneurial spirit, just cannot wait to try out their business idea. They run their businesses in an unplanned and responsive way, carrying out a difficult task without the necessary skills and expertise. It is possible that they might succeed – and many do. However, others would argue that 'failing to plan is planning to fail'.

RUNNING AND EXPANDING/DEVELOPING A BUSINESS

After the launch, entrepreneurs become engaged in the day-to-day running of the business. For many this involves working in production or delivering a particular service. For example, someone opening a hair salon will be cutting customers' hair, and someone setting up a chocolatier will be busy making chocolates. However, running a business requires owners to undertake a range of other tasks that are crucial to the success of the business. As the business expands and develops, more and more time will be spent attending to these 'functional' business activities.

- **Financial management.** The business needs enough money to fund its operations. This might require producing cash flow forecasts, arranging loans and overdrafts, making payments, chasing debts and monitoring cash movements into and out of the business.
- **Administration.** This usually involves accurate record keeping. For example, a business must record all of its transactions so that profit and tax liabilities can be calculated. It may be necessary to send out invoices, keep stock records, process wage slips, deal with

the tax authorities and comply with legislation. If an entrepreneur sets up a limited company there will be other administrative duties to perform.
- **Marketing.** Initially, depending on the nature of the business, marketing might involve obtaining an online business listing, developing an attractive website, using an email campaign, distributing leaflets, placing advertisements in a newspaper, organising promotions or giving special offers. It will also involve developing relationships with customers. However, as the business develops there may be a need to carry out more market research, investigate new distribution channels, raise the profile of the business by using social media and invest in some sophisticated promotions. Investment in marketing may be necessary to retain market share, launch new products and penetrate new markets.
- **Purchasing.** Businesses will have to buy resources all the time. They may also have to buy in commercial services, such as cleaning, printing and accountancy. Entrepreneurs need to get the best quality resources at the lowest possible price. Many business owners will develop relationships with their suppliers. However, it will also be important to explore new opportunities in the supply chain. Purchasing may require entrepreneurs to develop negotiating skills so that they can reduce their costs.
- **Managing people.** Some entrepreneurs run their businesses independently without the help of others. However, if a business is successful it will probably need staff to help out. This will involve spending time on recruitment, selection and training. Entrepreneurs may need to develop skills in managing people and motivating staff.
- **Production.** In manufacturing and construction, the production process is an important business function. For example, an entrepreneur setting up a small factory to make soft drinks will need to organise the various manufacturing processes, from mixing raw materials (such as sugar, water and flavourings) to bottling and packaging products for distribution. The entrepreneur will need to monitor product quality and consistency, consider health and safety issues in the factory, and ensure that production levels match orders.

It is clear that once the hard work of setting up a business has been done, it does not get any easier. The pressure on entrepreneurs can be considerable, and because their livelihoods depend on its success, running a business can be stressful. It is reckoned that more than half of new businesses fail within 5 years. However, some businesses survive and become established. If entrepreneurs develop and expand their businesses, their role is likely to change. They are less likely to be involved in production and spend more of their time addressing issues related to marketing, finance, administration, and so on. Eventually, when it becomes cost-effective, an entrepreneur is likely to organise the business into departments and employ specialists to handle marketing, finance, human resources, etc. The business owner will probably take on the role of leader in the organisation. This change in role from entrepreneur to leader is discussed in Chapter 18.

One example of a new business that expanded and developed successfully is OneMinuteLondon.com. This business was launched in 2013 by Nelson Sivalingam, a film and video production specialist. It provides an online guide to eating and drinking in London. Before making a booking, or prior to turning up at a venue, people can watch a 1-minute video clip of places under their consideration using their mobile phones or other Internet devices. Some high-profile venues, such as Hix,

Hyatt Group and Be At One, signed up to the platform and saw it as a way of converting visitors into bookings. The site was generating over 1500 bookings a month in 2013/14. OneMinuteLondon.com attracted attention from the *Guardian* and *Evening Standard* newspapers,

ACTIVITY 1   SKILLS   ANALYSIS, REASONING, INNOVATION

CASE STUDY: TRAVELIBRO

TraveLibro is a travel social networking site, which is designed to connect users with fellow travellers, bloggers, travel agents and other industry partners. It is based in Mumbai, India, and provides a research, planning and booking service for travellers. For example, it provides:

- customised holiday plans for a wide range of different holiday experiences such as family holidays and backpacking with friends
- simple and efficient planning tools linked to the information sources and an option to make bookings
- a social network that enables users to capture, save, share and relive their travel experiences
- advertisers in the travel industry the opportunity to target very specific audiences
- travel agents with a global marketplace to sell their products.

The business was launched in 2013 by Monish Shah. However, in 2014, he joined up with Malhar Gala who contributed a substantial amount of money to the business and became a co-founder. This helped to match the huge amount of money that Monish had already invested. In 2014, the two entrepreneurs rented their first office and hired some talented people from the technology, travel, research and digital sectors. In the first 2 years, the pair worked very hard developing the business. However, at the same time both were working as full-time employees – often sleeping for just 3 hours a night.

TraveLibro launched its website in August 2015 followed by its app in December 2015. Since then the portal has received over 400,000 unique visits and 20,000 app downloads from users in 49 different countries. However, Monish and Malhar are ambitious. They want TraveLibro to be the world's biggest travel social network.

1. Explain one role played by an entrepreneur when starting a business. Use an example from the case to illustrate your answer.
2. Explain how the roles of Monish and Malhar might change as their business grows into a much larger organisation.

which generated some positive publicity. The business planned to raise more finance, diversify into hotels and experiences, and expand into two other major cities.

INTRAPRENEURSHIP

Entrepreneurs are business owners and risk their own personal finances when developing a business idea. **Intrapreneurs** are employees, usually in large businesses, who use entrepreneurial skills to find and develop initiatives that will have financial benefits for their companies. These might be new products, services or systems. However, unlike entrepreneurs, intrapreneurs carry no financial risk. If their initiatives fail, the employer shoulders the financial burden.

Some businesses encourage the spirit of entrepreneurship through the whole of the organisation. It is set firmly within their culture. Examples of businesses that adopt this approach include Google, Apple and Zappos®. Such companies believe that entrepreneurial spirit helps a company to grow and evolve rather than become stale and stagnate.

Intrapreneurs are usually employed in product development. The advantages of employing intrapreneurial staff include the following.

- Intrapreneurs can drive innovation in a business and uncover new commercial opportunities. This can help a business gain a competitive edge and increase profits significantly. In some cases the discoveries and inventions made by intrapreneurs can have a huge positive impact on a business.
- It is a means of satisfying the self-actualisation needs of employees. Self-actualisation is the highest

ACTIVITY 2   SKILLS   ANALYSIS, INNOVATION

CASE STUDY: GOOGLE

Like many organisations in the technology sector, Google is a company that embraces intrapreneurship. Until quite recently, Google allowed its employees to spend 20 per cent of their time at work developing their own individual projects. This approach was to encourage innovation, creativity and original thinking. One such project, started by Paul Buchheit, was the development work for Gmail™, particularly the search function and increased storage capacity. Today, Gmail remains one of the most widely used email platforms on the web. It helps to direct key traffic towards Google's products.

Google introduced a programme called 'Innovation Time Off' to help develop an entrepreneurial spirit in the organisation. A number of years ago Google's founders, Larry Page and Sergey Brin, talked about how they had empowered their employees to be more creative and innovative by encouraging them to take 20 per cent of their day to work on ideas that would most benefit Google. This approach resulted in the development of some of Google's most successful products including Gmail, Google News™, Google Maps™, Google Talk, AdWords™, AdSense™, Driverless Cars and Google Glass™.

However, Google's approach to innovation has changed recently. It now has a more focused innovation programme, which is directed by senior management. This is because Google is now a huge global business. It has a number of highly profitable products that need to be fully exploited to maximise the financial benefits. As a result, a different approach to innovation is needed compared to the 'Innovation Time Off' programme taken when Google was an emerging force searching for new products. A different culture, and a workforce with slightly different characteristics is needed to take advantage of its current highly successful products.

However, there are risks to this change. Innovation will now involve fewer personnel selected for focused projects. This might mean that creative staff will be more difficult to recruit and the flow of innovative concepts and potential new products will diminish.

1. What is the difference between an entrepreneur and an intrapreneur?
2. Explain the possible benefits to Google of its 'Innovation Time Off' programme.
3. Explain why Google has reduced the role of intrapreneurs in recent years.

level of need, according to Maslow's hierarchy of needs. If staff adopt this role they are being given the opportunity to be creative and reach their full potential. This will help to motivate staff and hopefully raise their productivity.

- A number of awards can be won by businesses if they develop unique or ground-breaking products. For example, the Queen's Award for Enterprise, which has three categories, including one for innovation, is awarded each year for outstanding achievements by UK businesses. These awards are prestigious and can help to enhance the image of a business. Receiving one of these awards can also attract free PR, which will help to promote the business.
- Individuals benefit by getting the opportunity to experiment and be creative without having to meet the cost of failure. This should improve their job satisfaction and help them develop entrepreneurial skills which they might use in the future – perhaps by setting up their own business.

BARRIERS TO ENTREPRENEURSHIP

Many would argue that it is important for an economy to encourage entrepreneurship. This is because businesses are the main source of income, employment and wealth for a country. However, despite this, a number of barriers exist that discourage many people who aspire to be entrepreneurs from getting started.

Lack of finance: Some people with a good business idea do not start trading because they cannot attract the necessary finance. The main problem is that the providers of capital and loans may be reluctant to lend money to entrepreneurs. This is because the failure rate can be high for new businesses and financial institutions cannot afford to lose money. In 2015, around 581,000 new businesses were set up in the UK but 20 per cent failed in the first year. A further 50 per cent were not expected to survive for 3 years. The inability to get finance is one of the main barriers to entrepreneurship.

Lack of entrepreneurial capacity: To be successful in business people have to be equipped with the necessary entrepreneurial skills and characteristics. Running a business requires a wide variety of talents and skills, and needs considerable energy and commitment. These are discussed in Chapter 20. Many people lack the entrepreneurial capacity needed and therefore fewer businesses are set up. However, this may not prevent some people trying. Although some make a success of it, perhaps by learning from their mistakes, they may be a very small minority.

Becoming an employer: Employing a person for the first time is quite a big step in the development of a business. Employers have responsibilities to their employees. For example:

- employees have to be paid a regular wage
- employees may be entitled to sick pay and other benefits
- health and safety issues have to be considered
- employers have to pay National Insurance contributions
- new employees may have to be trained, which is expensive.

It is these responsibilities that often discourage employment and therefore prevent business development. Employees may also turn out to be unreliable and possibly damage the reputation of the business. Becoming an employer may be an unattractive proposition for some entrepreneurs.

Legal barriers (red tape): Bureaucratic 'red tape' can discourage potential entrepreneurs. Legislation and other regulations can be demanding – complying with legislation relating to employment, the environment, consumers, corporate governance, health and safety, taxation, property rights and competition costs money and diverts an entrepreneur's focus away from what is important to them – i.e. running the business and 'making money'. This can be a big barrier to entrepreneurship.

Lack of ideas: Some people would like to run their own business, but do not have any original ideas. A lot of markets are saturated or so competitive that the potential for profit is limited. It is possible to take out a franchise or copy the ideas of others. However, for many people this does not reflect the 'spirit' of enterprise.

Fear of failure: The failure rate for business start-ups can be high. Many new entrepreneurs may not realise that statistically their chances of success may be quite low. However, many do recognise that failure is a possibility and a fear of failure stops them from starting an enterprise. In many cultures failure has very negative associations and is best avoided if possible.

Aversion to risk: Entrepreneurs have to take risk. But many people are risk averse and are not inclined to undertake activities where the outcome is uncertain. This is a psychological barrier to enterprise and one that is difficult to overcome. It is hard to encourage a person to become an entrepreneur if risk taking is not a feature of their personality.

Corrupt and unsupportive environment: Some countries may have an unsupportive business environment. This might be because they are politically unstable, have contract and property laws that may be unclear, enforce regulations inconsistently or may be impacted by corruption and bribery. In these countries, some regulators and inspectors might act as predators. This means that entrepreneurs might have to develop friendly ties with government officials and bureaucrats to 'smooth the way' for their businesses to operate.

ANTICIPATING RISK AND UNCERTAINTY IN THE BUSINESS ENVIRONMENT

In Chapter 1 it was explained that businesses have to deal with both risk and uncertainty. The key difference between the two is that entrepreneurs have some control over risk. They make a conscious decision to take a risk and to a certain extent they can choose the levels of risk they take. In contrast, although it is known that uncertain events might occur, their timing is often impossible to predict. For example, no one can predict when an earthquake might occur. Also, the impact on businesses of some uncertain events can be devastating. Arguably, dealing with uncertainty is more challenging than dealing with risk.

Anticipating risk: Entrepreneurs understand the nature of risk right from the point when they first set up a business. For example, a significant number of entrepreneurs have probably sacrificed secure employment with a regular income to start their businesses. Also, most of them will have used some of their own money for start-up capital. Entrepreneurs know that if their business fails, they could lose their investment and they may not find another job easily. Even if entrepreneurs are successful, they are likely to take further risks in the future. For example, a business may grant trade credit to a new customer for a highly lucrative order. However, there is a risk that the customer might not pay once the order has been delivered.

Entrepreneurs can take measures to reduce the amount of risk they take. For example, before launching a brand-new product nationally, they could test it out in a smaller market. In the above example, before granting trade credit a business can undertake a credit search to check the likelihood a new customer will fail to repay their debt. Entrepreneurs can also deal with risk by using quantitative techniques, such as decision trees, when making important decisions. Using quantitative techniques often helps to measure the possible outcomes of actions, which makes them easier to evaluate.

Finally, entrepreneurs usually know that if they take more risk, the rewards could be greater – however, so could the losses. For example, a business might decide to export products. In overseas markets where these products might be completely new, sales, revenues and profits could be very high. However, different countries have different cultures, tastes and preferences.

As a result, a product that was successful in the domestic market may be a complete failure overseas. Such a failed venture could be very expensive.

Anticipating uncertainty: Dealing with uncertainty is more of a problem for entrepreneurs as they have no control over the nature or timing of some events. For example, when the UK voted to leave the EU in June 2016, there was a great deal of uncertainty regarding the possible economic consequences of BREXIT. A number of businesses think that leaving the EU could be a disaster. However, it may be 10 years or more before the outcomes are known. This level of uncertainty could result in businesses postponing or cancelling investment projects.

There is nothing that businesses can do to prevent uncertain events from happening, but they may be able to make some preparations to deal with their consequences, should they occur. For example, they may set aside funds to deal with unexpected events. Entrepreneurs might also use methods such as PESTLE analysis, SWOT analysis, risk assessment and scenario planning to help reduce uncertainty, prepare for unexpected events and improve the quality of decision making.

CHECKPOINT

1. Entrepreneurs are innovators. What does this mean?
2. What risks might an entrepreneur take in addition to putting personal money into a business start-up?
3. Describe the possible stages that need to be completed when setting up a business.
4. How important is the planning stage when starting a new business?
5. What is meant by financial management?
6. State three benefits to a business of employing intrapreneurs.
7. What is risk aversion?
8. State three other possible barriers to entrepreneurship.

SUBJECT VOCABULARY

entrepreneurs individuals who, typically, set up and run a business and take the risks associated with this.
intrapreneurs employees who use entrepreneurial skills, without having to risk their own money, to find and develop initiatives that will have financial benefits for their employer.

EXAM PRACTICE

PIOTR SANTOS

SKILLS › ANALYSIS, INTERPRETATION, DECISION MAKING

Piotr Santos came to the UK from Poland in 2006. He was a qualified chef and wanted to open his own Polish restaurant in Liverpool city centre. He had recently spent four months in his spare time researching the business idea. During this process he found two important pieces of information. There were around 10,000 Poles living in Merseyside and there was no restaurant serving only Polish food and currently operating in Liverpool. This suggested that there was a chance his business idea was viable. After collecting questionnaires from 250 people the results were encouraging. However, there was a problem. The cost of setting up the restaurant was going to be far more than he had imagined. Piotr had saved up £12,000 but needed a total of £20,000 to fund the start-up.

Piotr was not discouraged. He wrote a detailed business plan, attended a local business course funded by the Liverpool and Sefton Chambers of Commerce and made appointments with four different banks to discuss funding. Unfortunately his meetings with banks were unsuccessful. None of them was interested in lending him the £8000 he needed to start a business. He approached the Polish community to see if anyone would be interested in making a private loan. He had one offer of £5000 but the person wanted a 50 per cent share of the business and also insisted that Piotr employed two of his daughters in the restaurant. Piotr could not accept these terms and was on the verge of giving up on his idea when a friend mentioned peer-to-peer funding. This involves getting a loan from unrelated individuals online via a specialist website. If people are interested they can lend money in return for interest. Within 2 months of making the application Piotr had raised the money needed.

Piotr spent a lot of time finding a suitable location for the restaurant. He felt it was vital to find exactly the right place. He contacted 12 estate agents and got them to help with the searching. Eventually he found some suitable premises in a part of the city popular with the Polish community. It was also on a bus route popular with Polish people going into town. He left his full-time job and spent 2 months preparing for his restaurant launch. He employed an assistant chef to help him out in the kitchen, a general kitchen assistant and two waiting staff. On the opening night he invited 100 people who paid £5 each for a five-course meal. It was a huge success. After 12 months of trading Piotr had made £48,000 profit. What surprised Piotr most of all was the number of non-Polish customers that used the restaurant regularly.

In 2013, he opened a second restaurant in Manchester and started to dream of a restaurant chain – 'PIOTR'. This was also a success and, in 2014, he opened two more restaurants, another in Manchester and one in Leeds. By the end of 2014 Piotr was spending most of his time on financial management, marketing and business development. Each of his four restaurants had their own manager and three more openings were planned.

Q

(a) Explain one risk that Piotr has taken in this case.
   (4 marks)

(b) Explain one factor that could have affected where Piotr decided to locate the restaurant when setting up his business. **(4 marks)**

(c) Explain one barrier to entrepreneurship that almost prevented Piotr from setting up his business.
   (4 marks)

(d) Assess the impact on Piotr's role in the business as it started to expand. **(10 marks)**

20 ENTREPRENEURIAL MOTIVES AND CHARACTERISTICS

LEARNING OBJECTIVES

By the end of this chapter you should be able to understand:
- characteristics and skills required to be an entrepreneur
- reasons why people set up businesses: financial motives: profit maximisation and profit satisficing and non-financial motives: ethical stance, social entrepreneurship, independence and home working.

GETTING STARTED

Suzi Trebowic left the hospital where she worked because she felt overworked and unappreciated. She was employed operating an X-ray machine for 22 years. She now wants a complete change and plans to start her own business. Her passion is health food. She enjoys cooking exciting meals on a very small budget. She plans to set up a website showing how people can eat well and lose weight on a very small budget. She believes that if she can generate enough website traffic she can earn revenue from selling advertising space. At work Suzi was quiet, conscientious, and good at following instructions. However, although she had the skills needed to fulfill her role, she lacked drive and self-confidence, and did not seek promotion like most of her colleagues.

State three skills that might be needed to run an online business. State three characteristics that might be needed to be a successful entrepreneur. Do you think Suzi might be a successful entrepreneur? What might be Suzi's motive for setting up a business?

CHARACTERISTICS OF ENTREPRENEURS

Starting your own business is very common. Hundreds of thousands of small businesses are started each year. People give up their jobs to work for themselves or they start a new business alongside a normal full-time job. Not everyone is suited to becoming an entrepreneur, either because they lack the skills needed or because they do not want to cope with the risk involved in setting up a business. Business Link, a government agency in the UK that encourages business start-ups, identified seven characteristics of successful entrepreneurs.

- **Self-confidence.** Successful entrepreneurs are people who believe that they are going to succeed. They think they have a winning formula for their business. They can persuade other people, for example, to buy the product or help finance the business.
- **Self-determination.** Successful entrepreneurs are ones who think they can take control of events going on around them. They can influence those events and turn them into something that will benefit their business.
- **Being a self-starter.** Many people work best when being told what to do. But to be a successful entrepreneur, you have to be a self-starter. Entrepreneurs are able to work independently and can take decisions. They have their own ideas about how things should be done and they are able to develop those ideas.
- **Judgement.** The business environment is changing all the time. A successful entrepreneur is someone who gathers information and listens to advice. At the same time, they are able to see where the business might go in the future and what they want out of the business. This helps them to make judgements and decisions.
- **Commitment.** Many people think when starting up a business that it is going to be easier than working for someone else. All the evidence shows that entrepreneurs work longer hours than those with a normal job. Running your own business can sometimes be more stressful because of the risks that are always present. So successful entrepreneurs are ones who are committed to what they do.
- **Perseverance.** All businesses have successes and failures. There is always an element of risk that their business could perform poorly or even fail. Therefore, successful entrepreneurs have to show perseverance. They have to be able to get through the bad times and the setbacks.
- **Initiative.** Successful entrepreneurs are able to take the initiative in situations. They do not allow events to overwhelm them by doing nothing. They are able to change and be proactive.

Not every successful entrepreneur has all of these characteristics. Few entrepreneurs are strong in every area. But people who run their own businesses tend to show different characteristics from people who work for someone else.

One example of an entrepreneur is Namibian Tammy Knott. She founded Mbiri Natural Skincare – a 100 per cent natural skincare brand made from Namibian plant ingredients. These include Namibian myrrh, marula oil and Kalahari melon seed oil. Myrrh, which is endemic to Namibia, is harvested by the Himba people in the northern desert regions of Namibia.

Tammy got her business idea after spending a lot of time in the Namibian desert with her mother who was doing some research into indigenous plants and their traditional uses. The brand was launched in 2015 after Tammy had attended a soap making course.

However, just before that she entered a competition called Namibia's Essential Oil Challenge Fund Competition, designed to encourage the cosmetic use of *Commiphora wildii*. Entrants had to submit some product prototypes along with a packaging design and business strategy. Tammy won and got NAD 35,000 to start her business. She started with a product called Rare Scent, which she made by hand on a table in her garage with a stove and three pots. However, she knew that larger scale production was needed so she got a loan from the bank and started Mbiri. She had no entrepreneurial background. Her drive came from the passion for Namibia and its people and plants.

ACTIVITY 1　　SKILLS　ANALYSIS

CASE STUDY: KAVINDU KUMARA

Kavindu Kumara left school, in Sri Lanka, at the age of 16. He obtained GCE O/Ls in mathematics, English and business studies. However, he did not really enjoy school because he felt the education system did not meet his needs. Kavindu was not a trouble maker but he was never interested in schoolwork. He was very sporty, creative and enjoyed organising sports tournaments and small fundraising events for charity. In December 2016, he organised a big cricket competition in his local village. The event was well publicised. Kavindu put up posters in neighbouring villages and persuaded a local newspaper to write an article about the tournament. On the day of the event, ten teams from neighbouring villages near Galle, Sri Lanka, turned up and so did several hundred supporters and curious locals. Kavindu had organised a number of food vendors and stalls to help make some money. The competition was a huge success and Kavindu made SLR 9800. He donated one-half of this to his local primary school to buy cricket equipment.

Kavindu is now in the process of setting up his own events company. His final school report written by the head of year is shown in Figure 1 (written in May before his exam results were published in August).

Kavindu Kumara

Kavindu is a charming young man. He is loyal, honest, open and friendly. Unfortunately, his 5 years spent at the Galle Academy have all been somewhat wasted – although he will probably just about pass the exams in maths and business studies. Kavindu had plenty of ability but was not motivated to reach his full academic potential. It is a regret that he has chosen to leave and not register for one of our school's vocational courses, to which he might be better suited.

To his credit, outside the classroom Kavindu excelled. He was the captain of the school cricket team for 5 years in a row and led his team to win the Galle Schools Cup in 2015. He also organised sports tournaments and charity events working alongside school staff. He was well liked by everyone. He is full of self-confidence, shows initiative and when interested can be extremely determined.

I'm not sure what the future will be like for Kavindu. He says that he is going to start his own business. A little ambitious perhaps for a sixteen-year-old – but it wouldn't surprise me at all if he made a great success of it.

Good Luck Kavindu!

Dilani De Silva
Dilani De Silva (Head of Year)

▲ Figure 1 Kavindu Kumara's final school report

1. Discuss whether Kavindu has the characteristics to become an entrepreneur.

Later in the year she sent a batch of Mbiri to the USA and has begun to establish the brand in South Africa.

SKILLS REQUIRED BY ENTREPRENEURS

Not only do entrepreneurs need to possess a number of important characteristics to be successful, they also need to use a wide range of different skills. To begin with it helps if entrepreneurs are capable to some extent in their chosen line of business. For example, an entrepreneur setting up a flying school will need piloting experience and an instructor's certificate. Someone starting a commercial radio station may need some broadcasting, transmitting and programming experience.

However, it is possible to set up a business in unfamiliar fields. For example, the skills needed in retailing, window cleaning and running an online sales operation can be learned fairly quickly. There are also examples of entrepreneurs entering quite diversified lines of business without any relevant experience. For example, Sir Stelios Haji-Ioannou set up easyJet® after being involved in his father's shipping business. It is possible to do this by employing experts in the chosen field right from the start. Other important entrepreneurial skills include the following.

Organising: Entrepreneurs play an important organisational role. They have to project manage the setting up and running of their business ventures. This involves organising and co-ordinating a wide range of resources in order to get the business up and running. In this organisational role, entrepreneurs will be planning, scheduling, giving instructions, prioritising, setting up systems, monitoring, time managing and meeting deadlines. If things go wrong, entrepreneurs will sometimes be 'fire-fighting', that is resolving conflict, dealing with business issues and sorting out problems.

Financial management: This is a very important skill and if it is neglected can lead to the failure of the business. The main aim of financial management is to make sure that the business has enough money whenever it is needed. This might involve budgeting, cash flow forecasting, chasing debts, keeping up-to-date financial records, arranging loans and overdrafts, and analysing financial information (in business accounts, for example).

Communication: Entrepreneurs will need to interact with a wide range of different stakeholders. These might include customers, employees, suppliers, the local community and the authorities. Entrepreneurs will need to develop effective face-to-face communication skills to deal directly with people. Charm, courtesy, confidence, professionalism and a convincing manner are all useful entrepreneurial qualities. Entrepreneurs might also be required to write letters, memos and reports, fill in forms and design documents for both internal and external use. Presentational skills might also be needed – when making a sales pitch, for example. If entrepreneurs have good communication skills, their businesses are likely to perform better.

Managing people: As a business grows there will be a need to take on more staff. It is often said that managing people is one of the most difficult tasks when running a business. Individuals are all different and may require different approaches to motivation. Entrepreneurs need to recruit the 'right people' in the first place and then show clear leadership and direction. People should be easier to manage if their needs are met, and if they are treated with respect and valued.

Decision making: Running a business will require a lot of decision making. The level of decisions however will differ. Most decisions are about low-level, day-to-day issues such as what materials or stock to order, which tools to use and where to advertise for a new employee. In contrast, a small number of decisions are strategic. These are important and can have long-term effects on the business. An example might be whether to move premises to a new location. Entrepreneurs will also have to solve problems when they occur. Decision making and problem solving require entrepreneurs to process, analyse and evaluate information.

Negotiating: Inevitably entrepreneurs will spend some of their time negotiating. This often means agreeing the terms of a contract, such as agreeing a price for undertaking some work or completing an order for a customer. However, negotiation might also be needed when dealing with suppliers and employees. Entrepreneurs need to be able to get their points across in a calm and confident manner, develop arguments with reasoning, know when to compromise, and try to arrive at a settlement that is agreeable to both parties.

IT skills: Entrepreneurs will be able to run their business more efficiently if they have good IT skills. For example, they might need to:

- set up filing systems to store and manage business documents and other information
- communicate with stakeholders using email or conference calling
- use spreadsheets to prepare budgets and cash flow forecasts
- design documents, such as invoices, order forms, job descriptions, expense claim forms, flyers and newsletters
- set up a business website and provide a system for online purchases
- use social media to help raise the profile of the business and direct potential customers to the business website
- use computer software to give presentations
- use specialist software, for designing products, for example.

REASONS WHY PEOPLE SET UP BUSINESSES

People set up businesses for a wide range of reasons. For example, they may not want to work for an employer any more, they may want to develop a personal interest into a business or they may have been made redundant and want to start something new. These motives, and others, fall into one of two different categories: financial and non-financial.

Financial motives: Many people set up a business because they want to make money. They often think that they could earn far more if they worked for themselves. Profit is the driving force behind many entrepreneurs and most businesses would not exist if it was not for the desire to make a profit.

Two approaches to making profit can be identified.

- **Profit maximisation.** Some entrepreneurs try to make as much profit as possible in a given time period. This is called profit maximisation. These entrepreneurs are motivated by money and their key focus is the financial return on their efforts. It might be argued that entrepreneurs who try to maximise profits are likely to take bigger risks. This is because there is usually a direct relationship between risk and reward. For example, a small manufacturer might decide to replace some workers with a computer numerically controlled (CNC) machine costing US$250,000. However, if production levels cannot be raised sufficiently to cover the cost of the machine, the financial burden might cause extreme cash flow difficulties. It might also be argued that entrepreneurs that aim to maximise profits are more likely to ignore the needs of other stakeholders. For example, an entrepreneur might enforce zero-hours contracts and only pay the legal minimum wage.
- **Profit satisficing.** Some entrepreneurs might take a different approach to profit. For example, they

may aim to make just enough profit to maintain their interest in the business. This is called profit satisficing. One reason why some entrepreneurs do not seek to maximise profits is because they do not want to take on the extra responsibility of expanding their business – which is often required to make more profit. Also, some entrepreneurs run 'lifestyle' businesses. This means a business that generates enough profit to provide the flexibility needed to pay for a particular lifestyle. This type of business allows owners to spend more time pursuing other interests or with family. For example, a couple running a small seaside hotel might shut down for 4 months in the winter so that they can visit family in Australia.

Non-financial motives: For some people, other motives for setting up a business might be as important or more important than making money. They will obviously need to make enough profit in order for the business to continue in operation, but the main driving force is non-financial. A number of non-financial motives exist.

- **Ethical stance.** A minority of people set up a business in support of a moral belief they possess. For example, a vegetarian who believes that it is wrong to kill animals for meat may open up a vegetarian restaurant. By encouraging more people to use the restaurant, particularly if non-vegetarians can be attracted, fewer animals would be killed. Another example might be setting up a business to generate 'clean' electricity. A keen environmentalist might feel that setting up a solar farm could contribute towards the reduction of carbon emissions.
- **Social enterprise.** These are organisations that trade with the aim of improving human and environmental well-being. They are sometimes referred to as not-for-profit organisations. Generally, social enterprises have a clear social and/or environmental mission and generate most of their income through trade or donations. Fairtrade is an example of a social enterprise. It markets products produced by small-scale farmers and workers who are excluded from trade in a variety of ways. Fairtrade ensures that these people get a better price for their produce, such as coffee. Social enterprises are discussed in Chapter 26.
- **Independence.** A lot of people want to be 'their own boss'. This is an important non-financial motive for setting up a business. These entrepreneurs are driven by the desire to be independent. The freedom to make all the decisions when running a business is very appealing. Some people dislike being told what to do at work. Being able to make your own decisions is often regarded as the main

key benefit of being an entrepreneur. Nearly 90 per cent of respondents to a survey by Startups.co.uk said this was very important. However, in practice this independence may be limited. Work has to be done. Taxes have to be paid. Those financing the business, like a bank giving a loan, have to be kept satisfied that the business will continue to survive. But those who own their own business, in general, do have more independence than those who work for an employer.

- **Home working.** Quite a number of entrepreneurs set up their businesses from home. They may be tradespeople such as plumbers, painters or electricians that use their home as a base for their business. Or, increasingly, they may work from a room or an office at home. Examples include writers, accountants, software designers, app developers, artists, tutors and financial analysts. There are two key benefits for home workers. The time and expense spent travelling to and from work is eliminated. They also enjoy more flexibility. For example, they can take meals and breaks whenever they want and a parent may be able to fit work around the needs of their children.

CHECKPOINT

1. State three characteristics of an entrepreneur.
2. What is financial management?
3. State two communication skills that an entrepreneur might need.
4. Why will an entrepreneur need negotiating skills?
5. What IT skills might an entrepreneur need?
6. What is profit satisficing?
7. State two non-financial motives for becoming an entrepreneur.

SUBJECT VOCABULARY

profit maximisation an attempt to make as much profit as possible in a given time period.
profit satisficing making enough profit just to satisfy the needs of the business owner(s).

EXAM PRACTICE

MAMA'S SPICES & HERBS

SKILLS ANALYSIS, INTERPRETATION, INNOVATION, CRITICAL THINKING, REASONING

Mikie Monoketsi founded Mama's Spices & Herbs in 2012. The business, based in Johannesburg, South Africa, is now flourishing and supplies various seasonings, health teas, soups and diet drinks. The products are targeted at consumers in poorer South African neighbourhoods and are sold by agents directly to customers.

Mikie is passionate about healthy eating and living and this is how the business began. After a personal crisis, when Mikie's call centre business and marriage both failed at the same time, she carried out some research into the eating habits of people living in the neighourhoods of Diepsloot, Randfontein, Cosmo City and Lion Park. She found that the spices people used were cheap and contained high levels of salt and other unhealthy ingredients, such as MSG, preservatives and bulking agents. These were considered unhealthy and likely to contribute to high levels of illnesses, such as hypertension and diabetes. Mikie also discovered what people were cooking – skop, mogodu, maotwana, kota (cows head, intestines, chicken feet, bunny chow), potato chips, fish, braai, stews and curries and fried chicken. This gave Mikie the idea to create her own set of healthy spices that would go well with these particular foods. However, her herbs and spices offered better quality, with health benefits, and at an affordable price.

Mikie found a reliable manufacturer to make her blends and employed sales representatives on a commission basis to sell her products. She also sells to a dozen or so distributers, who have their own networks that pay up front for their stock. Mikie is now very wealthy and is worth considerably more than the ZAR 10,000 she used to get the business going.

Mikie points to a number of factors that helped her to be a successful entrepreneur. For example, she emphasised the importance of good communication and networking skills. Mikie used gyms to develop partnerships, get connected and meet people to help build her business. For example, she met a helpful spice company executive at a gym who gave her lots of useful advice. Mikie also appears on television and radio, which gives her the opportunity to explain her vision on health and fitness, demonstrate exercise routines and occasionally promote her business.

Another important skill that Mikie emphasised was financial management. She said it was very important to monitor spending and account for every single cost – especially labour, packaging, cost of sales and time.

Mikie discovered that a failure to record all costs meant that even though she was increasing sales she was not making more money. For example, she had failed to take into account the samples she was giving out. Samples are very important in the food industry and their costs must be recorded. Finally, she also recognised (eventually) that the business could not fund wasteful personal spending. Such transactions were much reduced when she realised that the business was suffering. To keep up to date with transactions, Mikie recorded all expenses in a notebook and invoiced all customers. Once she started doing this the performance of the business improved.

Today the business continues to flourish. Mikie is diversifying and targeting mainly women with a range of health products such as Flat Stomach Tea and Flat Stomach Power Oats. The business is growing strongly and now provides an online shopping facility. Mama's Spices & Herbs is currently looking to recruit additional agents in the Western Cape, Northern Cape, Eastern Cape (Port Elizabeth and East London), Free State, Mpumalanga, Limpopo and North West. Mama's Spices & Herbs also has a shop in Fontainebleau. Not only is Mikie making a lot of money for herself, she also helps to inspire other young entrepreneurs to set up in business.

Q

(a) Explain one characteristic that entrepreneurs must have to increase their chances of being successful.
(4 marks)

(b) Explain one reason why some entrepreneurs run their businesses from home. **(4 marks)**

(c) Analyse two important skills that entrepreneurs like Mikie Monoketsi need to run a business. **(6 marks)**

(d) Evaluate whether Mikie's motives for setting up Mama's Spices & Herbs were (i) financial or (ii) non-financial. **(20 marks)**

21 BUSINESS OBJECTIVES

UNIT 1
1.3.5

LEARNING OBJECTIVES

By the end of this chapter you should be able to understand:
- survival
- profit maximisation
- other objectives: sales maximisation, market share, cost efficiency, employee welfare, customer satisfaction and social objectives.

GETTING STARTED

Omar Anwan is a social media enthusiast from Halhul, Palestine. He wanted to set up an organisation advising small businesses on how to raise their profile and generate sales using social media. He wrote a comprehensive business plan, invested ILS 200,000 of his own money in the start-up and began designing his own website. The plan detailed three important business objectives.
- break even by the end of the first year
- generate ILS 400,000 sales by the end of the second year
- make customer satisfaction a business priority.

State two advantages of setting business objectives. Do you think Omar's business objectives are realistic? What other business objectives might you have if you set up in business?

BUSINESS OBJECTIVES

The **aims** of a business are what the business wants to achieve in the long term. Aims tend to be general and examples might be to be the 'best' in the market or the 'market leader'. The **objectives** of a business are the goals or targets that need to be met in order to achieve an aim. For example, a business might aim to grow and set annual sales targets as objectives to help achieve it. Businesses are more likely to be successful if they set clear objectives. Businesses need to have objectives for the following reasons.

- Employees need something to work towards. Objectives help to motivate people. For example, sales staff might get bonuses if they reach certain sales targets.
- Without objectives owners might not have the motivation needed to keep the business going. Owners might lose control and allow their business to become passive and aimless. This could result in business failure.

- Objectives help owners decide where to take a business and what steps are necessary to get there. For example, if a business aims to grow by 10 per cent, it might decide that launching products overseas would be the best way to achieve this.

It is easier to assess the performance of a business if the objectives set are SMART. This means that they should be:
- **S**pecific – stating clearly what is trying to be achieved
- **M**easurable – can be measured quantitatively
- **A**greed – have the approval of everyone involved
- **R**ealistic – able to be achieved given the resources available
- **T**ime specific – have a stated time by which they should be achieved.

An example of a SMART objective might be for a business to increase turnover by 8 per cent in the next 12 months. If the objectives are achieved it could be argued that the business has performed well.

SURVIVAL

All businesses will consider survival to be important. However, from time to time survival can become the most important objective. For example, when a business first starts trading it may be particularly at risk. It often takes time for people to recognise the existence of a new business. Entrepreneurs may lack experience and there may be a shortage of resources. Therefore, a target for a new business may be simply to survive in the first 12 months. A business might also struggle to survive if new competitors enter the market. If the new entrants have better or cheaper products, or more financial resources, entrepreneurs may need to focus on survival in the changed business environment at the expense of other objectives.

Many businesses struggle when trading conditions become difficult. For example, in the first 6 months of 2015, it was reported that 59 Greek companies were closing down everyday. This had resulted in 613 job losses and a loss of €22 million in national income every 24 hours. This was caused by the extreme austerity measures being imposed by Greece's creditors following the financial crisis in 2008. There has been a prolonged period of low business confidence during this time and many, many businesses found it extremely difficult to raise funds to keep trading. Since 2008, many businesses in Greece have just aimed to survive in the hope that the future will eventually bring improved trading conditions.

ACTIVITY 1 | SKILLS → ANALYSIS, ADAPTABILITY, CRITICAL THINKING

CASE STUDY: SEARS

Sears, one of North America's highest profile retailers, announced in 2014 that it would be closing a number of stores and taking out loans from the billionaire chairman and CEO, Eddie Lampert. Sears had seen its revenue fall for 8 years in a row. It had made losses for the last 4 of those years. The struggling superstore, which also owns Kmart, lost US$548 million in the quarter up to November 2014. Two main reasons were given to explain the decline of Sears. The slow economic recovery from a deep recession hit the store hard because its target market was middle- and low-income consumers, who may have been most affected by the recession. Also, stiff competition was reported from more efficient operators such as Walmart, Home Depot and Amazon. It was reported that Eddie Lampert thought that many of the Sears stores were too large and in the wrong locations.

In an effort to save the company the following measures were announced.

- More stores would be closed. Sears once owned 3523 stores. This figure reduced to fewer than 2000 by 2015.
- US$400 million would be borrowed from a hedge fund owned by Eddie Lampert.
- Between 200 and 300 buildings would be sold and rented back to improve liquidity.

1. Using an example from this case, explain one reason why Sears might have pursued survival as a business objective.
2. Discuss whether the measures Sears has taken to survive are likely to be successful.

PROFIT MAXIMISATION

Without profit most businesses would not exist. However, some businesses focus on profit more aggressively, usually because the owners want to make as much profit as they possibly can. This is called profit maximisation. This might be more likely if businesses are owned by institutional shareholders, such as pension funds and investment funds. These owners need to maximise the returns on their investments to meet the needs of their clients. Many entrepreneurs are unlikely to pursue profit maximisation, they are more likely to pursue profit satisficing. This is discussed in Unit 20.

If entrepreneurs want to maximise profit, they will focus on keeping costs as low as possible while raising prices as high as they can before customer loyalty is damaged. Skim pricing is often used by profit maximisers.

This strategy is usually used in the luxury goods market, for instance jewellery and designer clothes. The prices are set unnaturally high, as customers for these goods are wealthy and not price sensitive so do not object to such excessive values.

One criticism of this approach is that it is too short-termist. By focusing aggressively on maximising short-term profits, it is possible that more lucrative long-term opportunities are overlooked. Profit maximisation as an objective might also damage relationships with other stakeholders, such as employees and customers. Higher profits often mean lower wages for employees and higher prices for customers.

OTHER OBJECTIVES

Although survival and profit maximisation are two important business objectives, there are others.

Sales maximisation: Some entrepreneurs might try to increase sales as an objective. This is called **sales maximisation**. It involves a business selling as much as it possibly can in a particular period of time. Sales levels are an important measure of performance and generally growing sales is a healthy sign for a business. Most businesses can raise profits by selling more output.

Sales maximisation might be used by an entrepreneur to win a larger market share. This could be important when trading first begins. Also, as a business grows, specialist sales staff might be employed. If the pay of sales staff is linked to physical sales levels, a business is likely to pursue sales maximisation as sales staff try to maximise their earnings.

THINKING BIGGER

There is a difference between physical sales levels and sales revenue. Maximising physical sales levels is likely to benefit a business. However, it might be more appropriate to focus on sales *revenue* as an objective, i.e. the money generated by physical sales. It may be possible to sell more units by lowering the price. However, this might actually reduce sales revenue. The impact on revenue of reducing price to increase sales depends on price elasticity of demand. This is discussed in Chapter 7.

Consider this example. An entrepreneur currently sells 6000 units a month at US$5 per unit. This generates sales revenue of US$30,000. In an effort to sell more, the entrepreneur lowers price to US$4. As a result sales rise to 7000. However, sales revenue drops to US$28,000. This is likely to have a negative impact on profit. This example shows that an effort to maximise physical sales levels has actually resulted in lower levels of sales revenue.

Market share: Most businesses would prefer a large market share to a small one. Consequently, trying to increase market share is a common business objective. If a business can get a larger market share this should help to increase revenue and raise the profile of the business in the market. If a business can build a bigger market share than its rivals, it may be able to dominate the market. This might mean that it has more control over price. A larger market share also means that output levels will be higher so a business might be able to lower its costs. This will increase profit margins and generate more profit for the owners.

Cost efficiency: From time to time businesses may consider how to reduce their costs. It is an objective that might be pursued when trading conditions become difficult due to more competition or an economic downturn. However, some businesses look to cut costs all of the time. If costs are lower, profit margins will be higher. Businesses with lower costs might also gain a competitive edge in the market.

A business can use a variety of methods to cut costs. It might:

- lay off staff to cut labour costs
- find new suppliers to get cheaper resources
- increase the usage of recycled materials
- develop new working practices that use fewer resources
- develop ways of saving energy.

One of the drawbacks of cutting costs is that product quality or customer service might suffer. For example, if a cafe cuts down on staff to reduce costs, customers might get fed up waiting for their food and go somewhere else.

Employee welfare: In recent years a number of businesses have realised the benefits of meeting the needs of employees more effectively. If employee welfare is improved workers will be happier, better motivated, more productive, more co-operative, more flexible and less likely to leave. Therefore another objective might be to improve employee welfare. A number of measures can be taken to achieve this, including:

- improving the working environment by making it cleaner, less noisy and less crowded
- ensuring that staff are given proper breaks and somewhere comfortable to interact with colleagues during those breaks
- ensuring that staff are equipped with the necessary tools and equipment, providing ergonomically designed chairs for call centre workers, for example
- maintaining high standards of courtesy between all staff members
- encouraging regular exercise by organising fitness sessions or providing a staff gym, for example.

Improving employee welfare is also likely to reduce staff absenteeism through sickness, enhance the image of the business, help to comply with health and safety legislation, and make it easier to recruit and retain good-quality people.

ACTIVITY 2　SKILLS　ANALYSIS

CASE STUDY: FANCYTHAT

Fancy dress parties in Australia have been popular since the 1990s. Some Australians wear fancy dress costumes for staff Christmas parties and when attending important cricket matches.

Brad Jones runs FancyThat, a manufacturing company based in Adelaide that makes fancy dress costumes and accessories for shops and other outlets in South Australia. After a quiet start in 2010 the business is now enjoying record sales. Interest in fancy dress costumes has grown in recent years. Brad got the idea after going to sporting and social events, and talking to some people who had dressed up for the day. Brad could not believe what people were prepared to pay for fancy dress costumes. Also, there were whole groups of people in the crowd dressed in identical costumes. Brad saw a business opportunity.

When Brad first started he just wanted to survive in the first year. However, he was ambitious and by 2016 he was still in business and wanted to grow turnover to AUD 400,000. He succeeded; however he has noticed recently that costs are rising sharply. His objective now is to cut fixed costs by 20 per cent and variable costs by 25 per cent, both by the end of the year.

1. Explain what is meant by a SMART objective.
2. Explain how Brad might cut costs in his business.

Customer satisfaction: Most businesses will try to meet the needs of customers. The benefits are clear. If customers are satisfied they are more likely to return. Loyal customers are valuable to a business. In order to win their loyalty, some businesses aim to exceed customer expectations. How might they do this?

- Ensure that all customer-facing staff are trained to a very high level in communication. Their conduct must be polite, professional and friendly 100 per cent of the time.
- Provide a platform for customer feedback – an online review system, for example.
- Interact with customers using social media – encourage a two-way flow of information.
- Deal with customer complaints promptly and effectively – to the evident satisfaction of the customer.
- Monitor customer service regularly – using mystery shoppers, for example.

In order to have effective customer service, businesses must know what customers want, provide them with it consistently and receive feedback on how the business is doing.

Social objectives: A business that sets social objectives is one that shows concern for the local area. A business should aim to promote prosperity and develop a strong relationship with the local community so it can co-exist. This might involve:

- keeping noise levels down
- maintaining sensible opening hours
- demonstrating responsibility to the environment by minimising pollution
- providing employment for local people
- maintaining open channels of communication between the business and the local community so that issues can be raised and discussed
- making contributions to community life, such as visiting local schools, sponsoring local events or making donations to local charities.

It is not in the interests of a business to upset the local community. This is because collectively, the local population may be a powerful force should they submit any form of objection. A business has a duty to be considerate and respectful when operating in a residential area, for example.

CHECKPOINT

1. State two situations where survival is likely to be an important business objective.
2. What is profit maximisation?
3. Give one benefit of increasing market share as a business objective.
4. State three ways a business can cut costs.
5. Why might a business aim to improve employee welfare?
6. State three ways a business can improve employee welfare.
7. How important is customer satisfaction as a business objective?
8. What are the social objectives of a business?

SUBJECT VOCABULARY

aims what a business tries to achieve in the long term.
objectives the goals or targets set by a business to help achieve its long-term purpose.
sales maximisation an attempt to sell as much as possible in a given time period (or an attempt to generate as much sales revenue as possible in a given time period).

EXAM PRACTICE

SONY

Sony is a giant Japanese electronics multinational company with a base in Tokyo. It has been trading for more than 70 years and employs around 125,000 people worldwide. However, staff numbers at Sony have been reduced. In 2008, around 180,000 people worked for the company. Sony has 12 important product divisions such as television & video, audio, gaming & network services, semi-conductors, smartphone & Internet, medical, pictures, music and financial services.

The company has encountered some trading problems in the last 10 years. For example, it has faced very fierce competition for some of its electronic products from strong rivals such as Apple, Samsung and emerging Chinese operators. In 2014, one of its products, PlayStation 4, was selling very well. It had sold over 7 million consoles since its launch – this was 2 million more than the Xbox®, its closest rival. However, television sales were being hit hard, an area where Sony had once led the global market – smartphones was also another area where Sony was struggling. In 2014, Kazuo Hirai, the Sony CEO, planned to introduce an extensive cost-cutting programme and in 2015 Sony shareholders showed their support for the CEO by reappointing him at the AGM. At the meeting, Hirai apologised for the poor financial performance of the company and said that he and other senior executives would not be taking their bonuses for the year.

One area where Sony has been looking to improve its performance is customer service (CS). In Sony's 2016 annual report it said that Sony was introducing measures to improve its CS function. Sony announced an initiative called the Sony Pledge of Quality – 'Sony employees will always respect our customers' viewpoints in striving to deliver product quality and customer service that exceed their expectations.' With regard to CS this meant improvements in responding to changing customer needs and providing a high-quality repair service. To help support the pledge and achieve the CS improvements, Sony has:

- set up a network of bases around the world to meet the CS needs of local customers
- appointed CS officers to co-ordinate global CS operations
- introduced key performance indicators, such as repair improvement rates and repair completion times
- provided ongoing training for staff in CS operations
- provided more convenient and eco-friendly manuals. This will involve switching from paper to online manuals and using pictures for instructions rather than text (wherever possible).

In 2016, after a period of financial struggle, Sony returned to profit. Figure 1 shows the profits for Sony between 2008 and 2017.

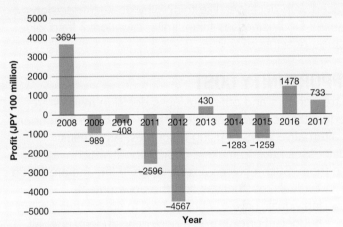

▲ Figure 1 Sony profit, 2008–17

(a) Explain why survival may have been a business objective for Sony between 2009 and 2015.

(4 marks)

(b) Explain how employee welfare might be a business objective. **(4 marks)**

(c) Discuss the importance of profit to a company like Sony. **(8 marks)**

(d) Assess the extent to which customer satisfaction is a business objective for Sony. **(10 marks)**

22 BUSINESS CHOICES

LEARNING OBJECTIVES

By the end of this chapter you should be able to understand:
- opportunity cost
- trade-offs.

GETTING STARTED

Imagine that you have received a gift of Rs 8000 (about £100 or US$130). Make a list of all the things you would like to buy with the money. Now arrange that list in order of preference. The item on the top will be the one you decide to spend the money on.

What have you sacrificed by choosing the preferred item at the top of the list? How often in life are you faced with decisions like this? Why do such decisions arise? Do businesses face similar situations? If so, give some possible examples.

OPPORTUNITY COST

Entrepreneurs and other business decision makers are frequently faced with **choices**. There are often a number of alternative ways of using resources. As a result businesses have to make a choice about which way to use them. Such choices are common in life and are faced by individuals, businesses and the government.

- Individuals have to choose how to spend their limited budgets. For example, a university student, after all living costs have been met, may have €50 left at the end of the week. This student would like to buy some new books (€20), get the train home for the weekend (€30), go out for a meal with friends (€30) or buy a new pair of designer jeans (€50). Clearly, a choice has to be made because all of these goods together would cost €130.
- Businesses may have to choose between spending €100,000 on an advertising campaign, retraining its workforce, redecorating the reception area or buying new vehicles for sales staff.
- A government may have to decide whether to spend €5000 million on increasing disability benefits, building new hospitals, providing better care for the mentally ill or building a new motorway.

Assume that a business placed its spending desires in the order of preference below.
1. Advertising campaign.
2. Retrain workforce.
3. Redecorate reception area.
4. Buy new vehicles for sales staff.

In this example, the advertising campaign is the preferred choice. Therefore the €100,000 will be allocated to this project. The other three options are sacrificed or given up. The benefit lost from the next best alternative is called the **opportunity cost** of the choice. In this example, it would be the benefit lost by not retraining the workforce. When making such choices, individuals, businesses and governments can identify and face the opportunity cost once their preferred spending choice has been made.

ACTIVITY 1

SKILLS   ANALYSIS

CASE STUDY: BRAZILIAN BIOFUELS

Brazil is the second biggest producer of biofuel (fuels made from plants) in the world. One Brazilian company, Jemerson EthoFuel, produces ethanol (a biofuel) from sugarcane. The company was successful for about 7 years, up until the oil price fell in 2014/15. Since then, like many other biofuel producers in the country, Jemerson EthoFuel has struggled as an increasing number of consumers have switched back to petrol as a fuel for cars. In 2017, Jemerson decided that some investment was needed to strengthen the company's financial performance. The company had BRL 40 million to invest and was able to identify a number of possible projects (all of which needed BRL 40 million). These projects are listed in order of preference below:
1. upgrade production facilities to improve efficiency by 25 per cent
2. merge with another biofuel company to cut costs
3. diversify into food production
4. develop a genetically modified type of sugar cane that could improve production by 30 per cent.

(a) Using this case as an example, explain what is meant by opportunity cost.

NON-MONETARY OPPORTUNITY COST

Opportunity costs can quite often be measured in monetary terms. In the above example, the opportunity cost of investing in the advertising campaign is the benefit sacrificed in order to retrain the workforce. The business might be able to calculate the value of the extra output generated by the workers after retraining. However, there may also be some non-monetary or intangible benefits of staff retraining. For example, many workers may feel more confident in their work and as a result they may be happier and more content. This may improve productivity further. However, such improvements, although real, would be very difficult to measure in monetary terms. Opportunity cost may also be difficult to quantify because such costs are incurred in the future and the future is so difficult to predict.

Opportunity cost can sometimes be personal. For example, an entrepreneur might decide to reinvest profits in the business at the expense of a family holiday. The opportunity cost of this decision might be overwork and disappointed children, which might be felt by the whole family. Clearly, increased happiness and a greater sense of well-being are additional factors that may contribute to opportunity costs.

BUSINESS CHOICES AND TRADE-OFFS

Businesses have to make countless decisions, and decision makers are frequently faced with **trade-offs**. This means that opting for one choice involves compromising another. For example, a company that prides itself on attention to detail must often sacrifice the speed of production. If a business wants to build up stock, it must sacrifice cash. There are many such examples in business.

One very important trade-off is that between risk and reward, as shown in Figure 1. It is often necessary to take bigger risks in order to receive higher rewards. However, with high risk there is the danger of large losses. For example, it was reported in the media that before 2008, banks granted mortgages to high-risk borrowers. The potential returns were high, but unfortunately when the property market collapsed many borrowers could not repay their loans. As a result some banks also collapsed.

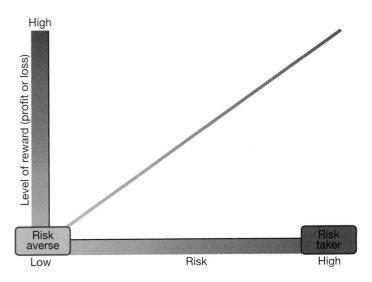

▲ Figure 1 The relationship between risk and reward

In 2001 Arsenal FC won approval to build a new stadium, increasing capacity from about 38,000 to over 60,000. The club invested about £400 million in the construction of the Emirates Stadium. The Arsenal manager, Arsène Wenger, was reported as describing it as the biggest decision in Arsenal's history since Herbert Chapman was appointed as chairman by the board. The Emirates opened in 2006 and up until 2014, when Arsenal won the FA Cup, the club failed to win a single trophy. For many of the club's supporters, this 8-year period of disappointing achievement on the pitch was an important part of the opportunity cost of the decision to build a new stadium as during this period the club appeared to have only limited resources to invest in new players and improve the quality of the playing staff. However, the true value of the opportunity cost is very difficult to quantify. How can you measure supporters' emotional disappointment at not winning any trophies? Also, if Arsenal had won some trophies their revenue would have been higher, but by how much? This example helps to highlight the difficulties in measuring the precise value of opportunity cost. You could use this example, or ones like it, when discussing the opportunity costs of business decisions.

Initially, one important decision for an entrepreneur is whether to set up a business in the first place. The benefits of running your own business may include:

- independence, as owners are in complete control and are free to make all decisions
- flexibility, as owners can choose a life balance between work and leisure that suits them
- the chance to make more money than might be earned in employment
- job satisfaction and a sense of achievement in building something from nothing
- the chance of becoming rich – some entrepreneurs become millionaires!

However, there is a trade-off. Many entrepreneurs leave their jobs to set up a business. They give up financial security that a regular salary from employment often provides. Employment may also offer health insurance, employee pensions, holiday pay and sick leave. Running a business is also very challenging, for the following reasons.

- Owners of small businesses are responsible for all day-to-day operations. Unless they have a reliable and trustworthy assistant, they have to be available whenever the business is open.
- The demands of running a business may result in a lack of free time. Also, if working from home the boundaries between work time and personal time may become blurred. Owners may spend too much time in 'work mode'.
- Business owners need a variety of skills to be successful. Advertising, marketing, interviewing, hiring, management, stock control and accounting are all part of an entrepreneur's responsibilities. This will be a lot more demanding than working in a specialised area as an employee.
- If owners operate as sole traders, they have unlimited liability. This means that personal assets are not protected if the business starts to run up debts.

ACTIVITY 2   SKILLS   ANALYSIS, DECISION MAKING, REASONING

CASE STUDY: BOEING DREAMLINER®

In 2013, a Boeing Dreamliner aircraft manufactured by Boeing Company, an American multinational corporation that designs, manufactures and sells aircraft, rotorcraft, rockets and satellites worldwide, caught fire at Boston Airport and all Dreamliners were grounded due to safety concerns. It was widely reported that the aircraft had experienced a variety of incidents up to that point, and that some felt there was an element of risk in Boeing's manufacture and operations decisions. The company chose to have the jet designed and built mostly by other companies. Although Boeing had a record number of orders, the process of designing and manufacturing the jet was problematic.

- The original delivery date of 2008 was significantly delayed, and the first Dreamliner was delivered in 2011.
- Many of the components used in the main body of the aircraft failed to match Boeing's specifications. This was expensive and caused delays.
- The first Dreamliner to arrive at the company's factory for assembly was missing thousands of parts.
- In January 2013 the entire fleet of 50 Dreamliner planes was grounded after planes had problems with their batteries. One company made the original batteries that were approved but the batteries that were later installed in the Dreamliner were made by another company.

Was Boeing right to outsource the design and production of the Dreamliner? Or did the company save money but at a risk that was too high and a cost that was too great?

Source: adapted from the *Financial Times* 11.01.2013.

1. What is meant by the trade-off between risk and reward?
2. Assess the possible costs incurred by Boeing as a result of outsourcing its design and production of the Dreamliner.

1.	Firms often have to consider the trade-off between holding liquid assets and investing more in productive assets, such as machinery. By reducing the amount of liquid assets held, there is a risk of cash flow problems. However, investing more in productive assets may increase profitability.
2.	Directors of public limited companies have to find the right balance when distributing corporate profits. They can reinvest profits and hopefully increase future profitability. However, shareholders may prefer higher current dividend payments and less reinvestment.
3.	Firms might choose to take a more ethical approach to their operations. However, this is likely to come at a cost, as investment in cleaner technology might be required, for example.
4.	A common trade-off is that between higher profit margins or higher turnover. Some businesses can often sell more and raise turnover, but this may come at the expense of lower prices and reduced profit margins.

▲ Table 1 Examples of common business trade-offs

Potential entrepreneurs would have to give this trade-off serious consideration before taking the risk. Some examples of common trade-offs in business are outlined in Table 1.

WEIGHING UP TRADE-OFFS

When businesses are faced with trade-offs similar to the ones shown in Table 1, the following actions might help to find the right balance.

- **Obtain information.** One approach would be to list the advantages and disadvantages of each choice and try to determine which carries the heaviest weight.
- **Balance short term with long term.** Try to determine what might be given up in the long run for some important short-term gain – and vice versa.
- **Measure support.** When weighing up alternatives, it might be appropriate for the decision maker to think about which key staff will support a particular idea and who will oppose it. The views of others can be a powerful influence.

CHECKPOINT

1. What might be the opportunity cost of a business giving workers a 6 per cent pay increase?
2. Give two possible examples of non-monetary opportunity costs.
3. What might be the consequences of a business investing too heavily in productive assets like machinery?
4. Give two examples of possible trade-offs in business.
5. What might be sacrificed by an entrepreneur starting a new business?

SUBJECT VOCABULARY

choices in business, deciding between alternative uses of resources.
opportunity cost when choosing between different alternatives, the opportunity cost is the benefit lost from the next best alternative to the one that has been chosen.
trade-offs in business, where a decision maker faces a compromise between two different alternatives; for example, between paying dividends to shareholders and reinvesting profits in the business.

EXAM PRACTICE

OBERTAUERN FARM

SKILLS ▶ ANALYSIS, INTERPRETATION, DECISION MAKING, REASONING

Marko and Carina Almer run a dairy farm in the Austrian Alps. They use most of the milk to make high-quality cheese, which they are able to sell to restaurants and other outlets at premium prices. The business is successful and in 2017 made a profit of €90,500. However, Marko and Carina could not agree on how to use the profit. Carina was keen to reinvest the profit into the business to help increase future profitability. However, in contrast, Marko wanted to buy a holiday home in Andalucia, Spain. The holiday home could be rented out to generate an income and provide a second home in one of their favourite holiday destinations. The options in order of preference are listed below.

1. Develop an Alpine campsite on the farm.
2. Buy a holiday home in Andalucia.
3. Set up a farm shop.
4. Buy new farm machinery.

Marko and Carina have become increasingly concerned about the use of chemicals such as pesticides and fertilisers in agriculture. They currently use both on their farm but have recently had their attention drawn to a report by the European Environment Agency (EEA) *European waters – assessment of status and pressures*. In this assessment, the agency reports that 48 per cent of streams and lakes in the EU will fail to meet good ecological status by 2015. One problem is the growth of small plants called algae that use up oxygen in the water and so kill fish and other plant life in waterways. However, the fight against pollution conflicts with concern about food security. There is growing global pressure for farmers to increase food supplies to help combat rising prices and rising population growth. The trade-off between higher production (using pesticides and fertilisers) and environmentally friendly farming methods (using less or no fertiliser and pesticides) is well known.

As a result of their concern Marko and Carina have been considering a switch to organic farming. This method does not use chemical fertilisers or pesticides. It relies upon more natural forms of farming such as

biological pest control. Farmers boosting the numbers of natural predators of a destructive insect is one example where a natural process replaces a chemical pesticide. However, organic farming is less efficient and so output is more expensive. Austria is one of the biggest producers of organic food in the world. But if incomes fall in the future consumers may prefer to buy non-organic produce because it is cheaper. Marko and Carina have agreed to meet a consultant to discuss the possibility of switching to organic farming methods. Some of the general advantages and disadvantages of organic farming are outlined in Table 2.

Advantages of organic farming	Disadvantages of organic farming
• Natural habitats are protected. • Soil condition is improved because natural fertiliser is used. • Healthier food is likely to be produced. • Fewer chemicals means more wildlife. • Organic retail sales were around €1300 million in 2015.	• Output may be lower due to crop damage by pests such as destructive insects. • The crop output has been reported as around 19 per cent lower on organic farms. • Control of unwanted weeds or other plants is very time-consuming and labour intensive. • Some organic pesticides, such as copper, can be harmful. • Some organic farming methods use more water, which can be costly.

▲ Table 2 General advantages and disadvantages of organic farming

(a) Explain what is meant by a trade-off when making a business decision. **(4 marks)**

(b) Explain the opportunity cost to Obertauern Farm of developing the campsite. **(4 marks)**

(c) Explain one way in which the business might find the 'right balance' when weighing up a trade-off. **(4 marks)**

(d) Assess the costs to Obertauern Farm of switching to organic production. **(10 marks)**

PLANNING A BUSINESS AND RAISING FINANCE

This first section in Unit 2 looks at the importance of planning in business and the content that might be included in a formal business plan. It also explores how businesses might raise finance. It features internal sources of finance, such as retained profit and owners' capital, and also external sources, such as bank loans, venture capital and crowd funding. The different forms of business organisation, such as sole traders, partnerships and limited companies are covered. And finally, the implications of limited and unlimited liability are also investigated.

23 PLANNING

LEARNING OBJECTIVES

By the end of this chapter you should be able to understand:
- ■ the content of a business plan
- ■ the relevance and uses of a business plan.

GETTING STARTED

Rahim Chandran is a trainee accountant at a firm of chartered accountants based in Pahang, Malaysia. Although he is doing very well at the practice, he feels dissatisfied. His real aim is to run his own business. Rahim has a degree in computer programing and an idea for an app. He thinks that people might benefit from having an app that shows instantly how much money they have available to spend. The app would be based on a weekly budget, which people would programme into their smartphones. It would show a spreadsheet of all planned spending, actual spending, money coming in (such as wages) and all money going out of their bank accounts. The app would also show all cash transactions and give an instant combined cash and bank balance. Rahim wants to set up a business to develop the app, bring it to market and then research into other finance-based apps.

He took his idea to a bank where he spent 20 minutes describing the app and how he needed a loan to get the business started. However, although the bank listened enthusiastically to Rahim they were quick to highlight some weaknesses in his business plan. Rahim had failed to think through with any accuracy his future sales or costs. He found it difficult to state clearly how any money invested in the business would be spent. He had not thought through how many staff he would need, nor what qualities they might require. He had also neglected to consider how he would launch and promote the app and whether there were any competitors in the market.

By the end of the appointment, Rahim felt he still liked the idea of the app. He also thought that the adventure of running his own business, and making lots of money, was very attractive. However, what would happen if the app did not take off? Could he tolerate the feeling of failure, was he prepared to work 7 days a week and what if he could not repay his investors? The bank was right to point out the weaknesses in the business plan and it seems that Rahim had underestimated the importance of planning. At that point, he gave up on any dream he had of becoming an entrepreneur. Perhaps a career in accounting was not so bad after all!

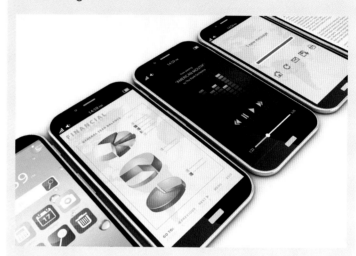

What evidence is there here to suggest that Rahim had failed to plan his business venture? What are the advantages to entrepreneurs of writing a business plan? What might be the consequences of starting a business without a proper plan? Is it a waste of time to write a business plan when afterwards you decide not to go ahead with the business idea?

WHY IS PLANNING IMPORTANT?

When organising an important event like a wedding, a holiday abroad or a house move, the event will be more successful if it is carefully planned. How many people would organise such events without making thorough plans before hand? If the planning process is not done things can go wrong and the consequences could be very unpleasant. For example, how good would a party be without 'proper' music? This could happen if the organiser had forgotten to book a DJ. It is sometimes said that 'failing to plan is planning to fail'.

Setting up a business can be a very complex and time-consuming. However, with careful planning the whole process is easier, less stressful and a number of expensive mistakes might be avoided.

THE CONTENTS OF A BUSINESS PLAN

A **business plan** is a plan of how the business will develop over a future period of time. It outlines the strategy of the business and helps to clarify what is needed to achieve its goals. It also helps entrepreneurs to think through their options, identifying the best opportunities and how to make the most of them. Business plans should be professionally documented and presented in a brief and clearly expressed manner. It is possible to download templates for business plans from the Internet – often free of charge. Guidance may also be obtained from banks or business advisory agents. There may be different styles but most business plans will contain some common and very important details. These include the following.

An executive summary: Some would argue that this is the most important part of the business plan. This is because anyone who reads only part of the plan, such as potential investors or banks, will always look at this particular section. It is an overview of the business start-up. It describes briefly the business opportunity to be exploited, the marketing and sales strategy, operations and then finance. Ideally, after looking at this section a reader will be keen to know more. The executive summary should be written last because it is a summary of the whole plan.

Elevator pitch: Entrepreneurs will be expected to tell others about their business idea – particularly investors, money lenders and potential customers. Therefore, a useful section in a business plan will be the elevator pitch. This is a summary that can be used in a 'pitch' about the business. The pitch should be quick and concise and delivered in the time an elevator ride would take. This is likely to be a 2-minute talk introducing the business – its name, what the business does, its aims, how it is different from competitors and who it is for. This should also be written after the business plan has been completed.

The business and its objectives: This section should state the name of the business, its trading address, its legal structure and its objectives. The whole planning process is driven by the firm's aims and objectives. When setting up a business it is much easier to make plans if the business has something specific to aim for. In the early stages of business development, the aim might be quite modest – perhaps to break even by the end of the first trading year. Survival is always an important objective for a new business.

The business opportunity: It is necessary to explain clearly what the business plans to sell. In some cases, this section is very important indeed because readers may not be familiar with the products. They may be of a highly technical nature or outside the field of readers' interests. It may be possible to provide some visual material in this section to show what products look like. In many developed countries businesses are likely to be selling services.

Owners' background: A number of people will be interested in the entrepreneur(s) who plan to set up the business. For example, potential investors, money lenders and suppliers will need to assess whether the owners should be offered credit. They will have to decide whether the people running the business are competent and trustworthy. Therefore, the business plan must include some details about the owners, such as the motives for setting up a business, their level of commitment, the nature of their training and work experience, their education and qualifications, and their hobbies and interests. Readers will want to know whether the owners have the skills and characteristics needed to run a successful business. Owners may provide CVs to support the business plan.

The market: In this section entrepreneurs need to show the size of the potential market. They will also need to identify the customer profile (the characteristics of individuals or other businesses that will be targeted). The nature of competition and the various marketing priorities will also have to be discussed. Many entrepreneurs will support this section with some market research. This might show, for example, where the typical customers are based, what causes customers to buy products and the factors that customers consider when buying a particular product. Entrepreneurs might use primary or secondary market research to gather information about the market (see Chapter 2).

It will be helpful in this section to show how the business plans to communicate with potential customers. For example, details about the following might be included:

- the methods of advertising and promotion that might be used
- the role played by social media
- the business website
- business literature, such as leaflets
- the role played by word-of-mouth advertising.

Personnel: When a business is first set up there may be very few, if any, other employees. However, in some cases other people will be needed and as the business grows, so will the need for help from other workers. Therefore, the business plan needs to clarify the number of employees needed and the skills, qualifications and experience that will be important. In the early stages of business development entrepreneurs often favour the use of part-time staff. This gives the business more flexibility.

Premises and equipment: Most new businesses will need a place from which to trade and a wide range of physical resources. For example, if opening a restaurant the business will need premises, furniture, decoration and refurbishment, cutlery (such as knives and forks), a cash register, computer, cookers, refrigerators, ovens, saucepans and other kitchen equipment. The restaurant will also need to be supplied with fresh produce, dry goods, drinks, gas, water, electricity and an Internet connection. This section of the business plan will need to list all the resources that will be needed by a new business.

Costing and finance: A very important part of the process when starting a business is working out how much it will all cost. This can be an intimidating task but entrepreneurs will find it almost impossible to raise capital or borrow money if they cannot say with some accuracy how much will be needed before trading can begin. This section may contain spreadsheets that list all the costs of setting up. Costs may be divided into 'one-off' start-up costs and ongoing expense (those which will continue to be incurred once the business is trading).

Once the set-up costs have been established business owners can work out how much money they will need to raise from potential investors. They will then need to identify some possible sources of finance. Many new businesses use bank loans and personal loans from friends and family. However, there are specialists that might lend money or provide capital for new businesses. These are discussed in Chapter 25. Finally, it is a mistake to be **undercapitalised** when starting a business. This means that a business has not raised enough money to get started. This may result in the business running out of cash and closing down. People reading a business plan may use this section to judge whether the owners are realistic about the amount of money needed to be successful.

Financial forecasts: A business plan is likely to contain a variety of financial forecasts. These might include a sales forecast, showing how the value of sales will change over a future time period, a cash flow forecast, which shows how money will flow into and out of the business on a week to week or month to month basis, a profit and loss forecast, showing when the business might move from making a loss into making a profit and how big a profit will, and a break-even analysis, showing the level of sales where total costs and total revenue will be exactly the same.

SWOT analysis: Some business plans might include a SWOT analysis. This involves looking at the internal strengths (S) and weaknesses (W) of the business idea and the external opportunities (O) and threats (T).

Finally, no two business plans will look the same. This is because both business ideas and entrepreneurs are all likely to be different in some way. There may also be variations between the styles used in different countries. Most of the sections discussed above are likely to be included but they may be ordered

differently and the importance of each section may vary. For example, the section describing the physical resources needed will contain far more depth and detail for a manufacturer than a service provider. Also, a manufacturer may include a section in the business plan with the title 'Production', in which production methods are described in more detail.

ACTIVITY 1 — SKILLS: ANALYSIS

CASE STUDY: TEACHING LANGUAGES

Emine Erkan is a retired teacher of modern languages. She lives in Ludwigshafen, Germany, and wants to set up a teaching agency. She thinks there is demand for private lessons in English and German. For example, she believes that academic students may want private English lessons to help pass their exams. She also reckons that money could be made by setting up short language courses for people wanting to learn German. She thinks that many of the economic immigrants arriving from Turkey (in particular) might be interested in 'language courses' to help them settle in Germany. Emine, whose family moved to Germany from Ankarra, Turkey, in 1978, has discussed the idea with friends. She has also spoken to some teachers who expressed an interest in using the agency to get work. In addition, she has met with a bank manager to discuss funding for the business. Emine reckons she might need around €15,000 to get started. A lot of this money would be used to market the business in the launch stage. However, the bank manager has said that to have any chance of getting funding she would have to write a business plan.

1. Explain the importance of planning to Emine when setting up a business.
2. Define a business plan.
3. What might be included in the costing and finance section of Emine's business plan?

THE PURPOSE AND RELEVANCE OF A BUSINESS PLAN

For many people, setting up a business is a life-changing decision and will have wide-ranging consequences. Therefore, it is necessary to spend some time carefully planning the whole process. Indeed, research has shown that start-up businesses that have prepared a business plan are more likely to succeed than those which have not. The business plan is how the business will develop over a period of time, like 1 or 2 years.

A business plan will also be needed to support applications for funding, both at the start-up stage and in the future. Money lenders and other investors are not likely to invest in a business unless owners can provide a clear vision of the future of the business. In particular, investors will want to know how the finance is going to be spent and when, and how it is going to be repaid. Also, when a company plans to raise money by floating on the stock market, it must publish a prospectus. This will contain important elements of a business plan. Investors have to be relatively confident that the company is going to be a success before buying shares.

A thorough and well-written business plan is likely to:
- force owners to take an objective, critical and unemotional look at the whole business idea
- provide a strategy for the development of the business
- provide an action plan that identifies key tasks that must be undertaken and goals which must be met to improve the chances of success
- highlight potential problems in advance so that solutions can be found
- help show money lenders and investors that the owner is realistic, responsible, serious and trustworthy.

CHECKPOINT

1. Give four examples of contents in a business plan.
2. What is a SWOT analysis?
3. What financial documents might be included in a business plan?
4. Who might read a business plan?
5. Outline one main reason for producing a business plan.

SUBJECT VOCABULARY

business plan a documented plan for the development of a business, giving details such as the products to be made, resources needed and forecasts such as costs, revenues and cash flow.
undercapitalised a business with insufficient capital to run effectively.

EXAM-STYLE QUESTIONS

INSTANT ROAD RESCUE

SKILLS   ANALYSIS
INTERPRETATION

In the last 10 years or so the Indian government has invested heavily in the nation's road networks. For example, in 2016/17 133 km of roads were constructed per day. This compares with the 2011–14 average of 73 km per day. India now has the second longest road network in the world – 4.7 million km. This infrastructure supports the transportation of more than 60 per cent of goods in India and 85 per cent of India's travellers. However, this growth in road development has contributed to an increase in road traffic accidents. For example, in one Indian state, Kerala, Thiruvananthapuram, there was a 20 per cent increase in the number of road accidents in the state during 2016 compared to 2015, rising from 39,014 to 49,329.

It was this information that motivated the Singh brothers, Jagbir and Kafar, to set up Instant Road Rescue in Kochi, Kerala. They wanted to provide an efficient breakdown and recovery service to the growing number of Indian vehicle owners. They wrote a comprehensive business plan before they started trading, which they used to help raise finance for the venture. Kafar said, 'Writing the business plan was a bit of a chore. It took a long time and all we wanted to do was to get trading. However, writing the plan ensured that we were well prepared when the launch eventually came. It made us think through a lot of important issues and helped us to avoid mistakes. For example, if we had not written the plan we would have overlooked the importance of social media in our marketing. The plan also helped us to get finance for the business. The bank could tell that Jagbir and I were thorough, committed, honest and realistic.' An extract from the business plan, the executive summary, is shown below.

INSTANT ROAD RESCUE

Executive summary: Instant Road Rescue (IRR) is a 24-hour breakdown recovery service based in Kochi (a city with a population of over 2 million), the largest city in Kerala. IRR will respond to breakdown calls within 30 km of Kochi and transport broken-down vehicles to any location within 200 km. IRR will have a transparent pricing policy. This is a unique selling point. Callers will be charged a Rs 2000 call-out fee plus Rs 20 per km.

Figure 1 shows that car ownership in India has more than doubled in 10 years. Further rapid growth in car ownership is to be expected as the Indian economy grows and people become wealthier. Research into the market concluded that 80 per cent of current breakdown operators were unreliable, unprofessional, rude, overpriced and unsympathetic. The market is growing rapidly. IRR will guarantee a response of time of 1 hour and deal with all customers in a friendly but highly professional manner. IRR will be promoted by listing the service in appropriate directories, using roadside posters highlighting the easily memorable contact number (IRR 0484 448844) and placing leaflets on parked cars in the city (in the hope that many drivers will see the leaflet). The use of social media by callers will be encouraged to inform friends and relatives about the service.

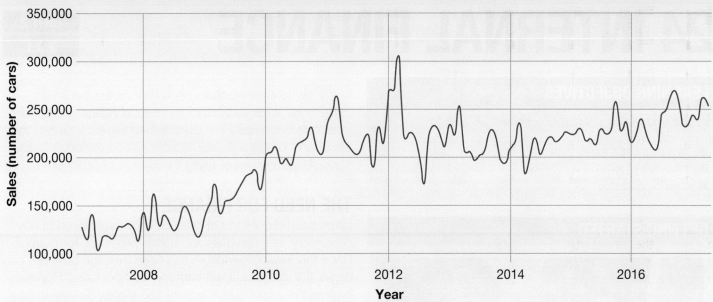

▲ Figure 1 Indian car sales, 2007–17
Source: Tradingeconomics.com | Centre for Monitoring Indian Economy

IRR will buy two breakdown vehicles initially and have a small network of subcontractors around the state to deal with unexpected surges in demand. The margins on subcontracted callouts will be small and a fee will have to be paid on a monthly basis to secure their loyalty. Subcontractors will also have to be trained in customer service. Initially two other people will be employed to share the work with Jagbir and Kafar.

Both Jagbir and Kafar have previous work experience working in the family second-hand car sales business. Jagbir is a qualified mechanic and Kafar has a degree in business management. Rs 2 million will be needed to set up the business and fund the first 9 months of trading. The Singh family will provide 50 per cent of this and a bank loan is needed for the other 50 per cent.

In the future IRR plans to:
- provide breakdown recovery insurance
- expand into nearby states in southern India
- set up an affordable and rapid motor repair operation.

(a) Define the term executive summary. **(2 marks)**
(b) Explain the purpose of an elevator pitch in a business plan. **(4 marks)**
(c) Discuss **two** important sections that should be contained in a business plan. **(8 marks)**
(d) Assess the purpose and relevance to Instant Road Rescue of a business plan. **(10 marks)**

24 INTERNAL FINANCE

LEARNING OBJECTIVES

By the end of this chapter you should be able to understand:
- owner's capital: personal savings
- retained profit
- sale of assets.

GETTING STARTED

Ahana Chaudhary started her own business after she was made redundant from her local hospital. She used her €6000 redundancy money and a further €4000 from her savings to start a business, providing a home care service for the elderly in her home town of Ghent, Belgium. The business was profitable from the start and 5 years later she recruited two full-time staff. Eventually, the demand was so great that she decided to operate a care agency, providing staff to deal with the needs of the elderly. She used €25,000 profit from the business as a deposit to buy an office for the agency.

Why do entrepreneurs need finance to start a business? What sources of finance did Ahana use to start her care business? How did she fund the expansion of the business into an agency? What might be the advantages and disadvantages of using this source of finance?

THE NEED FOR FINANCE

Firms need money to get started. They might need to buy equipment, raw materials and obtain premises, for example. Once this initial expenditure has been met, the business can begin. If successful, it will earn money from sales. However, business is a continuous activity and money flowing in may be used to buy more raw materials and settle other trading debts. If the owner wants to expand, extra money may be needed over and above that from sales. Expansion may mean larger premises, more equipment and extra workers. A business will need to find a way of raising this finance.

The items of expenditure above fall into two categories – **capital expenditure** or **revenue expenditure**. Capital expenditure is spending on items that may be used over and over again. A company vehicle, a cutting machine and a new factory all fall into this category. Revenue expenditure refers to payments for goods and services that have either already been consumed or will be very soon. Wages, raw materials and fuel are all examples of this category. Revenue expenditure also includes the maintenance and repair of buildings and machines.

OWNER'S CAPITAL

Capital is the money provided by the owners in a business. It is an example of **internal finance**. Internal finance is money generated by the business or the current owners. In most cases, a business cannot start unless the owners provide capital of their own. Providing capital is part of the risk taken by entrepreneurs when setting up a business.

Owners provide capital from their own personal resources. A common source is personal savings. Some entrepreneurs have deliberately saved up over a period of time so that they can start their own business. Sometimes, people who have lost their jobs may decide to go into business using their redundancy payments. These sources are personal and can be used by sole traders and partnerships. Owners of limited companies also provide their own capital. They have to find money to buy shares. Finally, owners can introduce fresh capital in the future if there is a need. Owner's capital is not just provided at the start-up stage.

RETAINED PROFIT

Retained profit is profit after tax that is put back into business and not returned to the owners. It is the single most important source of finance for a business. A lot of business funding comes from retained profit. It is the cheapest source of finance, with no financial charges, such as interest and administration. However, there is an opportunity cost. If retained profit is used by the business it cannot be returned to the owners. For a small business this might mean that owners and their families have less money to fund their lifestyle. For limited companies it means that shareholders receive lower dividends. In the case of a public limited company this may lead to conflict if the shareholders see that dividend payments have been frozen because the directors have used the profit in the business.

Retained profit is a flexible source of finance. It does not have to be used immediately. It can be collected gradually by a business and retained in a bank account where it will earn interest. A business can then use the retained profit at a later date. If a business does not make a profit, retained profit is not possible as a source of finance.

SALE OF ASSETS

An established business may be able to sell some unwanted assets to raise finance. For example, machinery, obsolete stock, land and buildings that are no longer required could be sold off for cash. Large companies can sell parts of their organisation to raise finance.

In 2017, LeEco, the Chinese tech conglomerate, planned to sell a prime property in Beijing for a price in excess of US$420 million. The money was needed by the company to invest in its core businesses such as automobiles, smartphones, television and its sports unit, LeSports.

Another option is to raise money through a **sale and leaseback** agreement. This involves selling an asset, such as property or machinery that the business still actually needs. The sale is made to a specialist company that leases the asset back to the seller. This is an increasingly popular source of finance. With such agreements instant cash is generated for the seller and the responsibility for the repair and maintenance of the asset passes to the new owner.

In 2016, the state-owned carrier Air India agreed a sale and leaseback deal for nine of its Dreamliner aircraft. Around 6000 crore was raised from the sale to Deutsche Bank, Bank of India, Export Import Bank of India and Industrial and Commercial Bank of China (ICBC). The sale proceeds were used to reduce Air India's debt. Air India will now lease the aircraft from the buying consortium.

ADVANTAGES AND DISADVANTAGES OF INTERNAL FINANCE

There are a number of advantages when using internal finance to fund business activity, though despite the attractive nature of internal finance, there may also be some drawbacks.

Table 1 summarises the advantages and disadvantages of using internal finance.

Advantages	Disadvantages
The capital is available immediately – there is no time delay between identifying a need for finance and obtaining it. For instance, retained profit will be in a bank account ready and waiting. Assets can be sold quickly if the price is competitive.	Internal finance can be limited – a business may not be sufficiently profitable to use retained profit or may not have unwanted assets to sell. Also, the current owners may not have any personal resources to contribute.
Internal finance is cheap – there are no interest payments, which means that costs will be lower and profit higher. Also, there are no administration costs.	Internal sources of finance cannot be subtracted from business profits to reduce tax owed. If external finance is used, the interest paid on a loan or leasing charges for assets, for example, can be treated as a business cost and subtracted from business profits to reduce tax owed.

The business will not be subject to credit checks. External finance often requires investigations into credit history of the borrowers.	Internal finance can be inflexible compared to external sources of finance. There are a wide variety of funding options for external finance, which can give the business flexibility.
There is no need to involve third parties.	There are no inflationary benefits with internal finance. Inflation can reduce the value of debt if external sources are used.
	Opportunity cost of using internal sources of finance can be high. For example, a plc considering the use of retained profits for funding will have to consider the reactions of shareholders if dividends are frozen or cut. Some shareholders may have a very short-term view and demand higher dividends now. This could result in conflict between shareholders and directors.

▲ Table 1 Advantages and disadvantages of internal finance

ACTIVITY 1   SKILLS   ANALYSIS

CASE STUDY: AVIGILON

In Canada, Vancouver-based Avigilon designs and manufactures video analysis equipment, security cameras and access control systems. Avigilon's products can be found in a wide variety of locations and sites. These include schools, transportation systems, healthcare centres, prisons, factories, airports, government organisations and shops. In 2016, Avigilon decided to sell its head office, a nine-storey building located in central Vancouver valued in excess of CAD 100 million. Avigilon are looking for a sale and leaseback deal that gives the company full use of the building. The building was purchased by Avigilon in November 2015 for CAD 42 million and the company is currently upgrading facilities. Avigilon will use the proceeds from the sale to reduce the company's debt, boost working capital (the liquid resources needed for the day-to-day running of a business) and increase shareholder value. According to Avigilon's CEO, 'Vancouver's real estate market is in a period of unprecedented growth. The building is located in one of the most desirable downtown locations. This presents a great opportunity for Avigilon to secure the space needed to support our growing business and increase shareholder value.' The sale would see Avigilon more than double their money on the purchase of the building.

1. Define sale and leaseback.
2. How did Avigilon plan to use the proceeds from the sale of its head office?
3. Explain **two** advantages to Avigilon of using sale and leaseback as a source of finance.

EXAM HINT

When answering a question on internal sources of finance, remember to consider carefully the financial circumstances of the case in the question. The sources and methods of finance used by a business will depend significantly on the nature of the business and its financial position. For example, smaller businesses may be forced to use internal sources because they present too much of a risk to external providers. In contrast, plcs have a much wider range to choose from because they are more secure and may have large quantities of collateral, which they can use to support a loan. Paying close attention to the business circumstances in the question will help you to show your skills in application.

SUBJECT VOCABULARY

capital money put into the business by the owners.
capital expenditure spending on business resources that can be used repeatedly over a period of time.
internal finance money generated by the business or its current owners.
retained profit profit after tax that is 'ploughed back' into the business.
revenue expenditure spending on business resources that have already been consumed or will be very shortly.
sale and leaseback the practice of selling assets, such as property or machinery, and leasing them back from the buyer.

CHECKPOINT

1. What is the difference between revenue expenditure and capital expenditure?

2. Give three examples of capital expenditure a farmer might undertake.

3. What is meant by capital?

4. State one advantage of using retained profit as a source of finance.

5. State two advantages of using the sale of assets to raise finance.

6. State two disadvantages of using internal finance.

EXAM PRACTICE

MUSCAT INTERIOR DESIGN

Muscat Interior Design (MID) was set up in 2010 by Qasim Al-Saadi. He worked for a top interior design company in New York for 10 years. However, the US company he worked for was taken over, and the integration of the two businesses meant that Qasim's services were no longer required. He received a very attractive redundancy package and decided to return home to Oman. Indeed, his ambition was always to return to the Middle East and start his own design business. Qasim is a talented designer and invested OMR 15,000 of his own money to set up the venture. The first few years were difficult. However, Qasim and his small team of highly skilled decorators eventually earned a reputation in the city of Muscat for producing high-quality interior designs and installation. The company specialised in bedroom designs and started to win some highly profitable contracts from hotel developers.

In 2017, MID won a contract to refit 30 rooms in a city hotel development. The contract was accepted by Qasim but he knew that the business would need to raise a further OMR 25,000 to fund the purchase of some specialist equipment and some high-quality imported raw materials. He would also need to meet the cost of recruiting another six or seven employees. Qasim was very keen to raise the funds internally even if it meant selling one or two vehicles owned by the business. Qasim did not want the company to go into debt, owing money

to investors and creditors. He wanted the business to be self-financing.

Figure 1 shows the profit made by the business between 2010 and 2016. Qasim is considering the use of some retained profit to finance the new contract.

(a) Define internal finance. **(2 marks)**

(b) Explain how Qasim might have raised the initial capital to start the business in 2010. **(4 marks)**

(c) Explain the opportunity cost to Muscat Interior Design of using retained profit for financing business activity. **(4 marks)**

(d) Assess Qasim's decision to use internal finance to fund the new contract in this case. **(10 marks)**

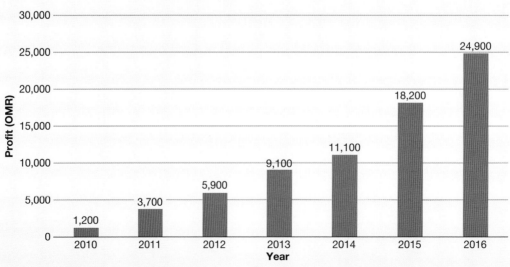

▲ Figure 1 Muscat Interior Design (MID) profit, 2010–16

25 EXTERNAL FINANCE

LEARNING OBJECTIVES

By the end of this chapter you should be able to understand:
- sources of finance and their suitability for different circumstances: family and friends, banks, peer-to-peer funding, business angels, crowd funding and other businesses
- methods of finance and their suitability for different circumstances: loans, share capital, venture capital, overdrafts, leasing, trade credit and grants.

GETTING STARTED

Nanchong Steelwork Ltd is a Chinese steel producer. The company has benefited in recent years from the government's massive investment in infrastructure projects, such as roads, bridges and tunnels. A number of years ago it won a government contract to carry out some steelwork on the new Olympic stadium. More recently it has undertaken work on motorway bridges. The business buys most of its raw materials from suppliers using trade credit – it gets 90 days to pay. The business has a 25-year mortgage on its premises (an office block and yard in Nanchong) and owes CNY 45,000 on a 2-year bank loan. It owns about one-half of its plant and machinery but the other half is leased. Finally, the company is owned by four family members who each invested CNY 200,000 10 years ago when the business was set up.

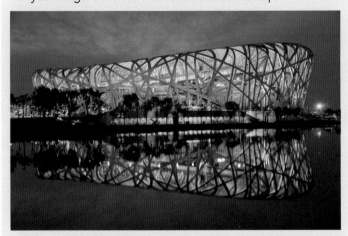

▲ The Olympic stadium, Beijing

Define external sources of finance. State five ways in which Nanchong Steelwork Ltd funds its business. Can you think of any other methods of business finance? How might the business raise CNY 4 million to buy an expensive machine?

EXTERNAL FINANCE

Few businesses can rely entirely on internal financing (see Chapter 24) to fund all business activity. Initially, **external finance**, which is finance from sources outside the business, may not be available. This is because new businesses have no trading record and present too much risk for many lenders. However, once a business has survived the initial 'uncertain' stages of business development, external sources of finance are likely to become a realistic option.

SOURCES OF FINANCE

There is quite a wide range of external sources that businesses can choose from.

Family and friends: A common source of finance, particularly for small businesses, is family members or close friends. This may be a cheap source because if the money is a loan, interest charges may be low, or possibly zero. In some cases money might be gifted to an entrepreneur. For example, a parent or grandparent might give their child or grandchild a sum of money as a present to help them get started. Another possible advantage of finance from friends or family is that they may not want to share in the ownership of the business. Consequently, they will not be able to interfere in the running of the business. However, serious problems could arise if a loan cannot be repaid or the terms of the arrangement are unclear. This could lead to the loss of friendship or a breakdown in family relations.

Banks: Commercial banks such as ANZ (Australia), State Bank of India, Commerzbank (Germany) and HSBC provide a range of different external funding arrangements for businesses. These include loans, overdrafts and mortgages. Most commercial banks have specialist departments or staff that deal exclusively with businesses. Banks will be involved in a business start-up because businesses need a bank account to facilitate financial transactions with customers and suppliers. Banks might also offer advisory services to businesses. These are often free. A formal application is required to get finance from banks and it will probably be necessary to provide a business plan.

Peer-to-peer lending: Peer-to-peer lending (P2PL) involves people lending money to unrelated individuals or 'peers' and therefore avoiding the use of a bank. Transactions are undertaken online and are organised by specialists such as Lendbox in India, Zopa in the UK and Pandai in China. Although this source of finance can be used by a business, it is not exclusive to businesses. Anyone can apply for a peer-to-peer loan. The key features of peer-to-peer lending include the following.

- All loans are unsecured, which means there is no protection for lenders. Therefore, lenders might lose their money if a borrower is unable to repay the loan.
- The whole financial arrangement is conducted for profit.
- All transactions take place online.
- No previous knowledge or relationship between lenders and borrowers is needed.
- Lenders may choose which borrower to lend to.
- Peer-to-peer sites make a charge – typically about 1 per cent.

The main attraction of P2PL is that interest rates are better for both borrowers and lenders than those offered by a bank. P2PL is also very convenient because it can be completed online fairly quickly. However, the main disadvantage is that in most countries there may be a lack of government protection for lenders. For example, in some countries there are compensation schemes that guarantee financial protection for money held in the bank accounts of recognised commercial banks. No such protection is provided for money lent using P2PL arrangements. Also, if you are a lender, access to cash may not be instant – each operator has different rules, but money might be locked away for months or longer.

Business angels: Business angels are individuals who typically may invest between £10,000 and £100,000+, often in exchange for a stake in a business. An angel might make one or two investments in a 3-year period, either individually or together with a small group of friends, relatives or business associates. Most investments are in business start-ups or in early stages of expansion. There are several reasons why people become business angels. Many like the excitement of the risk involved, or being part of a new or developing business. Others are attracted by the tax relief offered by the government. Some are looking for investment opportunities for their surplus income.

A problem with this source of finance for businesses is finding a suitable 'angel'. As angels normally take a stake in the business, the angel and the current business owners must have shared interests and a common vision for the future direction of the firm. For example, some owners might look for an angel with business experience hoping that they can provide some useful input into the running of the business. In contrast, many owners might want angels to keep their distance and just maintain a financial interest in the business. Also, business angels may be demanding individuals with considerable pressures on their time. They may be overwhelmed by business propositions and spend a lot of time selecting suitable targets for investment.

Business owners must present a clear and compelling business proposition. They must highlight the positive aspects of the venture, but with due regard to the risks involved. Business owners also have to be comfortable with sharing profits with the angel for as long as they are involved. Funding from business angels is popular in many countries around the world. For example, in 2016, it was reported that business angel investment in Ireland was estimated to be worth between €70 million and €120 million annually.

ACTIVITY 1 — SKILLS ANALYSIS

CASE STUDY: KHALID SPORTSGEAR LTD

Usman Ahmad Khalid runs Khalid SportsGear Ltd, a sports equipment manufacturing business in Abu Dhabi, UAE. After a successful start, Usman saw that the market was expanding and that an opportunity existed for growing the business. However, his current factory was too small and access was poor. Usman had found a new location but AED 350,000 was needed to complete the move and meet remodeling costs. He met with a bank manager and it was agreed that a good way forward would be to attract a business angel.

Usman was introduced to Rameez Raza, a wealthy retired businessman. He agreed to put AED 350,000 in the business for a 20 per cent stake. Rameez advised Usman that he would be looking to 'cash in' his investment in 5 years. In 2016, Usman said about the business angel: 'Throughout the last 4 years Rameez attended monthly meetings, making valuable contributions. With his prudent advice he guided the business through a recession and helped it to double in size. He had a number of useful contacts and was particularly helpful on the marketing side. I will miss him when he moves on next year.'

1. Define the term 'business angel'.
2. Explain two possible disadvantages of using business angels as an external source of finance.
3. Assess the impact Rameez has had on Usman's business.

Crowd funding: Crowd funding is similar to peer-to-peer funding in that banks are excluded and individuals can lend money to others without previous knowledge of them. However, the fundraisers tend to be businesses or groups who are involved in a particular venture such as putting on production, building a school or setting up a community project. The lenders or investors will be large numbers of individuals who collectively represent 'the crowd'. Transactions are conducted online. They are administered by a crowd funding specialist such as Ulule, Kickstarter and Tumblebug (based in Europe, the USA and South Korea, respectively). These websites allow those seeking finance to publish details of their business idea or project, including how much cash they need, how they will use it and how investors stand to profit (if at all) in future. Some of the sites carry out checks on the fundraisers but not all of them. In most cases the investors, who can usually pay as little as £10 towards venture, are offered shares in the business. In 2016, a total of KRW 18 billion (US$15.4 million) was raised from 7172 investors to fund 121 projects, according to the Financial Services Commission in South Korea.

THINKING BIGGER

There has been a huge growth in the number of sites offering P2PL and crowd funding since 2008. This is mainly because interest rates have been low for many years, so savers have been desperate to seek alternative ways of using their money to gain a good return. There has also been a 'credit crunch' since 2008, which has resulted in a reduction in the number of loans granted by traditional business lenders, such as banks. Furthermore, a string of financial scandals has led to a loss of trust in some banks around the world. In the future, if there is strong growth in these sources of finance, it may become easier for businesses to raise external finance. The market might become more competitive and business funding could get cheaper and more accessible.

You could use this information on sources of external funding in a variety of ways. It will be of use when answering questions on business finance. It might also be useful when discussing changes in technology, competition and business, business and the economy, business efficiency and the causes and effects of change.

Other businesses: Another external source of finance might be provided by other businesses. For example, a business might set up a fully funded subsidiary. This might occur when a manufacturer sets up a business to supply it with components. Some businesses set up joint ventures, where the businesses share the finance, costs and profits of a specific venture. Some plcs buy shares in other companies. This might be to earn an income, if they have surplus cash for example. Alternatively, plcs might buy shares in other companies to build a controlling stake, perhaps with a view to taking them over in the future.

METHODS OF FINANCE

Businesses can use a variety of different methods to raise finance.

Loans: A loan is an arrangement where the amount borrowed must be returned over a fixed period of time in regular equal payments. Loans tend to be inflexible and interest will be added to the total. There are different sorts of loan capital.

- **Bank loans** are probably the most common type of loan. They may be **unsecured loans**. This means that the lender has no protection if the borrower fails to repay the money owed. They can be used for long-term or short-term purposes depending on the needs of the business. However, the use of unsecured bank loans has probably diminished in recent years due to the high risk they carry for banks.

- **Mortgages** are **secured loans** where the borrower has to provide some assets as collateral to support the loan. This means that if the borrower defaults, the lender is entitled to sell the assets and use the money from the sale to repay the outstanding amount. Mortgages are long-term loans and are typically for 25 years or more. They might be used by a business to fund the purchase of premises or a large item of capital equipment. Mortgages are usually cheaper than unsecured loans because there is less risk for the lender.

- **Debentures** are a specialised method of loan finance. The holder of a **debenture** is a creditor (someone to whom the business owes money) of a company, not an owner. Debenture holders are entitled to a fixed rate of return, but have no voting rights. They must also be repaid on a set date – when the the term of the loan ends. Public limited companies use this long-term source of finance.

MATHS TIP

If a business takes out a 4-year bank loan for £50,000 with an interest rate of 10 per cent per annum, what will be the monthly repayments (including interest)?

Total interest = 10% × £50,000 = £5000 × 4
= £20,000.

$$\text{Monthly repayments} = \frac{£50,000 + £20,000}{4 \times 12}$$

$$= \frac{£70,000}{48} = £1,458.33 \text{ per month}$$

ACTIVITY 2

SKILLS | ANALYSIS, PROBLEM SOLVING

CASE STUDY: PETAR POPOV

Petar Popov runs a distribution company in Sofia, Bulgaria. He owns five lorries and has a contract with a supermarket chain. He distributes grocery products from suppliers to a network of supermarkets in the country. In 2017, he needed BGN 130,000 to replace one of the older lorries. He considered a number of sources but decided to take out a 5-year bank loan. The interest rate was 7.5 per cent per annum.

1. Define a bank loan.
2. Calculate the total interest charge on the 5-year loan.
3. Calculate the monthly repayments on the loan.

Share capital: For a limited company **share capital** is likely to be the most important source of finance. The sale of shares can raise very large amounts of money. **Issued share capital** is the money raised from the sale of shares. **Authorised share capital** is the maximum amount shareholders want to raise. Share capital is often referred to as **permanent capital**. This is because it is not normally redeemed, i.e. it is not repaid by the business. Once the share has been sold, the buyer is entitled to a share in the profit of the company, i.e. a dividend. Dividends are not always declared. Sometimes a business makes a loss or needs to retain profit to help fund future business activities. A shareholder can make a **capital gain** by selling the share at a higher price than it was originally bought for. Shares are not normally sold back to the business. The shares of public limited companies are sold in a special share market called the stock market or stock exchange. Shares in private limited companies are transferred privately. Shareholders, because they are part owners of the business, are entitled to a vote. One vote is allowed for each share owned. Voting takes place annually and shareholders vote either to re-elect the existing board of directors or replace them. Different types of shares can be issued.

- **Ordinary shares.** These are also called **equities** and are the most common type of share issued. They are also the riskiest type of share since there is no guaranteed dividend. The size of the dividend depends on how much profit is made and how much the directors decide to retain in the business. All ordinary shareholders have voting rights. When a share is first sold it has a nominal value shown on it – its original value. Share prices will change as they are bought and sold again and again.

- **Preference shares.** The owners of these shares receive a fixed rate of return when a dividend is declared. They carry less risk because shareholders are entitled to their dividend before the holders of ordinary shares. Preference shareholders are not strictly owners of the company. If the company is sold, their rights to dividends and capital repayments are limited to fixed amounts. Some preference shares also allow their holders to receive late-payment of dividends that were missed in years when dividends were not declared. Some are also redeemable, which means that they can be bought back by the company.

- **Deferred shares.** These are not used often. They are usually held by the founders of the company. Deferred shareholders only receive a dividend after the ordinary shareholders have been paid a minimum amount.

Venture capital: Venture capitalists are specialists in the provision of funds for small- and medium-sized businesses. Typically they invest in businesses after the initial start-up and often prefer technology companies with high growth potential. They prefer to take a stake in the company, which means they have some control and are entitled to a share in the profit. Venture capitalists raise their funds from institutional investors such as pension funds, insurance companies and wealthy individuals. They are also likely to exit after about 5 years. Examples of venture capitalists include MMC Ventures, Index Ventures and AXM Venture Capital. Businesses may turn to venture capitalists for funding when they have been refused by other sources.

Bank overdraft: This is an important source of finance for a large number of businesses. A **bank overdraft** means that a business can spend more money than it has in its account. In other words they go 'overdrawn'. The bank and the business will agree on an overdraft limit and interest is only charged when the account is overdrawn. The amount by which a business goes overdrawn depends on its needs at the time. This means that bank overdrafts provide a flexible source of funding to businesses. However, a bank has the legal right to call in the money owed at any point in time. This will happen if the bank suspects that the business is struggling and unlikely to repay what is owed.

Leasing: A **lease** is a contract through which a business acquires the use of resources, such as property, machinery or equipment, in return for regular payments. In this type of finance, the ownership never passes to the business that is using the resource. With a finance lease, the arrangement is often for 3 years or longer and, at the end of the period, the business is given the option of then buying the resource.

There are some advantages of leasing.

- No large sums of money are needed to buy the use of equipment.
- Maintenance and repair costs are not the responsibility of the user.
- Hire companies can offer the most up-to-date equipment.
- Leasing is useful when equipment is only required occasionally.
- A leasing agreement is generally easier for a new company to obtain than other forms of loan finance. This is because the assets remain the property of the leasing company.

However:

- over a long period of time leasing is more expensive than the purchase of equipment and machinery
- loans cannot be secured on assets that are leased.

Trade credit: It is common for businesses to buy raw materials, components and fuel, and pay for them at a later date, usually within 30–90 days. Paying for goods and services using trade credit seems to be an interest-free way of raising finance. It is particularly profitable during periods of inflation. However, many companies encourage early payment by offering discounts. The cost of goods is often higher if the firm does not pay early. Delaying the payment of bills can also result in poor business relations with suppliers.

Grants: Some businesses might qualify for financial support in the form of a grant. Both central and local government in most countries around the world back a wide range of schemes. A list of grants available can be accessed using the government's 'business finance support finder' tool. This allows firms to select specific funding options and search for grants by business location, size and type of business activity.

One example of a scheme in the Caribbean is Compete Caribbean. This supports innovative projects through its highly competitive 'innovation window' facility. Businesses can apply for up to US$500,000

for transformational, high-risk ventures that promise to advance economic development in the Caribbean. Another is the Arthur Guinness Projects scheme. This provides grants ranging from US$10,000 to over US$50,000 to social and high-impact enterprises. Businesses operating in areas such as technology, environment, social and community regeneration, culture and arts, and community well-being are favoured by this scheme.

Grants are usually available to small businesses providing they meet certain criteria. Most grants do not have to be repaid, so this is a significant advantage of this type of external finance.

ACTIVITY 3   SKILLS   ANALYSIS

CASE STUDY: SOUTH AFRICAN BUSINESS GRANTS

There are a number of government schemes in South Africa that provide grants for businesses. Examples include Automotive Investment Scheme, National Youth Development Agency and several others. One scheme, Black Business Supplier Development Programme, provides grants for existing businesses that are at least 50.1 per cent owned by black people (black, Indian or other non-white races). The main purpose of this fund is to support businesses that are owned by non-White South Africans.

This specialist funding arrangement offers non-repayable grants of up to ZAR 1 million to help businesses improve their competitiveness and sustainability. The aims of these business grants are to expand existing businesses and boost employment in the country. However, these grants are not available to business start-ups. Four-fifths (up to ZAR 800,000) of the total grant should be allocated specifically for tools, machinery and equipment and the remainder (up to ZAR 200,000) is intended for business development and training. The government hopes the money will be used to improve corporate governance, management, marketing, productivity and businesses will make more use of modern technology.

In order to qualify for these grants a business must ensure that:

- it is a CIPC (Companies and Intellectual Property Commission) registered company
- it is 50.1 per cent or more black owned (black, Indian or non-white)
- the management team is 50 per cent black
- it has a turnover of between ZAR 250,000 and ZAR 35 million per annum

- it has been trading for at least 1 year and can provide proof of turnover
- it has valid SARS tax clearance and IRT14 SARS document.

1. Explain **one** advantage to a South African business of getting one of these grants.
2. What measures must a business take in order to qualify for funding from the Black Business Supplier Development Programme.
3. Explain **one** reason why many governments around the world give grants to businesses.

CHECKPOINT

1. What is external finance?
2. What is the difference between crowd funding and peer-to-peer lending?
3. State two reasons why a business angel would invest in a business.
4. Bank overdrafts are flexible. What does this mean?
5. What is the main advantage of an unsecured bank loan for a business, when raising finance?
6. What is a capital gain?
7. State two advantages of leasing as a method of finance.
8. How might a business use trade credit as a method of finance?
9. What sort of businesses might venture capitalists look to invest in?

SUBJECT VOCABULARY

authorised share capital the maximum amount that can be legally raised.

bank overdraft an agreement between a business and a bank that means a business can spend more money than it has in its account (going 'overdrawn'). The overdraft limit is agreed and interest is only charged when the business goes overdrawn.

capital gain the profit made from selling a share for more than it was bought.

crowd funding where a large number of individuals (the crowd) invest in a business or project on the Internet, avoiding the use of a bank.

debenture a long-term loan to a business.

equities another name for an ordinary share.

external finance money raised from outside the business.

issued share capital amount of current share capital arising from the sale of shares.

lease a contract to acquire the use of resources such as property or equipment.

peer-to-peer lending (P2PL) where individuals lend to other individuals without prior knowledge of them, on the Internet.

permanent capital share capital that is never repaid by the company.

secured loans a loan where the lender requires security, such as property, to provide protection in case the borrower defaults.

share capital money introduced into the business through the sale of shares.

unsecured loans a loan where there are no assets to which the lender has a right if the borrower does not make repayments.

venture capitalists providers of funds for small- or medium-sized companies that may be considered too risky for other investors.

EXAM PRACTICE

NAPIER HOSPITALITY

SKILLS ANALYSIS, INTERPRETATION, REASONING

Napier Hospitality organises corporate hospitality in all the major cities on the North Island of New Zealand. They organise trips, visits and events for companies that want to entertain clients. Examples are taking guests to high-profile sporting events such as race meetings and international cricket, football and rugby matches. In the last 5 years a lot of business has been generated organising hospitality at rugby union stadiums, particularly for international matches. The market is growing very strongly and Jennifer Prince, the owner of the business, has always been able to get plenty of custom.

The business was started in a warehouse office in Napier. However, the business has reached a new stage in its development. There is now a need to relocate to a high-quality space in order to project a more 'upmarket' image. There are other investment needs. In total the business requires NZD 400,000 to:

- relocate to a new office
- redesign and upgrade the website
- set up a ticketing agency to buy and sell tickets for sporting events.

Jennifer is planning to use external funding for the business. Internal funding is not really an option because there are no assets to sell and Jenny has spent most of her profit on developing her home. Figure 1 shows the profit and retained profit for the business between 2011 and 2017. After a meeting with her accountant, the following funding options have been identified:

- a mortgage, using Jennifer's own house as security
- an unsecured bank loan
- set up a private limited company and sell shares to members of the family
- attract a business angel to invest in the company.

The method of funding preferred by Jennifer is the unsecured bank loan. She does not really want to risk any personal wealth by using her house as security for a mortgage. Also, although her father could easily provide much of the finance in a share issue, she is worried that he might try to interfere too much. She thinks the involvement of a business angel might be OK but wonders whether the right sort of investor could be found.

Q

(a) Define an unsecured bank loan. **(2 marks)**
(b) Explain one disadvantage to Napier Hospitality of issuing share capital. **(4 marks)**
(c) Explain one possible reason why Jennifer preferred external funding in this case. **(4 marks)**
(d) Assess which method of finance Napier Hospitality is likely to use in this case. **(10 marks)**

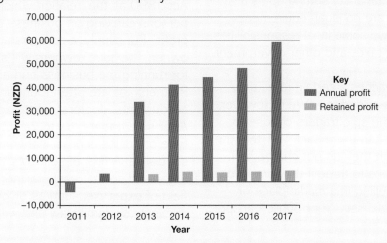

▲ Figure 1 Profit and retained profit for Napier Hospitality, 2011–17

26 FORMS OF BUSINESS

LEARNING OBJECTIVES

By the end of this chapter you should understand:
- sole trader, partnership and private limited company (Ltd)
- franchising, social enterprise, lifestyle businesses, online businesses.

GETTING STARTED

There are many kinds of business organisation. Some examples include your local hairdresser, Amazon, Samsung, a window cleaner, Nissan and Oxfam.

Who might own these businesses? How are these businesses different? What might be the advantages to a business like Amazon of operating an online business? Do all of these businesses aim to make a profit?

SOLE TRADERS

There are millions of businesses trading all over the world. For example, in the USA there are approximately 28 million, in the UK over 5 million, in India about 48 million and the EU around 26 million. They vary in their size, ownership and legal structure. A **sole trader or sole proprietor** is the simplest form of business organisation. It has one owner, but can employ any number of people. Sole traders can be involved in a wide range of business activity. In the **primary sector**, they may be farmers or fishermen. In the **secondary sector**, they may be small building or manufacturing businesses. However, most sole traders will be found in the **tertiary sector**. Many of these are retailers running small shops. Others may offer services such as web design, tutoring, hairdressing, taxi driving and garden maintenance. Setting up as a sole trader is easy, as there are no legal requirements. However, sole traders do have some legal responsibilities.

- They may have to pay taxes and other government charges.
- Once their turnover reaches a certain level, they must register for value added tax (VAT). However, in some countries some sole traders choose to register because they can claim back VAT that they have paid, even though they do not charge VAT.
- They may need a licence to trade if they are involved in activities, such as selling in a marketplace or street or supplying a taxi service or public transport.

- They may need planning permission – for example, a person may have to apply to the local authority for planning permission to convert a shop into a restaurant.
- They must comply with legislation aimed at business practice – for example, they are legally required to provide safe working conditions for their employees.

All sole traders have **unlimited liability**. This means that if the business fails, a sole trader can lose more money than was originally invested. This is because a sole trader can be forced to use personal wealth to pay off business debts. The advantages and disadvantages of operating as a sole trader are summarised in Table 1.

Advantages	Disadvantages
The owner keeps all the profit.	The owner has unlimited liability.
The business is independent and the owner has complete control.	The owner may struggle to raise finance, as lenders may consider them too risky to offer credit.
The business is simple to set up, with no legal requirements.	Independence may be a burden, for example if an owner is ill.
The business can be flexible and can adapt to change quickly.	The owner and any employees are likely to work very hard, with long hours.
The business can offer a personal service because it is small.	The business is usually too small to exploit economies of scale.
The business may qualify for government help.	The business cannot be continued if the owner passes away.

▲ Table 1 Advantages and disadvantages of sole traders

PARTNERSHIPS

A **partnership**, in the UK, is defined in the Partnership Act 1890 as the 'relation which subsists between persons carrying on business with common view to profit'. Put simply, a partnership has more than one owner. The 'joint' owners will share responsibility for running the business and also share the profits. Partnerships are often found in professions, such as accountants, doctors, estate agents, solicitors and vets. After sole traders, partnerships are the most common type of business organisation. It is usual for partners to specialise. A firm of solicitors with five partners might be organised so that each partner specialises in their own field of expertise, such as divorce, personal injury cases, criminal law, family law and wills probate.

There are no legal requirements to complete when a partnership is formed. However, partners may draw up a **deed of partnership**. This is a legal document that states partners' rights in the event of a disagreement. It covers issues such as:

- how much capital each partner will contribute
- how profits (and losses) will be shared among the partners
- the procedure for ending the partnership
- how much control each partner has
- rules for taking on new partners.

If no deed of partnership is drawn up the arrangements between partners will be subject to the Partnership Act. For example, if there is a dispute regarding the share of profits, the Act states that profits are shared equally among the partners.

The advantages and disadvantages of partnerships are shown in Table 2 on the next page.

Advantages	Disadvantages
The partnership is easy to set up and run, with no legal requirements.	Partners have unlimited liability.
Partners can specialise in their area of expertise.	Partners have to share the profit.
Partners share the burden of running the business.	Partners may disagree and fall out with one another.
More owners can raise more capital.	One partner's decision creates legal obligations for all partners.
The partnership does not have to publish financial information.	Partnerships have limited growth potential.

▲ Table 2 Advantages and disadvantages of partnerships

LIMITED PARTNERSHIPS

The Limited Partnerships Act 1907, in the UK, allows a business to become a **limited partnership**, although this is rare. This is where some partners provide capital but take no part in the management of the business. Such a partner will have **limited liability** – the partner can only lose the original amount of money invested. A partner with limited liability cannot be made to sell personal possessions to meet any other business debts. This type of partner is called a **sleeping partner**. Even with a limited partnership there must always be at least one partner with unlimited liability. The Act also allows this type of partnership to have more than 20 partners.

The Limited Liability Partnership Act 2000 allows the setting up of a limited liability partnership. All partners in this type of partnership have limited liability. To set up as a limited liability partnership, the business has to agree to comply with a number of regulations, such as sending annual reports to the Registrar of Companies.

CASE STUDY: UCHE OKAFOR ASSOCIATES

Uche Okafor Associates are a firm of chartered accounts based in Abuja, Nigeria. The partnership was formed in 2011 between Okafor, Ezuego and Amokachi, who each contributed NGN 8 million. A deed of partnership was drawn up and it was agreed that the profits from the business would be shared 40 per cent, 40 per cent and 20 per cent between Okafor, Ezuego and Amokachi, respectively. Amokachi's share was lower because he was a newly qualified accountant and therefore had less experience than the others.

One of the business's strengths is that each partner is a specialist in a particular field of accountancy. Okafor is a tax specialist, Ezuego is an investment analyst and Amokachi is in charge of external audits. This helped the business to serve a range of customers with different financial needs.

In 2016, the partners decided to expand. They needed to raise NGN 16 million to obtain more office space and upgrade their computer systems. The partners considered inviting a sleeping partner to contribute some capital. However, in the end, they borrowed the money from a bank.

1. (a) Why do you think Okafor, Ezuego and Amokachi drew up a deed of partnership?
   (b) In 2016, the partnership made a profit of NGN 25 million. In the absence of a deed of partnership, how much profit would Amokachi be entitled to?
2. Explain two advantages of a partnership illustrated by this case.
3. Discuss two possible reasons why Okafor Associates decided against inviting a sleeping partner into the business.

LIMITED COMPANIES

A **limited company** has a separate legal identity from its owners. The company can own assets, form contracts, employ people, sue people and be sued.

Certain features are common to limited companies.

- Capital is raised by selling shares. Each shareholder owns a number of these shares and is a joint owner of the company. They are entitled to vote on important business decisions, such as a choice of who should run the company. They also get dividends paid from profits. Shareholders with more shares will have more control and get more dividends.
- Unlike sole traders or partnerships, the owners (shareholders) have limited liability. If a limited company has debts, the owners can only lose the

money they originally invested. They cannot be forced to use their own money to pay any debts that have been run up by the business.

- Limited companies are run by directors who are elected by the shareholders. The board of directors, headed by a chairperson, is accountable to shareholders. The board runs the company as the shareholders wish. If the company performs badly, directors can be voted out at an annual general meeting (AGM).
- Unlike sole traders and partnerships, who pay income tax on profits, limited companies pay corporation tax.

Forming a limited company: To form a limited company, it is necessary to follow a legal procedure. This involves sending some important documents to the Registrar of Companies: these are the **memorandum of association** and the **articles of association**. These are shown in Figures 1 and 2 (below).

The memorandum of association sets out the constitution and gives details about the company. The following details must be included:
- name of the company
- name and address of the company's registered office
- objectives of the company and the nature of its activities
- amount of capital to be raised and the number of shares to be issued.

▲ Figure 1 Memorandum of association

This document deals with the internal running of the company. The articles of association include details such as:
- rights of shareholders depending on the type of share they hold
- procedures for appointing directors
- length of time directors should serve before re-election
- timing and frequency of company meetings
- arrangements for auditing company accounts.

▲ Figure 2 Articles of association

If the documents in Figures 1 and 2 are acceptable, the company gets a **certificate of incorporation**. This allows it to trade as a limited company. The shareholders have a legal right to attend the AGM and must be told of the date and venue in writing.

A limited company can be set up online, and a number of websites offer such services. Such websites provide templates for the memorandum of association and the articles of association, which makes the whole process easier.

PRIVATE LIMITED COMPANIES

Most private limited companies are small- or medium-sized businesses, though some are large businesses, similar in size to public limited companies. Private limited companies share the following features.

- Their business name ends in Limited or Ltd.
- Shares can only be transferred privately, from one individual to another. All shareholders must agree on the transfer and they cannot be advertised for sale.
- They are often family businesses owned by family members or close friends.
- The directors of private limited companies tend to be shareholders and are involved in running the business.

The advantages and disadvantages of private limited companies are outlined in Table 3.

Advantages	Disadvantages
Shareholders have limited liability.	Private limited companies have to publish their financial information.
More capital can be raised by issuing shares.	Setting-up costs have to be met.
Control over the business cannot be lost to outsiders.	Profits are shared between more members.
The owners have tax advantages. Owners may pay less tax, for example.	It takes time to transfer shares to new owners.
Private limited companies are considered to have a higher status than some other types of business organisations, such as a sole trader.	Private limited companies cannot raise large amounts of money like public limited companies.

▲ Table 3 Advantages and disadvantages of private limited companies

ACTIVITY 2　　SKILLS　REASONING, ANALYSIS

CASE STUDY: GroPak

The Netherlands is one of the largest exporters of food in the world. Kika van Lunteren owns GroPak, a food processing business in Pijnacker. Around 60 per cent of GroPak's output is for the export market. Kika buys vegetables in bulk from local farmers and then washes, cuts and packs them attractively before delivering them to customers. She set up as a sole trader in 2006, but the growth of the business has taken her by surprise. The success is down to a 'sale-or-return' policy that customers like. This results in some waste, but her premium pricing helps to compensate for any losses.

In order to meet the demands of rapid growth and to help expand into new markets, Kika needs to raise €400,000. She has approached a number of banks, but has found that they are reluctant to lend to her. Her accountant has suggested forming a private limited company to raise money by issuing some shares to members of her family and two key employees of the business.

1. Explain two advantages of becoming a shareholder in GroPak.
2. Explain who runs a private limited company.
3. Assess the likely impact on Kika of GroPak becoming a private limited company.

FRANCHISING

Starting up your own business carries a lot of risk. Most new start-ups have ceased to exist after 5 years of trading. One way of possibly reducing this risk is to buy a **franchise**. The franchisor is a company that owns the franchise. It has a track record of running a successful business operation. It allows another business, the franchisee, to use its business ideas and methods in return for a variety of fees. There are a number of successful global franchises. Examples include McDonald's, SUBWAY®, Pizza Hut®, Hertz® and Marriott International.

The franchisor provides a variety of services to its franchisees.

- It gives the franchisee a licence to make a product that is already tried and tested in the marketplace. This could be a physical product but is far more likely to be a service.
- The franchisor provides a recognised brand name which customers should recognise and trust. This helps generate sales from the moment the franchise starts trading.
- The franchisor will provide a start-up package. This will include help and advice about setting up the business. The franchisor might provide the equipment to start the business. It might help find a bank which will lend money. It will provide training for the new franchisee.

- Many franchises provide materials to use to make the product. A company like McDonald's, for example, sells food ingredients to its franchisees. If the franchisor does not directly sell to the franchisee, it might organise bulk-buy deals with suppliers to cut costs for all its franchise operation.
- It is likely to provide marketing support. For example, it might have national advertising campaigns. It may provide marketing materials like posters to place in business premises, or leaflets to send to customers.
- There should be ongoing training. This will be linked to issues such as maintaining standards, sales and new products.
- There is likely to be a range of business services available at competitive prices. For example, the franchisor might negotiate good deals on business insurance or vehicle leasing with suppliers.
- Many franchises operate exclusive area contracts. This is where one franchisee is guaranteed that no franchise deal will be signed with another franchisee to operate in a particular geographical area. This prevents competition between franchisees and so helps sales.
- Over time, the brand should be developed by the franchisor. For example, new products should be developed to appeal to customers.

In return for these services, the franchisee has to pay a variety of fees.

- There will be an initial start-up fee. Part of this will cover the costs of the franchisor in giving advice or perhaps providing equipment. Part of it will be a payment to use the franchise name.
- Most franchisors charge a percentage of sales for ongoing management services and the ongoing right to use the brand name.
- Franchisors will also make profit on the supplies they sell directly to their franchisors.
- There may also be one-off fees charged for management services such as training.

There are advantages and disadvantages of franchising. Table 4 shows some general advantages and disadvantages for the franchisee. Although one of the advantages is that the franchisor provides national advertising, some of it can be quite poor. Also, like any other business enterprise they can be successful or they can fail. For example, when buying a franchise, it is important for the franchisee to be careful when assessing the opportunities that the franchisor is offering. It is worth remembering that often 'you get what you pay for'. If someone who is not suited to running a business buys a franchise, the prospect of failure is still relatively high. Some of the advantages and disadvantages to franchisors of franchising are summarised in Table 5.

Advantages to the franchisee	Disadvantages to the franchisee
Franchises are lower risk, as they use an idea that has already been tried and tested.	A franchisee's profit is shared with the franchisor.
Franchisees get support from the franchisor.	Franchisees have to sign contracts with franchisors, which can reduce independence.
The set-up costs of a franchise are predictable.	Setting up a franchise can be an expensive way to start a business.
Franchisees can benefit from national marketing campaigns organised by the franchisor.	Franchisees lack independence and must follow strict operating rules.

▲ Table 4 Advantages and disadvantages to franchisees of franchising

Advantages to the franchisor	Disadvantages to the franchisor
Franchising is a fast method of growth.	Potential profit is shared with franchisees.
Franchising is a cheaper method of growth because growth is mainly funded by the franchisee.	Poor franchisees may damage the brand's reputation.
Franchisees take some of the risk on behalf of the franchisor.	Franchisees may get their supplies from elsewhere.
Franchisees are more motivated than employees.	The cost of supporting franchisees may be high.

▲ Table 5 Advantages and disadvantages to franchisors of franchising

ACTIVITY 3   SKILLS   REASONING, ANALYSIS

CASE STUDY: CARREFOUR

France-based Carrefour is an international retail chain with around 12,000 stores. It sells groceries, a few non-grocery lines and has three different types of stores – supermarkets, convenience stores, and cash and carry outlets. It also has online services that incorporate a click and collect operation. In 2016, the organisation had a turnover of €85,700 million and was Europe's largest supermarket chain.

A significant part of Carrefour's revenue results from a franchising operation. Over 7000 convenience stores are run by franchisees. For an initial cost of up to €280,000 people can become a Carrefour franchisee. One of the main advantages of taking on a Carrefour franchise is the reputation the group has for providing great value products, as well as a network of experienced service and operating staff. Carrefour

is a well-developed customer-focused chain and franchisees have the opportunity to exploit Carrefour's powerful purchasing operation and use their own skills to create a thriving business.

Another key benefit to Carrefour franchisees is the independence they enjoy. Although Carrefour is an international chain, franchisees are encouraged to identify and serve the needs of their local customer base. For example, Carrefour reckons that each of their French stores works with about 100 local producers. Finally, Carrefour offers management training programs, job training and training in merchandising. Carrefour has also created Teach, a specialist training centre designed to meet the specific needs of franchisees.

To ensure that the Carrefour brand is protected the group has a cautious recruitment policy for its franchisees. For example, the desired skills for opening a Carrefour franchise include:

- relevant management experience (ideally gained in food retailing)
- a desire to be an independent entrepreneur and business owner
- customer service skills
- management skills
- the ability to work independently
- strong communication skills
- a genuine interest in food distribution.

1. Explain the difference between a franchisor and a franchisee.
2. Discuss the key benefits to franchisees of taking out a Carrefour franchise.
3. Assess the benefits to the Carrefour Group of its franchising operation.

FINANCIAL PLANNING

This section looks at the different aspects of financial planning, beginning with the nature and calculation of sales revenue and costs, and methods of increasing sales volumes and revenues. The purpose and difficulties of sales forecasting are addressed as are the factors that affect sales forecasts. There is also coverage of break-even analysis and cash flow forecasting. The section ends with a look at the purpose and different types of budgets and how variance analysis can be used to help make business decisions.

29 SALES, REVENUE AND COSTS

LEARNING OBJECTIVES

By the end of this chapter you should be able to understand:
- calculation of sales volume and sales revenue
- calculation of fixed costs, variable costs, total costs and average costs
- ways of improving sales volumes and sales revenues.

GETTING STARTED

OzzyTrek organises specialised adventure holidays in Australia where customers can enjoy a range of outdoor activities, such as canoeing, walking, camping and kangaroo watching. The target market is young adults in the Benelux region (Belgium, the Netherlands and Luxembourg). In 2014, OzzyTrek lowered the price of its trips by 20 per cent to try to boost sales. Figures 1 and 2 show **sales volume** and **sales revenue** for the business between 2008 and 2017.

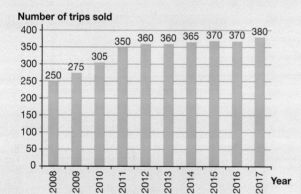

▲ Figure 1 Sales volume for OzzyTrek, 2008–17

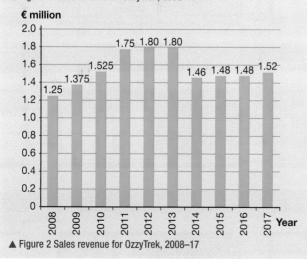

▲ Figure 2 Sales revenue for OzzyTrek, 2008–17

What is the difference between sales revenue and sales volume? What price was charged between 2008 and 2013? What price was charged after 2013? What impact did the price change in 2014 have on sales volume and sales revenue? What types of business costs might be incurred by OzzyTrek?

SALES VOLUME

The output produced by businesses is eventually sold. Businesses measure and monitor sales levels. One approach is to measure the sales volume. This is the number of units sold by a business. However, depending on the nature of the business, sales volume can be measured in different ways. Some examples are illustrated in Table 1.

Type of business	How sales volume is measured
Cereal farmer	Tonnes of wheat sold
Car manufacturer	Number of cars sold
Airline	Number of passengers carried
Oil company	Barrels of oil sold
Haulage business	Number of miles travelled
Hotel	Number of rooms let
Driving instructor	Number of hourly lessons given
Insurance company	Number of policies sold
Music tutor	Number of hourly lessons given
Dairy farmer	Litres of milk sold
Power generator	Megawatt hours sold

▲ Table 1 Measuring sales volume

When a business sells clearly recognisable units of output, such as the examples shown in Table 1, measuring or calculating sales volume is straightforward. However, in some cases it is difficult to identify single units of output. For example, how might you measure the sales volume of a supermarket that sells thousands of different products each day? Or how would you measure the annual sales volume of a construction company that builds 25 semi-detached houses, 5 apartment blocks, 2 warehouses, 2 office blocks, 2 tunnels, 5 different-sized factories and a bridge? In these cases the units sold are different – they are not standard. To overcome this problem it may be easier, and more meaningful, to calculate the sales revenue.

SALES REVENUE

Sales revenue is the *value* of output sold by a business. It may be calculated for a specific time period, such as a day, week, month or year. It can also be calculated for individual products when a business has a wide product range. Sales revenue, which is often called **total revenue**, is calculated using the following formula:

Sales revenue = Price × Quantity of output

WORKED EXAMPLE

In 2017, Gartex Mining Inc. sold 1,433,400 tonnes of stone to customers. The price per tonne was US$12.60. What is the sales revenue for 2017?

Sales revenue = US$12.60 × 1,433,400
            = US$18,060,840

All businesses have to calculate the value of their sales revenue each year. Sales revenue can be used as a measure of business performance. Most businesses would want to see their sales revenue grow each year.

BUSINESS COSTS

A business needs accurate and reliable cost information to make decisions. For example, a firm that is aiming to expand production or deliver more services to meet rising demand must know how much that extra output will cost. In the same way that you are familiar with your own personal costs – these are the regular expenses you have, such as travel to school or college – so businesses will know what their expenses are. These might include wages, raw materials, insurance and rent.

It is important to understand how the costs of a business change in the **short run** and the **long run**.

- The short run is the period of time when at least one factor of production is fixed. For example, in the short run, a firm might want to expand production in its factory. It can acquire more labour and buy more raw materials, but it has a fixed amount of space in the factory and a limited number of machines.

ACTIVITY 1   SKILLS   ANALYSIS, PROBLEM SOLVING

CASE STUDY: FC BARCELONA

FC Barcelona is one of the richest football clubs in the world. In the 2015/16 season it was reported in the media that the total revenue generated by the club was €620 million. Figure 3 shows the sales revenue for FC Barcelona between 2006/07 to 2015/16. However, the graph does not reflect the very wide range of revenue sources enjoyed by the football club. The three key revenue sources are: fees from broadcasting; commercial activities; and match day sales. For example, on a match day revenues are likely to be generated from the sale of match tickets, match programmes, food and drinks, hospitality boxes, special functions and concessions (revenue from vendors given the right to trade in or around the stadium). Sources of commercial revenues are also diverse. Examples include: the sale of merchandising, such as team shirts, clothes and almost anything containing the FC Barcelona logo; sponsorship; advertising; travel packages to overseas games; weddings; business meetings and other functions held at the stadium; stadium tours; and revenue from providing hospitality. In the 2015/16 season FC Barcelona received €40 million from Nike for kit sponsorship and €41 million from Qatar Airways for jersey sponsorship. The club is also beginning to generate revenue from its involvement in social media. In the 2014/15 season FC Barcelona enjoyed 89.6 million 'Likes' on Facebook and had 16.6 million and 26.6 million followers on Twitter and Instagram, respectively.

1. Why might FC Barcelona find it difficult to calculate sales volume?
2. If FC Barcelona play 19 games in La Liga in a season, calculate total revenue from programme sales if an average 23,500 programmes are sold at each match for €2.

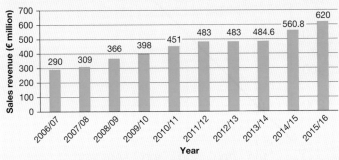

▲ Figure 3 FC Barcelona sales revenue, 2006/07–2015/16

- In the long run, all factors can vary. The firm can buy another factory and add to the number of machines. This will increase capacity (the maximum amount that can be produced) and begin another short-run period. In the service industry, an airline, for example, can buy or lease another plane in the long run to increase capacity. In the short run it may be able to fly more passengers by using its fleet of planes more frequently.

FIXED COSTS

Costs that stay the same at all levels of output in the short run are called **fixed costs**. Examples might be rent, insurance, heating bills, depreciation and business rates, as well as capital costs, such as factories and machinery. These costs remain the same whether a business produces nothing or is working at full capacity. For example, rent must still be paid even if a factory is shut for a 2-week holiday when nothing is produced. Importantly, 'fixed' here means costs do not change as a result of a change in output in the short run. But they may increase due to, say, inflation. Figure 4 shows what happens to fixed costs as a firm increases production. The line on the graph is horizontal which shows that fixed costs are £400,000 no matter how much is produced. The firm is a doll manufacturer.

What happens over a longer period? Figure 5 illustrates 'stepped' fixed costs. If a firm is at full capacity, but needs to raise production, it might decide to invest

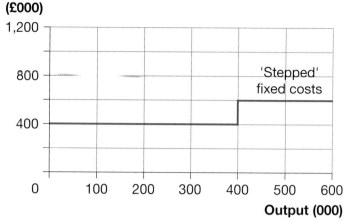

▲ Figure 5 Stepped fixed costs of a doll manufacturer

in more equipment. The new machines raise overall fixed costs as well as capacity. The rise in fixed costs is shown by a 'step' in the graph. This illustrates how fixed costs can change in the long run.

VARIABLE COSTS

Costs of production, which increase directly as output rises are called **variable costs**. For example, a baker will require more flour if more bread is produced. Raw materials are just one example of variable costs. Others might include fuel, packaging and wages. If the firm does not produce anything then variable costs will be zero.

Figure 6 shows the variable costs of the doll manufacturer mentioned above. Variable costs are £2 per doll. If the firm produces 100,000 dolls it will have variable costs of £200,000 (£2 × 100,000).

Producing 600,000 dolls will incur variable costs of £1,200,000 (£2 × 600,000). Joining these points together shows the firm's variable costs at any level of output. As output increases, so do variable costs. Notice that the graph is linear. This means that it is a straight line.

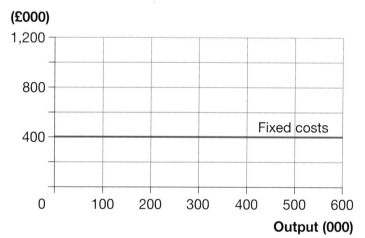

▲ Figure 4 Fixed costs of a doll manufacturer

EXAM HINT

When discussing or calculating fixed costs, it is important to remember that fixed costs will be incurred even if the business shuts down for a period of time. For example, if a sole trader operating a restaurant shuts down for 3 weeks in January when trade is low, fixed costs such as rent, insurance, interest on loans and business rates still have to be paid.

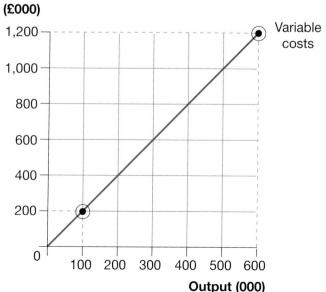

▲ Figure 6 Variable costs of a doll manufacturer

Finally, the equation for total variable cost is given by:

TVC = Variable cost per unit × Output

THINKING BIGGER

Some production costs do not fit neatly into our definitions of fixed and variable costs. This is because they are not entirely fixed or variable costs. Labour is a good example. If a firm employs a member of staff on a permanent basis, no matter what level of output, then this is a fixed cost. If this member of staff is asked to work overtime at nights and weekends to cope with extra production levels, then the extra cost is variable. Such labour costs are said to be **semi-variable costs**. Another example could be the cost of telephone charges. This often consists of a fixed or 'standing charge' plus an extra rate which varies according to the number of calls made.

TOTAL COST

If fixed and variable costs are added together they show the **total cost** of a business. The total cost of production is the cost of producing any given level of output. As output increases total costs will rise. This is shown in Figure 7, which again shows the production of dolls. We can say:

Total cost (TC) = Fixed cost (FC) + Variable cost (VC)

The business has fixed costs of £400,000 and variable costs of £2 per doll. When output is 0, total costs are £400,000. When output has risen to 300,000 dolls, total costs are £1,000,000, made up of fixed costs of £400,000 and variable costs of

THINKING BIGGER

Costs can also be divided into direct and indirect costs. Direct costs are costs that can be identified with a particular product or process. Examples of direct costs are raw materials, packaging and direct labour. Indirect costs or overheads result from the whole business. It is not possible to associate these costs directly with particular products or processes. Examples are rent, insurance, the salaries of office staff and audit fees. Indirect costs are usually fixed costs and direct costs variable costs, although in theory both direct and indirect costs can be fixed or variable.

£600,000 (£2 × 300,000). When output is 600,000, total costs are £1,600,000, made up of fixed costs of £400,000 and variable costs of £1,200,000 (£2 × 600,000). Figure 7 shows the way that total costs increase as output increases. Notice that as output increases fixed costs become a smaller proportion of total costs.

AVERAGE COST OR UNIT COST

The **average cost** is the cost per unit of production, also known as the **unit cost**. To calculate average cost, the total cost of production should be divided by the number of units produced, or output.

$$\text{Average cost} = \frac{\text{Total cost}}{\text{Output}}$$

WORKED EXAMPLE

Take the example of the doll manufacturer with fixed costs of £400,000 and variable costs of £2 per unit. If output was 100,000 units:

$$\text{Average cost} = \frac{£400,000 + (£2 \times 100,000)}{100,000}$$

$$= \frac{£600,000}{100,000} = £6$$

The importance of average cost is discussed in more detail in Chapter 37.

PROFIT AND LOSS

One of the main reasons why firms calculate their costs and revenue is to enable them to work out their **profit** or **loss**. Profit is the difference between revenue and costs.

Profit = Total revenue − Total costs

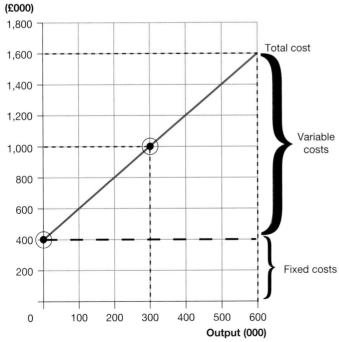

▲ Figure 7 Total cost of a doll manufacturer

For example, if the doll manufacturer produces and sells 300,000 dolls, they sell for £5, fixed costs are £400,000 and variable costs are £2 per unit, then:

Profit = £5 × 300,000 − (£400,000 + [£2 x 300,000])
    = £1,500,000 − (£400,000 + £600,000)
    = £1,500,000 − £1,000,000
    = £500,000

It is possible to calculate the profit for a business at any level of output using this method.

If the variable costs were £4 per unit, the business would make a loss.

Loss = £5 x 300,000 − (£400,000 + [£4 × 300,000])
    = £1,500,000 − (£400,000 + £1,200,000)
    = £1,500,000 − £1,600,000
    = − £100,000

WAYS OF IMPROVING SALES VOLUME

Most businesses will be keen to improve sales volumes providing they have enough capacity. A number of approaches could be used, some of which are discussed briefly below.

Advertising: Businesses will tend to sell more output if they increase expenditure on advertising. The main aim of all methods of advertising is to increase sales volume. Different businesses and industries are likely to have their own preferred methods. For example, many global car manufacturers like to use television adverts. This is because the performance of a car can be demonstrated using moving images. Many small businesses rely on much cheaper advertising media such as adverts in local newspapers. The different methods of advertising are discussed in detail in Chapter 11.

Promotion: Businesses can choose from a wide range of different methods of promotion to help increase sales volumes. Examples might be coupons, sponsorship, free gifts, loyalty schemes, PR, merchandising or direct mailing. One very popular method used in supermarkets to increase sales volume is BOGOF offers. This type of offer might even double sales volumes for a period of time. The different methods of promotion are also discussed in detail in Chapter 11.

Businesses must monitor carefully the impact on profit of increased expenditure on advertising and promotion when trying to lift sales volumes. Heavy expenditure on advertising and promotion may have a negative impact on profit even though sales volumes rise.

Improved targeting: Businesses are likely to increase sales volumes if their advertising and promotion is more targeted. That means that it should be aimed more accurately at the people who are most likely to purchase the product. For example, a golf equipment retailer could place a print advert in a national newspaper that sells several million copies per day. However, the same advert placed in a monthly golf magazine, with a much lower number of sales might be far more cost effective. This is because the advert is directed solely at golfers, that is, people who might be interested in buying golf equipment. The advert is more targeted. Many businesses are using social media to help make advertising more targeted.

Extend product range: Another approach to increasing sales volumes is to increase the range of products for sale. For example, a potato crisp manufacturer may be able to increase sales volumes by launching a new flavour. In 2016, Walkers introduced a range of sandwich flavoured crisps. These included Toasted Cheese and Worcester Sauce, Cheese, Cucumber and Salad Cream, Roast Chicken and Mayonnaise, and Sausage and Brown Sauce. One effect of this marketing strategy might be to persuade people who like sandwiches, but do not normally buy crisps, to make a purchase. This would help to increase sales volumes.

Extend distribution networks: If businesses are successful using one method of distribution, they might consider others to boost sales volumes. For example, an ever-increasing number of retailers are selling their goods online. In some cases, this enables businesses to sell to global markets. Such a move could have a very dramatic effect on sales volumes.

Develop relationships with customers: By engaging more with customers businesses might be able to improve customer retention and encourage repeat purchases. This would increase sales volumes. Ideally a business would want to attract a new customer and then keep them for life. In an effort to achieve this businesses try to develop relationships with them. To do this businesses would have to communicate effectively with customers, learn as much as possible about their customers, respond effectively to customer complaints, build customer trust and stay in regular touch without being intrusive. Many businesses have found that exchanging information with customers using social media has helped to develop relationships.

IMPROVING SALES REVENUE

Most of the methods discussed above to boost sales volumes can also help to raise sales revenue. For example, if a business increases sales volumes by 12 per cent after attending a trade fair, sales revenue may also rise by 12 per cent (assuming there is no change in price). However, businesses might use specific strategies to generate more sales revenue. Two additional methods can be identified.

Changing price: A change in price is likely to have an impact on sales revenue. Both a price increase and a price decrease might boost sales revenue. It depends on whether demand for a product is price elastic or price inelastic.

- **Raising price.** A business can increase revenue by raising price if demand is price inelastic. If PED = −0.8, a business can increase revenue by raising the price by 10 per cent even though sales volumes will actually fall by 8 per cent. For example, if the current sales volume is 100,000 and price is US$2, total revenue will be US$200,000 (100,000 × US$2). However, if the price is increased by 10 per cent to US$2.20, demand will fall by 8 per cent to 92,000. However, revenue will rise to US$202,400 (92,000 × US$2.20).

- **Lowering price.** A business can only increase revenue with a price cut if demand is price elastic. If PED = −2.4, a business can increase revenue by cutting the price by 10 per cent because demand rises by 24 per cent. For example, again, if the current sales volume is 100,000 and price is US$2, total revenue will be US$200,000 (100,000 × US$2). However, if the price is cut by 10 per cent to US$1.80, demand will rise by 24 per cent to 124,000. As a result revenue will rise to US$223,200 (124,000 × US$1.80).

Adding complementary services or products: A business can generate more sales revenue if it can persuade customers to buy additional services or products that are related to the core product. For example, revenue might be increased if a:

- shoe retailer can also sell shoe-cleaning materials and other footwear accessories
- car dealer can also sell a credit agreement and warranties
- short-haul airline charges extra for preferred seats, travel insurance, food and beverages during the flight and carrying extra luggage
- computer retailer can also sell software, insurance and protection from malware and viruses
- garden-maintenance provider can also sell plants, fertilisers and more specialist garden services such as tree felling or garden design.

CHECKPOINT

1. What is the difference between sales volume and sales revenue?
2. How is sales revenue calculated?
3. What is the difference between the short run and the long run in business?
4. Give two examples of fixed costs for a taxi driver.
5. Give two examples of variable costs for an online retailer.
6. What is a semi-variable cost?
7. How is profit calculated?

SUBJECT VOCABULARY

average cost or unit cost the cost of producing one unit, calculated by dividing the total cost by the output.
fixed cost a cost that does not change as a result of a change in output in the short run.
long run the time period where all factors of production are variable.
profit (loss) the difference between total costs and total revenue. It can be negative.
sales revenue the value of output sold in a particular time period. It is calculated by price × quantity of output.
sales volume the quantity of output sold in a particular time period.
semi-variable costs costs that consist of both fixed and variable elements.
short run the time period where at least one factor of production is fixed.
total cost the entire cost of producing a given level of output.
total revenue the amount of money the business receives from selling output.
variable costs costs that rise as output rises.

EXAM PRACTICE

RAZIA MALIK

SKILLS ANALYSIS, INTERPRETATION, PROBLEM SOLVING

Razia Malik operates as a sole trader. She offers 1-day courses in business start-ups for Urdu-speaking people in Toronto, Canada. There are about 90,000 Pakistanis living in Toronto who are targeted by Razia. The courses cover all aspects of business start-ups, such as writing a business plan, market research, financial management, negotiation skills and legal issues. Most of her work comes from local authorities.

The business charges CAD 600 for a 1-day course and can enrol up to 20 entrepreneurs. Razia rents function rooms in small hotels for CAD 150 per day to run the courses. The course fee also includes refreshments.

In 2016, the business provided a total of 200 courses and made a reasonable profit. However, Razia felt that she could improve the sales revenue of the business by marketing the business more aggressively in a wider geographical area. Her aim was to raise profit by 10 per cent. She thought that she could charge more and also reduce the amount of time travelling around the region. She spent CAD 3000 advertising on specialist Urdu websites and raised the price of the courses to CAD 900. As a result, the number of courses sold fell to 150 in 2017. Details of the costs incurred by Razia's business are shown in Table 2.

	2016	2017
Car lease per annum	5000	5000
Insurance per annum	1000	1200
Other fixed costs per annum	2000	2800
Special promotion	0	3000
Room hire fees per course	150	200
Refreshment costs per course	150	180
Training materials per course	50	50
Other variable costs per course	50	70
Price per course	600	900

▲ Table 2 Financial information for Razia Malik's business training courses (CAD)

 Q

(a) Define fixed costs. **(2 marks)**
(b) Define sales volume. **(2 marks)**
(c) Calculate the profit made by the business in 2016. **(4 marks)**
(d) Analyse two methods a business might use to increase sales volume. **(6 marks)**
(e) Price elasticity of demand for Razia's courses is estimated to be −1.2. Assess the extent to which Razia achieved her objective by raising the price of the courses from CAD 600 to CAD 900. **(10 marks)**

30 SALES FORECASTING

LEARNING OBJECTIVES

By the end of this chapter you should be able to understand:
- purpose of sales forecasts
- factors affecting sales forecasts: consumer trends, economic variables and actions of competitors
- difficulties of sales forecasting.

GETTING STARTED

All business organisations, from the smallest of sole traders to the largest multinational, must try to forecast future sales. Important decisions within the business will be based on these forecasts.

Marco Frederick owns and runs an ice cream manufacturer 'Chicago', which produces high-quality ice cream. Marco was sitting in his office late one evening preparing orders from his suppliers for the following 3 months. He was deciding how much of his key raw materials he needed to buy. Milk, sugar and ingredients such as fruit and cream are expensive and are an important cost for his business. But how much of each should he order? If he ordered too much the result would be waste. If he ordered too little he would not be able to meet demand and lose potential profit. He turned to the sales forecasts he had prepared before working out his order.

Why is it important for a business like this to have an idea of what its sales will be next month, next year or in 3 years? What problems might the business face if Marco did not attempt to forecast future sales? If we accept that this type of prediction is important, how might a business construct its forecasts?

PURPOSE OF SALES FORECASTS

Generating an accurate **sales forecast** is one of the most important tasks for a business, and one that will directly affect its efficiency and success. Imagine a business that did not carry out any sales forecasting. How much stock would it buy and hold? What would its staffing levels be? How would it know if it had enough funding? What would its marketing strategy be? Without some predictions of sales, these questions are impossible to answer. Businesses are keen to know about what might happen in the future. Anything a business can predict accurately will reduce uncertainty and enable it to plan more effectively.

Given the importance of sales forecasting, the next step is to understand how to produce forecasts that will be useful to any business.

Forecasting is a business process, assessing the probable outcome using assumptions about the future. Forecasts may be based on a variety of data, for instance current information provided by managers. Most forecasts are based on data gathered from a variety of market research techniques. The accuracy of forecasts will depend on the reliability of the data.

What might a business like to predict with accuracy? Examples include:
- future sales of products
- the effect of promotion on sales
- possible changes in the size of the market in the future
- the way sales change at different times of the year.

Time series analysis: A variety of techniques can be used to predict future trends. One of the most popular is time series analysis. This involves predicting future levels from past data. The data used are known as **time series data** – a set of figures arranged in order, based on the time they occurred. For example, a business may predict future sales by analysing sales data over the last 10 years, as shown in Table 1.

Year	2006	2007	2008	2009	2010	2011	2012	2013	2014	2015
Sales (US$ 000)	125	130	130	150	140	155	180	190	210	230

▲ Table 1 Yearly sales of a garden furniture manufacturer

The business is assuming that past figures are a useful measure of what will happen in the future. This is likely to be the case if trading conditions are stable or if the business needs to forecast trends in the short term. Consider Table 1. Based on the trend of sales during previous years, the business might reasonably forecast that sales will rise in 2016. But precisely what sales might the business expect? This forecast is important because it will determine orders of raw materials and component parts, which may need to be placed well in advance. In terms of capacity, if the forecast for 2016 is sales of US$250,000, the business will need to consider whether it has the physical capacity to produce this volume, and whether it has the staffing required to produce this. These considerations may require the business to look for additional production capacity, or to recruit more staff. In short, the sales forecast will trigger other decisions within the business.

Time series analysis does not try to explain data, only to describe what is happening to it or predict what will happen to it. There are likely to be four components that a business wants to identify in time series data.

- **The trend.** 'Raw' data can provide figures for many different things and it may not always be easy to see exactly what is happening from these figures. Consequently businesses often try to identify a trend. This shows the pattern that is indicated from the figures. For example, there may be a trend for the sales of a new product to rise sharply in a short period as it becomes very popular.
- **Seasonal fluctuations (variations).** Over a year a business is unlikely to have a constant level of sales. Seasonal variations are very important to certain businesses, such as ice cream producers or greetings card manufacturers, where there may be large sales at some times but not at others.
- **Cyclical fluctuations.** For many businesses there may be a cycle of 'highs and lows' in their sales figures over a number of years. These can be the result of the recession–expansion–recession of the trade cycle in the economy. In a recession, for example, people have less money to spend and so the turnover of a business may fall in that period.
- **Random fluctuations.** At times there will be surprising or unusual figures that stand out from any trend that is taking place. An example might be the sudden boost in sales of umbrellas in unusually wet summer months, or the impact on consumer spending of a one-off event, such as a summer music festival.

MATHS TIP

Sales forecasting necessarily involves statistics. It can be useful to show percentage changes in business statistics data.

Example

2016 sales = US$400,000
2017 sales = US$450,000

sales have increased by 12.5% between 2016 and 2017.

This is found by: $\dfrac{\text{Change in sales}}{\text{Original}} \times 100\%$

$$\frac{\text{US\$50,000}}{\text{US\$400,000}} \times 100\% = 12.5\%$$

ACTIVITY 1   SKILLS   INTERPRETATION

CASE STUDY: GARDEN FURNITURE SALES

Drawing on the data in Table 1, Table 2 shows seasonal fluctuations in the sales of garden furniture in Washington, USA.

2013		2014				2015			
Q3	Q4	Q1	Q2	Q3	Q4	Q1	Q2	Q3	Q4
75	30	25	65	80	40	30	65	95	40

▲ Table 2 Quarterly sales of a garden furniture manufacturer (US$000s)

1. Use the data from Table 2 to explain one reason why sales for this business are higher in Q3 than in Q1.
2. Explain why sales forecasting will be useful for this business in terms of: (a) staffing (b) buying supplies.

THE BENEFITS OF SALES FORECASTING

Using sales forecasts has some real advantages for businesses. In general it will help the business to plan ahead and avoid surprises. Having a clear idea of what sales will be in the next financial period provides a number of clear benefits.

- Forecasts inform cash flow predictions and give the business a clear idea of what cash inflows will be, so that finances can be managed
- They allow the business to plan orders of supplies and components. For some businesses, suppliers will need notice of large orders. Sales forecasts help build relationships with suppliers
- They enable the business to ensure it has the correct staffing levels for the predicted sales. From Table 1, if the business had a forecast for 2016 of US$250,000, this might mean that it needs to recruit more staff to meet these higher sales levels
- They enable the business to ensure that it has the capacity to meet the predicted orders. If forecasts are for higher sales, the business may need to buy additional equipment or rent/buy premises.

FACTORS AFFECTING SALES FORECASTING

Sales forecasting is extremely important for a business, but it can be an extremely difficult process to complete. Past data is useful in helping to predict future outcomes, but this is not entirely accurate. Unexpected things happen and there are other factors that need to be taken into account when trying to forecast future sales. Three crucial factors are consumer trends, economic variables and actions of competitors.

Consumer trends: Businesses aim to meet the needs of consumers by providing products and services. In a market economy successful businesses anticipate and meet the needs of consumers by supplying goods and services that are in demand at a point in time. Consumer tastes and preferences can and do change over time. Sometimes these changes can occur quickly. **Consumer trends** are the habits and behaviours of consumers around the products they buy and how they use them.

Today, the most popular use of a smartphone is not the 'phone' at all; it is to access the Internet, either through the phone's browser, or through apps. In the late 1980s, when the first mobile phones became widely available, this could not easily be predicted. Consumer behaviour has changed. This affects the decisions and marketing of smartphone producers. This is an example of a long-term trend in consumer spending behaviour. Many changes in consumer behaviour are more short term, and in response to factors such as seasonal variations and fashion.

- **Seasonal variations.** Some products are seasonal in that they are purchased in smaller or greater quantities at different times of the year. Some businesses that are affected by seasonal factors are obvious: coastal hotels and guest houses see a rise in sales during spring and summer months; power companies see a rise in sales of gas and electricity during the winter. Knowledge of the seasonal variation in sales is vital when constructing sales forecasts. This is important for the management of a business, for example when looking at cash flow. Businesses affected by seasonal factors use sales forecasts to inform cash flow forecasts and from these forecasts will recognise when lower sales will occur and therefore expect lower cash flow during certain times of the year. Knowing this is very useful. Businesses can put in place strategies to manage the periods when cash flow will be less strong.

  Time series data is used by businesses to identify seasonal variations. For example, gas companies know that in the winter months they need to have available larger quantities of gas to cope with the higher levels of demand from domestic and business consumers.

  Energy providers, such as the Naftogaz (Ukraine) and Gazprom (Russia), are very aware of this type

CASE STUDY: VAL THORENS

Val Thorens, located in the Tarentaise Valley, Savoie, France, is a popular ski resort in the French Alps. It is the highest in Europe and attracts skiers from several different countries. The resort is served by a number of hotels, one of which is the 50-room Hotel Prince. During the winter season the hotel is busy, often full in the weeks between November and March. However, when the snow melts and the skiers leave, the hotel is very quiet. The hotel owners have tried to boost 'off-peak' sales by marketing the hotel's facilities to businesses for conferences and other uses. However, competition is fierce and the owners doubt that they will ever fill the hotel during this time.

	2015	2016	2016	2016	2016	2017	2017	2017	2017
	Q4	Q1	Q2	Q3	Q4	Q1	Q2	Q3	Q4
Rooms sold	4040	4420	910	710	4110	4440	940	840	4090

▲ Table 3 Sales figures for Hotel Prince (rooms sold per quarter)

1. Use the data from Table 3 to explain the meaning of seasonal variations.
2. Calculate the percentage change in room sales at the Hotel Prince between:
   (a) 2016 quarter 1 and quarter 3
   (b) 2016 quarter 4 and 2017 quarter 4.
3. Assess **two** possible impacts on Hotel Prince of the seasonal variations shown in Table 3.

of data. These seasonal variations in consumption of energy – gas and electricity – have important implications for sales and cash flow.

- **Fashion.** Consumer tastes and preferences change and can be highly unpredictable. Fashion – particularly in the area of clothing – changes constantly. This can make accurate sales forecasting very difficult.

Any change in fashion will lead to businesses modifying their sales forecasts. Unpredictability is a feature of sales in some industries.

- **Long-term trends.** Whereas fashions can change in the short term, and with little notice, other changes to consumer behaviour are more long term. For example, the trend for consumers today to watch film and television on demand, and using mobile devices, has led to a growth of media platforms such as Netflix and Amazon Prime®, and the fall of operators such as Blockbuster (a video rental chain). Long-term changes affect sales forecasts, and business strategic responses based on investment and strategic planning. Consider the global demand for food. It is expected to grow by between 59 per cent and 98 per cent by 2050. This is due to growth in the global population and rising incomes in many developing countries.

  Data relating to the global growth in the use of electric cars will be used by car manufacturers when constructing sales forecasts, and also when deciding on corporate strategy. For example, by 2050 sales of electric cars are expected to reach around 100 million. This might influence decisions on what to produce and where. Consumer trends have changed over recent years to favour low-emission cars. This change is due in part to the cost advantage for motorists, and in part to the environmentally friendly aspect. These factors have probably led to a number of global car manufacturers to launching their own versions of battery electric vehicles (BEVs). For example, most major car makers, including GM and Volkswagen, have vowed to roll out more than one fully electric car by 2020.

Economic variables: What happens in the wider economy has some important implications for business sales forecasting. The economy is comprised of consumers (households), businesses and government. Economic variables are measurements of different aspects of an economy that give an indication of how that economy is performing. Economic performance has some important implications for businesses generally, and sales forecasting in particular. Important economic variables are as follows:

- **Economic growth.** Economic growth is measured using gross domestic product (GDP). This is a measure of the total output of an economy. When economic growth is rising, sales for many – but not all – businesses tend to increase. One reason for this is that consumer incomes generally increases during periods of economic growth, and this translates into higher spending. In a period of strong economic growth, sales forecasts will often be increased. A slowdown in economic growth leads to lower sales. In this situation, sales forecasts are often reduced. Many businesses

ACTIVITY 3

SKILLS ▶ ANALYSIS, INTERPRETATION, PROBLEM SOLVING

CASE STUDY: ORGANIC FOOD SALES

Sales of organic food in many countries has been rising since the 1990s. Figure 1 shows the rise in retail sales in Europe. Sales have grown from €11,900 million in 2005 to €26,200 million in 2014. However, organic food is more popular in some European countries than others. For example, Germany consumes more organic food than any other European country. Figure 2 shows retails sales of organic food in a selection of European countries.

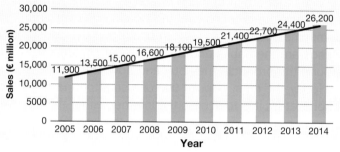

▲ Figure 1 European retail sales of organic food, 2005–14

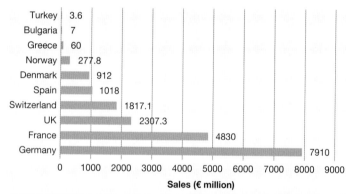

▲ Figure 2 Retail sales of organic food in a selection of European countries

1. Define consumer trends.
2. Calculate the percentage increase in retail sales of organic food between 2005 and 2014.
3. Discuss how some farmers in Europe might respond to the data shown in Figures 1 and 2.

expect to sell less in times of economic downturn. This will affect sales forecasts.

- **Interest rates.** These are charged by banks and other financial institutions for borrowing money. When interest rates are high, the cost of loans increases and the demand for loans falls. Loans are used by consumers and businesses to fund purchases. For example, when a household buys a new car, the chances are this will be purchased using a loan. When interest rates are rising, sales forecasts may be adjusted downwards. Businesses might expect that demand for their product will fall. In contrast, when interest rates fall the cost of loans also falls. This means they are more attractive for consumers. Sales forecasts may be adjusted upwards in response to such a change in interest rates.

- **Inflation.** The general rise in consumer prices over time. When inflation is rising this indicates that prices in the economy are rising also. In such periods consumers and businesses often choose to spend less. Sales forecasts are reduced at these times.

- **Unemployment.** The number of people who are out of work. During a recession, unemployment rises. During the economic crisis that started in 2008, unemployment rose in a number of countries, particularly in Europe. As a result, spending in many economies fell and this had a huge impact on business sales and orders. At such times sales forecasts are amended.

- **Exchange rates.** These reflect the value of one currency in terms of another. An exchange of £1 = US$1.45 means that £1 will buy US$1.45. If this exchange rate rises, say to £1 = US$1.60, it is cheaper for UK consumers to buy goods and services from the USA. As a result, UK businesses might find that sales fall due to the increased price competitiveness of the USA. The impact on sales forecasts would be to cause them to fall, as consumers are shifting their spending to US goods and services. In addition, UK goods become more expensive for USA consumers; something that used to cost US$1.45 now costs US$1.60. Demand will tend to fall in such situations.

Change in economic variable	Impact on business sales forecasts	
	Higher sales forecast	Lower sales forecast
Strong economic growth	X	
Slower GDP growth		X
Rising inflation		X
Falling inflation/deflation	X	
Rising unemployment		X
Falling unemployment	X	
Rising interest rates		X
Falling interest rates	X	
Higher exchange rate		X
Falling exchange rate	X	

▲ Table 4 Effect of economic variables

The analysis of economic variables in Table 4 assumes that businesses enjoy 'normal' patterns of demand. When incomes rise consumers tend to buy more of the product. This applies to a large majority of products. For example, the demand for new cars rises when unemployment falls and incomes rise. So does the demand for event tickets, books and magazines, fresh food, clothing, and so on. These products are likely to have a positive income elasticity of demand. This means that as incomes rise, demand also rises. For such businesses the impact on sales forecasts will be for them to increase.

However, for some businesses the opposite is true. When incomes rise some businesses expect their sales to fall. Value supermarkets, such as Aldi and Lidl, may grow in popularity when incomes are falling, for example during a recession. When incomes start to rise, consumers begin to shift to more expensive providers. The result for such businesses is that sales forecasts actually fall when consumer incomes are rising. However, this view of the current position of supermarkets in some countries may be too simple. It does not necessarily follow that value supermarkets, such as Aldi and Lidl, will simply accept that customers will move to competitors as soon as incomes begin to rise. In fact, these businesses have been not only trying to attract customers away from their original supermarket, but also trying to keep their custom. This is a competitive market and rivals are keen to capture and retain custom. There is some evidence that more affluent customers are now sticking with retailers that would previously have been regarded as perhaps lower in quality.

Actions of competitors: The actions of competitors can have a real impact on a business in many ways, from pricing to promotion. Sales forecasting is another area that can be affected by the actions of competitors. Where competitors use a strategy to capture market share from a rival, sales forecasts may need to be adjusted downwards.

The size of the impact on sales forecasts will depend on the type of strategy used by the competing business. A short-term promotion might affect sales for a short period of time only, and not lead to a change to next year's sales forecast. A rival restaurant opening next door to an existing restaurant is likely to have a greater, more long-term effect.

Any significant action by a competitor will affect the reliability of time series data, such as past sales. Effectively, the conditions within the market have been changed.

How the business responds to the actions of competitors is important. If a competing business opened a new branch close to a business, it might realistically be expected that sales at the existing business would fall.

Sales forecasts would need to reflect this. However, the dynamic nature of business means that a company does not ignore the actions of competitors. The response will influence sales forecasts. A response that aims to counter the action of the competitors may mean that sales predictions remain unchanged.

The effect of the actions of competitors cannot truly be known until some point in the future. Consider the following example.

Competitor enters market 2016						
Year	2013	2014	2015	2016 ↓	2017	2018 (forecast)
Sales (£ 000)	78	86	84	79	62	65

▲ Table 5 Yearly sales of a coffee shop

The data in Table 5 shows that sales from previous years are fairly stable, and these can be used by the business to forecast sales. The entry into the market of a competitor clearly had some impact on the business. Sales in 2017 fell sharply from the previous year and below the trend. In consequence, the sales forecast for 2018, based on the time series data, reflects the fact that sales are lower due to the entry into the market of a rival.

ACTIVITY 4   SKILLS ANALYSIS

CASE STUDY: CATHAY PACIFIC

In 2016, Cathay Pacific, the airline based in Hong Kong, China, announced a drop in profits. The airline's net profit in the first half of the year dropped to HKD 353 million. This was down 82 per cent from the same period last year. Revenue for the second six months of the year also fell – by 9.2 per cent to HKD 45,680 million.

The fall in revenue and profit was caused by a number of factors. However, the most important reason was increasing competition in the market. For example, Cathay Pacific faces a threat from other Chinese and Middle Eastern airlines that are expanding rapidly in the region. Airlines such as Air China and China Eastern are offering more direct services from other Chinese cities. This makes it less attractive for passengers to travel via Hong Kong. There is also competition from Middle Eastern airlines such as Emirates, Etihad and Qatar Airways.

In 2017, Cathay Pacific said it would review its hedging policy when buying aviation fuel, hedging for 2 years rather than 4, which would probably help to cut fuel costs. The airline also said it would review its staffing levels and attempt to reduce operating costs. One approach would be to assign employees

from some outdated roles to new jobs that required a sharper 'digital focus'. Chief Operating Officer Rupert Hogg said Cathay Pacific needs to 'become more agile and efficient in dealing with challenges ahead'.

1. Explain one impact on Cathay Pacific's sales forecast in response to growing competition in the market.
2. Why might time series data from Cathay Pacific – details of sales in previous years – be less reliable following the emerging competition on a number of fronts?

THINKING BIGGER

Sales forecasting is extremely important for businesses. Whether they do it formally, using statistical trend analysis and modelling, or less formally, using estimates based on sales from previous series or informed by previous experience, all businesses aim to forecast what sales will be in the next period.

There are lots of opportunities for questions requiring analysis and evaluation in this topic. The statistical element of sales data means that analytical considerations can be made.

A key thing to consider in this topic is the difficulty of forecasting in different industries. Whereas time series data may be useful for businesses in some sectors, such as energy or greeting cards, this is less useful for others. For example, industries where many new competitors enter the market, such as new technology businesses, may struggle.

Another consideration when analysing business cash flow is the nature of the business. Rising incomes in the economy would typically lead a business to expect higher sales and to therefore reflect this expectation in their sales forecast. However, for businesses that sell at the lower end of quality goods, the opposite may be true. This is an important consideration when analysing business sales forecasting due to changing economic variables.

THE DIFFICULTIES OF SALES FORECASTING

Predicting the future is not easy. This uncertainty applies in all areas of life. What will the weather be like next week? How will my football team perform next season? Will the value of my house rise or fall over the next 12 months? This affects many aspects of life, but especially business.

In this chapter we have explored how businesses can use techniques to help minimise this uncertainty, by using statistical methods and time series analysis to help predict with more certainty what might happen to sales in the future. In fact, some of the factors we have explored in this chapter cause the difficulties involved in sales forecasting.

Volatile consumer tastes and preferences: We have seen how a business can use past sales data to identify future sales. This is called **extrapolation**. This is often a good starting point and a reasonable basis on which to base forecasts. However, extrapolation is not a perfect method to base future predictions. If Chelsea wins the UK Premiership for 2 years in a row, does this mean they will win a third time? Possibly, but this is not guaranteed. Crocs® produce rubber shoes that were once very fashionable. Inaccurate sales forecasts from 2008 onwards nearly caused the collapse of the business. Sales from 2004 to 2007 were increasing steeply and it was therefore reasonable, based on extrapolation of this data, to forecast strong growth in subsequent years. Capacity and production were increased. Unfortunately, these decisions by the business happened at the same time consumer tastes changed. The view of Crocs changed from fashionable 'must have' to being out-of-date.

Range of data: There is a lot of data available to consumers, business and government. Which data is most important for a business to use? In addition to its own sales data, what about wider economic data, such as unemployment, average income growth, commodity prices, exchange rates and so on? This extensive range of data can be difficult enough for a large multinational business to make sense of, let alone a small business. A real difficulty of accurate sales forecasting lies in the sheer amount of data that exists which might inform the forecast.

Subjective expert opinion: However statistical and quantitative time series data might be, the final decisions around sales forecasts are often left to business experts, such as sales analysts. Experts will base their judgements in part on their own opinion and knowledge of the market and wider economic variables. These opinions are necessarily subjective and can be wrong. Crocs almost collapsed because of the professionally compiled but ultimately inaccurate sales forecasts of its marketing team.

CHECKPOINT

1. Why might a business want to predict future sales?
2. State three advantages to a business of using sales forecasts.
3. What is time series data?
4. What is meant by 'trend'?
5. State three economic variables that might affect the sales forecasts of a business.
6. Give three reasons why consumer trends might change.
7. State three difficulties in accurately forecasting sales.

SUBJECT VOCABULARY

consumer income the amount of income remaining after taxes and expenses have been deducted from wages.
consumer trends the habits or behaviours of consumers that determine the goods and services they buy.
economic growth the rise in output of an economy as measured by the growth in Gross Domestic Product (GDP), usually as a percentage.
economic variables measures within the economy which have effects on business and consumers. Examples include unemployment, inflation and exchange rates.
extrapolation forecasting future trends based on past data.
forecasting a business process, assessing the probable outcome using assumptions about the future.
sales forecast prediction of future sales revenue, often based on previous sales data.
time series data a method that allows a business to predict future levels from past figures.

EXAM PRACTICE

HYUNDAI HEAVY INDUSTRIES

SKILLS ANALYSIS INTERPRETATION

Shipbuilding in South Korea is an important industry. It is reckoned that more than half of the commercial ships built in world are made in Korean shipyards. For example, in 2016 Korea exported US$33,200 billion worth of ships and boats.

One important company operating in this sector, which employs over 21,000 people worldwide, is Hyundai Heavy Industries (HHI). In 2017, the company announced a huge 400 per cent increase in its orders resulting from an upturn in trade. Between January and May, HHI and its two associated companies, Hyundai Samho Heavy Industries (HSHI) and Hyundai Mipo Dockyard (HMD), received orders for 62 shipbuilding contracts. The orders were worth US$3800 million – a 416 per cent increase on the same period last year when the group received orders for 12 ships worth about US$1000 million.

The order value was more than half of the combined three companies' annual sales forecast of US$7500 million. In May, the HHI Group received orders for 20 ships worth US$1300 million. This could also rise to 29 ships and US$1900 million assuming that all the orders are completed. In April 2017, the three companies received 21 orders worth US$1000 million.

According to a report, HHI Group received about 67 per cent (28 ships) of the world's total orders for big tankers, and 50 per cent (14 ships) of the world's very large crude carrier orders. A HHI Group official said that given the current flow of orders HHI is likely to exceed its annual order target for the year. However, this was not necessarily a surprise since HHI had increased the intensity of its marketing efforts to meet clients' needs. This effort was also supported by a strong financial foundation and the company's reputation for shipbuilding expertise.

Another reason for the increase in orders might be the growth in international trade. During 2016, international trade growth was slow. However, the World Trade Organization has predicted that global growth in trade will be 2.4 per cent in 2017. In 2018, the forecast was for growth of between 2.1 per cent and 4 per cent. Orders for commercial ships may also have risen due to the lifting of sanctions in Iran. After a number of years where Iran was excluded from the majority of international trade (due to its position on the development of nuclear facilities), the nation is now allowed to trade freely again. Therefore more ships will be needed to transport goods – particularly oil.

(a) Define a sales forecast. **(2 marks)**
(b) Explain how the orders might affect future sales forecasts for HHI. **(4 marks)**
(c) Analyse **two** possible difficulties businesses might encounter when making sales forecasts. **(6 marks)**
(d) Assess the factors that might affect sales forecasts at HHI in the near future. **(10 marks)**

31 BREAK-EVEN

LEARNING OBJECTIVES

By the end of this chapter you should be able to understand:
- contribution: selling price – variable cost per unit
- break-even point: total fixed costs + total variable costs = total revenue
- using contribution to calculate the break-even point
- margin of safety
- interpretation of break-even charts
- limitations of break-even analysis.

GETTING STARTED

Eva Dlasková runs a company that provides a 24-hour taxi service from Václav Havel Airport Prague to Prague city centre, in the Czech Republic. Fixed costs each month are usually CZK 90,000 and variable costs are CZK 300 per trip. Eva charges CZK 1200 per trip. In the summer months (June to September) the business can make 250 trips a month.

Calculate the total cost of 250 trips to the airport in June (total cost = fixed costs + variable costs). Calculate the total revenue from 250 trips to the airport. How much profit is made from 250 trips? How many trips would be needed in a month for the business to break-even?

CONTRIBUTION

Craig Eckert sells second-hand cars. His last sale was £990 for a Golf GTI. He bought the Golf at a car auction for £890. The difference between what he paid for the car and the price he sold it for is £100 (£990 – £890). This difference is called the **contribution**. It is not profit because Craig has fixed costs to pay such as rent, insurance and administration expenses. Contribution is the difference between selling price and variable costs. In this case the selling price was £990 and the variable cost was £890. The £100 will **contribute** to the **total fixed costs** of the business and the profit.

CONTRIBUTION PER UNIT AND TOTAL CONTRIBUTION

A business might calculate the contribution on the sale of a single unit, or the sale of a larger quantity, such as a whole year's output.

Unit contribution: In the previous example the unit contribution was calculated. It was the contribution on the sale of one unit, a single car. The formula for calculating the unit contribution is:

$$
\begin{aligned}
\text{Contribution per unit} &= \text{Selling price} - \text{Variable cost} \\
&= £990 - £890 \\
&= £100
\end{aligned}
$$

Total contribution: When more than one unit is sold the total contribution can be calculated. For example, a clothing company receives an order for 1000 pairs of trousers. The variable costs are £7.50 a pair and they will be sold for £9.00 a pair. The total contribution made by the order is:

$$
\begin{aligned}
\text{Total contribution} &= \text{Total revenue} - \text{Total variable cost} \\
&= (£9.00 \times 1000) - (£7.50 \times 1000) \\
&= £9000 - £7500 \\
&= £1500
\end{aligned}
$$

The £1500 in this example will contribute to the clothing company's fixed costs and profit. The total contribution can also be calculated by multiplying the unit contribution by the number of units sold.

$$
\begin{aligned}
\text{Total contribution} &= \text{Unit contribution} \times \text{Number of units sold} \\
&= (£9.00 - £7.50) \times 1000 \\
&= £1.50 \times 1000 \\
&= £1500
\end{aligned}
$$

EXAM HINT

Contribution can be used to calculate the profit made by a business. The formula needed is:

Profit = Total contribution – Fixed costs

ACTIVITY 1   SKILLS   PROBLEM SOLVING

CASE STUDY: MÜLLER CAMPING-ANHÄNGER

Serge Müller runs Müller Camping-Anhänger, a Munich-based business in Germany, that manufactures camping trailers. The market conditions are favourable and in recent years the firm has invested heavily in developing its export business. As a result, around 70 per cent of the firm's trailers are now sold to other European countries – mainly France, Spain and Italy. The annual fixed costs of the business are €200,000 and the variable costs are €500 per trailer. The trailers are sold for €800 each.

1. Define the term contribution.
2. Calculate the contribution made by each trailer.
3. Calculate the profit made by Müller Camping-Anhänger if 2000 trailers are made and sold in a year.
4. A new company enters the market, and Müller Camping-Anhänger is forced to lower its price to €650 in the coming year. Calculate the impact the price cut will have on annual profit. (Assume that output stays the same at 2000.)

BREAK-EVEN POINT

Businesses, particularly those that are just starting up, often like to know how much they need to produce and sell to break-even. If a business has information about fixed costs and variable costs and knows what price it is going to charge, it can calculate how many units it needs to sell to cover all of its costs. The point where total costs (fixed costs + variable costs) are exactly the same as total revenue is called the **break-even point**. The level of output a business needs to produce so that total costs are exactly the same as total revenue is called the **break-even output**. It makes neither a profit nor a loss. For many businesses the break-even point is highly significant. It shows the level of output where all costs have been covered and that all future sales will generate a profit for the business.

WORKED EXAMPLE

A business produces 1000 units and sells them for £50 each. Total fixed costs are £10,000. Variable costs are £40 per unit. So total variable costs are £40 × 1000 = £40,000.

Therefore:
Total costs = £10,000 + £40,000 = **£50,000**
Total revenue = £50 × 1000 = **£50,000**

Total revenue and total costs are exactly the same at £50,000. Therefore the business will break-even at this level of output. So the break-even output is 1000 units.

CALCULATING BREAK-EVEN USING CONTRIBUTION

It is possible to calculate the break-even output if a firm knows the value of its fixed costs, variable costs and the price it will charge. The simplest way to calculate the break-even output is to use contribution. The following formula can be used.

$$\text{Break-even output} = \frac{\text{Fixed costs}}{\text{Contribution}}$$

WORKED EXAMPLE

Jack Cadwallader makes iron park benches. His fixed costs (FC) are £60,000 and variable costs (VC) £40 per bench. He sells the benches to local government bodies across the country for £100 each. Therefore contribution is given by:

Contribution = Selling price − Variable cost
Contribution = £100 − £40
Contribution = £60

Once the contribution has been calculated, the number of benches Jack needs to sell to break-even can then be determined.

$$\text{Break-even output} = \frac{\text{Fixed costs}}{\text{Contribution}}$$

$$= \frac{£60,000}{£60}$$

$$= 1000 \text{ benches}$$

Jack Cadwallader's business will break-even when 1000 park benches are sold.

ACTIVITY 2 — SKILLS — PROBLEM SOLVING

CASE STUDY: MARIAM NANJEGO

Mariam Nanjego assembles gift packs that she sells online. She operates from a small warehouse in Kampala, Uganda that she rents for UGX 1 million per month. She incurs other fixed costs of UGX 500,000 per month and sells the gift packs for UGX 50,000 each (including delivery and packaging). She employs two part-time staff and variable costs are UGX 40,000 per gift pack.

1. Calculate the monthly break-even output for Mariam Nanjego's business.
2. Calculate the total cost and total revenue at the break-even level of output.
3. Calculate the profit made by the business if 200 gift packs are sold in a month.

BREAK-EVEN CHART

The use of graphs is often helpful in break-even analysis. It is possible to identify the break-even point and break-even output by plotting the total cost and total revenue equations on a graph. This graph is called a **break-even chart**. Figure 1 shows the break-even chart for Jack Cadwallader's business.

Output is measured on the horizontal axis and revenue, costs and profit are measured on the vertical axis. What does the break-even chart show?

- **The value of total cost over a range of output.** For example, when Jack produces 1500 benches total costs are £120,000.
- **The value of total revenue over a range of output.** For example, when Jack produces 1500 benches total revenue is £150,000.
- **Break-even charts can show the level of fixed costs over a range of output.** For example, the fixed costs for Jack's business are £60,000.
- **The level of output needed to break-even.** The break-even point is where total costs equal total revenue of £100,000. This is when 1000 benches are produced. So the break-even output is 1000 benches.
- **The profit at a particular level of output.** If Jack produces 1500 benches, profit is shown by the vertical gap between the total cost and total revenue equations. It is £30,000.
- **At levels of output below the break-even output, losses are made.** This is because total costs exceed total revenue. At an output of 500, a £30,000 loss is made.
- **At levels of output above the break-even output, a profit is made.** This profit gets larger as output rises. At an output of 1500 a profit of £30,000 is made.

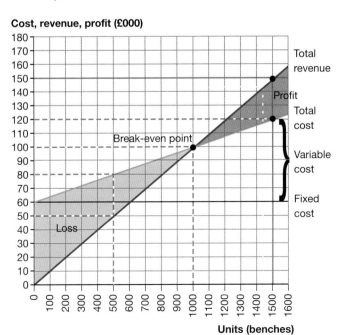

Cost, revenue, profit (£000)

▲ Figure 1 Break-even chart for Jack Cadwallader

- **The relationship between fixed costs and variable costs as output rises.** At low levels of output, fixed costs represent a large proportion of total costs. As output rises, fixed costs become a smaller proportion of total costs.

MARGIN OF SAFETY

What if a business is producing more than the break-even output? It might be useful to know by how much sales could fall before a loss is made. This is called the **margin of safety**. It refers to the range of output over which a profit can be made. The margin of safety can be identified on the break-even chart by measuring the distance between the break-even level of output and the current (profitable) level of output. For example, Figure 2 shows the break-even chart for Jack Cadwallader. If Jack produces 1200 benches the margin of safety is 200 benches. This means that output can fall by 200 before a loss is made. If Jack sells 1200 benches the chart shows that total revenue is £120,000, total cost is £108,000 and profit is £12,000.

Businesses prefer to operate with a large margin of safety. This means that if sales drop they still might make some profit. With a small margin of safety there is a risk that the business is more likely to make losses if sales fall.

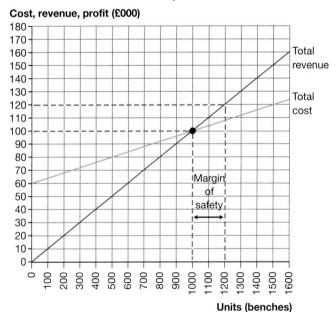

Cost, revenue, profit (£000)

▲ Figure 2 Break-even chart showing the margin of safety for Jack Cadwallader's business

Finally, the equation for calculating the margin of safety is given by:

MOS = Current output − Break-even output

USING BREAK-EVEN ANALYSIS

Break-even analysis is used in business as a tool to make decisions about the future. It helps answer 'what if' questions. For instance, what would happen in each of these situations.

- If the price went up, what would happen to the break-even point?

- If the business introduced a new product line, how many would the new product have to sell to at least break-even?
- If the business is just starting up, what has to be the level of output to prevent a loss being incurred?
- What will happen to the break-even point if costs are forecast to rise?
- Would the break-even point be lower if components were bought in from outside suppliers rather than being made in-house?

Break-even analysis is also found in business plans. Banks often ask for business plans when deciding whether or not to give a loan. So break-even analysis can be vital in gaining finance, especially when starting up a business.

LIMITATIONS OF BREAK-EVEN ANALYSIS

Break-even analysis does have some limitations. It is often regarded as too simplistic and some of its assumptions are unrealistic.

Output and stocks: It assumes that all output is sold, so that output equals sales, and no stocks are held. Many businesses hold stocks of finished goods to cope with changes in demand. There are also times when firms cannot sell what they produce and choose to accumulate stocks of their output to avoid making staff redundant.

Unchanging conditions: The break-even chart is drawn for a given set of conditions. It cannot cope with a sudden increase in wages and prices or changes in technology.

Accuracy of data: The effectiveness of break-even analysis depends on the quality and accuracy of the data used to construct cost and revenue functions. If the data is poor and inaccurate, the conclusions drawn on the basis of the data may be incorrect. For example, if fixed costs are underestimated, the level of output required to break-even will be higher than suggested by the break-even chart.

Non-linear relationships: It is assumed that the total revenue and total cost lines are linear (a straight line). This may not always be the case. For example, a business may have to offer discounts on large orders, so total revenues fall at high outputs. In this case the total revenue line would rise and then fall, and be curved. A business can lower costs by buying in bulk. So costs may fall at high outputs and the costs function will be curved.

Multi-product businesses: Many businesses produce more than one single product. It is likely that each product will have different variable costs and different prices. The problem is how to allocate the fixed costs of the multi-product business to each individual product. There are a number of ways, but none is perfect. Therefore, if the fixed costs incurred by each product are inaccurate, break-even analysis is less useful.

Stepped fixed costs: Some fixed costs are stepped. For example, in order to increase output a manufacturer may

need to acquire more capacity. This may result in rent increases and thus fixed costs will rise sharply. Under these circumstances it is difficult to use break-even analysis.

A break-even chart can be used to work out the price charged and the variable cost per unit. To calculate the price charged, look at the total revenue at the break-even level of output and divide this by the break-even output. To calculate the variable cost you need to look at the total cost at the break-even level of output, subtract fixed costs and then divide the answer by the break-even level of output.

CHECKPOINT

1. A product sells for UAH 300 and the variable costs are UAH 250. What is the contribution per unit?
2. A clothes retailer buys 240 jumpers for XOF 7500 each. The jumpers are sold for XOF 9600 each. What is the total contribution made by the jumpers?
3. If total contribution is FJD 300,000 and fixed costs are FJD 245,000, what is the profit?
4. If total variable costs are ILS 1.8 million and contribution is ILS 0.9 million, what is the total revenue?
5. How can the contribution be used to calculate the break-even level of output?
6. What is the equation for calculating the margin of safety (MOS)?
7. What effect will a price increase have on the margin of safety?
8. What effect will a fall in fixed costs have on the margin of safety?
9. State three uses of break-even analysis.
10. State three limitations of break-even analysis.

SUBJECT VOCABULARY

break-even when a business generates just enough revenue to cover its total costs.
break-even chart a graph containing the total cost and total revenue lines, illustrating the break-even output.
break-even output the output a business needs to produce so that its total revenue and total costs are the same.
break-even point the point at which total revenue and total costs are the same.
contribution the amount of money left over after variable costs have been subtracted from revenue. The money contributes towards fixed costs and profit.
margin of safety the range of output between the break-even level and the current level of output, over which a profit is made.

EXAM PRACTICE

GOWDA CHANDA INC.

SKILLS ANALYSIS, INTERPRETATION, PROBLEM SOLVING

Gowda Chanda runs a plastics recycling plant, which is located in Pittsburgh, Pennsylvania, USA. The business incurs quite high monthly fixed costs, which include leasing charges for premises and machinery. He also employs five staff. Figure 3 shows a monthly break-even chart for the business in November. The planned output of recycled plastic material for the month is 1000 tonnes and the margin of safety is also shown on the chart.

Unfortunately there was a machinery breakdown on 12 November and the monthly output was only 700 tonnes. Essential repairs had to be carried out which stopped production for several days.

Q

(a) Define margin of safety. **(2 marks)**
(b) Calculate the price charged for recycled plastic material per tonne. **(4 marks)**
(c) Calculate the variable cost per tonne of recycled plastic material. **(4 marks)**
(d) Explain one impact on Gowda Chanda Inc. of the machinery breakdown. **(4 marks)**
(e) Assess the usefulness of break-even analysis to Gowda Chanda Inc. **(10 marks)**

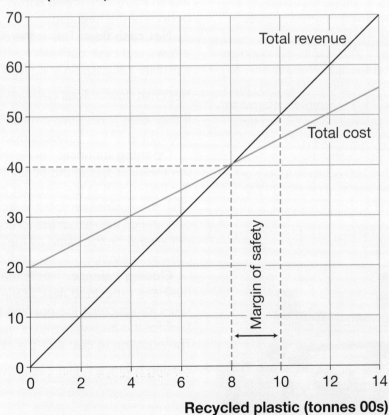

▲ Figure 3 Break-even chart for Gowda Chanda Inc.

32 CASH FLOW

LEARNING OBJECTIVES

By the end of this chapter you should be able to understand:
- construction and interpretation of simple cash flow forecasts
- use and limitations of cash flow forecasts.

GETTING STARTED

The Peruvian government is investing quite heavily in the nation's infrastructure. One of the biggest projects at the moment is the construction of Lima's metro system. Much of the construction work is being undertaken by Italian and Spanish companies. However, the supply of many materials and components, and the provision of some specialist services, has been contracted to Peruvian companies. One Peruvian company, Ramos Hormigón, is supplying some concrete units that are being used in the construction of a metro station on one of the lines.

In May 2017, Ramos Hormigón paid its 220 workers a total of PEN 1.3 million and spent PEN 2.3 million on raw materials. The business also spent PEN 1.98 million on other expenses and paid PEN 0.8 million interest to a bank. In the same month cash also flowed into the business. Ramos Hormigón received PEN 4.5 million from its main customer for work carried out on the metro station and a total of PEN 0.68 million from other smaller customers. The business also received PEN 0.5 million from a local government agency for work carried out 6 months ago.

What are examples of cash outflows and cash inflows for Ramos Hormigón? Calculate the net cash flow (cash inflows − cash outflows) for the business in May 2017. Explain why cash is very important for a business. Many businesses produce regular cash flow forecasts, explain what these statements might show.

CASH FLOW FORECASTS

Without cash a business cannot trade. Experts suggest that about 20 per cent of business failures are due to poor cash flow. Even when trading conditions are good, businesses can fail. A business must ensure that it has enough cash to pay staff wages and bills when they are due. One way for a business to help control its cash flow is to plan ahead by producing accurate cash flow forecasts. Such forecasts also form an important part of business plans.

INTERPRETING CASH FLOW FORECASTS

A **cash flow forecast** lists all the likely receipts (**cash inflows**) and payments (**cash outflows**) over a future period of time. All the entries in the forecast are estimated because they have not occurred yet. The forecast shows the planned cash flow of the business month by month. It also shows three key figures at the bottom of the forecast:

Net cash flow: This is the difference between cash inflows and cash outflows for the month. The equation to calculate net cash flow is given by:

Net cash flow = Total cash inflows − Total cash outflows

If this value is negative it means that more cash has flowed out of the business than has flowed in.

Opening balance: This is the amount of cash that the business has at the beginning of each month. For the first month in the forecast it will be the amount of cash the business has left over from the previous trading period. For the rest of the forecast the opening balance will always be the same as the closing balance from the previous month.

Closing balance: This is the amount of cash that the business expects to have at the end of each month. It takes into account the opening balance and the net cash flow for the trading month. It may be positive or negative. The equation to calculate the closing balance is given by:

Closing balance = Net cash flow + Opening balance

Table 1 shows a 12-month cash flow forecast statement for Fishan's Ltd, a grocery wholesaler.

What is predicted to happen to cash flow at Fishan's over the 12-month period?

January: The company will have an opening cash balance of £11,000 in January. In January receipts are expected to be £451,000 and payments £365,000. This means that an extra £86,000 (£451,000 – £365,000) will be added in this month – a positive **net cash flow**. The closing balance should be £97,000 (£11,000 + £86,000).

February: In February expected payments (£406,000) are greater than expected receipts (£360,000). This means that there will be a negative net cash flow of £46,000 in February. However, the opening balance of £97,000 will cover this and the business will not have a cash flow problem. It ends the month with a positive closing balance of £51,000 (£97,000 – £46,000).

March: In March payments again will be greater than receipts, giving a negative net cash flow of £92,000. However, this is now greater than the opening balance of £51,000. This means that the business faces a negative closing balance of £41,000 and will have a cash flow problem. It would have to find some way to finance this, perhaps by borrowing from a bank.

March to May: The business will have cash flow problems in March and April, when it faces negative closing balances, even though in April receipts are greater than payments (a positive net cash flow). In May, however, the negative opening balance of £26,000 is outweighed by the positive net cash flow of £113,000. The business will have a

positive closing balance of £87,000 and no cash flow problem.

June to December: In June and August, but not July, the business would have cash flow problems. From September on, when there will be positive closing balances every month, there appear to be no cash flow problems. This is because the owners plan to introduce £300,000 into the business in September.

CONSTRUCTING A CASH FLOW FORECAST

Constructing a cash flow forecast is a straightforward process. It can be done manually but is easier using a spreadsheet. As shown in Table 1 the forecast is divided into columns. The first column is used to describe the entries in the forecast and the remainder shows financial values for each month in a future trading period – 6 months or 12 months perhaps. The cash flow forecast is constructed by entering financial values in the three sections described below.

Cash inflows: Once the structure of the document has been prepared (dividing the paper into columns), the values for expected cash inflows for each month can be entered. This is the top section in the forecast. Examples of cash inflows are cash from cash sales, cash from credit sales, interest received from banks, fresh capital (introduced by the owners perhaps), cash from loans and cash from the sale of business assets such as an unwanted vehicle. Most of these values have to be estimated (forecast) by the business.

Once these values have been entered for each month in the forecast the total cash inflows can be calculated.

												(£000s)
	Jan	Feb	Mar	Apr	May	Jun	Jul	Aug	Sep	Oct	Nov	Dec
Cash inflows												
Cash sales	451	360	399	410	490	464	452	340	450	390	480	680
Capital introduced									300			
Total cash inflows	451	360	399	410	490	464	452	340	750	390	480	680
Cash outflows												
Goods for resale	150	180	150	180	150	180	150	180	150	180	220	250
Leasing charges	20	20	20	20	20	20	20	20	20	20	20	20
Motor expenses	40	40	40	40	40	40	40	40	40	40	40	40
Wages	100	100	100	100	100	100	100	105	105	105	125	125
VAT			126			189	187		187			198
Loan repayments	35	35	35	35	35	35	35	35	35	35	35	35
Telephone		11			12			12			14	
Other	20	20	20	20	20	20	20	20	20	20	20	20
Total cash outflows	365	406	491	395	377	584	552	412	557	400	474	688
Net cash flow	86	(46)	(92)	15	113	(120)	100	(72)	193	(10)	6	(8)
Opening balance	11	97	51	(41)	(26)	87	(33)	63	(9)	184	174	180
Closing balance	97	51	(41)	(26)	87	(33)	63	(9)	184	174	180	172

▲ Table 1 Cash flow forecast for Fishan's Ltd
Brackets show minus figures.

ACTIVITY 1 SKILLS PROBLEM SOLVING, ANALYSIS

CASE STUDY: SALIM AND AMJAD QADIR

Salim and Amjad Qadir own a thriving textile business located in the centre of the Karkhano market in Peshawar, Pakistan. The brothers buy textiles from a number of manufacturers in the country and sell to individual customers. However, the Qadirs have recently started to supply small dressmakers in the city. These traders are allowed to buy fabric on 60-day credit terms. Table 2 shows a 3-month cash flow forecast for the business in 2017. (Note that some of the figures are missing in the forecast.)

	May	June	July
Cash inflows			
Cash sales	104,000	110,000	98,000
Cash from credit sales	12,000	15,000	17,000
Bank interest	1100	1200	1200
Total cash inflows	**117,100**	**126,200**	**116,200**
Cash outflows			
Inventory purchases	67,500	70,100	62,100
Rent	10,000	10,000	10,000
Utilities	4000	4000	5000
Other expenses	7600	6100	7400
Total cash outflows	?	?	?
Net cash flow	?	?	?
Opening balance	15,900	?	?
Closing balance	?	?	?

▲ Table 2 Cash flow forecast for the Qadirs (PKR)

1. Using examples from this case, explain the difference between cash inflows and cash outflows.
2. Complete the cash flow forecast for Qadirs' textile business to show the:
   (a) total cash outflows for each month
   (b) net cash flows for each month
   (c) closing balance for each month
   (d) opening balance for June and July.
3. Explain the possible impact that the new credit sales to traders might have on the firm's cash flow.

This is done by adding the values in each column for each month. For example, in Table 1 the total cash inflows for January are £451,000. There is only one source of cash for January in this example.

Cash outflows: The middle section of the cash flow forecast is constructed by entering all the expected payments that the business plans to make each month. These payments represent cash outflows. This is likely to be the largest section and examples of monthly entries might include payments to suppliers for raw materials or goods for resale; payments for utilities such as gas, water and electricity; wages; payments to the tax authorities; loan repayments to banks and other expenses such as advertising, insurance, cleaning, rent, interest and motor expenses. Most of these payments will have to be estimated but some may be known in advance. For example, a business will usually know how much rent it has to pay each month in the next year.

Once these values have been entered for each month in the forecast the total cash outflows can be calculated. This is done by adding the values in each column for each month. For example, in Table 1 the total cash outflow for January is £365,000.

Closing balance: The bottom section of the forecast is used to calculate the expected closing balance. This is the cash that the business expects to have at the end of each month. It is calculated by adding together the net cash flow and the opening balance and may be positive or negative. For example, in Table 1 the closing balance in January is forecast to be £97,000. Note that the closing balance in January is also the opening balance for the next month – February in this case.

CHANGES IN CASH FLOW VARIABLES

Once a cash flow forecast has been prepared, it can be adjusted to show the effect on net cash flows of changes in some of the variables.

Table 3 shows a 6-month cash flow forecast for Patel Motors, a small garage and car service business. Mr Patel opened a shop inside his garage in May and hopes that this will help to boost his cash flow.

The forecast shows that by the end of the 6-month period the cash position of the business is expected to improve. The closing cash balance is forecast to rise from £1900 in June to £3550 in November.

However, after a couple of months it became clear that some of the figures in the forecast needed to be changed. In August Mr Patel had to buy computer equipment to help in the repair of newer cars. This cost £1200. He also had to employ more casual labour to help out in the shop. As a result, wages paid to casual labourers rose to £1100 per month from August on. Finally, Mr Patel received a £400 unexpected payment from a customer in September for work carried out 2 years ago. He had previously written off the debt, that is, declared the money lost.

The effects of changes to variables are shown in Table 4. There will be a negative impact on the cash balance of the business at the end of the 6 months. The closing cash balance is now expected to fall from £1900 in June to £1550 in November.

	June	July	August	September	October	November
Cash inflows						
Petrol and repairs	6700	6600	7200	6800	7100	7600
Shop and other sales	2250	2750	2300	3300	3850	4350
Total cash inflows	**8950**	**9350**	**9500**	**10,100**	**10,950**	**11,950**
Cash outflows						
Casual labour	800	800	800	800	800	800
Petrol and parts	4250	4300	4700	4500	4500	5000
Stock and other expenses	2450	2500	4500	5000	5600	5600
Total cash outflows	**7500**	**7600**	**10,000**	**10,300**	**10,900**	**11,400**
Net cash flow	**1450**	**1750**	**(500)**	**(200)**	**50**	**550**
Opening balance	**450**	**1900**	**3650**	**3150**	**2950**	**3000**
Closing balance	**1900**	**3650**	**3150**	**2950**	**3000**	**3550**

▲ Table 3 Cash flow forecast for Patel Motors

	June	July	August	September	October	November
Cash inflows						
Petrol and repairs	6700	6600	7200	6800	7100	7600
Shop and other sales	2250	2750	2300	3300	3850	4350
Debt repayment				400		
Total cash inflows	**8950**	**9350**	**9500**	**10,500**	**10,950**	**11,950**
Cash outflows						
Casual labour	800	800	1100	1100	1100	1100
Petrol and parts	4250	4300	4700	4500	4500	5000
Stock and other expenses	2450	2500	4500	5000	5600	5600
Computer equipment			1200			
Total cash outflows	**7500**	**7600**	**11,500**	**10,600**	**11,200**	**11,700**
Net cash flow	**1450**	**1750**	**(2000)**	**(100)**	**(250)**	**250**
Opening balance	**450**	**1900**	**3650**	**1650**	**1550**	**1300**
Closing balance	**1900**	**3650**	**1650**	**1550**	**1300**	**1550**

▲ Table 4 Amended cash flow forecast for Patel Motors

WORKED EXAMPLE

The effect of a change in one single variable in a cash flow forecast has a large effect on the rest of the forecast. The simple cash flow forecast for a retailer is shown in Table 5. The effect of an increase in stock purchases from £69,000 to £72,000 in June is shown in Table 6. The changes are shown in green. Note that the increase in the value of stock purchases has an impact on five other values – even in this very simple forecast.

	June	July
Cash inflow		
Sales revenue	98,000	107,000
Cash outflow		
Wages	25,000	25,000
Stock	69,000	74,000
Total cash outflow	94,000	99,000
Net cash flow	4000	8000
Opening balance	10,000	14,000
Closing balance	14,000	22,000

▲ Table 5 Simple cash flow forecast

	June	July
Cash inflow		
Sales revenue	98,000	107,000
Cash outflow		
Wages	25,000	25,000
Stock	72,000	74,000
Total cash outflow	97,000	99,000
Net cash flow	1000	8000
Opening balance	10,000	11,000
Closing balance	11,000	19,000

▲ Table 6 The effect of changes in one variable (shown in light green)

MATHS TIP

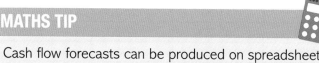

Cash flow forecasts can be produced on spreadsheets. This means that the effect of changes in some of the variables, such as in the examples above, can be shown very easily. Once the new figures are entered in the spreadsheet, the new totals and balances are calculated automatically.

THE USE OF CASH FLOW FORECASTS

Businesses draw up cash flow forecast statements to help control and monitor cash flow in the business. There are certain advantages in using forecasts to control cash flow.

Identifying the timing of cash shortages and surpluses: A forecast can help to identify in advance when a business might wish to borrow cash. At the bottom of the statement the monthly closing balances are shown clearly. This will help the reader to identify when a bank overdraft will be needed. For example, Table 1 showed that Fishan's would need to borrow money in March, April, June and August. In addition, if a large cash surplus is identified in a particular month, this might provide an opportunity; for example, to buy some new equipment. A business should try to avoid being overdrawn at the bank because interest is charged. If certain payments can be delayed until cash is available, this will avoid unnecessary borrowing.

Cash flow forecasts are particularly helpful for businesses that have seasonal demand. This is because cash inflows will be irregular, i.e. high during peak season and low at off-peak times. It will be important to delay some payments during periods where cash inflows are expected to be low.

Supporting applications for finance: When trying to raise finance, lenders often insist that businesses support their applications with documents showing business performance, outlook and **solvency**. A cash flow forecast will help to indicate the future outlook for the business. It is also common practice to produce a cash flow forecast statement in the planning stages of setting up a business. It is unlikely that any potential investor or lender will finance a business without a thorough business plan supported by a cash flow forecast.

Enhancing the planning process: Careful planning in business is crucial. It helps to clarify aims and improve performance. Producing a cash flow forecast is a key part of the planning process because it is a document concerned with the future. If business owners try to run a business without any forward planning, mistakes are more likely to be made and it is difficult to identify problems in advance. A lack of planning is likely to result in poor business performance.

Monitoring cash flow: During and at the end of the financial year, a business should make comparisons between the predicted figures in the cash flow forecast and those that actually occurred. This will help identify where problems have arisen. The business can then try to identify possible reasons for any significant differences between the two sets of figures. For example, it might be that an overpayment was made. Constant monitoring in this way should allow a business to control its cash flow effectively.

THE LIMITATIONS OF CASH FLOW FORECASTS

Although cash flow forecasts are extremely useful in helping to manage a business, it is important to recognise their limitations.

- Some of the financial information used in forecasts will be based on estimates. For example, even under normal trading conditions it is very difficult to predict sales revenue for a future time period – it has to be estimated. It is also difficult to estimate future costs – particularly variable costs. These will be dependent on future sales that are uncertain. Fixed costs, such as rent, rates and insurance are more predictable. Consequently, if the figures for cash inflows and cash outflows are not accurate, then the net cash flows and closing balances will be unreliable.
- Business activity is subject to external forces that are beyond the control of owners and managers. Changes in factors such as interest rates, the state of the economy, government legislation, exchange rates, competition and consumer tastes can have an impact on business costs and revenues. As a result, there will be an impact on a cash flow forecast. For example, the cash flow forecast for a wheat farm would be affected negatively if poor weather conditions reduced crop yields.
- A business uses resources in preparing a cash flow forecast. A business owner or employee will spend time gathering the information and assembling the forecast. It will also have to be regularly updated so that the monitoring process is meaningful. There might be a danger, for instance, that an owner spends too much time focusing on the cash flow forecast at the expense of meeting customer needs.
- A cash flow forecast only focuses on one important business variable – cash. Other variables are also important, such as profit, profit margins and productivity. The cash flow forecast cannot be used on its own to evaluate the performance of a business.

EXAM PRACTICE

CHARLTON PLASTICS LTD

SKILLS ▶ PROBLEM SOLVING, ANALYSIS, INTERPRETATION

Charlton Plastics Ltd manufactures materials for the packaging industry. It operates from a small processing plant in Edmonton, Canada. The family-run business is committed to the use of recycled materials and produces a range of plastic bags, sacks and sheets. In 2014, the business started to export its products and recently overseas sales have grown well.

In December 2016, Charlton's financial director produced a cash flow forecast for the following year. Table 7 shows part of that forecast, from January to April 2017.

	Jan	Feb	Mar	Apr
Cash inflows				
Home sales	124,000	124,000	125,000	128,000
Export sales	62,000	63,000	66,000	72,000
Interest	3000	3000	3000	3000
Total cash inflows	**189,000**	**190,000**	**194,000**	**203,000**
Cash outflows				
Wages	55,000	55,000	55,000	55,000
Materials	76,000	78,000	81,000	87,000
Insurance	4000	4000	4000	4000
Drawings	21,000	21,000	21,000	21,000
Other overheads	24,000	27,000	28,000	30,000
Total cash outflows	**180,000**	**185,000**	**189,000**	**197,000**
Net cash flow	9000	5000	5000	6000
Opening balance	12,300	21,300	26,300	31,300
Closing balance	21,300	26,300	31,300	37,300

▲ Table 7 Cash flow forecast for Charlton Plastics Ltd, 2017 (CAD)

At the end of January the firm's financial director notified the board that the forecast had to be updated to take into account the following changes.

- Wages would have to rise to CAD 57,000 from February on.
- Due to favourable market conditions, material prices would fall to CAD 71,000, CAD 75,000 and CAD 81,000 in February, March and April respectively.
- A payment of CAD 11,500 to the tax authorities would have to be paid in February to compensate for an underpayment in the previous tax year.

Q

(a) Explain one reason why a cash flow forecast is an important part of a business plan. **(4 marks)**

(b) Calculate the closing balances in the cash flow forecast resulting from the changes above. **(4 marks)**

(c) Discuss the impact of the changes in the cash flow forecast on Charlton Plastics Ltd. **(8 marks)**

(d) Evaluate whether or not the use of cash flow forecasts will benefit Charlton Plastics Ltd. **(20 marks)**

33 BUDGETS

LEARNING OBJECTIVES

By the end of this chapter you should be able to understand:

- the purposes of budgets
- the types of budget: based on historical figures and zero based
- variance analysis
- difficulties of budgeting.

GETTING STARTED

Rabih Shamsin runs a ladies hair salon in Beirut, Lebanon. He likes to keep control of business costs and uses budgets to help him. Table 1 shows the cost budget for a 6-month period.

	Jul	Aug	Sep	Oct	Nov	Dec	Total
Wages	4200	4200	4200	4200	4400	5000	26,200
Rent	1400	1400	1400	1400	1400	1400	8400
Materials	450	450	460	460	470	520	2810
Electricity	100	100	110	130	180	200	820
Advertising	500	500	500	500	500	500	3000
Other overheads	300	300	300	310	310	330	1850
Total	6950	6950	6970	7000	7260	7950	43,080

▲ Table 1 A cost budget for Rabih Shamsin's hair salon (LBP 000)

What is the total expected cost of running the business for the 6-month period? What is happening to planned costs over the time period? Why might costs be so high in December? How might this cost budget help Rabih?

PURPOSE OF BUDGETS

A **budget** is a financial plan that is agreed in advance. It must be a plan and not a forecast – a forecast is a prediction of what might happen in the future, whereas a budget is a planned outcome that the firm hopes to achieve. A budget will show the money needed for spending and how this might be financed. Budgets are based on the objectives of businesses. They force managers to think ahead and improve co-ordination. Most budgets are set for 12 months to match the accounting period, but there are exceptions.

Budgets are likely to be used by both large and small businesses. Small business owners often underestimate the importance of financial control when running their businesses and budgeting is a method of control that could easily be employed. This might help avoid problems in the future.

Budgets fulfil the following specific purposes.

Control and monitoring: Budgeting allows management to control the business. It does this by setting objectives and targets. These are then translated into budgets for a particular period; say, the coming year. How successful the business has been in achieving those targets can be found by comparing the actual results with the budget. Any reasons for failing to achieve the budget can then be analysed and appropriate action taken. For more effective control it is helpful to monitor budgets continually. Some businesses produce weekly budgets to allow managers to respond quickly.

Planning: Budgeting forces management to think ahead. Without budgeting, managers might work on a day-by-day basis, only dealing with opportunities and problems as they arise. Budgeting, however, plans for the future. It anticipates problems and their solutions.

Co-ordination: Larger businesses are often complex organisations. There may be many departments and different operating sites – for instance for production and administration. A multinational company will have sites and workers spread across the world. Budgeting is one way in which managers can co-ordinate and control activities of the many areas of business.

Communication: Planning allows the objectives of the business to be communicated to the workforce. By keeping to a budget, managers and workers have a clear framework within which to operate. So budgeting removes an element of uncertainty within decision-making throughout the business. Budgeting also shows the priorities of the business and highlights costs that need to be kept under control.

Efficiency: In a business with many workers, it becomes important for management to empower staff by delegating decision making. In a medium to large business, senior management cannot efficiently make every decision on behalf of every employee, department or site. Budgeting gives financial control to lower levels of management who are best able to make decisions at their point within the organisation.

Motivation: Budgeting should act as a motivator to the workforce. It provides workers with targets and standards. Improving on the budget position is an indication of success for a department or group of workers. Fear of failing to reach budgeted targets can be an incentive to the workforce.

TYPES OF BUDGET

Businesses might use a wide range of different budget types. However, some budgets are more frequently used than others. Two key types are the **sales budget** and the **production cost budget**. Budgets are often prepared using **historical figures**. This means that the data used to prepare the budgets is based on data that the business has gathered in the past. Obviously adjustments will be made to take into account future known events, such as planned changes in production or changes in costs or prices. Examples of budgets that make use of historical figures are shown in Table 2.

Budget	Description
Sales volume	A key budget – shows planned sales levels
Sales revenue	Uses sales volume budget and prices to show planned revenue
Production cost	Based on sales volume budget and shows all planned production costs
Overheads	Shows all planned indirect costs, such as insurance, rent and office wages
Total cost	Shows all planned business costs
Marketing	Shows planned spending on, for example, research, advertising, promotion and sales
R&D	Shows planned expenditure in research and development
Profit	Shows planned revenue, costs and profit
Cash	Shows planned cash inflows and outflows and cash balances
Master	Shows a summary of all budgets – including cost, revenue and profit

▲ Table 2 Types of budgets – some examples

WORKED EXAMPLE

Sales volume budget

Table 3 shows a sales volume budget for Emerald Artwork. The company produces four products: AD23, AD24, AE12 and AE13.

	Feb	Mar	Apr	May
AD23	100	100	100	100
AD24	50	80	80	100
AE12	40	50	40	50
AE13	30	30	50	50

▲ Table 3 Sales volume budget for Emerald Artwork

Sales revenue budget

The sales revenue budget for Emerald Artwork is shown in Table 4. The planned sales revenue for each month is calculated by multiplying the planned sales volume by the prices of each product. The prices for AD23, AD24, AE12 and AE13 are £12, £20, £25 and £30, respectively.

				(£)
	Feb	Mar	Apr	May
AD23	1200	1200	1200	1200
	(12 × 100)	(12 × 100)	(12 × 100)	(12 × 100)
AD24	1000	1600	1600	2000
	(20 × 50)	(20 × 80)	(20 × 80)	(20 × 100)
AE12	1000	1250	1000	1250
	(25 × 40)	(25 × 50)	(25 × 40)	(25 × 50)
AE13	900	900	1500	1500
	(30 × 30)	(30 × 30)	(30 × 50)	(30 × 50)
Total	4100	4950	5300	5950

▲ Table 4 Sales revenue budget for Emerald Artwork

Production budget

Emerald Artwork's production costs include materials, direct labour, indirect labour and overheads. Table 5 shows the production cost budget for Emerald Artwork. The budget shows that total production costs are planned to rise over the time period.

				(£)
	Feb	Mar	Apr	May
Cost of materials	660	780	810	900
(£3 per unit)	(3 × 220)	(3 × 260)	(3 × 270)	(3 × 300)
Direct labour costs	880	1040	1080	1200
(£4 per unit)	(4 × 220)	(4 × 260)	(4 × 270)	(4 × 300)
Indirect labour costs	440	520	540	600
(£2 per unit)	(2 × 220)	(2 × 260)	(2 × 270)	(2 × 300)
Production overheads				
(10% of direct & indirect costs)	1320 × 10% = 132	1560 × 10% = 156	1620 × 10% = 162	1800 × 10% = 180
Total	2112	2496	2592	2880

▲ Table 5 Production cost budget for Emerald Artwork

ACTIVITY 1　SKILLS　PROBLEM SOLVING, ANALYSIS

CASE STUDY: FIBRECRAFT LTD

FibreCraft Ltd produces three types of canoe for the New Zealand market – the Kayak, the Explorer and the Twin-seater. The products sell for NZD 200, NZD 220 and NZD 280, respectively. The financial director produces 6-monthly budgets to help control the business. Table 6 shows the sales volume budget for January to June 2017.

	Jan	Feb	Mar	Apr	May	Jun
Kayak	210	210	210	230	250	300
Explorer	100	100	110	110	120	130
Twin-seater	30	35	35	40	40	50

▲ Table 6 Sales volume budget for FibreCraft Ltd January–June 2017 (NZD)

1. Prepare the sales revenue budget for FibreCraft Ltd.
2. Use the sales volume budget to calculate total revenue for each month and for the whole 6-month budget period.
3. What does the budget show over the time period?

Zero-based budget: The financial information used in most budgets is based on historical data. For example, the cost of materials in this year's production budget may be based on last year's figure, with perhaps an adjustment for inflation. Production and manufacturing costs, such as labour, raw materials and overheads, are relatively easy to value and tend to be controlled using methods such as standard costing.

However, in some areas of business it is not so easy to measure costs. Examples might be certain marketing, administration or computer services costs. Where costs cannot be justified then no money is allocated in the budget for those costs. This is known as **zero-based budgeting (ZBB) or zero budgeting**. A manager must show that a particular item of spending generates an adequate amount of benefit in relation to the general objectives of the business in order for money to be allocated in a budget.

This approach is different to the common practice of extrapolating from past costs. It encourages the regular evaluation of costs and helps to minimise unnecessary purchases. The concept of **opportunity cost** is linked to ZBB. Opportunity cost is the cost of the next best alternative. When choices are made, businesses try to minimise the opportunity cost. ZBB also involves a cautious approach to spending, so that costs are minimised. Both approaches include an element of 'value for money'.

The main advantages of ZBB are that:
- the allocation of resources should be improved
- a questioning attitude is developed which will help to reduce unnecessary costs and eliminate inefficient practices
- staff motivation might improve because evaluation skills are practised and a greater knowledge of the firm's operations might develop
- it encourages managers to look for alternatives.

ZBB also has some disadvantages.
- It is time-consuming because the budgeting process involves the collection and analysis of quite detailed information so that spending decisions can be made.

- Skilful decision making is required. Such skills may not be available in the organisation. In addition, decisions may be influenced by subjective opinions.
- It threatens the existing way in which the business is run. This might adversely affect motivation.
- Managers may not be prepared to justify spending on certain costs. Money, therefore, may not be allocated to spending which could benefit the business.

To deal with these possible problems, a business might give each department a 'base' budget of, say, 50 per cent. Departments could then be invited to bid for increased expenditure on a ZBB basis.

USING BUDGETS

Budgetary control or budgeting involves a business using budgets to look into the future, stating what it wants to happen, and then deciding how to achieve these aims. The control process is shown in Figure 1 and explained below.

Preparation of plans: All businesses have objectives. If the sales department increases sales by 10 per cent, how does it know whether or not this is satisfactory? Targets are usually set which allow a business to determine whether its objectives have been met. The results it achieves can then be compared with the targets it sets.

Comparisons of plans with actual results: Control will be effective if information is available as quickly as possible. Managers need budgetary data as soon as it is available. Recent developments in information technology have helped to speed up the supply of data. For budgeting purposes the financial year has been divided up into smaller control periods – usually 4 weeks or 1 calendar month. It is common to prepare a budget for each control period. At the end of the period the actual results can then be compared with targets set in the budget.

Analysis of variances: This is the most important stage in the control process. **Variance analysis** involves trying to find reasons for the differences between actual and expected financial outcomes. Variances are explained in the next section. A variance might be the result of some external factor influencing the business. In this case the business may need to change its business plans and adjust the next budget.

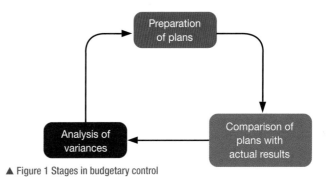

▲ Figure 1 Stages in budgetary control

VARIANCES

A **variance** in budgeting is the difference between the figure that the business has budgeted for and the actual figure. Variances are usually calculated at the end of the budget period, as that is when the actual figure will be known.

Variances can be favourable (F) or adverse (A). Favourable variances occur when the actual figures are 'better' than the budgeted figures.

- If the sales revenue for a month was budgeted at £25,000, but turned out to be £29,000, there would be a £4000 favourable variance (£29,000 – £25,000) as sales revenue was higher than planned.
- If costs were planned to be £20,000 and turned out to be £18,000, this would also be a favourable variance of £2000, as actual costs were lower than planned.

Adverse variances are when the actual figures are worse than the budgeted figures. Actual sales revenues may be lower than planned, or actual costs may be higher than planned. Managers will examine variances and try to identify reasons why they have occurred. By doing this they might be able to improve the performance of the business in the future.

TYPES OF VARIANCE

Variances can be calculated for a wide range of financial outcomes. Most budgets are set for expenditure (costs) and income (sales revenue). Consequently, variances will also focus on a firm's expenditure and income. This suggests that variance analysis provides a very good way of monitoring business costs. Examples of variances could be wages, materials, overheads and sales revenue. Variances can also be calculated for volumes. For example, it is possible to calculate a sales variance or a labour hours variance. One of the most important variances of all is the profit variance. The profit variance is influenced by all other variances. A change in any variance will affect profit. This is because all variances relate to either the costs or the revenue of a business, both of which affect profit levels. The number of possible variances is equal to the number of factors which can influence business costs and revenue.

WORKED EXAMPLE

Table 7 calculates the income variances for Wishart Ltd, a wooden furniture manufacturer. Most of the variances are favourable (F) and might be the result of:

- the ability to charge higher prices
- an increase in demand due to a marketing campaign
- improvements in the quality of the product
- an increase in consumer incomes
- a change in consumers' tastes in favour of wooden furniture.

							(£)
	Jan	**Feb**	**Mar**	**Apr**	**May**	**Jun**	**Total**
Budgeted income	16,500	17,000	17,500	18,000	19,000	20,000	108,000
Actual income	16,600	17,400	17,900	17,700	18,500	20,800	108,900
Variance	**100F**	**400F**	**400F**	**300A**	**500A**	**800F**	**900F**

▲ Table 7 Income budget, actual income and income variances for Wishart Ltd

WORKED EXAMPLE

Table 8 calculates the expenditure or cost variances for Wishart Ltd. Most of these variances are adverse (A) – possibly because:

- costs might be higher due to production being higher
- suppliers may have raised prices
- there may be some inefficiencies in production
- wages may have been higher due to wage demands by workers.

							(£)
	Jan	**Feb**	**Mar**	**Apr**	**May**	**Jun**	**Total**
Budgeted expenditure	11,400	11,900	12,500	13,000	14,000	15,000	77,800
Actual expenditure	11,500	11,600	12,700	13,500	14,200	15,600	79,100
Expenditure variances	**100A**	**300F**	**200A**	**500A**	**200A**	**600A**	**1,300A**

▲ Table 8 Budgeted expenditure, actual expenditure and expenditure variances for Wishart Ltd

WORKED EXAMPLE

Table 9 calculates the profit variances for Wishart Ltd. Over the 6-month period the variance is adverse – mainly because costs have been higher than planned.

							(£)
	Jan	Feb	Mar	Apr	May	Jun	Total
Budgeted profit	5100	5100	5000	5000	5000	5000	30,200
Actual profit	5100	5800	5200	4200	4300	5200	29,800
Profit variances	0	700F	200F	800A	700A	200F	400A

▲ Table 9 Budgeted profit, actual profit and profit variances for Wishart Ltd

ACTIVITY 2   SKILLS   ANALYSIS, PROBLEM SOLVING

CASE STUDY: US CORN BELT

The corn belt in the USA, a region which includes Iowa, Illinois, Indiana, southern Michigan, western Ohio, eastern Nebraska, eastern Kansas, southern Minnesota and parts of Missouri, is home to a large number of arable farms. Many businesses in this region serve the needs of these arable farmers. One such business is Bobby Beddoes, which maintains and services agricultural machinery for farmers around the Fort Dodge, Iowa, area. The business has a workshop in Fort Dodge but also does 'call-out' work to fix tractors, combine harvesters and other farm machinery on location. Table 10 shows the income (sales revenue) budget and actual income for the business between January and June 2017.

	Jan	Feb	Mar	Apr	May	Jun
Budgeted income (US$)	100,000	110,000	120,000	125,000	140,000	175,000
Actual income (US$)	90,000	110,000	128,000	129,000	152,000	197,000

▲ Table 10 Income budget and actual income for Bobby Beddoes, January–June 2017

1. Calculate the sales revenue variances for each month and the total sales revenue variance for the whole budget period.
2. Explain the variance in February.
3. Explain two possible reasons for the pattern of variances over the 6-month time period.

USING VARIANCES FOR DECISION MAKING

The final stage in budgetary control is the analysis of variances. It is important to identify the reasons why variances have occurred. If variances are adverse it will be necessary to take action to ensure that adverse variances are avoided in future. If variances are favourable the business can learn from understanding the reasons why this has occurred and can introduce strategies and systems to help continue performance improvements in the future.

When making decisions about how the business should be run, information about the causes of variances will be very helpful. For example, if a business has an adverse cost variance, it might discover that the cause was higher prices charged by suppliers. The business might then decide to look for new suppliers. A favourable sales revenue variance might be the result of an effective advertising campaign. The business might decide to make more use of the same or similar campaigns in the future. Variance analysis can help business decision makers because of the information it provides about financial outcomes and their causes.

DIFFICULTIES OF BUDGETING

Businesses may encounter problems when setting budgets and using them as tools for financial management.

EXAM HINT

When you have calculated a profit variance, you need to appreciate that if it is a favourable profit variance of £450,000 it could be made up of a favourable cost variance of £560,000 and an adverse income variance of £110,000. In this case the business would need to investigate why the income variance was adverse. This could help to improve performance further.

Setting budgets:

- Problems may arise because figures in budgets are not actual figures. The figures are plans based on historical data, forecasts or human judgement. A business might construct its budgets by adding a percentage to historical data without systematic analysis.
- The most important data in the preparation of nearly all budgets is sales data. If sales data are inaccurate, many of the firm's budgets will be inexact.
- The setting of budgets may lead to conflict between departments or staff. A business may only have limited funds and departments compete against each other for those funds. For instance, the marketing department may want to promote a product, but new machinery may be needed in the R&D department.
- The time spent setting budgets could have been spent on other tasks. For example, sales managers could be winning new customers and increasing revenue for the business instead of drawing up this year's budget.
- Sometimes businesses set over-ambitious objectives. When this happens, the budgeting process is pointless because budgets are being drawn up for targets that are unachievable. The budget then ceases to be a useful document against which outcomes can be compared.

Motivation: In some businesses, workers are left out of the planning process. If workers are not consulted about the budget, it could be difficult to use that budget to motivate them. Budgets that are unrealistic can also fail to motivate staff.

Manipulation: Budgets can be manipulated by managers. For example, a departmental manager might have great influence over those co-ordinating and setting budgets. The manager may be able to set a budget that is easy to achieve and consequently makes the department look successful, but ultimately that budget might not help the business achieve its objectives.

Rigidity: Budgets can sometimes restrict business activities. For example, departments within a business may have different views about when to replace delivery vehicles. The more often vehicles are replaced, the higher the cost. However, the newer the vehicle, the lower the maintenance cost and the less likely it will be off the road for repairs. The budget may be set so that older vehicles have to be kept rather than replaced. But this may lead to customer dissatisfaction and lost orders because deliveries are unreliable.

Short-termism: Some managers might be too focused on the current budget. They might take actions that damage the future performance of the business just to meet current budget targets. For example, to keep labour costs down in the current budget period, the manager of a supermarket might reduce staffing on customer service. This may well save costs now, but it could lead to customers leaving due to poor service. Consequently the long-term performance of the business would suffer.

CHECKPOINT

1. How might a budget improve managerial accountability?
2. Why is the sales budget such an important budget?
3. How might budgets motivate staff?
4. Give examples of three types of budget.
5. Why might a business use zero-based budgeting?
6. Describe the three steps in budgetary control.
7. How is a variance calculated?
8. What is adverse variance?
9. State two possible causes of a favourable sales revenue variance.
10. State two possible causes of an adverse cost variance.
11. State four benefits of using budgets.

SUBJECT VOCABULARY

budget a quantitative economic plan prepared and agreed in advance.
budgetary control a business system that involves making future plans, comparing the actual results with the planned results and then investigating the causes of any differences.
historical figures quantitative information based on past trading records.
opportunity cost when choosing between different alternatives, this is the benefit lost from the next best alternative to the one chosen.
production cost budget a firm's planned production costs for a future period of time.
sales budget a firm's planned sales for a future period of time – can be measured in terms of volume or revenue.
variance the difference between actual financial outcomes and those budgeted.
variance analysis the process of calculating variances and attempting to identify their causes.
zero-based budgeting or zero budgeting a system of budgeting where no money is allocated for costs or spending unless they can be justified by the fund holder (they are given a zero value).

EXAM PRACTICE

CAZADECOCHES.ES

SKILLS ANALYSIS, INTERPRETATION, PROBLEM SOLVING, REASONING

The website cazadecoches.es is an online business that brings together buyers and sellers of second-hand cars in Spain. The business charges car owners a fixed price to list their cars for sale on the site for 2 weeks. Anyone searching to buy a car can use the site free of charge. The business also earns a growing stream of income from selling advertising space on the site. The business is based in Gibraltar to take advantage of the very low corporation tax rate in the country. It is currently 10 per cent (this compares with 25 per cent in Spain).

In 2015, the directors took a decision to incorporate and develop a comparison site for second-hand cars. However, the decision was not unanimous because two of the directors thought that the level of expenditure needed to develop and launch the site was too high. They also thought that competition would be tough. Table 11 shows the budgeted expenditure, revenue and profit for 2015–19 and the actual figures for 2015–17.

	2015	2016	2017	2018	2019
Budgeted income	2.14	2.2	2.6	3	3.8
Actual income	**2.13**	**2.14**	**2.22**		
Budgeted expenditure	1.99	2.11	2.01	2.01	2.1
Actual expenditure	**2.01**	**2.21**	**2.3**		
Budgeted profit	0.15	0.09	0.59	0.99	1.7
Actual profit	**0.12**	**−0.07**	**−0.08**		

▲ Table 11 Budgeted expenditure, costs and profit, and actual figures 2015–19 (€ million)

 Q

(a) Define variance. **(2 marks)**

(b) Calculate the income, expenditure and profit variances for 2015, 2016 and 2017 for cazadecoches.es **(4 marks)**

(c) Discuss the possible impact of the new comparison site on cazadecoches.es. **(8 marks)**

(d) Assess the usefulness to cazadecoches.es of using variance analysis. **(10 marks)**

MANAGING FINANCE

Poor financial management can result in the collapse of a business. This important section looks at how to calculate and increase profit, and how profit is measured in a statement of comprehensive income (profit and loss account). It also examines the difference between profit and cash, and focuses on the liquidity of businesses. It explores the purpose and nature of the statement of financial position (balance sheet) and looks at the importance of cash and working capital management. At the end the different causes of business failure are addressed – both internal and external.

34 PROFIT

LEARNING OBJECTIVES

By the end of this chapter you should be able to understand:
- the calculation of gross profit, operating profit and profit for the year (net profit)
- ways to increase profits
- statement of comprehensive income (profit and loss account), and measuring profitability
- calculation of gross profit margin, operating profit margin
- profit for the year (net profit) margin and ways to improve profitability.

GETTING STARTED

AVI is an established producer of branded goods based in South Africa. The company is quoted on the Johannesburg stock exchange and sells more than 50 household brands, such as Five Roses® and Lavazza® (drinks), Bakers® and Willards® (snacks and biscuits), Yardley® (personal care) and Spitz® and Lacoste® (shoes and clothing). In 2016, AVI's operating profit was ZAR 2154.6 million on revenue of ZAR 12,188.9 million. This was an increase on 2015 when revenue was ZAR 11,243.7 million and operating profit was ZAR 1916.9 million.

▲ Some of AVI's brands

Calculate the percentage change in revenue and profit between 2015 and 2016. What might explain the differences in your answers? What measures might AVI take to improve their profitability further in the future?

EXAM HINT

The accounting ratios in the Pearson Edexcel specification use the term 'profit for the year (net profit)'. In business, you might see the terms 'profit for the year (net profit)' or 'net profit' used with the same meaning. The accounting ratios in the Pearson Edexcel specification use the term 'revenue'. In business, you might see the terms 'revenue' or 'turnover' used with the same meaning.

PROFIT

As explained in Chapter 29, if total costs are subtracted from total revenue this gives business's profit. This is the money left over after all costs have been met, and belongs to the owners of the business. Accountants calculate and define profit in a number of ways.

Gross profit: Gross profit is the difference between **revenue or turnover** and **cost of sales**.
- Turnover, also called revenue or sales revenue, can be calculated as price × quantity of sales.
- Cost of sales are the direct costs of a business.
- Gross profit is the profit made by a business after direct costs have been met.

For a retailer or wholesaler the cost of sales is the cost of buying in stock to re-sell. For a manufacturer the cost of sales is any costs associated directly with production, such as raw materials, factory wages and other direct costs. For a supplier of services it is any direct costs, such as direct labour. Gross profit is calculated by:

$$\text{Gross profit} = \text{Revenue} - \text{Cost of sales}$$

Operating profit: Operating profit is the difference between gross profit and business overheads. Overheads are indirect costs, such as selling and administrative expenses. Operating profit is calculated by:

$$\text{Operating profit} = \text{Gross profit} - \text{Operating expenses}$$

Profit for the year (net profit): Profit for the year or net profit is the profit made by the business for the year. It is the difference between operating profit and finance costs (interest paid on loans) and any other **exceptional costs**. Net profit may be calculated before or after the subtraction of taxation. It is calculated by:

$$\text{Profit for the year (net profit)} = \text{Operating profit} - \text{finance costs (and exceptional costs)}$$

Sometimes net finance costs are shown in the statement of comprehensive income. This is the difference between any interest paid by a business (on loans and overdrafts, for example) and any interest received by the business (from money placed in deposit accounts, for example).

WORKED EXAMPLE

HLD plc is a large Canadian paper manufacturer. In 2014, its turnover was CAD 46 million. Its cost of sales was CAD 23.5 million, operating expenses CAD 12.4 million and finance costs CAD 2.1 million. What was the gross profit, operating profit and net profit?

Gross profit = Revenue/turnover − Cost of sales
= CAD 46 million − CAD 23.5 million
= CAD 22.5 million

Operating profit = Gross profit − Operating expenses
= CAD 22.5 million − CAD 12.4 million
= CAD 10.1 million

Profit for the year = Operating profit − Finance costs (and
(net profit)   any exceptional items)
= CAD 10.1 million − CAD 2.1 million
= CAD 8 million

ACTIVITY 1   SKILLS   ANALYSIS, PROBLEM SOLVING

CASE STUDY: WEST RYDE HOTEL

West Ryde Hotel is an established and successful four-star hotel located in North Sydney, Australia. It has 43 rooms, employs 42 staff and its restaurant has a reputation for excellent meals. Some financial information for the hotel is shown in Table 1 for 2017 and 2016.

	2017 (AUD)	2016 (AUD)
Turnover/revenue	2,341,700	2,600,700
Cost of sales	1,090,000	980,500
Administration expenses	399,100	388,900
Finance costs	21,000	19,300

▲ Table 1 Financial information for West Ryde Hotel, 2016 and 2017

1. Calculate: (i) gross profit; (ii) operating profit; (iii) profit for the year for 2017 and 2016.
2. Calculate the percentage change in the profit for the year between 2016 and 2017.
3. Analyse whether the financial performance of the hotel has improved over the 2 years.

WAYS TO INCREASE PROFIT

Most businesses will want to increase their profits if it is possible. One approach is to increase profitability. This involves raising prices or lowering costs per unit. This is discussed later in this chapter. Also, a business might use one, or more, of the following approaches to raise the overall level of profits for the business.

Adjust the marketing strategy: A business could use a range of marketing techniques to increase its revenues. For example, it could:

- invest more in advertising
- invest in a new promotional campaign such as introducing a loyalty card
- exploit new distribution channels such as selling goods online
- increase commissions to sales staff
- improve customer targeting using social media
- accept a wider range of payment methods such as credit cards or PayPal
- encourage people to buy larger amounts or repeat their purchases more regularly.

Find new markets: A business could generate more sales by finding new markets for its products. For example, a local business may launch its products across the country. Some businesses sell more by exploiting overseas markets. For example, a number of Mexican businesses have started to sell more bananas and avocados to China and Europe.

Diversify: A business can increase its revenue and profit by extending its product lines or producing completely new products. For example, Google, which is globally famous for its search engine, is also developing business interests in wearable technology and driverless cars, among other things.

Mergers and takeovers: Some businesses try to grow their profits by joining together with others. They might, for example, choose to merge their business or take over rivals. A business may take over a rival in the same market so that it can grow quickly and lower costs by exploiting economies of scale. Alternatively, a business may diversify by acquiring another firm in a completely different field. For example, in 2015, US company J.M. Smucker, known for jams, peanut butter and coffee, bought Big Heart Pet Brands, maker of Milk Bone dog biscuits and Meow Mix cat food (among others), for US$3200 million.

Disposal of non-profitable activities: Some businesses may be in a position where they can increase profits by getting rid of poorer performing parts of their business. This is particularly the case if a business has a product or a division that is making a loss. For example, in 2017, GM motors announced its desire to sell its loss-making European arm Opel. France's PSA Group, which owns Peugeot and

Citroen, expressed an interest. It was reported that Opel had lost up to US$15,000 million for GM since 2000. In March 2017, it was reported that PSA had agreed to pay €2200 million for Opel. Clearly, if a business can 'off-load' a loss-making section of its operations, overall profit will improve immediately.

STATEMENT OF COMPREHENSIVE INCOME (PROFIT AND LOSS ACCOUNT)

At the end of the trading year, businesses produce documents that show key information relating to the financial performance of the business. One of these documents is the **statement of comprehensive income**. This shows the income and expenses of a business during the financial year. It is used to calculate gross profit, operating profit and profit for the year (net profit).The layout of the statement is important. The financial information must be presented in a standard way. An example from a statement for Forest Way Autotraders Ltd, a second-hand car dealer, is shown in Table 2.

	2017 (£)	2016 (£)
Revenue/turnover	561,000	498,200
Cost of sales	331,000	322,100
Gross profit	**230,000**	**176,100**
Selling expenses	45,300	38,200
Admin expenses	122,500	102,800
Operating profit	**62,200**	**35,100**
Finance costs	22,100	21,000
Profit for the year (net profit)	**40,100**	**14,100**
Taxation	8000	2800
Profit for the year (net profit) after tax	**32,100**	**11,300**

▲ Table 2 Selected information from the statement of comprehensive income for Forest Way Autotraders Ltd, year ending 31 January 2017

The statement always shows the figures for the current trading year and the previous year. This allows a comparison to be made. In this case, the statement shows that net profit before tax has increased from £14,100 to £40,100. This is a significant increase, probably because turnover has increased quite sharply. The statement in Table 2 also shows the taxation paid by the business and the net profit after tax.

CASE STUDY: APPGAME

AppGame is a new but rapidly growing South Korean software company. It designs children's game apps on mobile phones. During 2017, the company had some staff shortages and invested in an expensive recruitment campaign. Selected information from the statement of comprehensive income for AppGame is shown in Table 3 (three figures are missing).

	2017 (KRW 000 million)	2016 (KRW 000 million)
Revenue/turnover	6.444	5.871
Cost of sales	4.191	3.713
Gross profit	**?**	**2.158**
Selling expenses	1.223	1.112
Admin expenses	?	0.211
Operating profit	**0.796**	**0.835**
Finance costs	?	0.216
Profit for the year (net profit)	**0.595**	**0.619**
Taxation	0.120	0.121
Profit for the year (net profit) after taxation	**0.475**	**0.498**

▲ Table 3 Selected information from the statement of comprehensive income for AppGame, year ending 31 December 2017

1. What is meant by a statement of comprehensive income?
2. Calculate the missing figures in the statement for AppGame.
3. Assess the possible impact on AppGame of the staff shortages in 2017.

MEASURING PROFITABILITY

The information contained in the statement of comprehensive income can show how well a business is performing. As mentioned earlier, in Table 2 the statement for Forest Way Autotraders Ltd shows that net profit for the year has increased from £14,100 to £40,100. This is a significant increase. However, it is possible to measure the profitability of a business in a more meaningful way. This can be done by calculating profit margins, which measure the size of profit in relation to revenue/turnover. Three profit margins can be calculated.

Gross profit margin: The **gross profit margin** shows the gross profit made on sales turnover/revenue. It is calculated using the formula:

$$\text{Gross profit margin} = \frac{\text{Gross profit}}{\text{Revenue}} \times 100\%$$

Higher gross margins are usually preferable to lower ones because it means that more gross profit is being made per £1 of sales. The gross profit margin:

- may be increased by raising revenue/turnover relative to the cost of sales, by increasing price
- may be increased by cutting the cost of sales; this might be achieved by finding cheaper suppliers of key materials
- will vary between different industries. As a rule, the quicker the turnover of inventory, the lower the gross margin that is needed. So, for example, a supermarket with a fast stock turnover is likely to have a lower gross margin than a car retailer with a much slower stock (inventory) turnover. Some supermarkets are therefore very successful with relatively low gross profit margins because of the regular and fast turnover of inventory.

Operating profit margin: The **operating profit margin** shows the operating profit made on sales revenue/turnover. Operating margin is used to measure a company's pricing strategy and operating efficiency. It gives an idea of how much a company makes (before finance costs and taxes) on each pound of sales. It is calculated using the formula:

$$\text{Operating profit margin} = \frac{\text{Operating profit}}{\text{Revenue}} \times 100\%$$

A high or increasing operating margin is preferred. This is because more money is made on each £1 of sales. If the operating margin is increasing, the company is earning more per pound of sales. Operating margin shows the profitability of sales from regular business. Operating income results from ordinary business operations and excludes other revenue or losses, exceptional items, finance costs and income taxes.

Profit for the year (net profit) margin: The profit for the year (net profit) margin or net profit margin takes into account all business costs, including finance costs, other non-operating costs and exceptional items. It is also usually calculated before tax has been subtracted.

The profit for the year (net profit) margin can be calculated by:

$$\text{Profit for the year (net profit) margin} = \frac{\text{Net profit before tax}}{\text{Revenue}} \times 100\%$$

On the previous page, Table 2 shows the income statement for Forest Way Autotraders Ltd. The profit margins for 2017 can be calculated as follows.

$$\text{Gross profit margin} = \frac{\text{Gross Profit}}{\text{Revenue}} \times 100\%$$

$$= \frac{£230,000}{£561,000} \times 100\% = \textbf{41\%}$$

$$\text{Operating profit margin} = \frac{\text{Operating profit}}{\text{Revenue}} \times 100\%$$

$$= \frac{£62,200}{£561,000} = \textbf{11.1\%}$$

$$\text{Profit for the year (net profit) margin} = \frac{\text{Net profit (before tax)}}{\text{Revenue}} \times 100\%$$

$$= \frac{£40,100}{£561,000} = \textbf{7.1\%}$$

Table 4 provides a summary of the profit margins for both 2017 and 2016. Over the 2 years there is a clear improvement in all of the profit margins. This suggests that the business has performed well – improving efficiency and possibly raising prices.

	2017	2016
Gross profit margin	41%	35.3%
Operating profit margin	11.1%	7%
Profit for the year (net profit) margin	7.1%	2.8%

▲ Table 4 Profit margins for Forest Way Autotraders Ltd, 2017 and 2016

Again, higher margins are usually better than lower ones. The profit for the year (net profit) margin focuses on the so-called 'bottom line' in business. The bottom line refers to the very last line in the statement of comprehensive income, which shows the profit left after all deductions have been made. It is the final amount of profit left over for the owners.

ACTIVITY 3

SKILLS ANALYSIS, PROBLEM SOLVING, INTERPRETATION

CASE STUDY: CHAPPERTON LTD

Chapperton Ltd develops wearable technology. UK shoppers spent around £105 million on wearable tech devices during the Christmas shopping period in 2014, a massive increase of 182 per cent compared to the previous year. Fitness and activity monitors are the most popular wearable devices, selling over £29 million, followed by smart watches at £25 million, healthcare wearable devices at £22 million, and the remainder on other wearable devices. Table 5 shows the company's statement of comprehensive income at 31 March 2014.

	2014 £000s	2013 £000s
Revenue/turnover	7800	5700
Cost of sales	3780	2100
Gross profit	**4020**	**3600**
Admin expenses	1560	1800
Operating profit	**2460**	**1800**
Finance costs	70	45
Profit for the year (net profit)	**2390**	**1755**
Taxation	580	450
Profit for the year (net profit) after tax	**1810**	**1305**

▲ Table 5 Selected information from the statement of comprehensive income for Chapperton Ltd, 31 March 2014

1. Explain the difference between the gross profit margin and the profit for the year (net profit) margin.

2. Calculate the gross, operating and profit for the year (net profit) margins for 2013 and 2014. Present the information in a table.

3. Assess the financial performance of Chapperton Ltd in 2014.

EXAM HINT

Calculating the different profit margins is fairly straightforward. It is important, though, to interpret the answers correctly. You need to know that the gross margin will always be the highest and the profit for the year (net profit) margin the lowest. You also need to know that higher margins are better and that an increase in margins over time shows an improvement.

Profit margins can be used to make comparisons between businesses in the same industry, but only if the businesses being compared have similar trading activities. For example, using the gross margin to compare the performance of Sainsbury's and Marks & Spencer (M&S) may not be appropriate because many of their product lines and the proportions of types of retail product are different (M&S sell more clothes than Sainsbury's, for instance). You need to understand that profit margins are likely to vary considerably across different industries.

WAYS TO IMPROVE PROFITABILITY

All businesses will want to improve their performance. An improved performance is likely to benefit all stakeholders. The returns on capital can be increased by making more profit with the same level of investment. This might be achieved by growth funded externally. This means the business increases sales using fresh capital.

Increasing profit margins will also improve performance. If profit margins can be raised, the business will make more profit at the existing level of sales. The profit margins can be improved in two ways.

Raising prices: If a business raises its price it will get more revenue for every unit sold. If costs remain the same then profitability should improve. However, raising price might have an impact on the level of sales. Generally, when price is raised demand will fall. However, if demand is not too responsive to changes in price, the increase in price will generate more revenue even though fewer units are sold. Raising price is always risky because it is never certain how competitors will react.

Global Insolvency Data for Q1 2012

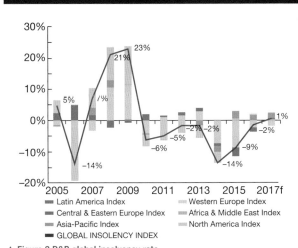

	D&B Global Insolvency Index	Year on year change (%) Q1 12	yr to Q1
World	90.2	−5.8	−3.8
Advanced economies	88.3	−8.3	−4.8
North America	75.0	−17.5	−13.9
Euroland	103.7	−1.9	2.6
Nordic Region	94.6	−6.2	−5.3
Emerging economies (ex. China)	105.5	14.7	4.8
Emerging Asia (ex. China)	103.2	2.3	−4.1
Eastern Europe	118.2	35.4	9.8

▲ Figure 2 D&B global insolvency rate
Source: National Statistics offices. D&B

Some of the common internal factors that cause business failure are outlined below.

Poor management of cash: Many businesses fail because they run out of cash. In some cases entrepreneurs focus too much on profit and neglect the importance of cash. There is a number of reasons why a business runs short of cash.

- **Investing too much in fixed assets.** In the initial stages of a business, funds are limited. Spending large amounts quickly on equipment, vehicles and other capital items uses up resources. It may be better to lease some of these fixed assets, leaving sufficient cash funds.
- **Allowing too much credit.** A great deal of business is done on credit. One of the dangers is that businesses allow their customers too long for payment. This means they have to wait for money and may be forced to borrow during this period. Failure to control debtors may also lead to bad debts.
- **Overborrowing.** Businesses may borrow to finance growth. As more loans are taken out, interest costs can rise. Overborrowing not only threatens a firm's cash position, but also the overall control of the business. It is important to fund growth in a balanced way, perhaps by raising some capital from share issues. It was reported that Disneyland Paris, France, has suffered for many years due to very high levels of debt. In 2014, it had to get financial help from its parent company to reduce its £1750 million debt.
- **Seasonal factors.** Sometimes trade fluctuates for seasonal reasons. In the agriculture industry, cereal farmers and fruit growers, for example, have a large cash inflow when their harvest is sold. For much of the year, though, they have to pay expenses without any cash flowing in. This situation requires careful management, although it is possible to predict these changes.

- **Unforeseen expenditure.** Businesses need to prepare for unforeseen expenditure. Equipment breakdowns, tax demands, strikes and bad debts are common examples of this type of emergency expense. In the early stages of business development, owners are often hit by unforeseen expenditure. This might be because they lack experience or have not undertaken sufficient planning.
- **External factors.** Sometimes events that are outside the control of the business cause cash flow problems. Examples include changes in consumer tastes, changes in legislation or a downturn in the economy. These are discussed in more detail later in this chapter.
- **Poor financial management.** Inexperience in managing cash or a poor understanding of the way cash flows into and out of a business may lead to cash flow problems. For example, if a business plans to spend heavily just before they receive large amounts of cash from customers that have bought on credit, it is likely to face problems. It is not advisable to spend cash when it is not definitely there. The control of cash flow will be improved if owners and managers produce regular cash flow forecasts, keep up-to-date financial records and operate an efficient credit control system.

Overestimating sales: Forecasting future sales is a very difficult process. This was explained in Chapter 30. For example, consumer tastes and preferences can change dramatically in short periods of time. There is also a large amount of data relating to consumer behaviour and other sales factors, which is sometimes difficult to analyse effectively even with modern analytical techniques. In addition, many entrepreneurs and business managers are optimistic. They are usually positive and confident people and expect things to turn out for the best. Consequently they may fall into the trap of overestimating sales.

If a business does overestimate sales the consequences can be serious enough to cause business failure. For example, a business might build up too much unsold stock and inadequate revenues may lead to cash flow problems. Once resources have been used to produce goods and services, if they remain unsold, a business might find that too much money has flowed out of the business and not enough has flowed back in. Consequently it may run out of cash and collapse.

Overtrading: Young and rapidly growing businesses are particularly prone to **overtrading**. Overtrading occurs when a business is attempting to fund a large volume of production with inadequate cash. Established companies trying to expand too quickly can also face this problem. Overtrading is most likely to occur if customers are given generous credit terms, if the business is undercapitalised or if profit margins are very slim. One important symptom of overtrading is the need to keep borrowing money to meet day-to-day expenditures.

Poor inventory control: Ineffective inventory control can cause problems for businesses. Poor inventory control may mean a business is holding too much stock, too little stock or the wrong sort of stock. If a business carries large quantities of inventory, money is tied up in unproductive assets. Inventories do not generate any return for a business until they are sold. Consequently, if inventories are built up, costs will be incurred and the flow of revenues may be insufficient. The costs of holding inventory can be significant and include storage, handling, labour, insurance, stock theft and stock becoming out of date.

If the wrong sort of stock is bought by a business this could cause serious problems. For example, if a retailer buys stock that cannot be sold because it is not in demand, it may eventually have to be sold at a loss.

If a business has too little stock it runs the risk of losing business. For example, if a manufacturer runs out of an important component, production may be stopped for a period. This might mean that customers are left waiting, go to rivals and never return.

Poor marketing: A range of marketing problems could be the cause of business failure. Businesses that launch new products that fail to meet customer needs are likely to have difficulties. The use of inappropriate pricing strategies could mean that prices are too high or too low. A business may invest too heavily in wasteful or inappropriate promotional campaigns. A business may fail to position itself correctly in the market, which can end up confusing customers to the point where they stop buying the product. Inappropriate or even offensive marketing messages or materials can also result in difficulties for businesses.

In 2017, Karachi-based KACS (Karachi Air-Conditioning Systems) in Pakistan, a specialist in the design, supply and installation of air-conditioning systems for offices, collapsed owing money to more than 180 suppliers and subcontractors. Up to 2015, the business had grown to PKR 4200 million sales and was trading profitably. The owners decided to grow the business further after several contract opportunities arose and during 2016 recorded sales of PKR 6700 million. However, the company was growing too quickly and resources became strained – it was unable to fund the additional working capital requirements of the new, larger business. This resulted in disastrous cash flow problems. The failure of the business resulted in the redundancy of 85 staff and debts of around PKR 1450 million.

1. Define overtrading.
2. Explain how it is possible for a profitable business like KACS to fail.

One example of a business failure caused by misunderstanding the market was India's Klozee. Klozee was a clothing rental operation, a business that tried to imitate similar operations in the USA such as Poshmark and Rent the Runway. Klozee borrowed money from venture capitalist TracxnLabs but closed down after 6 months. Klozee co-founder, Arman Haji, said that the Indian market was not ready for such a service. Demand was low with Klozee receiving just 12–15 orders per day. It seemed that there was not a culture in India for renting clothes. Apart from the concept itself, many Indians had concerns over hygiene, despite assurances of high-quality cleaning.

Poor quality: Supplying products which fail to meet customer quality expectations is likely to cause difficulties for businesses. Poor-quality products can result in lost customers and long-term damage to the reputation of a business. In 2016, Samsung had to completely withdraw its Samsung Note® 7 smartphone after serious issues with the batteries. There were numerous reports of the phones catching fire and causing damage to both people and property. The financial cost to Samsung of this quality defect in the Note 7 was widely discussed with some reports saying that it could have been up to US$17,000 million.

With the widespread and increasing use of social media around the world, news about poor-quality products can travel very quickly. As a result, quality assurance is now more important than ever. Quality is discussed in detail in Chapter 40.

EXTERNAL CAUSES OF BUSINESS FAILURE

It could be argued that failed business owners are quick to blame external factors for the problems their business faced – thereby taking blame away from themselves. However, it is reckoned by some that only about 20 per cent of business failure is due to external forces. Some of the most likely external factors to cause business failure are outlined below.

Market conditions: Markets are dynamic, which means they change all the time. For example, consumer tastes are not constant and businesses that cannot adapt to changes are more likely to fail. In the last 10 years or so there has been a huge growth in online shopping. Retailers that have failed to set up their own online operation have often struggled. Also, over time certain industries decline and are replaced by others. For example, the amount of coal used to generate electricity is decreasing rapidly, so the need for coal mining companies is drastically reduced. Society is increasing its demand for energy generated by environmentally friendly production methods. As a result a number of coal mining companies around the world have closed down.

Changes in market conditions can sometimes result in sharp fluctuations in prices. This might have a negative impact on businesses if prices fall sharply. In certain industries firms are 'price takers'. For example, oil producers have to sell their output at the global market price. Consequently, when oil prices fall marginal producers will leave the market. For example, the price of oil fell from around US$103 in late 2014 to US$30 in 2016. This caused a number of businesses in the oil industry to contract, and in some cases fail.

Competition: The strength and success of business rivals can be a cause of failure. Competitors might bring out superior products. They might read market conditions more effectively. They may charge lower prices because their costs are lower. They may be a powerful company and use predatory pricing to drive smaller rivals out of the market. In recent years many manufacturers in the west have been outcompeted by low-cost producers from China and other emerging nations. Many high street retailers have collapsed because people are doing more of their shopping online where the same products are often cheaper. For example, one of the reasons why SpoonRocket failed (see 'Getting started' above) was due to a very crowded marketplace. Numerous online food delivery services were setting up all over the USA at the time, which made the market very competitive.

Economic: The general state of the economy, both domestic and global, can have an impact on the success of businesses. Figure 2 shows that the level of business failures rose after the financial crisis in 2008. After this crisis many countries in the world went into recession and thousands of businesses in many countries collapsed as a result. The government's economic policies might also contribute to business failure. For example, in the last 5 years there have been cuts in government expenditure in some countries, such as Greece, which have resulted in job losses. Some taxes have been increased and the wages of some public sector workers have been frozen. This leads to a drop in disposable incomes, which results in lower demand and hardship for some businesses. Businesses that produce non-essential goods and services are likely to feel the effects of an economic downturn more severely.

Exchange rates: Businesses that import and export will be affected by changes in the exchange rate. For example, a business that relies heavily on the export market will suffer if the exchange rate rises sharply. Higher exchange rates mean that overseas customers have to pay more for goods and services. This could reduce demand and force marginal firms into administration. In 2017, the Egyptian pound fell sharply after it was devalued by the government. This meant that many businesses that had borrowed money from abroad faced a huge increase in fees and interest charges. As a result, a number of big Egyptian businesses placed a full-page advert in a newspaper appealing to President Abdel-Fattah El-Sisi to resolve the 'crisis' faced by companies. 'Firms are facing bankruptcy because banks are asking them to pay for letters of credit issued before the pound was devalued at the new exchange rates', the ad said.

Interest rates: In many countries interest rates have been historically low since the mid-2000s. However, a sharp increase in rates could cause difficulties for some businesses. Those with large debts would be at risk, as would those that depend on consumers using credit to fund their purchasing. Rising debt often causes problems for businesses and when interest rates rise the burden of that debt may 'crush' a company. For example, very tragically, there have been a large number of suicides by farmers in India. Between 2004 and 2012 it was reported that an average of 16,000 Indian farmers each year took their own lives. The Indian government reckoned that 80 per cent of farmers killed themselves in 2015 because of bankruptcy or debts after taking loans from banks and other moneylenders.

ACTIVITY 2   SKILLS   ANALYSIS, PROBLEM SOLVING

CASE STUDY: BRAZILIAN SOYBEANS

Since the mid-1990s, Brazil has experienced a huge investment in the growing of soybeans. Growers borrowed billions of dollars to set up farms in order to benefit from high soybean prices. The beans were shipped to markets all over the world to make cooking oil and cattle feed. However, market conditions have changed and the price of soybeans has fallen – as shown in Figure 3. As a result, many hundreds of businesses in the industry are struggling to come to terms with huge debts and a soybean surplus which has forced the global price down and resulted in Brazil's longest recession in a century.

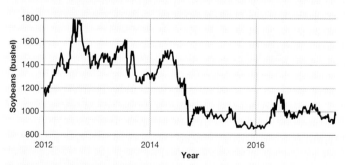

▲ Figure 3 Soybean price, 2012–17

One businessman, Nelson Vigolo, increased the size of his farm in Mato Grosso state by a scale of 15 before the downturn. However, in 2017 his company,

Grupo Bom Jesus, went bankrupt. The company owed US\$590 million that it could not repay. Strangely, soybean prices are expected to rise again in the near future as many growers have either gone bankrupt or reduced their growing capacity.

Soybean prices have fallen from US\$1800/bushel in 2012 to US\$1000/bushel in 2017.

1. Calculate the percentage change in soybean prices over this time period.
2. Explain how changes in market conditions have resulted in business failure in this case.
3. To what extent do you think economic conditions contributed to the failure of Grupo Bom Jesus?

Government regulations: Sometimes changes in government legislation can lead to business failure. For example, in 2014 a number of moneylenders withdrew from the market in the UK after the government passed legislation to control the supply of so-called 'payday loans'. In another example, Germany-based SolarWorld, which manufactures solar panels, went into administration in 2017. One of the main causes of its failure was cuts in government subsidies to the industry.

Governments all over the world can have a negative impact on businesses. This is likely to happen if they impose legislation that limits companies' ability to do business, reduce subsidies (as in the example above) or cut government expenditure.

Supplier problems: It is possible for a business to collapse if they are let down by suppliers. For example, if a key supplier fails to make deliveries, a business may not be able to meet customer orders. As a result customers might go to rivals and never return. For some business this could be a cause of failure.

BMW encountered supplier problems in 2017, which meant it had to pause production in two factories. BMW stopped production at its factory in Leipzig due to problems with an Italian supplier of a steering component. In the same year production was stopped at plants in Tiexi, China, and Rosslyn, South Africa, due to German supplier Bosch running out of steering gears. A large multinational like BMW may be able to deal with such problems because they have huge resources. However, smaller firms may be more vulnerable.

Supplier problems are likely to do more damage to businesses that use outsourcing or JIT manufacturing. This is because such businesses rely very heavily on supplier performance.

Natural phenomena: Some businesses can fail due to natural occurrences such as the weather. Obviously, many farmers are extremely vulnerable to weather patterns that result in poor growing conditions. One of the main problems for most farmers is long periods of lower than normal rainfall. For example, reports from South Africa said that the number of South African companies going bankrupt during the first quarter of 2016 rose from 119 to 182. Most of these were to be expected in the agricultural sector. According to reports, the lack of rainfall throughout South Africa in 2015/16 had, and will continue to have, a huge negative effect on South Africa's farm output.

Another problem caused by natural phenomena is disease. Again it is the agricultural sector that suffers from this problem. For example, in 2016 olive growers in southern Italy were ordered to cut down thousands of diseased olive trees. The disease, *Xylella fastidiosa*, was first discovered in Italy in 2013. However, since then it has infected millions of trees, many of which are hundreds of years old. The EU instructed officials to create empty zones throughout the olive groves to stop the disease spreading. This meant than many healthy trees also had to be destroyed. Hundreds of distressed Italian farmers stood and cried as the tree cutting and burning advanced. Many of them face bankruptcy unless the government provides financial compensation.

SUBJECT VOCABULARY

administration where a failing business appoints a specialist to rescue the business or wind it up.
bushel customary unit of weight or mass. Historically equal to 8 gallons (35 litres). Modern use: equal to a mass defined differently for each commodity.
external factors factors beyond the control of businesses, which can cause collapse.
internal factors factors that businesses are able to control, which can cause collapse.
overtrading a situation where a business does not have enough cash to support its production and sales, usually because it is growing too fast.

CHECKPOINT

1. What is the difference between the internal and external factors that cause business failure?

2. Why did the business failure rate around the world rise just after 2008?

3. What happens when a business goes into administration?

4. Describe why the management of cash is so important to the survival of a business.

5. Give four possible causes of cash flow problems for a business.

6. State two ways that marketing problems could result in business failure.

7. How can business failure be caused by poor inventory control?

8. State two ways in which competitors might cause business failure.

9. How might a change in interest rates result in business failure?

10. State two natural phenomena that might cause business failure.

EXAM PRACTICE

DICK SMITH

SKILLS ▶

Dick Smith began his business life by installing and maintaining car radios in Sydney, Australia. In 1968, he invested AUD 610 and founded the Dick Smith brand. In addition to his car radio business, Dick opened 'Dick Smith Wholesale'. The store was targeted at electronics enthusiasts like Dick himself, and sold a wide range of electronics components. It was hugely successful and Dick began to develop a chain of stores. By 1980, the chain consisted of 20 stores but in the next 30 years or so, new owners Woolworths opened hundreds more stores across the whole of Australia. This included numerous David Jones Electronics powered by Dick Smith stores, Dick Smith Powerhouse superstores and a Move concept store.

Unfortunately, in 2016 the business failed owing creditors more than AUD 260 million. The cause of the failure was explained by a number of factors. First of all the market was changing. An increasing number of customers were buying online and competition from rivals, such as Harvey Norman, was also fierce. According to the company's administrators the market changed. They said, 'The consumer electronics market is highly competitive with rapid changes in consumer demand patterns.' This resulted in low margins for Dick Smith, a decline in market share and slow revenue growth.

Another problem that contributed to Dick Smith's downfall was poor inventory control. In this case, the stock held by the stores did not meet customer needs. Consequently, the business was left with a lot of obsolete and unsellable stock. As a result, in 2015, Dick Smith announced that it was necessary for the business to declare that AUD 60 million of inventory was worthless.

Inventory management is crucial in the retail sector and if a business makes errors they can be very costly.

There was also the suggestion that Dick Smith was trying to grow too quickly. This led to a considerable financial commitment and rapid outflow of cash. As a result the business was forced to increase borrowings. Cash flow was also damaged by high running costs due to Dick Smith operating a much larger store network than its rivals. Also, the credit terms obtained by Dick Smith and the cost of other finance was said to be too high. This placed a further strain on the business.

Finally, in an effort to improve cash flow the business organised some big discount sales to raise cash levels. However, the low margins on these sales, and the rising cost of finance needed to support the business, eventually led to the failure of the business.

Q ━━━━━━━━━━

(a) Explain the difference between the internal and external causes of business failure. **(4 marks)**

(b) Evaluate whether the failure of Dick Smith was due to (i) internal factors or (ii) external factors. **(20 marks)**

RESOURCE MANAGEMENT

Businesses use a range of different resources. This section looks at how resources are used in production. It focuses on the different production methods, productivity, efficiency and the distinction between labour- and capital-intensive production. It also looks at how capital utilisation is calculated, the implications of under- and over-utilisation of capacity, and how capacity utilisation can be improved. The role played by inventory control in business is also explored and the importance of just-in-time production and waste minimisation is addressed. Finally, the section deals with the way businesses maintain quality using methods such as total quality management and kaizen.

37 PRODUCTION, PRODUCTIVITY AND EFFICIENCY

LEARNING OBJECTIVES

By the end of this chapter you should be able to understand:

- methods of production: job, batch, flow and cell
- productivity: output per unit of input per time period, factors influencing productivity, the link between productivity and competitiveness, and ways to improve productivity
- efficiency: production at minimum average cost, factors influencing efficiency and ways to improve efficiency
- the distinction between labour- and capital-intensive production
- competitive advantage from short product lead-in times.

GETTING STARTED

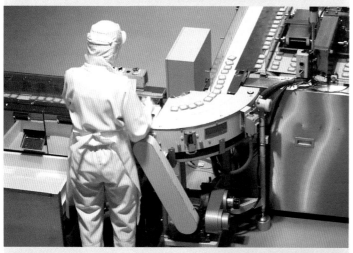

Describe the two different methods of production used in the photographs. Why are different methods necessary? Which do you think is the most efficient method of production? What might be the advantages of each method of production?

WHAT IS PRODUCTION?

Production takes place when resources, such as raw materials or components, are changed into 'products'. Land, labour, capital and enterprise, the factors of production, are used in the production process. The use of land and farm vehicles to grow cabbages is an example of production in primary industry. An example of secondary industry would be the use of wood, plastic, glue, screws, labour, drilling and cutting equipment to manufacture furniture.

Today production is often referred to more generally as those activities that 'bring a product into being'. Activities which are part of tertiary industry, such as services, would be included in this definition. A bank might talk about providing a 'product' in the same way as a carpet manufacturer. Examples of products in a bank's product portfolio might include mortgages, current accounts, house insurance and foreign currency. Direct services from the producer to the consumer, such as car repairs or decorating, can also be regarded as production in this sense.

JOB PRODUCTION

Job production involves the production of a single product at a time. It is used when orders for products are small, such as 'one-offs'. Production is organised so that one 'job' is completed at a time. There are a wide variety of goods and services which are produced or provided using this method of production. Small-scale examples include the baking of a child's birthday cake, a dentist's treatment session or the construction of an extension to a house. On a large scale, examples could include the building of a ship, the construction of the Wuhan Tianxingzhou Yangtze River bridge in China or the manufacture of specialised machinery. Job production is found in both manufacturing and the service industries. Because the numbers of units produced is small, the production process tends to be labour intensive.

The workforce is usually made up of skilled workers or specialists and the possibility of using labour-saving machinery is limited. Many businesses adopt this method of production when they are 'starting up'. The advantages and disadvantages of job production are shown in Table 1.

Advantages	Disadvantages
Quality is high because workers are skilled	High labour costs due to skilled workers
Workers are well motivated because work is varied	Production may be slow – long lead times
Products can be custom made	A wide range of specialist tools may be needed
Production is easy to organise	Generally an expensive method of production

▲ Table 1 The advantages and disadvantages of job production

ACTIVITY 1 **SKILLS** ANALYSIS

CASE STUDY: ARMANDO SOUSA

Armando Sousa is an accountant. He runs a small practice from an office based in Maputo, Mozambique. Most of his work involves producing final accounts for sole traders, partnerships and small limited companies in the city. He has a client base of around 260 businesses and employs a secretary and a young trainee accountant. In addition to preparing accounts he offers other services such as:

- completing tax returns
- taxation planning
- advice on the financial management of businesses
- advice on investment
- auditing.

1. Use this case as an example to explain what is meant by job production.
2. Explain why job production might help to motivate Armando and his trainee.

BATCH PRODUCTION

Batch production may be used when demand for a firm's product or service is regular rather than a 'one-off'. An example might be a furniture factory, where a batch of armchairs is made to a particular design. Production is divided into a number of operations. A particular operation is carried out on all products in a batch. The batch then moves to the next operation. A baker uses batch production when baking bread. The operations in the baking process are broken down in Table 2.

1. Combine ingredients in a mixing container until a dough is formed.
2. Mix the dough for a period of time.
3. Leave the dough to rise for a period of time.
4. Divide the dough into suitable units (loaves) for baking.
5. Bake the loaves.
6. Allow loaves to cool.

▲ Table 2 Operations involved in the production of a batch of bread

These operations would be performed on every batch of bread. There is some standardisation because each loaf in the batch will be the same. However, it may be possible to vary each batch. The ingredients could be changed to produce brown bread or the style of baking tin could be changed for different-shaped loaves.

A great number of products are produced using this method, particularly in manufacturing, such as the production of components and food processing. For example, in a canned food plant, a firm may can several different batches of soup, each batch being a different recipe. Products can be produced in very large or very small batches, depending on the level of demand. Larger production runs tend to lower the unit or average cost of production. New technology is increasingly being introduced to make batch production more efficient. The advantages and disadvantages of batch production are shown in Table 3.

Advantages	Disadvantages
Workers are likely to specialise in one process	More complex machinery may be needed
Unit costs are lower because output is higher	Careful planning and co-ordination is needed
Production is flexible since different orders can be met	Less motivation because workers specialise
More use of machinery is made	If batches are small, costs will still be high
	Money may be tied up in work-in-progress

▲ Table 3 The advantages and disadvantages of batch production

---

ACTIVITY 2 **SKILLS** ANALYSIS

CASE STUDY: WANNASRI GARMENTS

Wannasri Garments makes clothing for work, leisure and promotional activities for European customers. In 2013, the company moved to a new factory in Ho Chi Minh City, Vietnam. The company has an excellent reputation in the industry. This is because it:

- provides a wide choice of quality clothing at low prices

- provides excellent customer service
- is flexible and can meet orders quickly.

Like most companies in the clothes industry, Wannasri Garments uses batch production. The company can meet a wide range of different orders due to the flexibility of their machinery and multiskilled workforce.

▲ Textile industry machinery at work

1. What is meant by batch production?
2. Explain why batch production is common in the clothes industry.
3. Explain one way in which Wannasri Garments might have overcome some of the typical problems associated with batch production.

FLOW PRODUCTION

Most people will have some idea of **flow production** from pictures of motor car factories. Production is organised so that different operations can be carried out, one after the other, in a continuous sequence. Vehicles move from one operation to the next, on a production line.

The main features of flow production are:

- the production of large quantities
- a simplified or standardised product
- a semi-skilled workforce, specialising in one operation only
- large amounts of machinery and equipment
- large stocks of raw materials and components.

Flow production is used in the manufacture of products as varied as newspapers, food and cement. It is sometimes called mass production, as it tends to be used for the production of large numbers of standard products, such as cars or confectionery. Certain types of flow production are known as continual flow production, because products such as clothing material pass continually through a series of processes. Repetitive flow production is the

manufacture of large numbers of the same product, such as plastic toy parts or metal cans.

The advantages and disadvantages of flow production are shown in Table 4. In the 1990s, flow production processes were changed in an attempt to solve some of the problems. Japanese manufacturers setting up businesses in the UK introduced methods to improve efficiency. Just-in-time manufacturing, for example, helped to reduce the cost of holding stocks. Some vehicle manufacturers attempted to introduce an element of job production into flow processes by customising products for clients. For example, a range of different cars was produced on the same production line. Cars in the same model range differed in colour, engine size and interior design.

Advantages	Disadvantages
Very low unit costs due to economies of scale	Products may be too standardised
Output can be produced very quickly	Huge set-up costs before production can begin
Modern plant and machines can allow some flexibility	Worker motivation can be very low – repetitive tasks
Production speed can vary according to demand	Breaks in production can be very expensive

▲ Table 4 The advantages and disadvantages of flow production

CELL PRODUCTION

Flow production involves mass producing a standard product on a production line. The product undergoes a series of operations in sequence on a continuous basis until a finished product rolls off the 'end of the line'.

Cellular manufacturing or **cell production** adopts a different approach and involves dividing the workplace into 'cells'. Each cell occupies an area on the factory floor and focuses on the production of a 'product family'. A 'product family' is a group of products that requires a sequence of similar operations. For example, the metal body part of a machine might require the operations cut, punch, fold, spot weld and dispatch. This could all be carried out in one cell. Inside a cell, machines are grouped together and a team of workers sees the production of a product from start to finish.

Take the example of a furniture manufacturer making parts for a kitchen range in a cell. The raw material, such as wood, would be brought into the cell. Tasks such as cutting or shaping would be carried out at workstations. The part would then be assembled and passed on to stock. The cell may also be responsible for tasks such as designing, schedule planning, maintenance and problem solving, as well as the manufacturing tasks which are shared by the team.

Here are some advantages of cellular manufacturing:

- floor space is released because cells use less space than a flow production line
- product flexibility is improved
- lead times are cut
- movement of resources and handling time is reduced
- there is less work-in-progress
- teamworking is encouraged
- there may be a safer working environment and more efficient maintenance.

PRODUCTIVITY

Output can be increased if **productivity** is raised. Productivity is the amount of output that can be produced with a given input of resources. It is common to measure the productivity of specific resources in a period of time. A business may measure **labour productivity** – this is output per worker per period of time. For example, a factory producing standard mobile homes employed 40 workers in 2017. During the year a total of 1200 mobile homes were produced. Therefore labour productivity was 30 homes per worker (1200/40).

This ratio is a useful measure of labour productivity, but there are some problems that need to be recognised. For example, which workers should be counted? Should maintenance crew, management and administrative staff be counted, or should the ratio concentrate on direct labour only, i.e. shop floor workers? How should part-time workers and the long-term sick be treated? How can the ratio describe a multi-product plant, where the efforts of an employee might contribute to the production of more than one product?

A business may be interested in the productivity of its capital. This is becoming increasingly the case as more firms become capital intensive. A **capital productivity** ratio can be calculated by dividing output by the amount of capital employed in a given period. For example, if a factory used 10 sewing machines and a total of 900 garments were completed in a day, the productivity of capital would be 90 garments per machine each day.

EXAM HINT

You need to be careful not to confuse production with productivity. Remember that production involves transforming resources into useful goods and services that meet customer needs – it refers to the **level** of output produced. Productivity is the **rate** of production. It is the amount of output that can be produced with a given quantity of resources in a period of time. Productivity will increase if more output can be made with the same amount of resources.

FACTORS INFLUENCING PRODUCTIVITY

Over time a business wants to improve productivity if possible. This is because costs will be lower and profit will be higher. Some of the key factors that can be used to influence productivity are outlined below.

Specialisation and the division of labour: One feature of modern business is **specialisation**. This is the production of a limited range of goods by an individual, business, region or nation. For example, Coca-Cola specialises in soft drinks, Toyota® makes cars and Emirates provides air travel. Specialisation inside a business is also common. Departments specialise in different activities, such as marketing, production, finance, personnel and purchasing. Workers will also specialise in certain tasks and skills. This is called the **division of labour**. It allows people to concentrate on a limited range of tasks. For example, in construction an architect will draw up plans, a bricklayer will build walls, a roofer will lay the roof, and so on.

Education and training: The government can help improve the quality of labour by investing in education. This might involve providing more equipment for schools or improving the quality of teaching. Firms can also improve the productivity of their workers by providing their own training.

Motivation of workers: If people are motivated at work they will be more productive. Firms might use financial incentives, such as piece rates. Workers who are not motivated by money may respond to other incentives. For example, job rotation might be introduced. This involves an employee changing jobs from time to time. If people are trained to do different jobs, their time at work may be more interesting because there is more variety.

Working practices: The way labour is organised and managed can affect productivity. Working practices are the methods and systems that employees adopt when working. For example, productivity might be increased by changing the factory layout – moving workstations or reorganising the flow of production. Such changes may improve productivity because workers do not have to move around as much, for example.

Labour flexibility: Labour can be more flexible if workers are trained to do different jobs and can switch from one to the other at short notice. For example, some supermarkets train most of their staff to operate checkouts. Then, during a busy period, workers can be switched from other jobs to operate checkouts to prevent long queues from forming. Some businesses use flexitime where workers can choose their own hours of work (within limits). For example, a call centre can be kept open from 7.00 a.m. to 8.00 p.m. if individual workers choose to work at different

39 INVENTORY CONTROL

LEARNING OBJECTIVES

LEARNING OBJECTIVES

By the end of this chapter you should be able to understand:

- interpretation of inventory control diagram
- buffer inventory
- implications of poor inventory control
- just-in-time (JIT)
- waste minimisation
- competitive advantage from lean production.

GETTING STARTED

Why do you think the business in the photograph holds such large amounts of inventory? What might be the opportunity cost of holding inventory? What other costs might be incurred when storing inventory like this?

WHAT IS INVENTORY?

Businesses purchase raw materials, semi-finished goods and components. A washing machine manufacturer, for example, may buy electric motors, computer chips, rubber drive belts, nuts, bolts, sheet metal, and a variety of metal and plastic components. These inventories, also called stocks, are used to make products, which are then sold to customers. Some businesses also hold inventories of their finished goods before they are delivered to customers. In practice a variety of inventories are held, for different reasons.

Raw materials and components: These are purchased from suppliers before production. They are stored by firms to cope with changes in production levels. Delays in production can be avoided if materials and components can be supplied from stores rather than waiting for a new delivery to arrive. Also, if a company is let down by suppliers it can use stocks to carry on production.

Work-in-progress: These are partly finished goods. In a television assembly plant, work-in-progress would be televisions on the assembly line which are only partly built.

Finished goods: The main reason for keeping finished goods is to cope with changes in demand. If there is a sudden rise in demand, a firm can meet urgent orders by supplying customers from inventory holdings. This avoids the need to step up production rates quickly.

INVENTORY CONTROL

One of the most important tasks in inventory control is to maintain the right level of inventories. This involves keeping inventory levels as low as possible, so that the costs of holding them are minimised. At the same time inventories must not be allowed to run out, which can result in production being stopped and customers being let down. A number of factors influence inventory levels.

Demand: Sufficient stocks need to be kept to satisfy normal demand. Firms must also carry enough inventory to cover growth in sales and unexpected demand. The term buffer stocks is used to describe inventory held to cover unforeseen rises in demand or breaks in supply. This is discussed later in this unit.

Stockpile goods: Toy manufacturers, for example, build up stocks in the few months up to December ready for the Christmas period. Coal-fired power stations build up inventory of fuel in the summer when demand for electricity is low so less coal is needed and the price of coal is lower. This means they have inventory ready for higher demand in the winter, and they have made savings on the cost.

The costs of inventory holding: If inventory is expensive to hold then only a small quantity will be kept. Furniture retailers may keep low inventory levels because the cost is high and sales levels are uncertain.

The amount of working capital available: A business that is short of working capital may not be able to purchase more inventory, even if it is needed.

The type of inventory: Businesses can only hold small stocks of perishable products. The inventory levels of food items and fresh ingredients will be very small. Almost the entire inventory of finished goods is often sold in 1 day. The 'life' of inventory, however, does not solely depend on its perishability. Stocks can become out of date when they are replaced by new models, for example.

Lead time: This is the amount of time it takes for a stock purchase to be ordered, received, inspected and made ready for use. The longer the lead time, the higher the minimum level of inventory needed.

External factors: Fear of future shortages may prompt firms to hold higher levels of raw materials in inventory as a precaution.

INTERPRETATION OF A STOCK CONTROL DIAGRAM

The flow of stock in a business can be illustrated using a stock control diagram like the one shown in Figure 1. The diagram focuses on the **re-order quantity** (the amount of stock ordered when a new order is placed) and the **re-order level** (the level of stock currently held when an order is placed).

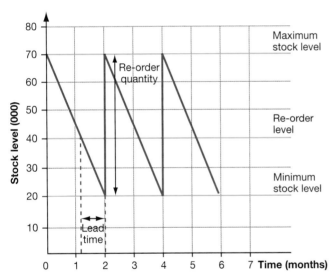
▲ Figure 1 Stock control diagram

The stock control diagram shown in Figure 1 assumes that:
- 50,000 units are used every 2 months (25,000 each month)
- the maximum stock level, above which stocks never rise, is 70,000 units
- the minimum stock level, below which stocks should never fall, is 20,000 units, so there is a buffer against delays in delivery
- stock is re-ordered when it reaches a level of 40,000 units (the re-order level)
- the re-order quantity is 50,000 units – the same quantity is used up every 2 months

- the lead time is just under 1 month. This is the time between the order being placed and the date it arrives in stock.

This is a theoretical model, which would be the ideal for a business. In practice deliveries are sometimes late, so there is a delay in stock arriving. Firms may need to use their buffer stock in this case. It is likely that re-order quantities will need to be reviewed from time to time. Suppliers might offer discounts for ordering larger quantities. The quantities of stock used in each time period are unlikely to be constant, for instance because production levels fluctuate according to demand.

ACTIVITY 1   SKILLS   ANALYSIS, PROBLEM SOLVING

CASE STUDY: MELCO ELECTRONICS

MelCo Electronics operates from a factory in Marseilles, France, and assembles control panels for computer games. The company imports a number of components from around the world – mainly China. One supplier in Shanghai ships a particular computer chip to the company. This is a new supplier and was given the contract to supply chips because they were 19 per cent cheaper than the original supplier. The change in supplier occurred 12 months ago. Figure 2 shows stock movements of this component over an 8-month period.

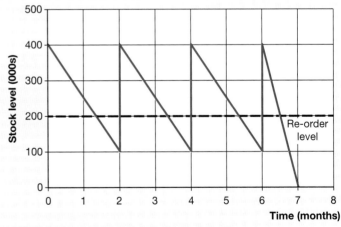
▲ Figure 2 Stocks of computer chips at MelCo Electronics

1. Calculate the (a) minimum stock level, (b) re-order level, (c) re-order quantity, (d) lead time for the computer chips.
2. Explain one reason for the change in stock level after the sixth month.
3. Discuss the possible consequences of the change in stock level after the sixth month for MelCo Electronics.

BUFFER STOCKS

Some businesses keep buffer stocks. This is an emergency stock held in case there is a stock shortage. A business might hold buffer stocks of finished goods in case there is a sudden increase in demand. If a business is not able to meet a surge in demand it will miss out on sales opportunities. There is also the fear of losing regular customers, which is a serious long-term problem. Businesses that need to hold buffer stocks of finished goods are those that experience sharp fluctuations in demand.

Some businesses need to hold buffer stocks of important raw materials or components. This is to protect themselves from a break in supply, which can lead to a break in production. With some production processes this could be disastrous. For example, if there was a break in the supply of soda ash for sheet glass production, this could involve stopping an enormous plant with hundreds of millions of pounds worth of labour and capital resources being left inactive. Some coal-powered electricity generators keep large buffer stocks of coal so that they can deal with surges in demand for electricity – if there is unusually cold winter, for example. Finally, some businesses may keep buffer stocks to give them a competitive edge – if they can respond to customer orders quickly, they may get more custom.

IMPLICATIONS OF POOR INVENTORY CONTROL

Businesses need to hold the 'right' amount of inventory. Holding too much or too little inventory can both have a negative impact on the business.

Holding too much inventory: If too much inventory is held a business will incur unnecessary costs.

- **Storage.** Inventory of raw materials, components and finished goods occupy space in buildings. A firm may also have to pay heating, lighting and labour costs if, for example, a security guard is employed to protect stores when the business is closed. Some products require very special storage conditions. Food items may need expensive chilled storage facilities. A firm may have to insure against fire, theft and other damages.
- **Opportunity cost.** Capital tied up in inventory earns no rewards. The money used to purchase inventory could have been put to other uses, such as new machinery. This might have earned the business money.
- **Spoilage costs.** The quality of some inventory may deteriorate over time, for example perishable goods. In addition, if some finished goods are held too long they may become out-of-date and difficult to sell.
- **Administrative and financial costs.** These include the cost of placing and processing orders, handling costs and the costs of failing to anticipate price increases.
- **Unsold inventory.** If there is an unexpected reduction in demand, the firm may be left with inventory that it cannot sell.
- **Shrinkage.** Very large stocks might result in an increase in theft by employees. They may feel the business would not miss a small amount of stock relative to the total inventory.

Holding too little inventory: To reduce the costs of holding too much inventory a business may fall into the trap of holding too little. There are several problems with holding too little inventory.

- The business may not be able to cope with unexpected increases in demand. This might result in lost customers if they are let down too often.
- If inventory deliveries are delayed, the firm may run out of inventory and have to stop production. This can lead to inactive labour and machinery while the firm waits for delivery.
- The firm is less able to cope with unexpected shortages of materials. Again, this could result in lost production.
- A firm which holds very low inventory may have to place more orders. This will raise total ordering costs. It might also miss out on discounts from bulk buying.

JUST-IN-TIME (JIT) MANAGEMENT OF INVENTORY

Just-in-time (JIT) manufacturing is an important part of lean production and the kaizen approach. It was developed in the Japanese shipbuilding industry in the 1950s and 1960s. The industry recognised that a great deal of money was tied up in inventory. Traditionally, 1 month's supply of steel was held by a shipyard. However, as the industry became more competitive, shipbuilders insisted that steel suppliers deliver orders 'just-in-time', i.e. a few hours or less before the steel was needed. This reduced the need for high levels of working capital and improved the financial performance of the business. JIT was extended to every stage of production. For example, raw materials were delivered JIT to be made into parts, parts were delivered JIT to be made into goods and goods were produced and delivered JIT to be sold.

JIT was introduced in other Japanese industries, such as the car industry, and then spread to other parts of the world, such as the USA and Europe. JCB® has used JIT in its Rochester, UK, plant. When JCB excavators (a large digging machine) are manufactured, every machine on the production line has already been sold. Supplies of components, such as engines from Perkins, and raw materials, such as steel plate, arrive on the day they are needed. JIT manufacturing requires high levels of organisational skills and reliable suppliers.

Table 1 shows the advantages and disadvantages of JIT manufacturing.

Advantages	Disadvantages
• It improves cash flow since money is not tied up in stock	• A lot of faith is placed in the reliability and flexibility of suppliers
• The system reduces waste, obsolete and damaged stock	• Increased ordering and administration costs
• More factory space is made available for productive use	• Advantages of bulk buying may be lost
• The costs of stockholding are reduced significantly	• At risk of a break in supply and machinery breakdowns
• Links with and the control of suppliers are improved	• Difficult to cope with sharp increases in demand
• The supplier base is reduced significantly	• Possible loss of reputation if customers are let down by late deliveries
• More scope for integration within the factory's computer system	
• The motivation of workers is improved. They are given more responsibility and encouraged to work in teams	

▲ Table 1 Advantages and disadvantages of JIT

THINKING BIGGER

Many firms using JIT stock control make use of **kanban** systems. Kanban is a Japanese term that means signs or cards. The kanban system is a method used to control the transfer of materials between different stages of production. The kanban might be a solid plastic brick or coloured ping-pong ball used to, for instance:

- inform employees in the previous stage of production that a particular part must be taken from stock and sent to a specific destination (conveyance kanbans)
- tell employees involved in a particular operation that they can begin production and add their output to stock (production kanbans)
- instruct external suppliers to send parts to a destination (vendor kanbans).

Kanbans are used to trigger the movement or production of resources. Used properly, they will be the only means of authorising movement. Kanbans are an important part of JIT manufacturing as they prevent the build-up of stock or parts in a factory.

WASTE MINIMISATION

A failure to control inventory adequately can result in wasted inventory. This is most likely to happen if inventory is perishable. Perishable stocks or goods are those which physically deteriorate after a certain amount of time and therefore cannot be used. Consequently they have to be thrown away. Examples include fresh produce, such as fruit, vegetables, meat, cakes and flowers, ready-mix concrete, airline meals and some medical products, like stored blood, vaccines and biological medicines.

Inventory can also be wasted if it has a limited lifetime and becomes obsolete after a certain amount of time. Examples might include newspapers and magazines, seasonal goods, such as Mother's Day cards, and merchandising produced for specific events like a concert or sports competition. It is important for businesses that produce these types of goods to control inventory levels very carefully. They may adopt some of the methods outlined below to minimise waste.

- If goods are perishable they must be placed in chilled storage. Fridges or freezers can prolong the life of perishable goods – particularly in warm weather.
- Businesses have to be especially conscientious when forecasting demand patterns for perishable goods. If they overestimate demand they could be left with a lot of unsold stock. Some businesses use complex quantitative techniques to predict the demand of perishable goods. Such techniques use historic data relating to demand, the shelf life of products, lead times and storage costs.
- A suitable **stock rotation** method should be adopted. With perishable goods the FIFO method (first in first out) is used. This means that the inventory that was delivered first must be issued first. Using this method ensures that older inventory is used up first.
- Many businesses use computers to manage inventory control. Computerised systems are programmed to automatically order inventory when the re-order level is reached. In supermarkets, computerised checkout systems record every item of inventory purchased by customers and automatically subtract items from total inventory levels. Most very large businesses use computerised stock control.
- Some businesses might be able to adjust product prices to help minimise waste. For example, if inventory remain high as the 'sell-by date' approaches, prices might be reduced to encourage purchases.
- Perishable goods need to be transported rapidly. If transportation can be speeded up then goods will

ACTIVITY 2   SKILLS   ANALYSIS, REASONING

CASE STUDY: LEAN PRODUCERS

Lean producers like US companies Whirlpool and Caterpillar use a JIT approach in their operations. However, a few years ago they encountered a serious problem that disrupted their supply chains. They had to make some expensive adjustments to their operations as a result of poorly maintained and deteriorating road surfaces in America. The poor quality of some US roads was holding up deliveries of finished goods, components and other materials to sites belonging to Whirlpool and Caterpillar. The companies came up with a number of solutions to deal with the problem.

Some decided to keep more inventories and vehicles on the road for longer periods of time. Others set up 'just-in-case' warehouses and guarded parking sites at strategic locations between suppliers and assembly plants. For example, Whirlpool has established a number of guarded car parks on the outskirts of major cities, such as Chicago, Milwaukee and Minneapolis. This means that a washing machine being transported from a regional distribution centre to a customer via a local distribution centre now sits overnight in a lorry park. Therefore the delivery is delayed by a whole day and extra inventories have to be held. The hold-ups in delivery, and the resources used to deal with the problems, obviously raise costs for these companies. Overall it is reckoned that the poor condition of the US road network is costing businesses millions of dollars per year. One transport authority said the cost of wasted fuel and driver time caused by road congestion amounts to about US$27,000 million per year.

To save money Caterpillar, which is one of the world's largest shippers by weight, often delivers very large machines in parts. For example, when transporting orders to ports for export it breaks some of its heaviest machines into parts and then reassembles them on the dock side before loading onto ships. This sounds expensive but according to a spokesperson from Caterpillar it is cheaper than obtaining the heavy-load permits that are required to transport very heavy machines on poorly maintained roads. The capacity of US roads has been reduced due to a lack of maintenance in recent years.

1. Explain **two** advantages of just-in-time production.
2. How does this case highlight one of the key problems with just-in-time production?
3. Explain how some companies have dealt with the problem identified in question 2.

reach the marketplace more quickly and be available for sale in the best condition. Some perishable goods, such as food and flowers, are flown to customers to increase the speed of delivery.

- To minimise waste, a business might find creative methods in the disposal of goods that have passed their sell-by date. For example, food products might be given to charities or sold as animal feed. Newspapers and magazines are likely to be recycled.

COMPETITIVE ADVANTAGE FROM LEAN PRODUCTION

The use of JIT stock control is often an important element if a business is adopting lean production. Lean production aims to use fewer resources in production. A range of production techniques, such as kaizen, cell production, flexible manufacturing, teamworking, empowerment and multiskilling, are used to minimise waste. Lean producers use less time, less inventory, fewer materials, less labour, less space and fewer suppliers. Lean producers are likely to have a competitive advantage because the reduction in waste and resource use will lower production costs. Specifically, competitiveness will be improved because lean production:

- raises productivity
- reduces costs and cuts lead times
- lowers the number of faulty products
- improves reliability and speeds up design time.

With these improvements businesses will be able to charge lower prices, offer better quality and reliability, and fight off rivals in the global marketplace.

THINKING BIGGER

Inventory control has been improved by the use of computers. Many businesses hold details of their entire inventory on computer databases. All additions to and issues from inventory are recorded and up-to-date inventory levels can be found instantly. Actual levels of inventory should be the same as shown in the computer printout. A well-managed firm will carry out regular inventory checks to identify differences. Some systems are programmed to automatically order inventory when the re-order level is reached. Access to inventory levels is useful when manufacturers are dealing with large orders. The firm might need to find out whether there are enough materials in stock to complete an order. If this information is available, then the firm can give a more accurate delivery date.

SUBJECT VOCABULARY

buffer stocks stock held as a precaution to cope with unforeseen demand.
kanban a card or an object that acts as a signal to move or provide resources in a factory.
lead time the time between placing the order and the delivery of goods.
re-order level the level of current stock when new orders are placed.
re-order quantity the amount of stock ordered when an order is placed.
stock rotation the flow of stock into and out of storage.
work-in-progress partly finished goods.

CHECKPOINT

1. Why do businesses prefer to minimise inventory holdings?

2. What is meant by work-in-progress?

3. State four costs of holding inventory.

4. Why are buffer stocks held by firms?

5. State two drawbacks of holding too little inventory.

6. State two possible disadvantages of just-in-time inventory management.

7. What types of inventory are most likely to be wasted?

8. What method of stock rotation is most suitable for perishable goods?

9. State two ways of minimising waste inventory.

10. How might lean production improve competitiveness?

EXAM PRACTICE

TOYOTA

SKILLS ANALYSIS INTERPRETATION

Toyota, the Japanese car manufacturer, has developed a production system that aims to completely eliminate waste. The Toyota Production System (TPS) is based on JIT production, but also uses other lean production methods, such as kaizen, in an attempt to completely eliminate seven sources of waste:

1. over-production (largest waste)
2. time on hand (waiting)
3. transportation
4. processing itself
5. stock at hand
6. movement
7. making faulty products.

Building on the JIT method of production, Toyota has produced an efficient system that reduces waste and demands on the production line, meaning that the vehicle can be built in the shortest period of time possible. The following principles help Toyota to achieve its aims.

1. When a vehicle order is received, a production instruction must be issued to the beginning of the vehicle production line.
2. The assembly line must be stocked with the required number of all needed parts so that any type of ordered vehicle can be assembled.
3. The assembly line must replace the parts used by collecting the same number of parts from the part-producing process.
4. The part-producing process must be stocked with small numbers of all types of parts. Also, they should only produce what was taken by an operator from the assembly process.

TPS has helped Toyota to keep improving the way it manufactures vehicles. It has also developed a corporate culture where employees have to deal constantly with challenges and problems, and must come up with fresh ideas. TPS has been so successful over the years that Toyota has gained a competitive advantage in the car industry. Indeed, many other manufacturers have adopted TPS or adapted it to meet their own needs.

Reproduced with permission from Toyota (GB) PLC.

(a) Define just-in-time stock management. **(2 marks)**
(b) Explain one reason why Toyota does not hold buffer stocks. **(4 marks)**
(c) Discuss the importance to Toyota of minimising waste. **(8 marks)**
(d) Assess the extent to which lean production has helped Toyota to gain a competitive edge. **(10 marks)**

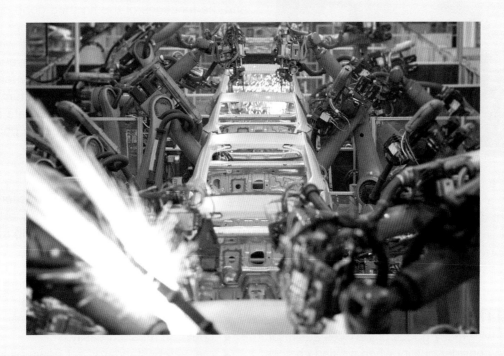

40 QUALITY MANAGEMENT

LEARNING OBJECTIVES

By the end of this chapter you should be able to understand:
- quality: control, assurance and circles
- total quality management (TQM)
- continuous improvement (kaizen)
- competitive advantage from quality management.

GETTING STARTED

Michelin stars are awarded to restaurants for the excellence of their food and service. There is no higher honour for a chef or a restaurant than to be awarded a Michelin star. After France, Japan has more restaurants with Michelin stars than any other country in the world. Perhaps this should not be a surprise since Japan has a culture that fully embraces quality, accuracy and simplicity. In 2016, 25 restaurants in Japan had been awarded three Michelin stars. This compares with just 3 in the UK and 13 in the USA. One of these Japanese three-star restaurants is Kohaku in Tokyo. The head chef is Koji Koizumi and his menu focuses on *kaiseki* meals, which are high-quality traditional Japanese multi-course dinners.

Define quality to a customer in this business. Why would the award of a Michelin star be desirable for a chef or restaurant owner? What are the advantages of selling quality products? Why might **quality** be increasingly important to businesses?

WHAT IS QUALITY?

Consumers, faced with many goods or services at similar prices, are likely to consider quality when making choices. Quality could be described as those features of a product or service that allow it to satisfy customers' wants. Take an example of a family buying a television. They may consider:
- physical appearance – they may want a certain style
- reliability and durability – will it last for 10 years?
- special features – does it have surround sound?
- suitability – they may want a portable television
- parts – are spare parts available?
- repairs – does the shop carry out maintenance?
- after-sales service – how prompt is delivery?

They may also consider features which they perceive as important, such as:
- image – is the manufacturer's name widely recognised?
- reputation – what do other consumers think of the business or product?

The importance of quality has grown in recent years. Consumers are more aware. They may get information from specialist publications and websites, which contain reports on the quality of certain products. They also have more disposable income and higher expectations than ever before. Legislation and competition have also forced firms to improve the quality of their products.

Businesses, faced with competition, are also concerned about the quality of their:
- design – the ideas and plans for the product or service
- production processes – the methods used to manufacture the goods or provide the services.

Poor designs may lead to problems with the materials and the functions of the finished good or service. It costs time and money to redesign poor products. Clients are unlikely to use businesses with poor designs again. Problems also occur with poor-quality production processes. Faulty products are costly for a business. Machinery that breaks down or constantly needs to be repaired will also be expensive. Late delivery and ineffective productivity that results in poor quality can harm a business's reputation.

QUALITY CONTROL

Traditionally, in manufacturing, production departments have been responsible for ensuring quality.

Their objectives might have been to make sure that products:
- satisfied consumers' needs
- worked under conditions they were likely to face
- operated in the way they should
- could be produced cost effectively
- could be repaired easily
- met safety standards set down by legislation and independent bodies.

At Kellogg's, for example, samples of breakfast cereal have, in the past, been taken from the production line every 30 minutes and tested. The testing took place in a food review room twice a day and was undertaken by a small group of staff. Each sample, about 50 in total, was compared with a 'perfect' Kellogg's sample and given a grade between 1 and 10: 10 was perfect but between 9.8 and 7, although noticeable to the trained eye, was acceptable to the customer. Below 7 the consumer would notice the reduction in quality. The cereals were tested for appearance, texture, colour, taste, etc. More sophisticated tests were carried out in a laboratory where the nutritional value of a sample, for example, was measured.

Quality control in many organisations, in the past, often meant quality controllers or quality inspectors checking other people's work and the product itself after production had taken place. By today's standards this is not quality control, but a method of finding a poor-quality product (or a problem) before it is sold to the consumer.

QUALITY ASSURANCE

Today businesses are less concerned about 'Has the job been done properly?' than 'Are we able to do the job properly?' In other words inspection is carried out during the production process. This means that problems and poor-quality products can be prevented before final production.

Such a preventative approach has been used by Japanese businesses and is known as total quality management. It is now being adopted by many businesses around the world. It involves all employees in a business contributing to and being responsible for ensuring quality at all stages in the production process. Quality assurance is a commitment by a business to maintain quality throughout the organisation. The aim is to stop problems before they occur rather than finding them after they occur.

Quality assurance also takes into account customers' views when planning the production process. For example, customers may be consulted about their views through market research before a product is manufactured or a service provided. They may also be part of a consultation group involved at the design and manufacturing stage.

EXAM HINT

You need to avoid confusion between quality assurance and quality control. Remember that quality assurance aims to prevent defects with a focus on the **processes** used to make the product. It is a **proactive** quality task. Quality control aims to identify (and correct) defects in the finished **product**. Quality control, therefore, is a **reactive** task.

ACTIVITY 1   SKILLS   ANALYSIS, INTERPRETATION

CASE STUDY: NESTLÉ®

In 2016, Swiss company Nestlé opened a new US$31 million quality assurance centre in Ohio, USA. At 82,000 square-feet (7820 m²) it is Nestlé's largest quality assurance centre and has been opened to explore the increasing threat of foreign bodies in the production of confectionery such as chocolate bars and other sweets. The centre has a 32,000 square-feet (2970 m²) biology lab, an upgraded chemistry lab and related facilities where 60 per cent of food testing will take place.

According to a spokesperson for Nestlé, the company's main concern regarding confectionery production is the salmonella bacteria, that can cause severe food poisoning. The company has to ensure that ingredients such as cocoa, nuts and sultanas are free from any bacteria that could cause illness. Nestlé is also concerned about the growing threat from allergens. The spokesperson said that Nestlé focuses on the development of safe products for young consumers who are growing up with allergies. For example, in the new quality assurance centre chemists are using up-to-date technology to monitor the levels of bacteria in both raw materials and finished products.

Nestlé claims it is working hard to eliminate foreign bodies getting into products. If a product contains a foreign body from the agricultural environment it may be potentially dangerous to many confectionery customers but particularly children. Compared to bacteria and allergens, the possible dangers posed by foreign bodies are often overlooked. The Nestlé spokesperson said that it is an emerging challenge and something the industry should seek to address.

▲ Inside Nestlé's quality assurance centre, Ohio

1. Define quality assurance.
2. Explain why quality assurance is such an important issue for Nestlé.
3. What evidence is there In this case to suggest that Nestlé takes quality assurance seriously?

QUALITY CIRCLES

Quality control circles or **quality circles** are small groups of workers (5–20) in the same area of production who meet regularly to study and solve production problems. In addition, such groups are intended to motivate and involve workers on the factory floor. They allow the workforce directly to improve the nature of the work they are doing.

Quality control circles started in the USA, where it was felt workers could be motivated by being involved in decision making. The idea gained in popularity in Japan and was taken up by Western businesses. Examples of their use can be found in Japanese companies setting up plants in the UK in the 1990s. For example, Honda at Swindon had 52 teams of six people looking at improvements that could be made in areas allocated to the groups, such as safety.

Quality control circles are only likely to work if they have the support of both management and employees. Businesses have to want worker participation and involvement in decision making, and set up a structure that supports this. Workers and their representatives also need to support the scheme. Employees must feel that their views within the circle are valued and must make a contribution to decisions.

ACTIVITY 2   SKILLS   ANALYSIS
CASE STUDY: WINNEBAGO®

Winnebago, based in Iowa, USA, is a well-known producer of recreational vehicles (RVs). It has a reputation among RV enthusiasts for high quality and innovation, dating back to its founding in 1958. Every Winnebago RV integrates superior construction, design and comfort. In its effort to maintain very high quality standards, Winnebago has used quality circles for many years. Indeed, the company has won the Recreational Vehicle Dealers Association's prestigious Quality Circle Award every year since it started in 1996.

Winnebago designs and manufactures components to high specifications. It has been able to deliver high quality at competitive prices. Higher quality is also the result of ongoing testing. Winnebago has a state-of-the-art, 40,000-ft^2 (3716 m^2) testing facility. The computerised model road (known to staff as 'The Shaker') and the nearly 1-km test track can reproduce the effects of years of normal driving in just a few days. Components are checked under hot, cold, wet and dry conditions, and every Winnebago RV goes through a high-pressure water tunnel and is checked for leaks before shipping.

1. Define quality circles.
2. Assess the importance of quality circles to Winnebago.

TOTAL QUALITY MANAGEMENT (TQM)

Errors are costly for business. There are benefits if something is done right the first time. **Total quality management** (TQM) is a method designed to prevent errors, such as the creation of poor-quality products, from happening. The business is organised so that the manufacturing process is investigated at every stage. It is argued that the success of Japanese companies is based on their superior organisation. Every department, activity and individual is organised to take into account quality at all times. What are the features of TQM?

Quality chains: Great stress is placed on the operation of **quality chains**. In any business a series of suppliers and customers exists. For example, a secretary is a supplier to a manager, who is the customer. The secretary's duties must be carried out to the satisfaction of the manager. The chain also includes customers and suppliers outside the business. The chain remains complete if the supplier satisfies the customer. It is broken if a person or item of equipment does not satisfy the needs of the customer. Failure to meet the requirements in any part of the quality chain creates problems, such as delays in the next stage of production.

Company policy, accountability and empowerment: There will only be improvements in quality if there is a company-wide quality policy. TQM must start from the top with the most senior executive and spread throughout the business to every employee. People must be totally committed and take a 'pride in the job'. This might be considered as an example of job enrichment. Lack of commitment, particularly at the top, causes problems. For example, if the managing director lacks commitment, employees lower down are unlikely to commit themselves. TQM stresses the role of the individual and aims to make everyone accountable for their own performance. For example, a machine operator may be accountable to a workshop supervisor for their work. They may also be empowered to make decisions.

Control: Consumers' needs will only be satisfied if the business has control of the factors that affect a product's quality. These may be human, administrative or technical factors, shown in Figure 1 on the next page. The process is only under control if materials, equipment and tasks are used in the same way every time. Take the example of a firm making biscuits. Only by cooking in the same way can the quality be the same every time.

These methods can be documented and used to assess operations. Regular audits must be carried out by the firm to check quality. Information is then fed back from the customer to the 'operator' or producer, and from the operator to the supplier of inputs, such as raw materials. For example, a retailer may return a batch of vehicles to the manufacturer because the gears were faulty. The manufacturer might then identify the person responsible for fitting the gears. An investigation might reveal that the faulty gears were the responsibility of a component supplier. The supplier can then be contacted and the problem resolved. Quality audits and reviews may lead to suggestions for improvements – a different material, perhaps, or a new piece of equipment.

Monitoring the process: TQM relies on monitoring the business process to find possible improvements. Methods have been developed to help achieve this. **Statistical process control** (SPC) involves collecting data relating to the performance of a process. Data is presented in diagrams, charts and graphs. The information is then passed to all those concerned.

SPC can be used to reduce variability, which is the cause of most quality problems. Variations in products, delivery times, methods, materials, people's attitudes and staff performance often occur. For example, statistical data may show that worker attitudes may have led to variations in output late on Friday afternoon. Discussion might result in a change in the working hours to solve the problem.

Teamwork: TQM stresses that teamwork is the most effective way of solving problems. The main advantages are:

- a greater range of skills, knowledge and experience can be used to solve the problem
- employee motivation is often improved
- problems across departments are better dealt with

- a greater variety of problems can be tackled
- team 'ideas' are more likely to be used than individual ones.

TQM strongly favours teamwork throughout the business. It builds trust and motivation, improves communications and co-operation, and develops a culture of collaboration. Many firms in the past have suffered by not sharing information and ideas. Such approaches have often led to division between sections of the workforce.

Consumer views: Firms using TQM must be committed to their customers. They must respond to changes in people's needs and expectations. To do this, information must be gathered on a regular basis and there must be clear communication channels for customers to express their views. Consumers are often influential in setting quality standards. For example, holiday companies issue questionnaires to their customers on the way back from a package holiday. The information can be used to identify the strengths and weaknesses of their operations. Such information can be used to monitor and upgrade quality standards.

Zero defects: Many business quality systems have a zero-defect policy. This aims to ensure that every product that is manufactured is free from defects. A business that is able to guarantee zero defects in customers' orders is likely to gain a good reputation. This could lead to new clients and improved sales.

Quality circles: TQM stresses the importance of teamwork in a business. Many businesses have introduced quality circles into their operations. In order for quality circles to be successful certain conditions must exist.

- A steering committee should be set up to manage the whole quality circle programme.
- A senior manager should ideally chair the committee. Managers must show commitment to the principle of quality circles.
- At least one person on the committee should be accountable for the programme.
- Team leaders should be properly trained.

Using TQM: TQM helps companies to:

- focus clearly on the needs of customers and relationships between suppliers and customers
- achieve quality in all aspects of business, not just product or service quality
- critically analyse all processes to remove waste and inefficiencies
- find improvements and develop measures of performance
- develop a team approach to problem solving
- develop effective procedures for communication and acknowledgement of work
- continually review the processes to develop a strategy of constant improvement.

There are, however, some problems.
- There will be training and development costs of the new system.
- TQM will only work if there is commitment from the entire business.
- There will be a great deal of bureaucracy and documents, and regular audits will be needed. This may be a problem for small firms.
- Stress is placed on the process and not the product.

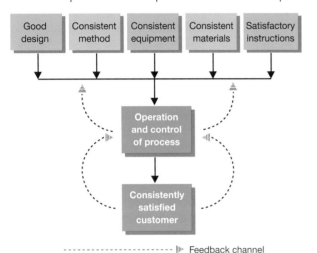

▲ Figure 1 The systematic approach to quality management

KAIZEN

Kaizen is perhaps the most important concept in Japanese management. It means continuous improvement. Every aspect of life, including social life, working life and home life, is constantly improved. Everyone in the business is involved. Kaizen is said to be an 'umbrella concept'. A wide range of different production techniques and working practices must be carried out for it to be effective. Figure 2 shows examples of the techniques, principles and practices. They should result in ongoing improvements. This approach argues that a day should not pass without some kind of improvement being made somewhere in the business.

There are a number of features of kaizen that affect a business.

Continuous improvement: Kaizen has been the main difference between the Japanese and the Western approaches to management in the past. The attempts of Western businesses to improve efficiency and quality have tended to be 'one-offs'. In Figure 3 the solid line illustrates the Western approach. Productivity remains the same for long periods of time, then suddenly rises. The increase is followed by another period of stability, before another rise. Increases in productivity may result from new working practices or new technology. The dotted line shows the Japanese approach. Improvements are continuous. They result from changes in production techniques, which are introduced gradually.

▲ Figure 2 The kaizen umbrella

Eliminating waste: The elimination of waste (called *muda* in Japan) in business practices is an important part of kaizen. Waste is any activity that raises costs without adding value to a product. Examples may be:
- time wasted while staff wait around before starting tasks, such as waiting for materials to arrive
- time wasted when workers move unnecessarily in the workplace, such as walking to a central point in the factory to get tools
- the irregular use of a machine, such as a machine which is only used once a month for a special order
- excessive demands upon machines or workers, such as staff working overtime seven days per week which causes them to be tired and work poorly.

Firms that adopt the kaizen approach train and reward workers to continually search for waste and to suggest how it might be eliminated.

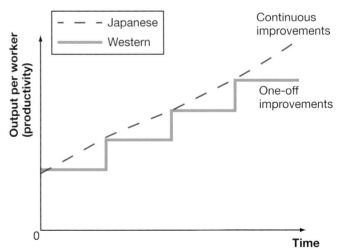

▲ Figure 3 The Western and Japanese approaches to improvement

Implementing continuous improvement: It is often difficult for workers in a business to look for continuous improvement all the time. Japanese businesses tried to solve this problem by introducing the PDCA (Plan, Do, Check, Action) cycle. It is a series of activities that lead to improvement.

- **Plan.** Businesses must identify where improvement is needed. Data must be gathered and used to develop a plan which will result in improvement.
- **Do.** Once the plan has been finalised it must be carried out. The plan is likely to be implemented by workers, on the production line perhaps.
- **Check.** The next stage in the cycle is to check whether or not there has been an improvement. This task may be carried out by inspectors.
- **Action.** If the plan has been successful, it must be introduced in all parts of the business.

COMPETITIVE ADVANTAGE FROM QUALITY MANAGEMENT

Supplying high-quality goods and services can have a huge positive impact on businesses. The main one is that product quality should be improved, which should help to increase sales. Also, business costs may be cut if faults in products are identified before the product reaches the market. The costs of failure once the product has reached the market are likely to be much higher than those during manufacture.

Some businesses use quality as a means of developing a USP. If a business can differentiate its product on grounds of quality and persuade the customer that their product is superior to its rivals, it may enjoy some benefits, particularly the ability to charge a higher price. This gives a business more flexibility in pricing.

Inevitably a business that can deliver quality will develop a competitive advantage. This will allow firms to win customers from rivals, increase market share, raise revenue and improve profitability. A number of British firms have been successful in overseas markets due to the competitive edge they have gained as a result of marketing quality products. Examples include Rolls-Royce®, Burberry®, Jaguar Land Rover (owned by Tata), British Airways and Jimmy Choo.

ACTIVITY 3 | SKILLS | ANALYSIS, PRODUCTIVITY

CASE STUDY: CFKS

CFKs (Clothes For Kids), based in Turin, Italy, produces high-quality children's clothing and the family-owned company has been trading for over 100 years. Their total commitment to quality and innovative design has seen the company produce products that are often featured in magazines and even sometimes purchased by celebrities for their children to wear.

As a company that is always looking to improve processes, the managing director, Daniela Girelli decided to introduce kaizen. She had read about how the car industry used kaizen to improve their productivity and felt that their product could be treated the same in many respects as each product was made from the same basic body shape. She also wanted to look at how the company could gain profit at each step. In the year after introducing kaizen productivity rose 5 per cent, which helped them increase their profit by 10 per cent as well.

To make kaizen work for their business Daniela looked at each point of the production chain and identified ways it could be improved. This included additional staff training so staff members could take on different tasks, to better purchasing negotiations with their material suppliers. They even looked at the way the product was sold. They identified that users on their website were not completing their purchases and investigated reasons why. They realised that their 'checkout' button was not very clear and resolved the issue, pushing online sales up 10 per cent.

Daniela thinks that their productivity will continue to grow and estimates that they can increase it by at least another 5 per cent. By increasing the number of garments made at each stage, they will make the company more profitable as the costs per item of manufacture will decrease.

1. Explain one way in which kaizen can help a business improve productivity.
2. Explain one way in which CFKs has benefited from the introduction of kaizen.

THINKING BIGGER

Despite the benefits from improving quality, it is important to recognise the costs.

- **Designing and setting up a quality control system.** This might include the time used to 'think through' a system and the training of staff to use it.
- **Lost production.** When a business introduces a major new system there can be some serious disruption while the new system is introduced. This could lead to a loss of output and damage to customer relations if orders are not met.
- **Improving the actual quality.** This may be the cost of better materials, superior methods, new machinery or training staff in new working practices. If the whole quality system fails, there may be costs in setting it up again. Time may be needed to rethink or adjust the system. Retraining might also be necessary.
- **Training.** Quality initiatives will only be successful if the people involved in their application are properly trained. This can be very costly. For example, if TQM is introduced the entire workforce will have to be trained. This may involve sending all staff on specialist training courses or outsourcing training to an expert in TQM.

It has been suggested that 10–20 per cent of the revenue of a business is accounted for by quality-related costs. The vast majority of these costs are related to assessment and failure, which add very little to the quality of the product. Eliminating such failure would help to reduce these costs, saving businesses significant sums.

CHECKPOINT

1. What is meant by the quality of a product?
2. What is the difference between actual and perceived quality?
3. What is the difference between quality control and quality assurance?
4. What is the main purpose of using quality circles?
5. State five implications of TQM for a business.
6. Why is teamwork so important in TQM?
7. What is meant by the kaizen umbrella?
8. Describe the purpose of the PDCA cycle.
9. What are the costs and benefits of ensuring quality?

SUBJECT VOCABULARY

quality features of a product that allow it to satisfy customers' needs. It may refer to some standard of excellence.

quality assurance a method of working for businesses that takes into account customers' wants when standardising quality. It often involves guaranteeing that quality standards are met.

quality chains when employees form a series of links between customers and suppliers in business, both internally and externally.

quality circles groups of workers meeting regularly to solve problems and discuss work issues.

quality control making sure that the quality of a product meets specified quality performance criteria.

statistical process control the collection of data about the performance of a particular process in a business.

total quality management (TQM) a managerial approach that focuses on quality and aims to improve the effectiveness, flexibility and competitiveness of the business.

EXAM PRACTICE

THE POWARTH GROUP

SKILLS   ANALYSIS, INTERPRETATION, CRITICAL THINKING

The Powarth Group owns a small chain of 23 hotels in Europe. Up until 2013 the group's performance had been poor with flat sales for 5 years in a row. However, in 2013 the group signed a deal with an online booking company in the hope that sales would increase dramatically, raising occupancy rates above the current 52 per cent. This turned out to be a disaster. The booking site also has a customer review system where people can give feedback about their experience. The review below is typical of the many posted on the site relating to Powarth Group hotels.

The Globe – Milan

This is one of the worst hotels my husband and I have ever stayed in. The main problem was the staff – they were totally uninterested and as guests we felt that we were an inconvenience. When we arrived there was a queue to check in and only one youngster on duty who could not speak English. The whole process took 55 minutes and the receptionist tried to charge us again even though we had paid in advance. There was quite a heated argument and communication was difficult – the hotel manager, who could speak English, was on a break and could not be contacted.

Things did not get better. Our room was dark, damp and in a very poor decorative state. There was no toilet roll, the towels did not look clean, the furniture was old and the television did not work. I could go on but the next day my husband and I checked out even though we had paid for two nights in advance.

Mrs T. Ellington

After several emergency board meetings the directors decided that some drastic action was necessary. They decided to invest in total quality management (TQM) to try and improve the quality of the hotel service. In 2016,

they took the following measures to introduce TQM at a total cost of €5.6 million:

- organised an outside agency to train all staff in TQM
- employed another agency to train staff in customer service
- set up a suggestions box to encourage staff ideas. €1000 was given to a member of staff if their idea was implemented by management
- organised the staff into teams
- kept records of all guest complaints and followed every single one up with a personal letter from the manager.

The group also invested €4.3 million in refitting of half of the hotels – planned another €5 million in investment in 3 years' time for refitting the remainder. The group also upgraded their website, changed the mission statement to emphasise the quality of their service and purchased a smart new hotel uniform. All staff were consulted on the uniform design and the wording of the mission statement.

At the end of 2014 profits rose from €120,000 to €1.67 million, guest complaints fell by 82 per cent, staff motivation improved and hotel occupancy rates had increased to 74 per cent.

 Q

(a) Define total quality management.   **(2 marks)**

(b) Explain how the use of teamworking might improve the quality of service at the Powarth Group hotels.   **(4 marks)**

(c) Discuss the possible benefits to the Powarth Group of total quality management.   **(8 marks)**

(d) Assess the extent to which the introduction of total quality management at the Powarth Group was a success.   **(10 marks)**

EXTERNAL INFLUENCES

The final section in Unit 2 addresses how external factors might impact on businesses. Some external factors are economic, such as interest rates, exchange rates and the rate of inflation. A second group of external factors is legislation, such as consumer protection, environmental protection, health and safety legislation, and competition policy. The third external factor is competition and the effect that large numbers of competitors and very large organisations have on businesses. The ways small businesses compete in markets is also covered.

41 ECONOMIC INFLUENCES

LEARNING OBJECTIVES

By the end of this chapter you should be able to understand:
■ the effect on businesses of, and how they can best respond to, changes in: the rate of inflation, exchange rates (appreciation, depreciation), interest rates, taxation and government spending and the business cycle.

GETTING STARTED

MUJI is a Japanese retail business with over 700 stores worldwide. It supplies fashionable products for the home while offering good quality, low cost and simplicity at the same time. MUJI stores sell a fairly wide range of stock including clothes, household goods and food. MUJI has a developed a reputation for being resource-saving, low-priced, simple and environmentally friendly. The company has performed very well, increasing revenue every year from JPY 178,186 million in 2012 to JPY 307,532 million in 2016.

Give four examples of external influences that might affect the performance of MUJI. How might a cut in personal income tax affect MUJI? How might MUJI react to a downturn in the global economy? Would MUJI benefit from higher interest rates?

EXTERNAL INFLUENCES

Business activity is influenced by a number of external influences. These are factors beyond the control of businesses. In some cases they restrict a business's

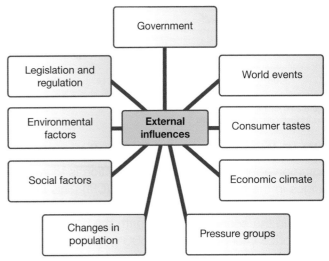

▲ Figure 1 External influences on businesses

decisions and may prevent its growth and development. Examples of these external influences are summarised in Figure 1.

Economic influences, such as inflation, exchange rates, interest rates, taxation, government expenditure and the business cycle can have many effects on a business. The government is responsible for the management of the economy. The aim of many governments is to keep prices stable, keep unemployment down, keep borrowing down and help the economy grow. The measures a government might use to achieve these aims can have an impact on businesses.

INFLATION

A government will want to keep prices stable in the country's economy. This means that **inflation** must be kept under control. Inflation is when the general price level is rising. For example, if a basket of goods cost €100 on 1 January 2016, and the same basket cost €103 on 1 January 2017, prices have gone up by 3 per cent. This means that the inflation rate is 3 per cent. If inflation is too high it can harm the economy. Figure 2 shows inflation rates in the EU between 2008 and 2017. The graph shows that the rate of inflation has been quite low, fluctuating between 0 and 4 per cent. It was even negative in 2010 which meant that prices in the EU were actually falling. Inflation rates at these levels are not problematic. However, in the 1970s, inflation reached levels of 25 per cent in some countries, which was a serious threat to businesses and the economy.

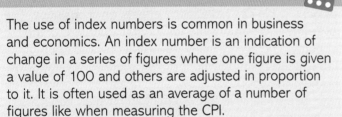

▲ Figure 2 EU inflation rates, 2008–17
Source: Tradingeconomics.com I Eurostat

HOW IS INFLATION MEASURED?

A common approach to measuring inflation is to calculate changes in the **consumer price index (CPI)**. This involves gathering information about the prices of goods and services in the economy. Each month the government records price changes of about 600 goods and services. From these records an average price change is calculated and converted into an index number. The month's figures can then be compared with the previous month's, or that of 12 months ago, to calculate the percentage change in prices (i.e. the inflation rate) over the time period. The inflation rates shown in Figure 2 use the CPI.

MATHS TIP

The use of index numbers is common in business and economics. An index number is an indication of change in a series of figures where one figure is given a value of 100 and others are adjusted in proportion to it. It is often used as an average of a number of figures like when measuring the CPI.

HOW DOES INFLATION AFFECT BUSINESSES?

Inflation rates between 0 and 4 per cent, like those in the EU between 2008 and 2017, are not likely to have a big impact on businesses. However, once the CPI gets into double figures and beyond, inflation can have some damaging effects on businesses.

High and particularly fluctuating inflation is likely to be damaging to businesses for a number of reasons.

Increased costs: High or fluctuating inflation imposes a variety of costs on businesses.

- With suppliers' prices rising all the time, but at different rates, time must be spent researching the market for the best deals. Equally, more time has to be spent monitoring the prices of competitors to decide when and by how much to increase your own prices. These costs are called shoe leather costs, because before the age of the telephone and the Internet, businesses would have to send their employees round on foot to gather this information.
- Raising prices costs money. Customers have to be informed of the new prices. Brochures might have to be reprinted and sent out. Websites might have to be updated. The sales force has to be made familiar with new prices. These costs are called menu costs because, for a restaurant, increasing prices means that it has to reprint its menus.
- Management is likely to have to spend more time dealing with workers' pay claims. Instead of being able to sign a 2- or 3-year deal, annual pay negotiations are likely to be the norm. If there is hyperinflation, where inflation is running into 100 per cent per annum or over, pay negotiations may have to take place each month. There is also a much larger risk of strikes because workers and managers will probably have different views of future inflation rates. Workers will be worried that any deal they make will leave them worse off after inflation. So they might be more willing to take industrial action to get high pay settlements.

Uncertainty: With high and fluctuating inflation, businesses do not know what prices will be in 3 or 6 months' time, let alone in 1 or 5 years. But decisions have to be made now which will affect the business in the long term. For example, businesses need to invest to survive. But how much should they invest? The price of a new machine, a shop or a new computer system will probably be higher in 6 months than today. But are they worth buying if interest rates are at very high levels? What if the new machine is bought, financed by very high cost borrowing and there is a recession, where demand for goods and services falls?

Another problem with uncertainty is linked to entering long-term contracts. A customer might approach a business wanting to buy products on a regular monthly basis for the next 2 years. How can the supplier put a price on this contract if it does not know what the inflation rate will be over the next 24 months?

Borrowing and lending: Borrowing and lending becomes an opportunity and a problem for businesses. On the one hand, the real value of debts incurred in the past can become quickly reduced by inflation. If inflation is 100 per cent per annum, the real value of money borrowed a year ago falls by 50 per cent in 1 year. Inflation initially benefits borrowers and harms lenders.

But in an inflationary environment, interest rates rise to match inflation. If there is prolonged inflation, interest rates are likely to become **index linked** – linked to the index of prices. So interest might be charged at the rate of inflation plus 5 per cent or plus 10 per cent.

Consumer reactions: Consumers react to inflation as well as businesses. Prolonged inflation tends to lead to more saving. Inflation makes consumers less confident. They become less willing to borrow money, not knowing what will happen in the future. The value of savings tends to fall as inflation reduces their real value. So people react by saving more to make up savings to their previous real value. Increased saving means less spending and so businesses will sell less.

If inflation is very high, consumers will adopt different spending patterns which may affect businesses. For example, if there is hyperinflation, prices will be changing by the day. Consumers will then tend to spend wages or interest as soon as they receive them. On 'pay day' there can be huge activity in shops. Supermarkets have to be prepared to sell most of the weekly or monthly turnover in just a few hours. Suppliers of fresh produce to supermarkets have to be ready to deliver most of their goods on one specific day of the week.

International competitiveness: High inflation can have an impact on businesses that import or export goods and services. For example, if a country has higher inflation rates than its trading partners, businesses in that country will become uncompetitive. As a result, they are likely to lose sales and shares in overseas markets. Also, businesses facing competition from overseas will lose out because imports become relatively cheaper. For example, consumers in a particular country may buy foreign goods instead of domestic goods because their prices are rising less quickly than those at home. The impact of changes in the price of imports and exports are discussed in more detail later in this chapter.

HOW MIGHT BUSINESSES RESPOND TO INFLATION?

Although inflation rates around the world were fairly low between 2008 and 2017, there is always a chance that inflation will start to rise again. Some businesses would probably respond to an increase in inflation in an effort to protect their profits. For example, they might take any of the following action:

- search for cheaper suppliers if costs of materials and other resources start to rise
- increase prices to compensate for the higher costs resulting from inflation
- negotiate hard with employees and their representatives when inflation-proof wage demands are made. For example, they might insist that higher wages can only be granted if there are improvements in productivity
- build up inventories ahead of further inflation so that products are sold at future higher prices
- look to outsource or relocate production overseas if domestic costs continue to rise.

EXCHANGE RATES

Different countries in the world have their own currencies. For example, the USA uses the dollar, Japan uses the yen, many EU countries use the euro and the UK has the pound. When countries use different currencies transactions between people and businesses are affected. For example, an Indian visitor to the UK cannot use rupees, they would have to buy some British pounds. How many pounds would the Indian visitor get for INR 150,000? This depends on the **exchange rate** between the pound and the rupee. If it were £1 = INR 100 the visitor would get £1500 (INR 150,000 ÷ INR 100). The exchange rate shows the price of pounds in terms of rupees. When businesses buy goods and services from other countries, payments are usually made in the supplier's currency. Some examples are given below.

WORKED EXAMPLE

1. How much will it cost a French business to buy goods from a British business which cost £400,000 if £1 = €1.25? The cost to the French business in euros is:

   £400,000 × 1.25 = €500,000

2. How many Sri Lankan rupees will it cost a Chinese business buying LKN 5.5 million of goods from a Sri Lankan business if LKN 1 = CNY 0.043? The cost to the Chinese business will be:

   LKN 5.5 million × 0.043 = CNY 236,764.7

3. How much will it cost an Indian business in Indian rupees to buy SAR 2.5 million of goods from a business in Saudi Arabia if INR 1 = SAR 0.058? The cost in Indian rupees is:

   SAR 2.5 million ÷ SAR 0.058 = INR 43,072,253.

4. How many pounds can a Japanese business person buy with JPY 100,000 when visiting London if £1 = JPY 190?
   The quantity of pounds that can be bought is:

   JPY 100,000 ÷ 190 = £526.32

THE IMPACT OF AN APPRECIATION IN THE EXCHANGE RATE ON IMPORTS AND EXPORTS

The exchange rate is the price of one currency in terms of another. Like all prices the exchange rate can change. This is because prices are determined by market forces, and supply and demand conditions can change at any time. For example, if the demand for UK exports rises, there will be an increase in the demand for pounds. This is because foreigners need pounds to pay for exports. The increase in demand for pounds will raise the exchange rate (i.e. raise the value of the currency, the pound, against that of another currency). When it rises, the exchange rate has **appreciated**.

Changes in the exchange rate can have an impact on the demand for exports and imports. This is because, when the exchange rate changes, the prices of exports and imports also change.

WORKED EXAMPLE

What happens when the exchange rate rises (i.e. the value of the pound rises) from, say, £1 = US$1.50 to £1 = US$2?

Impact on exports: If a UK business sells goods worth £2 million to a US customer, the dollar price at the original exchange rate is US$3 million (£2 million × 1.50). When the exchange rate rises the dollar price of the goods also rises to US$4 million (£2 million × 2). This means that demand for UK exports is likely to fall because they are now dearer.

Impact on imports: If another UK firm buys goods worth US$600,000 from a US supplier, the price in pounds at the original exchange rate is £400,000 (US$600,000 ÷ 1.50). When the exchange rate rises the price in pounds for the importer falls to £300,000 (US$600,000 ÷ 2). This means that demand for imports is likely to rise, because they are cheaper.

THE IMPACT OF A DEPRECIATION IN THE EXCHANGE RATE ON IMPORTS AND EXPORTS

When the exchange rate falls it has **depreciated**. The impact on the demand for imports and exports is the opposite.

WORKED EXAMPLE

What happens when the exchange rate falls (i.e. the value of the pound falls) from, say, £1 = US$1.50 to £1 = US$1.20?

Impact on exports: If a UK business sells goods worth £2 million to a US customer, the dollar price at the original exchange rate is US$3 million (£2 million × 1.50). When the exchange falls the dollar price of the goods also falls to US$2.4 million (£2 million × 1.20). This means that demand for UK exports is likely to rise because they are now cheaper.

Impact on imports: If another UK business buys goods worth US$600,000 from a US supplier, the price in pounds at the original exchange rate

is £400,000 (US$600,000 ÷ 1.50). When the exchange rate falls the price in pounds for the importer rises to £500,000 (US$600,000 ÷ 1.20). This means that demand for imports is likely to fall because they are dearer.

The effects of changes in the exchange rate on the demand for exports and imports are summarised in Table 1.

Exchange rate	Price of exports	Demand for exports	Price of imports	Demand for imports
Falls	Falls	Rises	Rises	Falls
Rises	Rises	Falls	Falls	Rises

▲ Table 1 Summary of the effects of changing exchange rates

HOW ARE BUSINESSES AFFECTED BY EXCHANGE RATES?

The preceding examples show what happens to the prices of imports and exports when exchange rates appreciate and depreciate. Sometimes these changes will benefit a business, other times they will not. For example, if the value of the rupee falls, Indian exporters will benefit because the price of exports falls and demand should increase. However, Indian importers will lose out because their purchases will be more expensive.

Fluctuating exchange rates cause uncertainty. Businesses do not know what is going to happen to exchange rates in the future. This means that it is difficult to predict demand for exports and the cost of imports. This makes planning and budgeting more difficult. Another problem is that it costs money to switch from one currency to another. There is usually a commission charge of around 2 per cent. This represents a cost to importers and therefore reduces profit.

HOW MIGHT BUSINESSES RESPOND TO A CHANGE IN EXCHANGE RATES?

The response by businesses to a change in exchange rates will depend on whether they are exporters or importers and whether the exchange rate appreciates or depreciates.

Appreciation: An export business will find that the prices of its products will be higher for overseas customers when the exchange rate appreciates. Therefore trading conditions have worsened. They might respond by lowering their prices to compensate for the increase in the exchange rate. They may also consider improving the quality of products and customer service. They may offer more favourable payment terms – extending the credit period perhaps. Generally they will provide a range of incentives in an effort to retain the loyalty of overseas customers. A business might also try to increase domestic sales or find new markets where exchange rates have not appreciated.

Importers will benefit from an appreciation in the exchange rate. Goods from overseas will be cheaper. They may respond by building up inventories of goods from abroad. They may take the opportunity to lower prices to win a larger market share. If the appreciation in the exchange rate is likely to be sustained they may consider expanding their operations. For example, a manufacturer that is able to buy much cheaper materials and components from overseas might be in a position to increase sales. The supply of goods and services will tend to increase when costs are lower (see Chapter 5).

Depreciation: An export business will find that the prices of its products will be lower for overseas customers when the exchange rate depreciates. Therefore trading conditions have improved. They might respond by raising prices to increase their profit margins since overseas customers would not feel the impact. They might use the lower prices to boost overseas sales and win a larger market share. If the depreciation is sustained they may try to grow faster by expanding their operations.

Importers will face higher prices when they buy from abroad. They may be forced to accept lower margins or raise their prices. If the depreciation is sustained they might have to consider some of the measures listed above that might be taken by businesses in the face of higher inflation.

ACTIVITY 1   SKILLS   ANALYSIS, PROBLEM SOLVING

CASE STUDY: BAUMER FAMILY HOLIDAY

In 2017, the Baumer family, who live in Texas, USA, took a 3-week holiday to Japan. They paid for their flights and accommodation in dollars online. However, before they left the USA they bought some Japanese currency. The exchange rate they got from their bank was US$1 = JPY 110.

1. Explain why exchange rates are necessary.
2. Calculate how much Japanese currency the Baumer family were able to purchase for US$4500.
3. Assess the impact on the cost to US tourists to Japan if the exchange rate depreciated to US$1 = JPY90.

INTEREST RATES

If a business or an individual borrows money, they usually have to pay interest on the loan. Equally, if they put their savings into a bank or building society, they expect to receive interest.

The interest rate is the price of borrowing or saving money. For example, if a small business borrows US$10,000 from a US bank for 1 year, and the interest rate is 7 per cent, it has to pay US$700 in interest. Equally, if a business has US$1 million in the bank for 1 year, which it

uses as working capital, and the rate of interest the bank offers is 3 per cent, it will earn US$30,000 in interest.

In recent years interest rates in many countries around the world have been very low. Figure 3 shows the level of interest rates in the US between 2008 and 2017. Since 2009 the base rate has been close to zero – although in 2017 they rose very slightly. Many predict that rates in the USA will continue to rise (perhaps slightly) in the future.

Finally, the use of interest rates to help control the economy is called **monetary policy**. For example, a government might raise interest rates to reduce demand in the economy if they thought that inflation was being caused by demand rising too quickly.

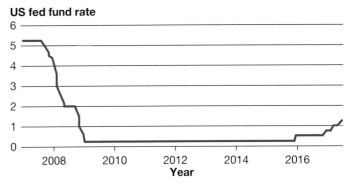

▲ Figure 3 US interest rates, 2008–17
Source: Tradingeconomics.com | Federal Reserve

EFFECT OF INTEREST RATES ON COSTS

Changes in interest rates are likely to affect the overheads of a business. Interest charges are part of overhead costs. If interest rates rise, businesses are likely to have to pay higher interest payments on their borrowing. For example, a business might borrow US$10,000. The annual payments on this would rise from US$600 to US$700 if the rate of interest rose from 6 to 7 per cent per year.

Not all borrowing is at variable rates of interest. Variable rates mean that banks or other lenders are free to change the rate of interest on any money borrowed. Many loans to businesses are at fixed rates of interest. This is where the bank cannot change the rate of interest over the agreed term (the time over which the loan will be paid off) of the loan. A rise in interest rates in the economy will not affect the overheads of a business with only fixed-term loans. But, if a business wanted to take out new loans, it would have to pay the higher rates of interest the bank or other lender was now charging. So overhead costs would rise.

EFFECT OF INTEREST RATES ON INVESTMENT

Changes in the rate of interest affect the amount that businesses invest, for example in new buildings, plant and machinery. There are four main reasons for this.

The cost of loans: Investment projects are often financed through loans. A rise in interest rates increases the cost of borrowing money. So projects financed this way will find that the total costs have risen, reducing profitability. This might be enough to persuade some businesses to cancel their investment plans. Total investment in the economy will then fall.

Attractiveness of saving: Businesses have the alternative of putting their funds into savings schemes rather than investing in machinery or buildings, for example. A rise in interest rates makes putting money into financial assets relatively more attractive. For example, if interest rates rise from 5 to 8 per cent, a business might decide to cancel an investment project and save the funds instead.

Paying off existing loans: A rise in interest rates will increase the cost of existing variable rate borrowing. A business could choose to pay off existing loans rather than increase its investment. This will reduce its costs. It also reduces the risk associated with borrowing.

A fall in demand: A rise in interest rates is likely to reduce total spending in the economy, as explained below. This might affect the profitability of many investment projects. For example, a business might forecast that an investment project would be profitable with 20,000 sales per year. But if sales were forecast to be only 15,000 per year because of a downturn in demand, then the investment project could be unprofitable and might not go ahead.

EFFECT OF INTEREST RATES ON DEMAND

The level of interest rates affects aggregate demand (i.e. total demand) for goods and services in the economy. A rise in interest rates will tend to push down aggregate demand. A fall in interest rates will tend to increase demand.

Businesses are directly affected by changes in demand. When demand falls, their sales go down because less is being bought. If demand rises, businesses receive more orders and more sales.

There are many different ways in which changes in interest rates lead to changes in the sales of businesses.

Domestic consumption: Consumers will be hit by a rise in interest rates. The cost of loans will rise. This will discourage consumers from buying goods bought on credit, such as cars, furniture and electrical equipment. These goods are known as consumer durables because they are 'used up' over a long period.

People who have a mortgage (a loan to buy a house) are also likely to see their monthly repayments rise because many mortgages are variable rate loans. Existing mortgage holders will then have less to

spend on other goods and services. Some potential new home buyers will be put off because they cannot afford the repayments, directly hitting the new housing market. If unemployment begins to rise because of less spending, consumer confidence will fall. This will make consumers even less willing to take out loans and spend.

Domestic investment: As explained above, businesses are likely to cut back plans for new investment if interest rates rise. Investment goods, like new buildings or machines, are made by businesses. So these businesses will see a fall in their demand.

Stock: Businesses keep stocks of raw materials and finished goods. Stock costs money to keep, because a fall in stock levels could be used to finance a fall in borrowing and interest payments. So a rise in interest rates will increase the cost of keeping stock. This will encourage businesses to destock, i.e. reduce their stock levels. This will be especially true if the rise in interest rates has hit demand in the economy. With fewer sales, less needs to be produced. So less stock needs to be kept. But cutting stock reduces orders for businesses further up the chain of production. For example, a retailer cutting stock affects demand from its suppliers. Destocking due to higher interest rates will therefore cause a fall in demand throughout much of industry.

Exports and imports: A rise in interest rates tends to lead to a rise in the value of one currency against others. A rise in the rupee, for example, will make it harder for Indian businesses to export profitably. At the same time, foreign firms will find it easier to gain sales in the domestic market because they will be able to reduce their prices. The result is likely to be a fall in exports and a loss of sales to importers in the domestic market. Both will reduce demand and hit Indian businesses.

ACTIVITY 2   SKILLS   ANALYSIS, REASONING

CASE STUDY: MICHEL PAPIN

In 1990, Parisian restaurateur Michel Papin was declared bankrupt. His restaurant business went into liquidation when he failed to pay interest owing on a mortgage. The interest payments on his €155,000 mortgage were €2400 per month. The mortgage, taken out on his home, had been used to help fund the restaurant. However, the restaurant struggled and was not generating enough revenue to meet the high mortgage payments. Michel lost everything. He borrowed €2000 from his father and went to New Zealand. Fifteen years later, after working as a chef in various hotels in Wellington and Queenstown, he returned to France with €30,000 of savings.

Michel invested €20,000 setting up a new catering venture specialising in the provision of food for weddings, business functions and parties. The business went very well and even grew between 2009 and 2015 where economic growth in France was very low and sometimes negative. In 2016, Michel decided to expand his business and invest some retained profit in an outdoor catering operation. His idea was to provide 'instant party facilities'. This included a large tent, music system and full catering service. The idea worked very well. He took on four more employees and since interest rates were at historic lows decided to borrow €10,000 to double the size of his outdoor catering operation.

1. Explain one effect that high interest rates can have on businesses.
2. Explain why a business like Michel's is likely to invest more when interest rates are low.

HOW MIGHT BUSINESSES RESPOND TO CHANGES IN THE INTEREST RATE?

The response by businesses to a change in interest rates will depend on whether they rise or fall.

Higher interest rates: Higher interest rates are generally bad for businesses. The cost of borrowing rises and demand for goods bought with borrowed money is likely to fall. Businesses may respond in the following ways:

- reduce the amount they borrow by cutting back on loans and overdrafts – this will help to compensate for the higher cost of borrowing
- postpone or cancel marginal investment projects. Higher interest rates mean that marginal projects become unprofitable
- if higher interest rates are sustained, and the economic situation starts to weaken, some businesses might react by modifying growth targets or even scaling down operations by releasing resources. They may lay off staff for example
- businesses with a wide range of financial assets might begin to put more money into deposit accounts since returns will be greater.

Lower interest rates: Business will generally prefer lower interest rates since the cost of borrowing will be lower and demand for goods bought with borrowed money, such as cars, will rise. Businesses may respond by:

- increasing investment since the returns will be higher if the cost of borrowing is lower. Firms may borrow more money to replace worn-out machinery, update technology, invest more in R&D, launch new products, make some acquisitions and grow their operations, for example
- since demand for some goods will rise, firms affected by this increase will have to prepare to increase production. They may need to recruit more staff and increase their productive capacity. This may mean they need to expand the scale of their operations – moving to larger premises for example
- some businesses may decide that they can increase their prices if demand is growing fast. This will help to boost revenue and profits – particularly if demand is inelastic.

TAXATION

Governments can affect business decision making using **fiscal policy**. This involves changing **taxation** and **government expenditure** to influence the economy. Taxes vary from country to country but are paid by both businesses and individuals. The main taxes in the UK are shown in Table 2. Most countries have a range of taxes which are either the same, or very similar, to those in Table 2.

Direct taxes (taxes on income)	
Income tax	Paid on personal income and that from paid and self-employment
National Insurance contributions	Paid by businesses and individuals on employee's earnings
Corporation tax	Paid by companies based on how much profit they make
Capital gains tax	Paid on the capital gain (profit) made when selling an asset
Inheritance tax	Paid on money transferred to another individual, usually after death
Indirect taxes (taxes on spending)	
Value added tax (VAT)	Paid mainly when buying goods and services (except food)
Excise duties	Paid when buying certain goods such as petrol
Customs duties	Paid when buying certain goods from abroad
Council tax	Paid by residents to the council to help fund local services
Business rates	Paid by businesses to the council to help fund local services

▲ Table 2 The main taxes in the UK

THE EFFECT ON BUSINESSES OF CHANGES IN TAXATION

How might changes in taxation affect businesses?

Consumer spending: Changes in certain types of taxation are likely to increase the income consumers have left after tax. These include reductions in income tax rates, increases in personal allowances and an increase in the limits on which inheritance tax is paid or a reduction in the rate of inheritance tax. If consumers have more income left they might increase spending on the products of businesses. Increases in income tax, National Insurance contributions and council taxes are all likely to leave consumers with less income and could reduce spending on products.

Prices: An increase in VAT or excise duty will raise the costs of a business. Businesses often pass this on to customers by raising the price of goods. An increase in customs duty will increase the price of goods being imported into a country.

Business costs, revenue and profits: Increases in some taxes might raise the costs of business. For example, VAT will raise costs. A business might try to raise prices to cover this and maintain profit. However, higher prices can reduce sales and so profit could still be affected if revenue falls. Rises in corporation tax, business rates, employers' National Insurance contributions and landfill tax will all tend to reduce business profits. Reductions in taxes are likely to increase the profits of a business.

Business spending and investment: Increases in costs and reduced profits mean that businesses have less retained profit. This can affect the ability of the business to pay its debts, buy stocks and meet other expenses. It can also affect whether it invests in new factories or machinery.

Shares: Changes in capital gains tax and stamp duty might affect shareholding. For example, an increase in capital gains tax might discourage people from becoming shareholders or delay sales of shares.

Importing and exporting: Increases in customs duties can affect businesses. For example, if a country raised customs duties on imported products a domestic business might benefit because imports against which it competed would then have a higher price. However, domestic businesses buying imported supplies would have to pay higher prices.

Business operations and employees: Increases in National Insurance contributions of employers might discourage employers from recruiting extra workers. Changes in taxation on company cars or allowances for staff using their own vehicles for work purposes might also change how a business offers these benefits to employees.

Other effects: Certain types of business might be affected by changes in tax. For example, an increase in landfill tax might encourage businesses to recycle. A rise in passenger duty could discourage holidaymakers and reduce the demand for holidays.

Tax avoidance and evasion: Increases in taxation often lead businesses to try to avoid paying the tax. For example, they might not hire workers to avoid higher National Insurance contributions or switch from buying imports to avoid customs duties. In some cases they might even try to evade the law, for example dumping waste in the countryside to avoid landfill taxes, which is illegal.

HOW MIGHT BUSINESSES RESPOND TO CHANGES IN TAXATION?

Businesses will prefer lower taxes to higher taxes. If taxation in general is increased there is likely to be a fall in demand and businesses might respond defensively. If business taxes are increased businesses might take action to avoid taxes. For example, if there is an increase in the rate of corporation tax businesses might decide to relocate their operations in a country where corporation taxes are lower. The difference in corporation tax rates around the world is significant. For example, in the UAE the highest marginal rate of corporation tax is 55 per cent. But in Paraguay and Qatar it is only 10 per cent. Higher taxes on business profits are likely to discourage investment since businesses will have less profits available to invest.

If taxes on spending are increased businesses might react by scaling back production. The impact of higher indirect taxes on supply is explained in detail in Chapter 5. If taxes on personal incomes are raised disposable income will fall so there is likely to be a fall in demand. This will lower business confidence and possibly result in less production and less investment.

Businesses are likely to respond more positively to lower taxes. Since demand is likely to rise businesses may increase production, grow and invest more. A country with a low tax system is likely to attract relatively more foreign direct investment than those with higher taxes.

GOVERNMENT EXPENDITURE
The government is responsible for spending in the public sector. It provides a range of services, such as education, defence, welfare benefits, transport and healthcare. In Australia, the government planned to spend AUD 464.4 billion in 2017/18. Figure 4 shows the categories of planned expenditure.

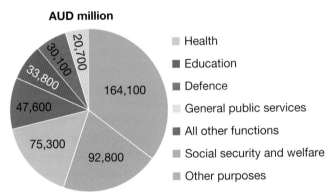

AUD million

- Health
- Education
- Defence
- General public services
- All other functions
- Social security and welfare
- Other purposes

164,100
92,800
75,300
47,600
33,800
30,100
20,700

▲ Figure 4 Planned government spending in Australia, 2017/18

THE EFFECT OF CHANGES IN GOVERNMENT EXPENDITURE ON BUSINESSES
Levels of government expenditure can influence business activity. If the government increases spending to more than it raises in taxes, total spending in the economy will rise. The exact impact of such a measure is complex. Although many businesses may benefit from higher spending levels in the economy, too much spending can lead to other problems, such as inflation and higher interest rates.

In several countries around the world governments have tried to reduce levels of government expenditure. For example, in Greece, where the size of the government's debt was becoming unmanageable, there have been some quite serious cuts. When government debt becomes too large the interest payments rise and are seen as a burden. Many would argue that the opportunity cost of interest is too high. Money could be better spent on education and health care, for example. Cuts in government expenditure are generally bad for businesses because it usually means a fall in demand. For example, if the government reduces the number of public sector employees, there will be a fall in demand for many goods and services. The way businesses might respond to changes in government spending is discussed below.

HOW MIGHT BUSINESSES RESPOND TO CHANGES IN GOVERNMENT EXPENDITURE?
Many businesses will react positively to higher levels of government expenditure. This is because demand in the economy tends to rise when the government spends more. For example, if a government employs more teachers, police officers, civil servants and social workers, there will be an increase in demand in the economy. Consequently businesses might increase production and expand. In contrast, lower levels of government expenditure will tend to have the opposite effect.

However, some businesses are likely to benefit more than others from changes in government spending patterns. It depends on how the government spends money. For example, in many countries around the world in recent years, governments have spent money trying to encourage the production of renewable energy. Therefore, businesses in sectors such as solar and wind power have invested heavily in growth. Also, when governments announce more spending in infrastructure, it is construction companies that are likely to gain the most and are therefore more positive in their response.

However, one possible impact on businesses is that too much spending in the public sector reduces development in the private sector. This might be because higher levels of government spending attract more resources into the public sector. This might mean that private sector businesses find it harder to attract resources. Consequently, the response by private sector businesses might be to raise prices rather than to invest and expand.

CASE STUDY: INDIAN GOVERNMENTAL TAXATION AND EXPENDITURE

In 2017, the Indian government announced a range of changes in taxation and levels of government spending that were predicted to have a significant impact on the Indian business community. For example, according to the 2017/18 budget the government proposed to:

- cut the rate of income tax by 50 per cent to just 5 per cent for those earning between INR 250,000 and INR 500,000 – according to the government about 79 per cent of the 37 million Indian people who submit income tax returns earn less than INR 500,000
- cut corporation taxes for small- and medium-sized businesses
- increase spending to build and modernise ports, railways, airports and roads – a record INR 3.96 trillion was reserved for this expenditure
- increase loans to farmers up to INR 10 trillion – it also allocated INR 480,000 million for a rural job guarantee programme and the electrification of villages (farm vehicle makers such as Mahindra & Mahindra Ltd and fertiliser manufacturer Coromandel International Ltd, are examples of businesses expected to benefit from this spending)
- spend INR 100,000 million on the construction of a high-speed Internet network designed to connect about 150,000 villages
- extend an affordable housing programme for another 5 years
- build more airports in smaller cities in partnership with private companies
- increase the number of railways by forming ventures with transportation companies to provide better connections to ports – rail equipment manufacturers such as Bombardier Inc. and General Electric Co. are among companies already investing in setting up operations in India to help improve the infrastructure.

In contrast, a minority of businesses might not benefit from some of the announcements made by the government. For example, the government planned to change rules relating to the sale of pharmaceuticals. It wanted to reduce the price of healthcare to make it more affordable by encouraging the production of unbranded medicines. The government also planned to increase the taxes on tobacco by 6 per cent.

1. Evaluate whether the proposals outlined in the budget will have (a) a positive, or (b) a negative impact on businesses on the country.

THE BUSINESS CYCLE

Over a period of time **gross domestic product (GDP)** (output in the economy) is expected to grow. However, the rate of growth is rarely smooth; there are likely to be some fluctuations. It is also possible for GDP to fall. These fluctuations are often referred to as the **economic, trade or business cycle**. Figure 5 shows these fluctuations and identifies four different phases in the cycle.

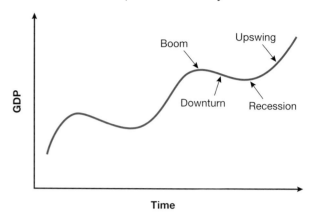

▲ Figure 5 The economic, trade or business cycle

Boom: The peak of the cycle is called a **boom**. During a boom GDP is growing fast because the economy is performing well. Existing firms will be expanding and new firms will be entering the market. Demand will be rising, jobs will be created, wages will be rising and the profits made by firms will be rising. However, prices may also be rising. For example, in some countries, the price of houses rose sharply when GDP was growing rapidly in the 1990s and 2000s.

Downturn: A boom will be followed by a **downturn**. The economy is still growing, but at a slower rate. Demand for goods and services will flatten out or begin to fall, unemployment will start to rise and wage increases will slow down. Many firms will stop expanding, profits may fall and some firms will leave the market. Prices will rise more slowly.

Recession or depression: At the bottom of the business cycle GDP may be flat. If GDP starts to fall, the bottom of the cycle may be referred to as a **slump or depression**. Such a period is often associated with hardship. Demand will start to fall for many goods and services – particularly non-essentials. Unemployment rises sharply, business confidence is very low, bankruptcies rise and prices become flat. The prices of some things may even fall. A less severe version of a depression is a **recession**.

Recovery or upswing: When GDP starts to rise again there is a **recovery or upswing** in the economy. Businesses and consumers regain their confidence and economic activity is on the increase. Demand starts to rise, unemployment begins to fall and prices start to rise again.

THE IMPACT OF THE BUSINESS CYCLE ON BUSINESS

The uneven pattern of growth, shown by the business cycle, can have an impact on businesses. However, the size of the impact will depend on the financial position of the business and what it produces.

Output: During a boom, businesses increase output to meet rising demand. Some will increase capacity. Businesses providing non-essential products and luxury items will benefit more than those that produce necessities. Businesses operating in the holiday, restaurant, air transport, jewellery and fashion industries are likely to benefit most. In contrast, during a recession or a depression output will fall. Businesses respond by reducing output and cutting capacity. Businesses that trade in essential items, such as supermarkets, will avoid the worst of the downturn.

Profit: During a boom business profits are likely to rise. This is because demand is rising and it is easier to raise prices. However, when national income starts to decline, it is harder to make a profit. Businesses may cut their costs to maintain profit levels. Many will have to tolerate lower profits and some will make losses.

Business confidence and investment: During an economic recovery and into a boom, business confidence is high. Business owners are optimistic about the future and are prepared to take more risks. For example, they are more inclined to launch new products, enter new markets and expand. In contrast, during a recession business confidence is low and business owners are pessimistic, cautious and anxious about the future. Consequently, they are not likely to take risks and are more inclined to contract their businesses. Investment is likely to fall. For example, instead of replacing out-of-date machinery they will continue to make do with what they have.

Employment: During a boom unemployment falls because businesses are taking on more workers to cope with rising demand. Sometimes firms might struggle to recruit the quantity and quality of staff that they need as there are fewer people seeking work. However, during a recession the opposite happens. Businesses lay off workers and unemployment rises.

Business start-ups and closures: In a boom more people are prepared to set up a new business. This is because demand is rising and it is easier to make a profit. Business confidence will be high so new entrepreneurs will be more enthusiastic. However, a recession is not a good time to start a new business. Business closures will be rising and inefficient businesses, those with cash flow problems and those producing non-essential products, are most at risk.

HOW MIGHT BUSINESSES RESPOND TO THE DIFFERENT PHASES IN THE BUSINESS CYCLE?

During a boom most business owners will be full of confidence and probably looking for opportunities to expand their operations and increase their profitability. They might invest more in product development and explore riskier ventures such as diversification, for example. Businesses will have a greater tendency to recruit more staff, borrow more money and make some acquisitions. In some sectors businesses will seek to raise prices to take advantage of favourable trading conditions.

Once a boom is over, and economic growth slows down, businesses may become more cautious. Confidence may be lower and there will be less incentive to invest and expand. In some sectors businesses might begin to look for ways of cutting costs and 'tightening' their operations – selling off or closing down marginal divisions, for example.

If the economy slides into a recession or a depression, many businesses will lack confidence and may become anxious. If unemployment is rising sharply and demand in the economy is falling, firms will respond by scaling back operations. They may lay off staff, mothball some of their resources, downsize operations and even begin rationalisation programmes. During this phase very few businesses will consider new ventures and most investment will involve the replacement of worn out or broken down machinery. Inevitably, some businesses will not survive a recession.

Finally, once an economy starts to recover from a recession, businesses and consumers start to feel more confident again. During the recovery unemployment starts to fall and demand starts to rise. This will help to stimulate business activity and owners will start to take a 'longer view' which means they are far more likely to invest.

When answering questions about the impact of events on a business, it may be useful to distinguish between whether they are internal or external. Credit may be given to answers which distinguish clearly between influences that a business can control and those that it cannot. For example, if a business is performing well it might be because it is being well managed. However, it might also be because a key rival has left the market. Evaluation marks may be awarded for answers that recognise this distinction.

CHECKPOINT

1. What is meant by an external influence on business?

2. How is inflation measured?

3. State three drawbacks of inflation for businesses.

4. How might deflation affect a business?

5. Why does the government impose taxes on individuals and businesses?

6. What is the difference between direct and indirect taxes?

7. State four examples of direct taxes.

8. What might be the impact on businesses of a fall in corporation tax?

9. What is the link between business investment and the interest rate?

10. How will a business be affected by a depreciating exchange rate if it exports 80 per cent of its output?

11. If £1 = AUD 1.85, how much will a British tourist pay in pounds for a meal in a Sydney restaurant that cost AUD 245.00?

12. What is meant by a boom in the economy?

SUBJECT VOCABULARY

appreciated (of a currency) a rise in the value of a currency.
boom the peak of the economic cycle where GDP is growing at its fastest.
consumer price index (CPI) a common measure of price changes used in many countries.
depreciated (of a currency) a fall in the value of a currency.
downturn a period in the economic cycle where GDP grows, but more slowly.
economic, trade or business cycle regular fluctuations in the level of output in the economy.
exchange rate the price of one currency in terms of another.
fiscal policy using changes in taxation and government expenditure to manage the economy.
government expenditure the amount spent by the government in its provision of public services.
gross domestic product (GDP) a common measure of national income, output or employment.
index linked the linking of certain payments, such as benefits, to the rate of inflation.
inflation a general rise in prices.
monetary policy using changes in the interest rate and money supply to manage the economy.
recession a less severe form of depression.
recovery or upswing a period where economic growth begins to increase again after a recession.
slump or depression the bottom of the economic cycle where GDP starts to fall with significant increases in unemployment.
taxation the charges made by government on the activities, earnings and income of businesses and individuals.

EXAM PRACTICE

ZOOMAIR SKILLS ANALYSIS, INTERPRETATION, REASONING

ZoomAir, a budget airline with bases in leading airports, is the largest airline in France by the number of passengers carried. In 2017 it had 500 routes, 160 aircraft, 20 bases and carried 50.7 million passengers. The airline serves over 35 countries.

Like other low-cost airlines in the European market, ZoomAir performs better than long-distance operators because it keeps its planes in the air for as long as possible every day. It also charges passengers for extra services, such as baggage check-in, food and hotel hire. Costs are kept low by buying fuel-efficient aircraft in bulk with aggressive discounts, reducing baggage-handling costs by charging passengers for check-in luggage and operating a younger, more efficient fleet of aircraft. Similar airlines in the US have fleets with an average age of around 12 years. The average age of an ZoomAir plane is just over 5 years. Finally, ZoomAir has a good record for their flights being on time and they have easy-to-use web and mobile sites, which attract over a million visits each day. Some operating information is shown in Figures 6, 7 and 8. Figure 9 shows some economic data.

 Q

(a) Define upswing in the business cycle? **(2 marks)**
(b) Explain one reason why a business like ZoomAir might be affected by a cut in income tax. **(4 marks)**
(c) Look at Figure 9. Discuss how European businesses, such as ZoomAir, might have responded to the pace of economic growth between 2013 and 2015. **(8 marks)**
(d) Evaluate whether or not Zoomair will benefit from an appreciation in the exchange rate. **(20 marks)**

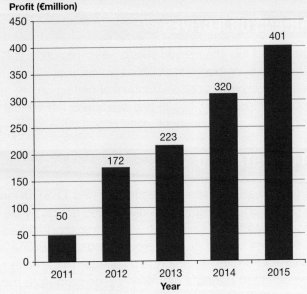

▲ Figure 7 ZoomAir profit, 2011–15

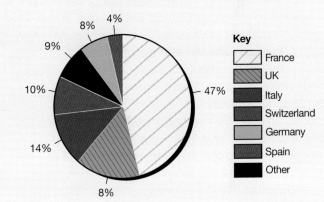

▲ Figure 8 ZoomAir passengers by country, 2016

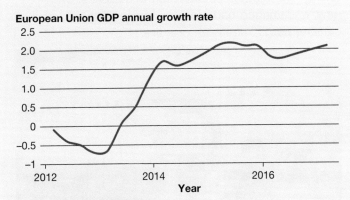

▲ Figure 9 EU growth rates, 2012–17
Source: Tradingeconomics.com ¦ Eurostat

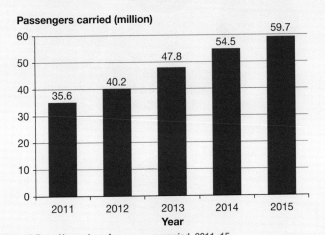

▲ Figure 6 ZoomAir number of passengers carried, 2011–15

42 LEGISLATION

LEARNING OBJECTIVES

By the end of this chapter you should be able to understand:
■ the effects on businesses of: consumer protection, employee protection, environmental protection, competition policy, health and safety and intellectual property rights (copyright, patents and trademarks).

GETTING STARTED

In 2016, Seattle-based Amazon was fined £65,000 in the UK for attempting to ship dangerous goods by air. Amazon was found guilty of trying to transport lithium-ion batteries and other dangerous goods. The online retailer had broken air safety regulations. The articles were detected during a monitoring process before they were loaded onto a plane. The company was taken to court by the UK Civil Aviation Authority under the Air Navigation (Dangerous Goods) Regulations 2002. This legislation outlines how such items must be classified, packed, marked, labelled and documented when being transported by air. This is in addition to the dangerous goods training which must be completed by the people sending them.

Amazon claimed that the breaches of the rules were 'inadvertent' and 'neither wilful nor reckless'. The company said the problem was the result of human error. However, the prosecutor said there was a potential risk if the items had been flown to their intended destination. The prosecutor also said, 'Under the right circumstances the batteries, even new, undamaged batteries, could overheat potentially causing burns, explosion or a fire.'

How has Amazon been affected by government legislation? What is the purpose of legislation in this case? State two other areas where businesses might be affected by government legislation. How might businesses benefit from any government legislation aimed at them?

THE NEED FOR LEGISLATION IN BUSINESS

Without legislation it is possible that some businesses could neglect the needs of certain stakeholders. For example, workers might be paid low wages or forced to work in an uncomfortable or even dangerous environment. One of the roles of the government is to provide a legal framework in which businesses can operate and ensure that vulnerable groups are protected.

It is important for the government to find the 'right balance'. Too much legislation will discourage enterprise and foreign investment. This might reduce growth in national income, reduce job creation, decrease tax revenues and reduce consumer choice. Too little, and some stakeholders' best interests might be neglected.

CONSUMER PROTECTION

Consumers want to buy good-quality products at fair prices and receive good customer service. They also want clear and accurate information about products. They do not want to buy goods that may be dangerous, overpriced or sold to them on false grounds. Without government legislation some firms would exploit consumers. Some of the consumer issues affected by government legislation are summarised in Figure 1. Some examples of legislation introduced by the government to protect consumers is summarised in Table 2 at the end of the chapter.

▲ Figure 1 Consumer issues affected by legislation

HOW DOES CONSUMER LEGISLATION AFFECT BUSINESSES?

The increase in the number of consumer laws and the concern about protecting consumers has a number of possible implications for firms.

Increases in costs: Improving the safety of a product or ensuring that measuring equipment is more accurate can increase the costs of a firm. For example, an electrical firm producing table lamps may find that its product failed to comply with legislation. The firm would have to change or improve the components used to make the lamps or redesign the lamp itself. Such changes would be likely to raise the firm's costs.

Quality control: Many firms have needed to improve their quality control procedures as a result of legislation. For example, firms involved in bagging or packaging goods must ensure that the correct quantities are weighed out. Failure to do so could result in legal action against the business. In addition, businesses must be careful not to sell substandard or damaged products.

Dealing with customer complaints: Many businesses now have a customer service or customer complaints department to deal with customers. These allow firms to deal with problems quickly and efficiently, and to deal with any problems before the customer turns to the legal system.

Changes in business practice: Attempts to ensure that customers are treated fairly by a business may place pressure on it to become more market orientated. The firm would attempt to ensure that it is actually meeting the needs of those people it is attempting to serve. Such a change, for example, may lead to greater use of market research.

EMPLOYEE PROTECTION

In many countries, employers have a responsibility towards their employees, but legislation is necessary to ensure that minimum standards are applied. Without legislative protection some businesses could exploit their workers. For example, they might pay low wages, make them work long hours, deny them employment rights, discriminate against certain groups and dismiss them unfairly. Businesses have a number of legal obligations when employing people.

Employment contract: Workers are entitled to a contract of employment. This is a legal agreement between the employer and the employee. It is likely to contain details including the start date, term of employment, job title and duties, place and hours of work, pay and holiday entitlement, pension and sickness absence, termination conditions (saying how the contract can be ended) and details relating to disciplinary, dismissal and grievance procedures.

Discrimination: Businesses have to make a choice when recruiting staff or selecting employees for promotion or training. Businesses will evaluate candidates in order to choose which one to employ or promote. It is usual to choose the person that is most experienced or better qualified; this is legal discrimination. However, it is illegal in most countries to discriminate on grounds of gender, race, disability, sexual orientation or age. This is unfair discrimination. When employing and promoting people, employers must base their decisions on the ability of candidates, and not, for example, whether they are male or female. There have been a number of Acts addressing discrimination in many countries around the world. One example in the UK is the Equality Act 2010 – which replaced the Sex Discrimination Act 1975 – the original legislation that made it illegal to discriminate either directly or indirectly against someone on the grounds of their gender or whether or not they are married.

Unfair dismissal: The UK Employment Relations Act 1999 states that employees who have worked for an employer for a year have the right not to be unfairly dismissed. Employees may have grounds to claim unfair dismissal if they were dismissed because they:

- were trying to join a trade union
- became pregnant
- refused to work on a Sunday
- were made redundant without a proper procedure.

Employees can be dismissed fairly if they are incapable of doing their job, found guilty of misconduct (wrongful or illegal actions), become ineligible to work (drivers losing their driving licence, for example), are made redundant or for any other substantial reason, such as giving false details on an application form. However, if employees feel that they have been unfairly dismissed in some countries they can take their case to an employment tribunal. If the tribunal finds in favour of the employee, it has the power to return that worker to their job. Some examples of legislation designed to protect people at work are summarised in Table 2 at the end of the chapter.

Equal pay: Historically, in many countries women have not received the same pay as men in lots of professions and occupations. To address this issue in the UK the government introduced the Equal Pay Act 1970. This stated that an employee (whatever their gender) doing the same or 'broadly similar' work as a member of staff of the opposite sex is entitled to equal rates of pay and conditions. The Act aimed to eliminate discrimination in wages and other conditions of work, such as holidays, overtime, hours and duties. The Act was updated in 1983 to allow female workers to claim for work of 'equal value' to that done by a man.

HOW DOES EMPLOYMENT LEGISLATION AFFECT BUSINESSES?

Businesses often complain about the burden of employment legislation. Many say that the legislation discourages them from taking on staff. Some of the negative effects of employment legislation are outlined below.

Compliance costs: The expenses incurred by a business in meeting the requirements of employment and related legislation can be significant.

- When taking on a new employee a business must check that the person is entitled to work in that particular country. For example, in the UK this involves checking a passport, or any other means of identification, which shows that a person is a national of an EU country. If the person was born in the UK then documents, such as their birth certificate, and tax forms, such as a P60 and a P45, must be inspected and their National Insurance number provided. A business must also check that the documents belong to the applicant. If a business only checks the documents of people whom they suspect might not be entitled to work in the UK, they may face a claim for discrimination. Copies of the documents must also be made.
- Employers are responsible for the well-being of employees at work. They must take out the necessary insurance policies and guard against discrimination or harassment. They may also have to deal with matters such as health and safety, discipline and grievances, discrimination in the workplace, bullying, annual leave and redundancy.
- Businesses must also deal with the tax authorities. For example, in the UK, they must tell Her Majesty's Revenue and Customs (HMRC) whenever someone is employed, deduct tax and National Insurance contributions (NICs) from earnings, provide employees with a P60 tax form every year and a P45 if they leave the business's employment. They also have to provide HMRC with an annual return for every employee.

These are just a few of the legal requirements when employing someone. These tasks and responsibilities take time and money to manage. Large businesses have specialists employed in this field to deal with compliance and the necessary administration. Costs will also be incurred if a business gets involved in a dispute with an employee. For example, a business might need to employ a legal team.

Higher labour costs: Some employment legislation has resulted in certain businesses having to meet higher labour costs. For example, in many countries there is a **national minimum wage**. This is designed to boost the earnings of very low-paid workers taking some people out of poverty. The legal minimum wage is reviewed and updated each year. This usually means that it goes up. As a result, businesses paying the minimum wage rate to employees have to meet this increase by law.

Changing working practices: In many countries, as a business employs more people it will have to introduce systems to deal with compliance and human resource management. It will also have to ensure that job advertisements do not discriminate on the basis of gender or whether or not candidates are married. For example, job titles should be gender neutral, as in 'fire fighter' or 'salesperson'. There will be a greater need for job descriptions and person specifications. For example, generally speaking, a person specification must not restrict the job to men or women, although there are exceptions. It is possible to offer a job to someone of a particular sex if the work is not covered by gender discrimination legislation. This could include teaching in single-sex schools, jobs in welfare services, e.g. the right to employ a female in a women's shelter, and acting roles. Interviews must be carried out in a structured way to help limit any prejudice that an interviewer might have. Selection procedures must not discriminate against certain groups. For example, a test style must not be used if it is unfamiliar to a particular ethnic culture.

Loss of flexibility: Some businesses argue that sections of the legislation make it more difficult to run a business because the laws are too inflexible. For example, in the EU employees can ask for flexible working arrangements that suit them if they have worked continuously for 26 weeks or if they have a child under the age of 6 (or a disabled child under the age of 18). Reasons for refusing an employee flexible working must be set out in writing and be legally justified.

Penalties: If businesses fail to comply with the laws outlined above there may be penalties. For example, fines can be imposed and the image or reputation of a business might be damaged. Businesses might also be forced to backdate claims from employees where 'wrongdoing' is proven. This can be very expensive. For example, an employee may receive all the lost pay resulting from unfair dismissal.

Positive effects: Employment legislation can also have a positive effect on businesses. For example, legislation creates a 'level playing field' when employing people. This means that immoral or improper businesses that want to exploit workers to lower costs so that they can gain a competitive edge in the market are prevented from doing so. Complying with employment legislation is also likely to improve worker motivation and employee welfare, which will help raise productivity, reduce levels of staff absence and cut staff turnover. It might also help to create a more positive and friendly culture within organisations. This can improve the image of businesses and make it easier to recruit and retain high-quality staff.

ACTIVITY 1 — SKILLS ANALYSIS, REASONING

CASE STUDY: IKEA®

In 2016, IKEA, the giant Swedish furniture and household goods retailer, was ordered by an employment tribunal to pay one of its employees €30,000. The employee, Ian Fortune, had been unfairly dismissed by IKEA from its Ballymun store in Dublin. In the circumstances of the case, IKEA employees are allowed to drink tea, coffee and soda fountain drinks free of charge in the bistro. However, Mr Fortune was dismissed by his manager for drinking a €1.25 milkshake without paying for it. This act was treated as gross misconduct by the manager and Mr Fortune was sacked.

Mr Fortune failed to attend investigation and disciplinary meetings because he was on a pre-booked holiday with his family. He also said that he had not received any information about the meetings. The tribunal did not agree that the matter was 'substantial ground justifying dismissal'. An IKEA HR manager said that the case was treated as 'gross misconduct' as in any case of theft. Mr Fortune had been employed by IKEA for 5 years and said that he was happy with the outcome.

1. Define unfair dismissal.
2. Explain the impact of employment legislation on IKEA in this case.

ENVIRONMENTAL PROTECTION

Without regulation, business activity can have a negative effect on the environment. For example, governments are becoming concerned about global warming and resulting changes in weather patterns and climates. Some of the greenhouse gases that contribute to global warming come from businesses, such as power generators. As business activity increases there is more gas emission. Also, economic development means that car ownership and air travel increases. The emissions from cars and aircraft also add to global warming. Some specific problems include the following.

- **Pollution.** There are different types of pollution. Water pollution may be caused by businesses dumping waste into rivers, streams, canals, lakes and the sea. An example would be warm water or chemicals being leaked into rivers. Air pollution may be caused by businesses releasing hazardous waste or gases into the air. Noise pollution can also be a problem. Noise from factory machinery and low-flying aircraft by airports are examples.
- **Destruction of wildlife habitats.** Some business development destroys wildlife habitats and spoils the natural environment. For example, around half of the forests that once covered the planet are now gone. Forests are vital for the ecological balance of the planet. It is also reckoned that more than half of the world's primates, such as monkeys and apes, will become extinct due to habitat destruction. Many other species are under threat from human activity, such as tigers, pandas and a wide range of plant and insect species.
- **Traffic congestion.** Extra traffic caused by commercial vehicles or workers travelling to and from work can cause congestion resulting in delays and accidents. For example, in one Indian city, Bangalore, traffic congestion costs about 5 per cent of its economic output.
- **Resource depletion.** Non-renewable resources, such as oil, coal, gas and minerals, cannot be replaced. Therefore, as business development accelerates these resources are depleted. Once they have run out, future generations will have to do without. High-quality soil, which is needed to grow food, is also being lost. The condition of around 40 per cent of the world's agricultural land has significantly declined. This is due to poor farming practices, overuse, the increased size of urban areas and land pollution. Also, some businesses waste resources. For example, many argue that some of the packaging used by businesses is unnecessary and that not enough use is made of recycled materials.

One approach used by many governments to minimise the damage done by businesses to the environment is to pass new laws. Much of the pressure for environmental legislation has emerged due to the growing concerns about global warming. If businesses fail to comply with environmental laws they may be fined or forced to close until the problem is resolved. Examples of environmental legislation are shown in Table 2 at the end of the chapter.

HOW DOES ENVIRONMENTAL LEGISLATION AFFECT BUSINESSES?

Environmental issues offer both threats and opportunities to businesses. Businesses which may benefit the most from growing environmental regulation are those selling pro-environmental and anti-pollution products. These businesses range from engineering companies selling equipment designed to reduce emissions, to service companies which advise other businesses on how they can comply with regulations, to businesses selling environmentally friendly products, such as managed wood.

Those which may lose the most are companies which are high polluters and who face competition from other businesses which don't face similar problems. For example, a specialist chemicals company may cease trading because there are many good substitutes to its products which have a much smaller environmental impact in production. Or a heavily regulated EU company may face competition from a producer in a developing country whose government places little restriction on its activity.

Marketing: Environmental issues can be a highly effective marketing tool for some businesses. Some companies, such as IKEA, which uses sustainable forestry techniques when sourcing wood for its products, and Johnson & Johnson®, which uses mainly solar energy in its production processes, have made a particular point of pursuing environmentally friendly policies, and feature these on their websites. Many businesses claim on their packaging to be environmentally friendly in some way. However, some businesses have found that environmental issues pose a marketing threat. Oil companies, for example, are frequently accused by pressure groups, such as Greenpeace, of harming the environment. Shell® has been heavily criticised for its oil exploration projects in the Arctic and it was widely reported that partly as a result of pressure from Greenpeace, Lego® ended its co-promotion with Shell after a 50 years' association. Such examples show that businesses must take quick and positive action when an environmental issue suddenly arises. It also shows that some businesses

have to work constantly to protect and improve their environmental image.

Finance: In some cases, responding to environmental concerns or new laws and regulations can have a positive financial impact on a business. Energy-saving measures, for example, can lead to a business having lower costs than before because of previous inefficiencies. In most cases, though, taking environmental action is likely to lead to higher costs. If all businesses in the industry also face these higher costs, prices are likely to rise to reflect the higher costs. Profits would then be largely unaffected. But if higher costs fall more heavily on one business than another, then some will gain a competitive advantage and others lose it. This in turn will have different impacts on profitability. Installing expensive new equipment will also have a negative impact on cash flow. In the nuclear power industry and the car industry, businesses must also make investment decisions knowing that there will be heavy costs at the end of a product's life. In the case of the nuclear power industry, this is in terms of safely making plants inoperative. For motor manufacturers, they have to take back old cars for recycling. This will affect the outcomes of appraisal methods like the payback method and discounted cash flow.

Operations management: Pollution controls and other environmental measures could have an impact on how a product is made. This could range from changes in the type of materials used, to production methods, to storage and after-sales service. For example, asbestos was widely used in industry years ago but its use today is severely restricted. Industries such as electricity generation and chemicals have had to introduce much cleaner production methods to reduce emissions. The landfill tax encourages businesses to reduce the amount of waste they produce.

Human resources: Environmental concerns and policies have human resource implications. Staff will need to be recruited and trained to deal with ever increasing government regulations concerning the environment. Some businesses may choose to outsource the guidance they need. Larger businesses are likely to put environmental policies in place. This could include an environmental audit where key measures relating to the impact of the business on the environment are audited each year and the results are made public. Implementing policies means that staff throughout the organisation are aware of the policies and what they must do to comply with the policies. As with any policy, unless there are good procedures and training in place to ensure compliance, staff will tend to interpret the policies as they see fit. Effective communication up and down the hierarchy is therefore essential. The very

ACTIVITY 2   SKILLS   ANALYSIS, REASONING

CASE STUDY: BUSINESS DAMAGING THE ENVIRONMENT

The rapid pace of economic growth in India in recent years has resulted in a noticeable amount of environmental damage. As a result, the Indian government has increased its efforts to reduce the impact of business activity on the environment. For example, in 2017, action was taken by India's National Green Tribunal (NGT), a body responsible for bringing actions against those that damage the environment. The NGT imposed a fine of INR 1 million each on three industrial units in Uttar Pradesh for releasing untreated waste and the use of underground water resources without permission. In addition to the fines, the three units were forced to close down their operations until further notice from the NGT.

The NGT ordered the three companies – ASP Sealing Product Ltd, Umang Dairies Ltd, and Dairy India Private Ltd, to deposit the fine with the Central Pollution Control Board. In one case, an inspection report said that ASP Sealing Product Ltd had stored waste in a holding tank and that oil scum had been detected. Samples of waste taken for analysis failed to comply with pollution norms, it was stated at the hearing.

In a report, it was said that the tribunal was very surprised that Umang Dairies Ltd, in operation since 1994, did not have permission from the Central Ground Water Authority for the use of underground water resources.

1. Explain how the three businesses discussed in this case have been affected by legislation.
2. Explain why environmental legislation is needed.

small minority of businesses which make environmental concerns an important business objective can use this as a way of motivating staff. Over time, it will tend to attract employees who are interested in this aspect of business. However, a tension between meeting financial targets such as profit targets and meeting environmental targets is likely to arise. For a business to survive, it must at least break-even. In this sense, financial targets tend to be more important than environmental targets. This tension between targets could demotivate staff who want to see environmental targets as the most important for the business.

COMPETITION POLICY

There is a need to monitor the activities of monopolies and markets that are dominated by a small number of large businesses. Without government regulation some businesses would exploit consumers by using **anti-competitive or restrictive practices** to reduce competition in the market. Such practices might include the following.

- **Increasing prices.** Raising prices to levels above what they would be in a competitive market. For example, some manufacturers supply goods to retailers and insist that they are retailed at a fixed price.
- **Restricting consumer choice.** A manufacturer of a strong brand might refuse to supply a retailer if that retailer stocks rival products. This will reduce choice for the consumer.
- **Raising barriers to entry.** By spending huge amounts of money on advertising, for example, a dominant firm can squeeze others out of the market. It might also lower its price for a temporary period. This would make it difficult for a new business to get established in the market. Once the new business disappears the price would go up again.
- **Market sharing.** This might occur if there is **collusion.** When a market is shared out between the dominant firms, choice is restricted and prices rise.

In the UK, the Competition and Markets Authority (CMA) is responsible for serving the interests of consumers and protecting them from restrictive practices. This body was formed in 2014 and replaced the Office of Fair Trading (OFT) and the Competition Commission. Its responsibilities are summarised in Table 1.

• Investigating mergers which could restrict competition
• Conducting market studies and investigations in markets where there may be competition and consumer problems
• Investigating where UK or EU laws against anti-competitive agreements and abuses of dominant positions may have been be broken
• Bringing legal action against individuals who commit the cartel offence
• Enforcing consumer protection legislation to tackle practices and market conditions that make it difficult for consumers to exercise choice
• Co-operating with sector regulators and encouraging them to use their competition powers
• Considering regulatory references and appeals

▲ Table 1 Responsibilities of the Competition and Markets Authority for protecting consumers from restrictive practices
Source: www.gov.uk

HOW DOES COMPETITION POLICY AFFECT BUSINESSES?

It might be argued that competition policy will have both a positive and a negative impact on businesses.

Positive: Businesses might get frustrated if their restrictive practices are judged to be illegal and they are forced to comply with the law. This is because such practices are often very highly profitable. However, since competition policy is designed to promote competition, many firms will actually benefit from it. For example, if dominant firms construct barriers to entry, this will make it very difficult for smaller firms to break into the market. Thus, if such barriers are made illegal then it is easier for new firms to break into the market. This will give opportunities to more businesses.

A more competitive business environment will benefit the economy. Competition will encourage innovation and improve efficiency as businesses try to survive in the market. As a result, businesses are more likely to develop new products, reduce costs and make progress in overseas markets. This will help businesses to generate more revenue and profit from exports. It will also raise income and employment.

Negative: Some businesses might argue that competition policy restricts their activities. For example, if a proposed merger or takeover is investigated by the CMA, this might slow down the whole process. This could cause delays and cost the businesses involved a lot of money. In 2014, a proposed merger between soft drinks companies Britvic and AG Barr was investigated by the authorities. The decision was delayed for about 4 months.

Sometimes, after an investigation, a merger or takeover might be permitted, but with conditions. For example, in 2014 a merger between two large cement producers, Lafarge and Holcim, was approved by the European Union. However, the EU directed Lafarge to sell all of its German and Romanian business activities, and instructed Holcim to sell all of its Slovak business and cease most of its activities in France.

HEALTH AND SAFETY

Figure 2 shows that work can be a dangerous environment. Although the graph shows that fatalities at work in Australia have fallen during the period shown, people are still being killed at work in large numbers. Because of the danger to employees, governments aim

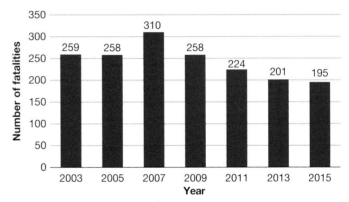

▲ Figure 2 Fatalities at work in Australia, 2007–15

to protect workers by passing legislation that forces businesses to provide a safe and healthy workplace. This might involve:

- providing and maintaining adequate safety equipment and protective clothing, such as fire extinguishers, aprons, hard hats, ear plugs and safety goggles
- ensuring workers have enough space to do their jobs
- guaranteeing a hygienic environment with adequate toilet and washing facilities
- maintaining workplace temperatures and reasonable noise levels
- providing protection from hazardous substances
- providing protection from violence, bullying, threats and stress in the workplace
- providing adequate breaks for rest.

In most countries around the world, there are numerous laws designed to protect people at work. There are also many regulations concerning health and safety at work that are regularly updated. In addition, businesses may follow codes of practice designed to protect workers. Some examples of health and safety legislation are given in Table 2.

Legislation	Date	Brief description and example
Sale of Goods Act (Consumer legislation)	1979	Products must be undamaged, usable and fit for purpose Example: a garment sold as 'waterproof' must not let in the rain
Food Safety Act (Consumer legislation)	1990	Food should be fit for human consumption and comply with safety standards Example: food should not be sold if decaying
Equal Pay Act (Employment legislation)	1970	Pay and conditions must be the same for all people doing the same or 'broadly similar' work Example: male and female bus drivers must be paid the same rates
National Minimum Wage Act (Employment legislation)	1998	It is illegal to pay a worker a wage rate below the set minimum wage rate Example: in 2014 a wage of £6.00 per hour would be illegal (£6.50 was the minimum wage)
Environment Act (Environmental legislation)	1995	Set up the Environment Agency to monitor and control pollution Example: it is unlawful to release emissions into the air (above certain levels)
Environmental Protection Act (Environmental legislation)	1990	Controls pollution caused by the disposal of waste into land, water and air Example: an unlicensed carrier of waste can be fined
Competition Act (Competition policy)	1998	Prohibits agreements, cartels or practices that restrict or prevent competition Example: it is illegal for a group of businesses to charge an agreed price
Enterprise Act (Competition policy)	2002	Established the Office of Fair Trading (OFT)* as an independent body Example: the OFT can refer investigations to the Competition Commission**
Health and Safety at Work Act (Health and safety)	1974	Aimed to raise the standard of health and safety at work Example: employers must provide a written statement of policy on health and safety
Working Time Regulations Act (Health and safety)	1998	Clarifies hours of work and break entitlements for workers Example: 48 hours is the maximum working week

▲ Table 2 Examples of UK legislation directed at businesses

* The Office of Fair Trading was replaced by the Competition and Market Authority in 2014
** The Competition Commission was replaced by the Competition and Market Authority in 2014

HOW DOES HEALTH AND SAFETY LEGISLATION AFFECT BUSINESSES?

The Health and Safety at Work Act 1974 requires businesses to prepare a written statement of their general policy on health and safety. Businesses also have to give training, information, instruction and supervision to ensure the health and safety of workers. Many businesses also follow codes of practice to meet health and safety standards at work. Meeting these requirements will raise business costs. Many large businesses, for example, employ a health and safety officer whose sole responsibility is ensuring that health and safety issues are addressed in accordance with the law. Smaller firms are likely to attach health and safety duties to the job description of a senior member of staff, to ensure compliance. Finally, health and safety inspectors have the right to enter business premises to ensure that health and safety measures are being carried out by businesses.

Penalties: Failure to comply with the law can be serious. At worst, employees' safety might be compromised, which could lead to accidents – in some cases fatal. Businesses can also be fined if they fail to comply with legislation. For example, in China in 2015, 66,000 people died at work. This was in spite of amendments to health and safety laws. Recently, an amendment to the Work Safety Law included a tiered list of penalties that increase according to the severity of the accident. The most serious accidents can attract fines of up to CNY 20m (around £2.3 million). In 2017, Or Kim Peow Contractors (OKP) and its safety co-ordinator and site supervisor, Victor Tan Kok Peng, were convicted and fined $250,000 and $12,000 respectively in relation to a workplace accident resulting in the death of a worker and the injury of three others in 2015.

Sources: Based on Warburton, C. China's rapid growth comes at a human cost and Ang, J. Or Kim Peow Contractors fined S$250k after workers fell 6.4 meters.

Benefits: Although complying with health and safety legislation imposes costs on businesses, there are some considerable benefits that result from it. For example, a good health and safety record will help to improve the image of a business. This will make it easier to attract and retain high-quality staff – especially in industries with 'hostile' working conditions where health and safety issues are of the utmost importance. Also, if businesses are genuinely committed to maintaining high standards of health and safety, workers will feel protected and more secure. As a result they may be better motivated and more loyal. This will benefit the business as workers will be more productive. Absence through injuries at work will be reduced, as might staff turnover.

INTELLECTUAL PROPERTY RIGHTS

In many industries protection is required for the creation of new products, technology and other original work such as a piece of music. Protection is needed to stop others from copying or profiting from the work and efforts of people or businesses that have created something new and unique. In some cases, businesses for example, may have invested huge sums of money in the development of a new product. Therefore, legislation is needed to ensure that inventors, writers, developers and other creators are not exploited. Technically, **intellectual property** is something unique that is physically created. Intellectual property can be owned if:

- it is created (and it meets the requirements for copyright, a patent or a design)
- the intellectual property rights are purchased from the creator or a previous owner
- you have a brand that could be a trademark, e.g. a well-known product name.

EXAM HINT

It is not necessary to learn all the legislative acts that relate to the protection of consumers, employees and the environment. However, it might be useful if you can remember, generally, the issues that are addressed by the acts. You do need to be fully aware of the impact that the legislation has on businesses. Also, remember that the legislation can have both positive and negative effects on business.

Intellectual property can have more than one owner and belong to a person or a business. It can also be sold or transferred to another owner. If it is protected it will be easier to take legal action in the event of theft. Such protection may take several forms.

Automatic protection: With some types of creations such as writing and literary works, art, photography, films, television, music, web content and sound recordings, protection is automatic. This means that the creator is automatically entitled to **copyright** protection. Copyright protects the creator's work and stops others from using it without their permission. There is no register of copyright and it is not necessary to make an application or pay a fee. The protection is completely automatic and extended across any countries in the world where copyright agreements already exist between nations. Copyright prevents others from copying work, distributing copies (whether free of charge or for sale), renting or lending copies, performing, showing or playing work in public, making adaptations of work and posting it on the Internet.

Applying for protection: For some types of intellectual property, such as patents or trademarks, it is necessary to apply for protection. For trademarks, such as the name of a product or any other words, sounds, logos, music or any combination of these, it is necessary to check first to see whether a trademark already exists. There is likely to be a trademark database that will help in the search process. Provided the trademark is unique owners can then follow the registration process. Once a trademark has been registered owners can take legal action against anyone who uses the trademark without permission. Owners can also put the ® symbol next to the trademark. This shows that the brand, for example, is already owned and cannot be used by others. Different countries are likely to have different registering processes for trademarks. Owners should be aware that a trademark has to be registered separately in each country where it will be used.

Patents are used to protect inventions. Patents will only be granted if an invention is new. Patents will not be granted for modifications to something that already exists. In many countries patents are more difficult to obtain. Indeed, in some countries only around 1 in 20 applications are successful. It is also necessary to pay a fee – £4000 in the UK – and it can take up to 5 years to secure a patent. Patent owners must also pay an annual fee on top of this and meet the costs of any legal action to defend a patent. Finally, a patent has a limited life – perhaps up to 20 years. After this others are allowed to copy the invention for their own gain. It may be helpful to get professional advice before applying for a patent.

HOW DO INTELLECTUAL PROPERTY RIGHTS AFFECT BUSINESS?

If businesses and people can protect their original work from theft, creativity is likely to be encouraged. In the wider economy everyone benefits from the work done by businesses to develop new products and new technology because they can enjoy more choice and lower prices. Also, the quality of life is improved if there are more books, films, music and other works of art. Therefore, the protection of intellectual rights has a positive impact.

Also, with the protection, through research and development businesses are likely to gain a competitive edge and make more profit. In some industries protection is absolutely vital. For example, in the pharmaceuticals industries, where billions are spent on research and development, such investment would not take place if businesses could not obtain patents. Patents reward businesses for their investment because they can exclude competition from others for up to 20 years. This helps the flow of new drugs and medicines onto the market and generates large amounts of profit for successful investors.

CHECKPOINT

1. State four consumer issues covered by consumer legislation.

2. How might a food producer be affected by consumer legislation?

3. How might business adverts be affected by consumer legislation?

4. What is the main purpose of the Sale of Goods Act?

5. What is a contract of employment?

6. How might an employee claim unfair dismissal?

7. State two restrictive practices that a business might try to engage in.

8. State three responsibilities of the CMA.

9. Why do businesses often regard legislation as a burden?

10. State two benefits to a business of complying with health and safety legislation.

11. Give two ways in which intellectual property might be protected.

12. Give one benefit of legislation designed to protect intellectual property rights.

SUBJECT VOCABULARY

anti-competitive or restrictive practices attempts by firms to prevent or restrict competition.
collusion two (or more) businesses agreeing to a restrictive practice, such as price fixing.
contract of employment a written agreement between an employer and an employee in which each has certain obligations.
copyright a legal right that grants the creator of an original work exclusive rights for its use and distribution. Usually only for a limited time.
discrimination favouring one person over another. For example, in the EU it is unlawful to discriminate on grounds of race, gender, age and disability.
employment tribunal a court that deals with cases involving disputes between employers and employees.
intellectual property an idea, design, or artistic work which a person or organisation has invented or created and on which they have obtained a copyright, trademark or patent.
national minimum wage a wage rate set by the government below which it is illegal to pay people at work.
unfair dismissal the illegal dismissal of a worker by a business.

EXAM PRACTICE

PADWELL ELECTRONICS PLC

SKILLS ANALYSIS, INTERPRETATION, PROBLEM SOLVING, REASONING

Padwell Electronics manufacture electrical components such as diodes, resistors, capacitors and transistors to standard sizes and standard electrical specifications. The Walsall-based UK company employs 4800 people in a large factory on an industrial estate. Most of the components are sold to the manufacturers of mobile phones. Padwell Electronics has a reputation in the industry for being one of the cheapest producers. However, its image in the local area is not very positive. Although it is a large employer, people often see jobs at Padwell Electronics as a 'last resort'. This is mainly because the pay is low, the work is very boring and working conditions are harsh. The factory is said to be noisy, cold and dark. Staff turnover is 39 per cent.

In October 2014, the national legal minimum wage rate in the UK was increased by 3 per cent from £6.31 to £6.50. At Padwell Electronics, 90 per cent of employees are paid the national minimum wage for a standard 36-hour week (four shifts of 9 hours). After the increase, Business Secretary Vince Cable said, 'The National Minimum Wage provides a vital safety net for the lowest paid, ensuring they get a fair wage while not costing jobs. This year's rise will mean that they will enjoy the biggest cash increase in their take-home pay since the banking crisis, benefiting over one million people in total.' However, Sally Castle, the CEO at Padwell Electronics, had this to say when talking to the local press: 'This pay increase is very bad for us. We try to be efficient here at Padwell, we keep our costs low, we aim to be the cheapest in the industry – it's what keeps us going. The government is always creating new demands. Just last month we had to spend £100,000 on a new toilet block for staff. There was nothing wrong with the old block until the HSE [Health and Safety Executive] got involved.'

Sally also mentioned the proposed merger with Deptford Electricals as an example of government legislation that's 'gone too far'. When the merger was proposed the authorities said that an investigation may be necessary because the two businesses together would dominate the market. The two companies were still waiting for an official announcement from the authorities 7 months after the initial proposal.

Sources: adapted from www.gov.uk and www.hse.gov.uk

(a) Calculate the increase in the weekly wage bill as a result of the increase in the minimum wage. **(4 marks)**

(b) Explain the main impact of the national minimum wage on Padwell Electronics. **(4 marks)**

(c) Explain one way in which the proposed merger with Deptford Electricals might be affected by competition policy. **(4 marks)**

(d) Evaluate whether or not the costs of complying with legislation outweigh the benefits to a business like Padwell Electronics plc. **(20 marks)**

43 THE COMPETITIVE ENVIRONMENT

LEARNING OBJECTIVES

By the end of this chapter you should be able to understand:
- the effects on businesses of competition in terms of competitor: numbers, size and behaviour
- ways for a small business to compete in a competitive market.

GETTING STARTED

In 2016, a report in the USA stated that air fares in America should be lower in 2017. According to the report fares for shorter journeys would probably fall by 3 per cent, while long-distance airfares would drop by around 1.5 per cent. The main reason for this downward pressure on prices was competition between airlines. Although, lower fuel costs and some overcapacity were also to blame.

The number of seats for sale has been growing faster than the number of passengers wishing to fly. The market is now highly competitive with budget carriers, such as Spirit Airlines Co., adding cheap services at the same airports as larger rivals. They are now adding routes from medium-sized airports. Some of the larger operators, such as American Airlines Group and United Continental Holdings, plan to fight back by offering cheap but higher-restriction fares. This should help to push prices lower still in 2017.

Draw a supply and demand diagram to show the effect on airfares of more airlines entering the market. Define a highly competitive market. Describe two measures that an airline might take to compete in the market. How might an airline reduce competition in the market?

THE COMPETITIVE ENVIRONMENT

One of the most important external influences faced by a business is the threat posed by competitors. The majority of markets are competitive and some are extremely competitive. For example, the European market for clothes, which is worth over €100,000 million, is highly competitive. There are many thousands of businesses competing to sell a wide range of clothes to the European population. Table 1 shows the turnover and the number of stores operated by the top ten clothes retailers in Europe. In addition to these large chains there are many thousands of independents which are often quite specialised, and cater for particular market niches. For example, an independent store might specialise in clothes for babies or wealthy shoppers looking for exclusivity. An increasing number of supermarkets are also selling clothes in addition to their traditional food and household goods lines. Finally, competition in this market has become more intense in the last 10–20 years due to the arrival of online clothes sellers. Many online suppliers belong to the stores mentioned in Table 1. However, there are a growing number online retailers that sell solely from a website. Examples of these are the two global giants Amazon and Alibaba.

	Operator	Turnover (€ million)	Stores	Base
1	H&M	15,900	2876	Sweden
2	Inditex	13,000*	4989	Spain
3	M&S	11,600	1109	UK
4	C&A	7200*	1579	BE/DE
5	Primark	6700	330	UK
6	Next	4900*	649	UK
7	Arcadia	2500*	2700*	UK
8	Debenhams	1900*	204	UK
9	Esprit	1300	290	Germany
10	Benetton	1000*	2600*	Italy

▲ Table 1 Top ten fashion/clothes retailers in Europe, 2016
*Estimated

In a minority of markets there is very little competition. For example, in many countries the supply of water is organised on a regional basis. In each region there is usually only one supplier. For example, in the south-west of England, the supply of water in Dorset, Somerset, Bristol, most of Wiltshire and parts of Gloucestershire and Hampshire is provided by one business, Wessex Water. The company, which is owned by the Malaysian company YTL Power International, serves a total of 2.7 million customers. People in this region cannot obtain a domestic water supply from any other provider, consequently Wessex Water operates as a monopoly. This arrangement is typical of the supply of water in many countries.

THE EFFECTS ON BUSINESSES OF COMPETITION

Operating in a competitive market is likely to have a number of implications for a business. Businesses will be challenged and forced to monitor the activities of rivals in order to minimise the threat they pose. The impact on businesses might be influenced by the numbers of competitors, the size of competitors or their behaviour.

Numbers: The number of rivals in a market can have an important influence on the level of competition. In some markets there may be a very large number. For example, in the restaurant industry there are huge numbers of operators. Even in quite small towns there may be dozens of restaurants. In global markets there will obviously be more firms competing. Owing to the process of globalisation, the number of potential rivals has increased enormously. However, it is not just multinationals that can operate in global markets. Even small firms can access global markets because they can often sell their products online to anywhere in the world. National markets will clearly have fewer firms competing than global markets. And the numbers of rivals in regional markets will be smaller still. Finally, in local markets the number of competitors will be small. Businesses in these markets serve small areas such as villages, small towns and specific residential areas. In some cases there may only be one business serving a local market. For example, many rural villages are served by just one shop. However, this does not mean that they do not face any competition. Most people in rural areas have cars and can travel to other shops in other locations.

Generally, the level of competition will tend to become more intense as the number of rivals in a market grows. This can have several effects on businesses.

- **Price.** In a highly competitive market, where there are large numbers of competitors, businesses have less control over the prices they charge. Prices are likely to be forced down. A business that charges a price that is significantly higher than those of its rivals risks losing sales. This is because consumers can switch easily from one supplier to another.

However, if a business can effectively differentiate its product there may be some scope for price increases. For example, in the fashion industry, businesses such as Burberry, Prada and Gucci can charge higher prices than rivals because the quality of their products is perceived to be superior.

- **Profit.** The profit available in a highly competitive market has to be shared between a greater number of contestants. Profit margins are likely to be squeezed because prices will be forced down. However, businesses that can operate more efficiently and reduce their costs may be able to enjoy higher profits than rivals that operate with a higher cost base.
- **Communication with customers.** Businesses will be under pressure to meet customer needs. Those businesses that meet customer needs effectively are more likely to survive in the market. This competitive pressure may mean that businesses make more of an effort to communicate with their customers. They may carry out more market research for example. They may also use social media to keep in touch with consumer sentiment. For example, comments relating to what people think about products can be picked up on Twitter accounts. An important part of good customer service is effective communication with customers. It is reckoned by some that forming strong relationships with customers will overtake productivity as a key driver of profitable growth.
- **Innovation.** In highly competitive markets innovation will be encouraged. This is because if a business can design new products, they may be of more interest to consumers and allow a business to gain a competitive edge in the market. The development of a USP can go a long way to aid survival in a competitive market. Many people prefer to buy products that are differentiated from those of rivals

Size: The size of rivals can have an important influence on the level of competition in a market. Running a business in the shadow of a large multinational is clearly going to be challenging. Large businesses can be very powerful. They can exploit economies of scale and lower their costs. They have the resources to recruit the best staff in the world, take risks, dominate suppliers and other stakeholders, change prices in markets and influence political decision making. They can take on large-scale contracts that smaller rivals could not hope to manage. For example, only large construction companies have the resources to build giant bridges, power stations, motorways and sports stadiums. However, it is not impossible for smaller businesses to survive profitably in markets alongside much larger rivals. The ways in which smaller businesses can operate in competitive markets is discussed below.

Generally, smaller rivals pose less of a threat in business than larger ones. The size of competitors though can have a number of effects on a business.

- **Price.** In markets that are dominated by large rivals, smaller businesses have little control over price. In many markets dominated by large firms, the strongest, or the lowest-cost producers, will tend to set the price. Other firms in the market are often happy to copy these prices. However, if a business is able to differentiate its product, there may be scope for higher prices.

- **Profit.** Larger firms will tend to enjoy both higher levels of profits and higher profit margins. Smaller firms may not be able to exploit economies of scale so their costs will be higher and their margins lower. Also, the level of profits made by smaller firms in the market will be lower. This is because they will have a much smaller share of the market compared to their much larger rivals.

- **Communication with customers.** In some respects smaller firms can communicate more effectively with customers than their larger rivals. This might be because smaller organisations are likely to be more personal and much closer to their customers. In contrast, very large companies often encounter problems communicating with customers. For example, they may use automatic answering services to deal with telephone queries. Many people do not like these systems. They may keep customers on 'hold' for long periods, fail to identify specific customer needs or direct them from one service to another without ever providing an adequate response. Because of these problems smaller firms may have a competitive edge over their larger rivals when it comes to communication. However, larger companies are employing social media to interact with customers which has helped to improve communications in recent years.

- **Innovation.** It could be argued that large businesses pose a threat to their smaller rivals in the development of new products and technology. This is because they have more resources. For example, Samsung spent US$13 billion on R&D in 2016. Small firms would never be capable of matching such expenditure levels. However, small firms can still be innovative. Because of their size they can be flexible and adaptable which often means they can respond to changes in customer demands quickly.

Behaviour: Businesses are likely to be directly affected by the behaviour of their rivals. In a competitive environment businesses will try to develop strategies to 'outcompete' their rivals. They might use a wide range of tactics to win a larger market share at the expense of their business opponents. Some key examples are outlined below.

- **Pricing.** One way a business will be affected by the behaviour of a competitor is when they change prices. Most consumers are sensitive to price changes and will buy the cheapest products on the market (assuming that quality is the same). For example, in 'Getting started' above, in the US domestic airline industry, Spirit Airlines started to provide cheap flights at the same airports as larger rivals. In response, some of the larger operators, such as American Airlines Group and United Continental Holdings, planned to fight back by offering cheap services of their own. This shows that businesses can be directly affected by the behaviour of a rival.

- **Marketing.** Businesses usually monitor the marketing activities of rivals such as the methods of promotion and advertising they use. If a rival introduces a new and effective promotional strategy, or places an imaginative advert on television, for example, this might boost their sales and market share. This will affect the sales of others in the market and is likely to illicit a response from them. Quite often businesses will adapt, copy or imitate the successful marketing campaigns of their rivals. For example, in 2016, the Kylie Cosmetics Instagram® account shared a promotional image of a red-lipped model with gold-coated fingers covering her face. LA make-up artist Vlada Haggerty used a similar image during the previous September and accused Kylie of stealing the idea.

- **Product differentiation.** If possible many businesses will try to differentiate their products from those of rivals. If they can do this effectively they may hold a more prominent position in the market and charge a higher price. Once a business has 'broken away from the pack' this puts pressure on rivals to make their own attempts at product differentiation. If they are not able to do so they are likely to lose market share.

- **Product development.** If competitors develop improved versions of their products, or launch brand new products, businesses can be negatively affected. New and improved products are often very attractive to consumers and businesses risk losing market share if they fail to innovate. In some industries, particularly technology-based industries such as mobile phones, gaming and other electronic goods, companies can gain a significant competitive edge by being a 'first-mover'. They can also expect to charge premium prices by selling to 'early adopters'.

- **Collusion.** In a minority of industries a number of firms might work together and behave like a monopoly. They might form a cartel and fix prices or share out the market. This behaviour can have a very damaging effect on the remaining firms in the industry. It is very difficult to compete with a monopolist because of the power they have over the market. However, in many countries cartels and collusion are not permitted because they are anti-competitive. In recent years, some firms have been discovered operating cartels and been penalised. For example, in 2017, Aschehoug, Cappelen Damm, Gyldendal and the former Schibsted Forlag, Norway's four largest publishers, were fined a total of NOK 32 million for engaging in anti-competitive practices. The competition authorities branded the behaviour as 'illegal co-operation'. The four companies were working together to avoid using their fierce rival distributor Interpress and were sharing competitively sensitive information.

- **Barriers to entry.** In some markets, it is easy for a new business to set up. For example, many entrepreneurs open small shops selling everything from groceries to toys. This is because barriers to entry are low. It does not cost too much to open up a shop and the amount of knowledge and expertise needed is minimal. However, in some industries setting up as a new competitor is very difficult. There are difficult barriers to overcome. In some industries such as broadcasting and air transport, a government licence is needed before trading can begin. In some industries, such as pharmaceuticals,

competition is prevented by patents. In others, such as car manufacturing, aircraft building or oil refining, the set-up costs can be huge and impossible with the financial resources of most entrepreneurs. Finally, in some industries it is possible for businesses to develop barriers to entry. For example, some large companies spend huge amounts of money advertising their products and developing very strong brand loyalty. Coca-Cola and McDonald's are good examples. It is difficult for new businesses and existing rivals to break into the markets of such firms when this behaviour is effective.

WAYS FOR A SMALL FIRM TO COMPETE IN A COMPETITIVE MARKET

The vast majority of firms in many countries are small. The number of small firms, along with self-employment, has also grown in the last 30 years. Governments in many countries have encouraged the development of small businesses. In developed countries, the growth in the tertiary sector has also helped. This is because the provision of many services can be undertaken more effectively on a small scale. Finally, even in markets where large firms are dominant there are ways in which small firms can compete. Also, in some cases it might be argued that small firms can have advantages over their larger rivals. Some of the ways in which small firms can compete in a competitive market are outlined below

Develop a market niche: A niche market is a small market segment – a segment which has sometimes gone 'untouched' by larger businesses. Niche marketing involves selling to a small customer group, sometimes with specific needs. Small firms can often survive in a competitive markets by supplying a niche. They may also avoid competition. It is also a lot easier to focus on the needs of the customer in a niche market. Also, if there is no competition it may also be possible to charge premium prices. For example, in the highly competitive holiday industry, some Malaysian companies are offering specialist holiday experiences in niche markets. Packages include visits to Sabah (known in Malaysia for its beaches, rainforests, diving and wildlife) for eco-tourists and hotels offering Muslims from the Middle East all that they require, including halal food and iftar (the meal to break their fast during Ramadan).

Flexibility: Small firms can adapt to change more quickly. This is because the owners, who tend to be the main decision makers, are actively involved in the business and can react to change. For example, a small baker can produce a personalised birthday cake for individual customers. A large, national cake manufacturer may not be able to do this.

Personal service: As firms get bigger it often becomes difficult to offer customers an individual personal service.

ACTIVITY 1   SKILLS   ANALYSIS, PROBLEM SOLVING

CASE STUDY: BOLT

In 2015, two entrepreneurs, Satyajeet Mohanty and Ronak Kumar Samantray, set up their own business, Bolt, in Hyderabad, India. They invented and developed a device for charging mobile phones while riding a motorbike. The device, called the Bolt Red Streak, is a small, waterproof mobile charger designed to charge any mobile safely and quickly on the bike. The unique removable design makes it easy to unplug and carry around when not riding. The device also tracks the entire ride on a route map and calculates total distance and average speed using the Bolt Riders App. It sells for INR 1599 and can be purchased online or from around 30 dealers.

The business, which was funded with about INR 25,000,000 raised from family and friends, has a lot of potential. In 2015 around 16 million two-wheeler vehicles such as scooters, motorcycles and mopeds were sold in India alone. Bolt currently employs five people with primary focus on production quality and after-sales service with customers.

The business hopes to sell 350 units per month in 2016.

1. Calculate the expected revenue in 2016 if sales targets are achieved.
2. What evidence is there in the case to suggest that Bolt is a small business?
3. Explain **two** ways in which a small businesses like Bolt can compete in the market.

Some people prefer to deal with the owner of a firm directly and are prepared to pay a higher price for the privilege. Owners are far more accessible in small firms than larger ones. They are more likely to take a personal interest in their customers and develop strong relationships with them over time.

Lower wages: Many workers in small firms do not belong to trade unions. As a result their negotiating power is weaker and the owners are often able to restrict wages to the legal minimum wage. Also, employees in small businesses may have lower expectations for their earnings. This might be because employees appreciate that the owner has limited resources due to the size of the business.

Better communication: Since small firms have fewer employees, communication tends to be informal and more rapid than in larger organisations. The owner will be in close contact with all staff and can exchange information

rapidly. As a result decision making will be faster and workers may be better motivated.

Innovation: Although small firms often lack resources for research and development, they may be surprisingly innovative. One reason for this is because small firms face competitive pressure to innovate. For example, if they fail to come up with new ideas for products they will lose their market share. It may also be because small firms are more prepared to take a risk. Perhaps they have less to lose than large firms.

CHECKPOINT

1. Give two examples of competitive markets.
2. Give two examples of markets that might lack competition.
3. Give an example of a market that is made up of a very large number of firms.
4. Why are firms likely to be price takers in markets with very large numbers of firms?
5. What is collusion?
6. How might a business be affected by the existence of a cartel in an industry?
7. Give two ways in which small businesses can compete in a highly competitive market.

EXAM HINT

Remember that in a minority of large markets there may be a lack of competition. For example, the energy markets in most countries are huge. However, there is often a lack of proper competition and it has been alleged that many of the operators in the industry are exploiting consumers.

EXAM PRACTICE

TESLA AND THE GLOBAL CAR MARKET

SKILLS ANALYSIS, INTERPRETATION, CRITICAL THINKING

The global car market is very competitive. It is dominated by some large and powerful multinationals such as Toyota, GM, VW, Renault-Nissan. In the first quarter of 2017 a total of 21.24 million passenger cars and light commercial vehicles were sold around the world. The pie chart in Figure 1 shows the market shares of the largest manufacturers in the first quarter of 2017. Figure 2 shows the amounts of money spent on advertising by a selected group of car manufacturers in 2015.

One of the small manufacturers operating in the car industry is the electric car producer, Tesla. The founders of Tesla wanted to prove that electric cars could be better than petrol-powered cars. Electric cars can accelerate instantly and have incredible power, and zero emissions. The founders wanted Tesla's products to be affordable and without compromise. Tesla's mission is to accelerate the world's movement to sustainable energy.

The market for electric vehicles is currently a very small proportion of the total market for cars. In the first quarter of 2017 Tesla sold just 25,418 cars. However, Tesla sold more electric cars than any other car manufacturer. Sales of electric cars are expected to rise significantly in the coming years but at the moment only about 0.2 per cent of all passenger cars sold around the world are electric. Sales of electric cars will be boosted in the future by cheaper batteries, improved infrastructure for battery charging and government commitments to phase out petrol- and diesel-powered cars.

The motor industry has been criticised in recent years due to some bad trading practices. For example, a number of manufacturers have been caught using defeat devices to cheat on emissions tests. In July 2017, it was announced that Porsche would have to meet the expense of recalling 22,000 3-litre Cayenne models to remove illegal emissions-controlling software. This came after VW refitted over 1 million diesel cars for the same reason. In 2015, VW admitted that some of its diesel cars were fitted with these 'cheating' devises.

In another development in 2017, three German car makers, VW, BMW and Daimler, were accused of colluding for many years. It was revealed in a report that the three companies may have secretly worked together on technology, forming a cartel that could have led to the emissions-test scandal. These allegations come just days after Daimler recalled more

than 3 million of its Mercedes Benz cars to adjust emissions software. Prior to that, VW-owned Audi recalled 850,000 vehicles.

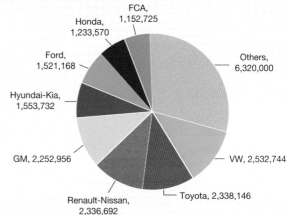

▲ Figure 1 Global car sales by manufacturer, 2017 (1st quarter)

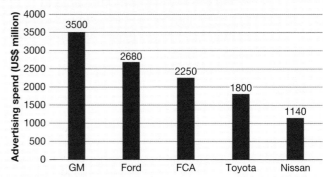

▲ Figure 2 Advertising expenditure by a selection of car manufacturers, 2015

Q

(a) Define a competitive environment. **(2 marks)**

(b) Explain one way in which Tesla aims to compete in the global car market. **(4 marks)**

(c) Discuss how the size of competitors in the car industry might affect Tesla. **(8 marks)**

(d) Assess how the behaviour of competitors in the car industry might affect Tesla. **(10 marks)**

INDEX

Locators in **Bold** indicate a definition.

4 Ps 62–3

acid test ratio (liquidity) 251, **254**
advertising 74–5, **81**
  and branding 78
  influence on
    demand 33
aesthetics, design mix component 69
agents (distribution channels) 91–2, **94**
assets 173, 248–50, 252, **254**
authority (of management) 115, **119**

B2B *see* business-to-business (B2B)
B2C *see* business-to-consumer
  (B2C)
balance sheet 249–50, 251, **254**
bank overdraft 180–1, **182**, 201
batch production 265
bonuses 126, **130**
boom (business cycle) 304, **306**
Boston matrix 60–2, **66**
bottom line 244
brand names 5, **9**
branding 58, 78–9
  emotional 80
  exam practice 82
  influence on demand 33
  influence on PED 48
  influence on pricing strategies 86
break-even 222–4, **224**
  exam practice 225
brokers (distribution channels)
  91–2, **94**
budgets 233–4, 238
  control 235
  variances 236–7
buffer stocks 281
business cycle 304–5, **306**
  exam practice 307
business objectives 155–8
  exam practice 159
business plans 166–9, **169**
  exam practice 170–1
businesses, failure of 256–61
  exam practice 262
business-to-business (B2B) 64–5
  and online distribution 93
business-to-consumer (B2C) 63–4
  and online distribution 93

capacity utilisation 274–7, **277**
  exam practice 278

capital 172, 249–50, **254**
  working 253–4, **254**
cash 248–9, 253–4, 257
cash flow
  exam practice 232
  forecasts 226–31
  variables 228–9
cell production 266–7
centralisation (in organisations) 116–17, **119**
chain of command 115, **119**
charities 189
CMA *see* Competition and Markets
  Authority (CMA)
commission (payment) 125–6, **130**
competition
  influence on markets 8
  influence on PED 48
  influence on pricing strategies 86
Competition and Markets Authority (CMA)
  313
competition policy (legislation) 313–14
competitive advantages 25–6, **28**
competitive markets 320–1
  exam practice 324
  and small firms 322–3
competitive pricing 85, **87**
  see also prices
competitors 319
  and business failure 259
  exam practice 324
  influence on sales forecasting 217–18
complementary goods 32, **34**
comprehensive income, statement of 243
consultation 128, **130**
consumer panels 12–13
consumer price index (CPI) 296, **306**
consumer protection (legislation) 308–9
consumer trends **219**
  influence on sales forecasting 215–16
consumers 11–12, 20
  behaviour 33
  income 32–3, 48
  socio-economic groups 24–5, **28**
contracts of employment 309, **317**
contribution 221, 222, **224**
control (distribution channels) 92
co-operatives 189, **191**
copyright 316, **317**
corporate social responsibility 72
cost, design mix component 69
cost plus pricing 83–4, **87**
  see also prices

costs 207, 210
  fixed 208, 221, 222
  influence on distribution channels 92
  and interest rates 299
  and profitability 246
  variable 208–9, 221
CPI *see* consumer price index (CPI)
crowd funding 178–9, **182**, 201
current ratio (liquidity) 251, **254**
curriculum vitae (CV) 104, **111**
customers
  loyalty 65–6
  satisfaction 158
  see also consumers

Data Protection Act 16
decentralisation (in organisations)
  116–17, **119**
delegation 116, **119**, 128, **130**
demand 11, 31–4, **34**, 42
  exam practice 35, 45
  excess 43, **44**
  and interest rates 300
demand curves 31–2, **34**, 41–2
demographics
  influence on demand 33
  influence on markets 7, 24
depression (business cycle) 304, **306**
design mix 68–73, **72**
differentiation (pricing strategies) 86
direct selling 90–1, **94**
discretionary expenditure 53, **54**
discrimination 309, **317**
disequilibrium 43–4
dismissal 100
distribution channels 89–92, **94**
  exam practice 95
  online 93–4
  services 94
downturn (business cycle) 304, **306**

e-commerce 5–6, **9**
economic variables **219**
  and business failure 259
  influence on markets 7
  influence on sales forecasting
    216–17
efficiency 269–70, **272**
employee protection (legislation) 309–11
employer/employee relationships 100–2
employment tribunals 309
empowerment 128–9, **130**

entrepreneurs 141–5, **147**
    barriers to 146–7
    characteristics 149–51, 152
    exam practice 148, 154
    risk 147
    skills 151–2
    uncertainty 147
entrepreneurship 135–7
environmental protection (legislation)
    311–13
Equal Pay Act 1970 309
Equality Act 2010 309
equilibrium price 41–2, **44**
ergonomics 69, **72**
e-tailing *see* online retailing
exchange rates 297–9, **306**
    and business failure 259–60
excise duties 38
expenditure 41–2, **44**
exports 297, 298, 299, 300, 302
external shocks
    influence on demand 34
    influence on supply 39

finance
    external 177–82, **182**
    internal 172–5
    raising it 172–4, 200–3
financial position, statement of 249–50
first-movers 271–2, **272**
flexible working 129
floatation 194, **197**
    exam practice 198
flow production 266
focus groups 12–13
forecasts
    cash flow 226–31
    sales 213–19, **219**
franchises 187–8, **191**
function, design mix component 68–9

GDP *see* gross domestic product (GDP)
government expenditure 303–4, **306**
government subsidies (supply) 38–9
grants 181, 201
gross domestic product (GDP) 216,
    304, **306**
Growth Share matrix *see* Boston matrix

Health and Safety at Work Act 1974 315
health and safety (legislation) 314–16
Herzberg (two-factor theory) 124–5, **130**
hierarchical organisations 113–15, **119**

imports 297, 298, 299, 300, 302
income elastic 52, **54**
income elasticity of demand (YED)
    52–4, **54**
    exam practice 55
income inelastic 52, **54**
industrial action 101, 103, **103**

inferior goods 33, **34**, 53, **54**
inflation 295–7, **306**
innovation (markets) 7
intellectual property rights (legislation)
    316–17, **317**
interest rates 299–301
    and business failure 260
intrapreneurs 145–6, **147**
inventories 252, 253, **254**, 279–80
    and business failure 258
    control 281–3
    exam practice 285
investment 8
    and interest rates 299–300

JIT *see* just-in-time (JIT)
job descriptions 105, **111**
job enlargement 130, **130**
job enrichment 129, **130**
job production 264–5
job rotation 129–30, **130**
just-in-time (JIT) 252–3, 266, 270, 281–2

kaizen 270, **272**, 290–1

leadership 132–8, **138**
    exam practice 139
lean production 270, **272**, 283–4
leasing 181, **182**
legislation
    competition policy 313–14
    consumer protection 308–9
    employee protection 309–11
    environmental protection 311–13
    health and safety 314–16
    influence on markets 7
    intellectual property rights 316–17
liabilities 249–50, **254**
liability (personal)
    limited 185, **191**, 195, 199, 200, 201–2
    unlimited 184, **191**, 199–200, 201
lifestyle businesses 189, **191**
limited companies 185–6, **191**
    exam practice 204
    private 186–7
    see also public limited companies
    (PLC)
liquidity 249, 250–3, **254**
loans 179, **182**, 201
    exam practice 183
luxuries (YED) 53

margin of safety 223, **224**
    exam practice 225
market clearing price *see* equilibrium price
market orientation 20–1, **28**
market research 8, 11–18, **18**
    exam practice 19
marketing 3–4, **9**
    exam practice 67
    influence on demand 33

leading to business failure 258–9
    objectives 57–8
    strategies 63–5
marketing mix 62–4, **66**
    exam practice 67
markets 3–4, 6–9
    and business failure 259
    competitive 320–3
    exam practice 10, 29
    growth 61
    influence on distribution channels 92
    mapping 22–3, **28**
    positioning 22, **28**
    segmentation 23–5, **28**
    share 5, **9**, 58, 61, 157
mark-up 83, **87**
mass market 4, **9**
    marketing strategies 63–4
Maslow (hierarchy of needs) 123–4, **130**
Mayo (human relations) 122–3
merchandising 77, **81**
monopolies 313
motivation
    exam practice 131
    methods 125–30
    theories 121–5
mutual organisations 189, **191**

national minimum wage 96, 310, **317**
necessities (YED) 53
niche market 4, 8, **9**
    marketing strategies 64
normal goods 33, **34**, 53, **54**

online businesses 190, **191**
    exam practice 192
online retailing 5–6, **9**
opportunity cost 160–1, **163**, 235
    exam practice 164
organisations 113–18, 120
output levels 223
outsourcing, workforce 99, **103**
overtrading 258

P2PL *see* peer-to-peer lending (P2PL)
partnerships 184–5, **191**
    limited 185, **191**
patents 316
PED *see* price elasticity of demand
    (PED)
peer-to-peer lending (P2PL) 177–8, **182**,
    201
penetration pricing 84–5, **87**
    see also prices
performance-related pay (PRP)
    126–8, **130**
person specifications 105, **111**
piecework 125, **130**
place, marketing mix component 63
PLC *see* public limited companies (PLC)
PR *see* public relations (PR)

predatory pricing 85, **87**
  see also prices
price elasticity of demand (PED) 46–9, **50**
  and branding 78
  exam practice 51
  influence on pricing strategies 86
price inelastic demand 46, **50**
prices 32–3, 37, 41–4
  and branding 78
  exam practice 45
  influence on YED 53
  marketing mix component 63
  and PED 48–9
  and profitability 245
pricing strategies 83–8, **87**
  exam practice 88
private equity companies 197
product design 11, 68
  exam practice 73
product orientation 20–1, **28**
product portfolios 60, 62, **66**
production 264–7, **272**
  capital-intensive 270–1
  costs 37, 234
  exam practice 273
  labour-intensive 270–1
productivity 267–9, **272**
products
  added value 26–7
  differentiation 26, **28**
  extension strategies 59–60
  influence on distribution channels 92
  influence on PED 48
  lead-in times 271–2
  life cycle 58–9, 63, 86
  marketing mix component 62–3
profit 241–3, 248–9
  influence on pricing strategies 86
  and loss 209–10
  maximisation 156
profit and loss account *see* comprehensive
    income, statement of
profit margins 243–4, 245–6, **246**
  exam practice 247
profit sharing 126, **130**
profitability 243–6
promotion **81**
  exam practice 82
  marketing mix component 63, 74–7
PRP *see* performance-related pay (PRP)
psychological pricing 85, **87**
  see also prices
public limited companies (PLC) 193–7,
    197
  see also limited companies
public relations (PR) 76–7, **81**

qualitative data 11, 12, 16–17, **18**
quality
  advantages 291–2
  assurance 287

and business failure 259
  circles 288
  control 206–7
quantative data 11, 16–17, **18**

recession (business cycle) 304, **306**
recovery (business cycle) 304, **306**
recruitment 104–8
  exam practice 112
recycling, design for 71, **72**
redundancy 100
  exam practice 103
responsibility (in management)
    115, **119**
retailers 90, **94**
retained profit 173, 201, 202
  exam practice 176
re-use, design for 70
revenue 58, **246**
  expenditure 172
  total 41–2, **44**, 49, 206–7, 222
risk, in the market 9

sales
  budgets 234
  forecasts 213–19, **219**
  maximisation 156
  promotions 76, **81**
  revenue 206–7, 210–11
  volume 206, 210
seasonality (demand) 34
services, distribution channels 94
share capital 180, **182**, 202
  exam practice 183
skimming (price) 84, **87**
sleeping partners 185, **191**
slump (business cycle) 304, **306**
small firms (competitive markets)
    322–3
SMART objectives 58, 155
social enterprises 189, **191**
  exam practice 192
social media (branding) 79–80
social trends
  and branding 79–80
  and design mix 70–2
  influence on distribution channels
    93–4
  influence on markets 7
  influence on pricing strategies 87
  and promotion 79–80
sole traders 184, **191**
sourcing, ethical 71–2, **72**
span of control 115, **119**
SPC *see* statistical process control (SPC)
sponsorship 79, **81**
staffing 96–7
  exam practice 103
start-ups 141–2, 152–3
  development 143–5
  exam practice 154

statistical process control (SPC) 289
stock control 280
  perishable goods 282–3
stock market 193, **197**
substitute goods 32, **34**
supply 36–9, **39**, 43
  exam practice 40, 45
  excess 44, **44**
supply curves 36, **39**, 41–2
survival (of a business) 155–6
  exam practice 159

taxation 301–3, **306**
  influence on supply 38
Taylor (scientific management)
    121–2, **130**
teamworking 129, **130**
technology (supply) 37–8
time (PED) 48
time series analysis 213–14, **219**
total quality management (TQM) 288–90
  exam practice 293
trade credit 181
trade unions 101, 102, **103**
trademarks 316
trade-offs (in business) **163**
  exam practice 164
training 109–11, **111**
  exam practice 112

UK Employment Relations Act
    1999 309
unfair dismissal 309, **317**
unique selling points (USP) 22, **28**, 63, 69,
    72
  and branding 78
  influence on pricing strategies 86
upswing (business cycle) 304, **306**
USP *see* unique selling points (USP)

value added tax (VAT) 38
variance analysis (budgets) 237
  exam practice 239
venture capital 180, **182**, 202
viral marketing 79, **81**
  exam practice 82

waste minimisation **72**
  design for 70
  of inventories 282–3
wholesalers 90, **94**
workers' rights 96–7, 98
workforce
  flexible 97–100, **103**
  outsourcing 99, **103**

YED *see* income elasticity of demand
    (YED)

zero-based budgets 235
zero-hours contracts 96, 98, **103**